RICHARD II
AND THE REVOLUTION
OF 1399

To Masni and Amy

RICHARD II
AND THE REVOLUTION
OF 1399

MICHAEL BENNETT

SUTTON PUBLISHING

First published in the United Kingdom in 1999 by
Sutton Publishing Limited · Phoenix Mill
Thrupp · Stroud · Gloucestershire · GL5 2BU

British Library Cataloguing in Publication Data
A catalogue record for this book is available from the British Library.

ISBN 0-7509-2283-4

 ALAN SUTTON™ and SUTTON™ are
the trade marks of Sutton Publishing

Typeset in 11/13 pt Bembo.
Typesetting and origination by
Sutton Publishing Limited.
Printed in Great Britain by
Butler & Tanner, Frome, Somerset.

CONTENTS

ACKNOWLEDGEMENTS

It is over a decade ago that I proposed a book focusing on the events surrounding the revolution of 1399. My interest in Richard II, though, stretches back to my earliest engagements with history, and was greatly nourished in the late 1960s and early 1970s by the publications of Caroline Barron, Tony Goodman, Richard H. Jones, John Palmer and Anthony Tuck. In the 1990s there has been a second renaissance in Ricardian studies. The National Gallery's exhibition of the newly restored Wilton Diptych in 1993 provided one important focus of scholarly and popular interest. Another focus was a series of panels on the reign of Richard II organized by the White Hart Society at the Congress of Medieval Studies at Kalamazoo. It is a pleasure to acknowledge debts, general and particular, to Caroline Barron, Doug Biggs, Barrie Dobson, Jim Gillespie, Chris Given-Wilson, Tony Goodman, Jeff Hamilton, Alison McHardy, Mark Ormrod, Nigel Saul, Jenny Stratford, George Stow, Antony Tuck and Simon Walker, and not least to that Maecenas of the out-of-the-way reference, Philip Morgan. I would like to thank the University of Tasmania for several research grants and periods of study leave; Dr David Smith, Director of the Borthwick Institute, York, and the President, Dame Gillian Beer, and the Fellows of Clare Hall, Cambridge, for electing me to visiting fellowships in 1988 and 1996; and my sister, Stella Thirsk, for providing me with a home away from home on so many occasions. In Tasmania I thank the students who have shared my interest in Richard II, especially Andrew Rayner and Clive Willingham, whose assistance and encouragement in the final stages of the enterprise were invaluable. I am grateful to Tristan Taylor, Olivia Harman and Dr Teodor Flonta for advice on points of translation; Robyn Murfet for assistance with proof-reading; Peter McLaren for proof-reading and indexing; and Lyn Rainbird, Secretary of the School of History and Classics, for general support. Above all, I thank Fatimah and the dedicatees, my daughters, for their love and support.

Michael Bennett
Hobart, August 1999

Dramatis Personae

RICHARD II

His father
Edward of Woodstock (eldest son of Edward III), prince of Wales, d. 1376

His mother
Joan of Kent (daughter of Edmund earl of Kent, third son of Edward I), princess of Wales, d. 1385

His wives
Anne of Bohemia (daughter of the Emperor Charles IV), d. 1394
Isabelle of Valois (daughter of Charles VI, King of France)

His brother
Edward of Angoulême, d. 1371

His half-brothers
Thomas Holland (son of Joan of Kent by Sir Thomas Holland, d. 1360), earl of Kent, d. 1397
John Holland (son of Joan of Kent by Sir Thomas Holland, d. 1360), earl of Huntingdon, duke of Exeter 1397, d. 1400

His nephew
Thomas Holland (son of Thomas Holland earl of Kent, d. 1397), earl of Kent 1397, duke of Surrey 1397, d. 1400

His uncles
Lionel of Antwerp (second surviving son of Edward III), duke of Clarence, d. 1368
John of Gaunt (third surviving son of Edward III), duke of Lancaster, duke of Guyenne, d. 1399
Edmund of Langley (fourth surviving son of Edward III), earl of Cambridge, duke of York, d. 1402
Thomas of Woodstock (fifth surviving son of Edward III), earl of Buckingham, duke of Gloucester, d. 1397

His cousins
Philippa of Clarence (daughter of Lionel of Antwerp), countess of March, d. 1380

Henry of Bolingbroke (son of John of Gaunt), earl of Derby, duke of Hereford, duke of Lancaster, King Henry IV, d. 1413

John Beaufort (son of John of Gaunt), earl of Somerset, marquis of Dorset, d. 1410

Edward (son of Edmund of Langley) earl of Rutland, duke of Albemarle, duke of York, d. 1415

Richard (son of Edmund of Langley) earl of Cambridge, d. 1415

Select magnates

Michael de la Pole, earl of Suffolk, d. 1389

Robert de Vere, earl of Oxford, marquis of Dublin, duke of Ireland, d. 1392

Richard FitzAlan, earl of Arundel, d. 1397

Thomas Beauchamp, earl of Warwick, d. 1401

Thomas Mowbray, earl of Nottingham, earl marshal, duke of Norfolk, d. 1399

Roger Mortimer, earl of March, d. 1398

Henry Percy, earl of Northumberland, d. 1408

John Montagu, earl of Salisbury, d. 1400

Ralph Neville, earl of Westmorland, d. 1425

Thomas Percy, earl of Worcester, d. 1403

William Scrope, earl of Wiltshire, d. 1399

Thomas Despenser, earl of Gloucester, d. 1400

CHAPTER ONE

TREASON AND TRUTH

In August 1399 Master Pietro da Verona, a notable scribe and illuminator, crossed to England. His business was with Richard II, and related to a splendid Bible produced in his workshop. It may be that the work had been commissioned by the king, or that it was being brought on approval. In the event Master Pietro was disappointed, though not in the prince to whom he looked for patronage. What he learned to his surprise and dismay in London was that England was in rebellion, and that Richard was the captive of Henry of Bolingbroke, duke of Lancaster, in Ireland. His intelligence was only a little awry. Richard had been campaigning in Ireland when news of Bolingbroke's invasion led him to return to Wales. Finding the military position hopeless he surrendered to the rebels at Flint in north Wales. A country consumed by civil commotion was no place for an artist and a foreigner. Da Verona wisely headed straight back across the Channel. He subsequently succeeded in selling the Bible to the duke of Berry.[1]

Over the summer and autumn the French court received disturbing reports from England. Charles VI knew some of the background to the crisis, and had significant interests at stake. Richard's problems with his magnates were well enough known. They had been compounded by his policies of peace and collaboration with France, which had been sealed by Richard's marriage to Isabelle of Valois, Charles's young daughter, in 1396. Henry of Bolingbroke was also well known in France. After his banishment from England in the autumn of 1398, he had come to Paris and taken the Hôtel de Clisson as his residence. The princes of the blood had entertained him, and joined him in mourning his father John of Gaunt, duke of Lancaster, when he died early in 1399. The king's brother Louis, duke of Orléans, may have known of Bolingbroke's resolution to return to England to seek his inheritance. Still, the French court professed to be caught by surprise by Bolingbroke's invasion. Dispersed in their castles and hunting-lodges over the summer, Charles and his uncles, the dukes of Burgundy and Berry, found themselves anxiously waiting for news from across the Channel. By September the reports sounded ominous, and Charles VI sent an urgent embassy to Bolingbroke to express his concerns, not least with respect to his daughter.[2]

This formal mission confirmed that Henry of Bolingbroke was not only master of the kingdom but had replaced Richard on the throne. A number of Frenchmen who had been in England in 1399 found that on their return to France they had a story to tell. The anonymous author of *Traison et Mort* seems to have come to England in 1398, and may have been attached to the household of the earl of Huntingdon, Richard's half-brother. He was at Coventry in September 1398 when Richard halted the duel between Bolingbroke and Mowbray, and condemned both lords to exile. His narrative of the betrayal and death of Richard, surviving in thirty-seven manuscripts, was widely read in France in the fifteenth century. Yet his account of the events of the summer of 1399 is

Detail, portrait of Richard II. (© Dean & Chapter of Westminster)

almost entirely derived from another narrative written in France around 1402, Jean Creton's *Metrical History of the Deposition of Richard II*. Creton was a *valet de chambre* of the duke of Burgundy, and crossed to England in May 1399. Since he followed Richard to Ireland and witnessed his surrender in north Wales, he provides unique insight into the last months of Richard's regime.[3]

Both narratives focus on Richard and the acts of betrayal that laid him low. French readers found confirmation in the writings of Creton and the author of *Traison et Mort* of their belief that the English were 'readily disposed to treason' and tended to support 'the most powerful, and him that maketh the best shew, without regard to right, law, reason, or justice'. 'Neither is this any new thing,' Creton continues, 'for many a time have they undone and destroyed their king and lord, as may be known from divers histories and chronicles.'[4] Yet Creton provides little background to the dramatic events that he witnessed. His *Metrical History* begins breathlessly with his setting out from Paris to join Richard's expedition to Ireland. The author of *Traison et Mort* does only slightly better. He begins his account in 1397 and shows some awareness of the rancour and division, the plots and counter-plots of Richard's last years. To obtain a larger perspective, however, French readers would have looked to the great chronicler of European chivalry, Jean Froissart.

* * *

It is not known when Jean Froissart, canon of Chimay, laid down his pen, or when, for that matter, he breathed his last. He continued his chronicle of the affairs of the French-speaking world to 1400, and he may well have lived some years beyond this date. But he had lived beyond his time, and in his last years he heard little from his steadily narrowing world that would have either inspired or consoled him. He had seen the passing in his own lifetime of a heroic age of 'honourable enterprises, noble adventures and deeds of arms', and had a powerful sense of the decadence of the times.[5] There was little to celebrate in France. From 1392 Charles VI suffered recurrent bouts of mental illness, and presided over an increasingly factious court in which his wife Isabelle of Bavaria, his brother the duke of Orléans, and his uncles the dukes of Berry and Burgundy plotted and intrigued. At no time in history did leadership from the 'most Christian' king of France seem so necessary. Two lines of popes, one at Rome and one at Avignon, vied for the allegiance of the faithful. As the Turks advanced through south-east Europe, encircling and throttling the Byzantine Empire, western Christendom was leaderless and divided. The emperor-elect, Wenceslas of Luxembourg, king of Bohemia, had little standing or credit in Germany, let alone in Christendom at large.

In the mid-1390s Richard of England seemed Christendom's best hope. Peace between England and France offered the prospect of common action in the cause of Christian unity. In October 1396 Richard's marriage to Isabelle of Valois sealed an agreement to a thirty-year truce and collaboration in a number of spheres. There was talk of a crusade led by the two kings, and indeed an advance force under Burgundian leadership set out earlier in the year. There was to be a joint approach to the popes in Avignon and Rome, and some commitment to press them to accept a compromise. Within two months of the marriage celebrations, however, there came grim news from Nicopolis. The crusading army had been defeated by the Turks, and some of the most distinguished knights of the age had been either slain or made captive.[6] Charles VI suffered a severe mental relapse. In England Richard's accord with France played a role in 1397 in opening up old wounds in the body politic. The fourteenth century ended in a series of unprecedented crises. In 1398 France took the momentous step of unilaterally withdrawing allegiance from the pope at Avignon. It was an awesome act, in a sense the deposition of a pope. Two years later the German princes came together and formally deposed the emperor-elect Wenceslas. In the mean time there had been a deposition in England. The official report had it that Richard II had voluntarily renounced the throne, but no one in Europe believed it.

Froissart had in some sense been acquainted with Richard all his life. Born in Valenciennes around 1337, he had known both Richard's grandfather, Edward III, and his grandmother, Philippa of Hainault. It was in the service of that distinguished lady that he had first acquired a larger vision of the world. In the course of his career as chronicler and man-of-affairs he was able to turn to advantage his acquaintanceship with England's leaders. Edward, prince of Wales, Richard's father, is one of the heroes of his chronicle. Froissart was actually at Bordeaux in 1367 when Richard was born. From 1377, when he succeeded his grandfather on the throne, Richard himself was a natural focus of interest. Froissart may not have fully understood the workings of English politics, but his chronicles provide useful information and insight on people and events. He knew the king's uncles, especially John of Gaunt, duke of Lancaster, Edmund of Langley, duke of York, and Thomas of Woodstock, duke of Gloucester, and his comments on their characters and especially how they were perceived in France cannot be ignored. None the less over the years he became increasingly out of touch. In July 1395 he decided to renew his acquaintance with England, and found his way to the court of Richard II. A great deal had changed, naturally enough, but he found men in the household who remembered him, and brought him up to date with events, most especially the success of the king's recent expedition to Ireland. He presented Richard with a book of love-poems, which was graciously received. Froissart did not leave empty-handed: the king dispatched Sir John Golafre to present him with a valuable goblet.[7]

The visit to England was the last occasion when Froissart sought out information at first hand. What prompted him, at around sixty years of age, to cross the Channel and seek out the English court was more than mere sentiment. It was precisely the perception that in the mid-1390s a great deal hinged on the person of the English king. Froissart's visit, and his gift of love-poems, may be seen in the context of the proposed marriage between Richard and Isabelle of Valois, a marriage designed to convert the series of truces between England and France into a lasting peace, a peace that in itself might set the scene for the healing of the schism and a new crusading offensive against the Turks. Already preliminary terms had been agreed between the two courts, but there was a great deal still to be achieved. Froissart may well have been priming himself for the main event. The marriage, and all that might flow from a final peace, would have proved a fitting end to Froissart's chronicles. The central theme of his long and sprawling chronicle had been the wars between England and France, wars which had begun with Edward III's claim through his mother, Isabelle of France, to the French crown. The long and fruitless conflict that had arisen with one marriage between an English king and a French princess would end with another.

For this reason, the fall of Richard II affected Froissart deeply. His account of Richard's last years shows that his sources were no longer sound, and on some points he was wildly and unaccountably inaccurate. He was writing in a hurry. He probably heard many rumours, and then compounded confusion by seeking to make sense of some of them. The impression is that he felt a duty to his readers and to himself to comprehend a major turn of events. As he wrote, he began to recall fragments from the past that now seemed relevant. He had been in Bordeaux when Richard was born, an event that he had reported in his chronicle. What he had not mentioned then, but included in his account of Richard's overthrow, was the tale told by Sir Bartholomew Burghersh. Apparently, prior to their departure for Bordeaux, Richard's father and mother had received a visit from Edward III at Kennington. While the members of the royal family made their farewells, the knights and ladies of the two households had gossiped among themselves. There had been some excited talk, it seems, about a prophecy of Merlin indicating that neither the prince nor any of his issue would ever succeed to the throne, but that the crown would pass instead to the house of Lancaster.[8] In a speech attributed to Bolingbroke, Froissart recalled, too, innuendoes about the chastity of Joan of Kent, the prince's wife, and thus about the paternity of Richard.[9] It all seemed to reflect the degeneracy of the times.

The events of 1399 likewise prompted Froissart to look back over, and rework, some of his earlier writings. He was looking for the larger patterns. He was drawn again to events in the decade before he was born, especially to the fateful marriage of Edward II and Isabelle of France.[10] It was no longer simply the seeds of the conflict between England and France that he saw, but some anticipation of the tragedy unfolding before him. It had been from France that the queen and her son had launched the invasion in 1325 which would overthrow Edward II and set his son on the throne. It was to this particular episode that Froissart now returned, expanding and reworking the first book of his chronicles. The events of 1325–7 and 1399 were so linked in his mind that some of the detail became confused. For Froissart, the Londoners played a key role on both occasions in leading the resistance to their feckless rulers, and Bristol was the place where both Edward and Richard made their last stands.[11] It was in reflecting on events in England in 1399 that Froissart made his final revisions and drew his history to a close.

★　★　★

In England the events of 1399 prompted a number of men to take up their pens. An anonymous clerk from around Bristol wrote a remarkable alliterative poem known by its first words as *Richard the Redeless*.[12] Professedly written in the wake of Henry's return to England and prior to his usurpation of the throne, the poem has an immediacy that is almost breathless. It addresses itself to Richard, and explains how through the lack of good counsel he has lost the love of his subjects. While it cannot have been completed until 1400, it captures some of the mood of 1397–9. In a passionate but rambling denunciation of Richard's regime it makes specific allusion to events of the time. The famous description of a parliament cravenly acquiescing to Richard's demands is clearly inspired by the meeting at Shrewsbury in February 1398. Some members 'sat there like a nought in arithmetic, that marks a place but has no value in itself'; some 'slumbered and slept and said very little'; some had been bribed; some told tales to the king about his foes, who were in truth his friends; some babbled in praise of the king and council; some tacked to the prevailing winds; some cared more for the king's promise of reward 'than about the interests of the commons'.[13]

Writing in a different genre, John Gower gave voice to the same concerns as the author of *Richard the Redeless*. Like Froissart, Gower was a poet whose work had found favour with Richard II. According to the prologue of the *Confessio Amantis*, he had been asked to write his masterpiece by the king himself as they talked about poetry on the royal barge. Like Froissart, Gower felt he had seen it all before. As he watched the events of 1397–9, he regarded them as the third and final crisis of a miserable reign. In the aftermath of the Peasants Revolt of 1381, he had written *Vox Clamantis*, a powerful invective against the disorder and degeneration of the age. He now extended this work to include an account of the crisis of 1386–8, during which Richard had first been brought under restraint, as a background to the king's acts of revenge in 1397. Completed early in 1400, his *Tripartite Chronicle* is a searing indictment of Richard's tyranny.[14] It is true that Gower was an unabashed admirer of Bolingbroke. He even rewrote the prologue to *Confessio Amantis*, excising the reference to Richard and replacing it with an encomium to Henry. Yet it is a mistake to dismiss him as merely a

Lancastrian propagandist. The revision to *Confessio Amantis* was made before 1393.[15] His disaffection with Richard was deep-seated and probably well grounded.

Adam Usk likewise attests to some hostility to Richard II in his last years. A native of south Wales, Usk was an ambitious canon lawyer who came to play a by no means negligible role in the events of 1399.[16] His professional association with Thomas Arundel, archbishop of Canterbury, who returned from exile with Bolingbroke, probably prompted him to join the rebel host at Bristol. Thereafter he was in a position to provide a first-hand account not only of Bolingbroke's advance north through the Welsh marches to Chester but also of the surrender of Richard II and the deliberations regarding the transfer of power. In October 1399 he was appointed to a committee of legal experts to consider the options. His account of this time reveals all too clearly the real confusion about how to proceed, and how a number of pretexts for deposition were actively canvassed. The deposition, according to his report, took place in two stages. On 29 September representatives of the various estates, in this case the bishops, the titled nobility, the lower prelates, the barons, the lower clergy and the commons, went to Richard in the Tower and received the surrender of the crown. Regrettably, Usk was not among this group, but he was presumably in the larger assembly which heard both the renunciation and articles of deposition, and then approved Henry's claim to the vacant throne.

Adam Usk's role in the revolution required him to look back at the historical record. He makes reference to the examination of a number of chronicles, including his own copy of *Polychronicon*. His role as a participant-observer in the stirring times led him to write his own continuation. Over the next few years he wrote an account of Richard's reign which was obviously informed by knowledge of how it ended. The pattern he imposed on the reign was not unlike that imposed by Gower. He identified crises in 1381, with the Peasants Revolt and the challenge of Lollardy; in the late 1380s, with aristocratic opposition to the court; and in the late 1390s, with Richard's tyranny and deposition. Like Gower, he presents the reign as a three-act play, with the events of 1386–8 setting the context for Richard's destruction of his opponents in the last years of his reign. For Gower the patterning is explicit and contrived. Usk simply cross-references the two sets of events in an otherwise loose narrative.[17]

Gower was a layman, Usk a secular clerk, but for the most part history writing in England was in the hands of monks. The events of the late 1390s stirred a number of monks to unwonted activity. In the case of three chronicles composed in Cistercian houses in the north of England it appears that the stimulus came as much from Richard's regal ambition as from his overthrow. At Dieulacres abbey in north Staffordshire a monk began a retrospective account of Richard's reign by describing him as 'the noble and most excellent king of all the kings of the world', and recording a whole series of prophecies about him.[18] A chronicler at Kirkstall abbey near Leeds was stirred by Richard's assertion of royal authority in autumn 1397. His presentation of the king as the sun lately concealed by the cloud, now revealed in all its brightness, may be derived from some Ricardian newsletter.[19] A continuation of the *Polychronicon* at Whalley abbey in Lancashire was likewise inspired by the dramatic conclusion to Richard's reign.[20]

The impress of the revolution of 1399 on monastic chronicles was varied. Thomas Burton, abbot of Meaux, wrote a compendious Latin chronicle beginning in 1396, but his focus of interest was the abbey, its land and the Humberside region. Richard's overthrow is briefly related, but only, it would seem, because Bolingbroke landed at Ravenspur, at the mouth of the Humber.[21] It is regrettable that two major chroniclers – Henry Knighton at Leicester, and an unknown monk at Westminster abbey – finish in the mid-1390s. There was some dislocation, and probably some destruction, of monastic chronicles in 1399. Henry allegedly requested monasteries to send him copies of their chronicles for inspection in September 1399. It has been surmised that part of a Glastonbury chronicle relating to Richard was destroyed at this time.[22] The *Liber Regius*, a major royal chronicle commissioned by Richard and kept at Westminster, seems likewise to have been lost.[23] Predictably enough, some of the major extant chronicles tend to be energised by their animosity towards Richard. The monk of Evesham and the continuator of the *Eulogium Historiarum*, possibly a Franciscan from Canterbury, both graft on to earlier works extended and more hostile accounts of Richard's reign.[24] The most important single source for the late 1390s, *Annales Ricardi Secundi et Henrici Quarti*, was compiled at St Albans, and is usually attributed to Thomas Walsingham.[25] Whether written by Walsingham or a colleague, it reflects both the good sources of information and the anti-curial prejudices generally associated with the St Albans scriptorium.

★   ★   ★

Almost all the narratives of the last years of Richard's reign are coloured by the politics of the time. Writing in the early 1430s, John Capgrave saw the problem and outlined his own approach to the history of the revolution of 1399:

> Forasmuch as different writers have given different accounts of the deposition of King Richard and the elevation of King Henry to the throne – and no wonder, since, in so great a struggle, one took one side, and one the other – I, who stand as it were in the middle between the two parties, consider that I hold a better and a safer path, since, having investigated both sides of the question, I set myself diligently to elucidate the truth alone, not, indeed, to the prejudice of any one who may write of these things after me, if he shall undertake to discuss this matter with more accuracy and clearness.[26]

It is a truism that the victors write the history. In the wake of the usurpation Henry had an interest in promulgating a particular version of events. The so-called 'Record and Process' provides an official record of the proceedings by which Richard abdicated and was then deposed by the estates of the realm. It includes a number of misleading, if not mendacious, statements. The notion that Richard freely offered to renounce the crown at Conway, and then formally abdicated 'with smiling countenance' in the Tower of London, cannot be accepted as the simple truth. The account is not only at variance with the French sources and some English chronicles, it is also at odds on crucial particulars with another quasi-official record of proceedings, the 'Manner of King Richard's renunciation'.[27] The 'Record and Process' was widely disseminated, and was incorporated into the St Albans and other chronicles. Its influence can be seen not only in narratives of the abdication and deposition but also in accounts of the last years of

Richard's reign. Walsingham, for example, offers a great deal of information on how Richard 'tyrannized' the realm. Some of what he says, however, can be regarded as a writing back into the historical record of the 'articles of deposition' of 1399.

Henry sent embassies to European courts to announce the circumstances of his accession. On their return to France, Jean Creton and the author of *Traison et Mort* were able to offer to the world an account of events from Richard's point of view. For Creton, who was with Richard at Conway, there was no free promise to renounce the crown. For the author of *Traison et Mort* and himself, the revolution of 1399 was a story of opportunistic rebellion, treason, betrayal and, ultimately, regicide. Their version gains a measure of support from some minor English chronicles. According to the Dieulacres chronicle, for example, Richard was tricked into surrender at Conway and then locked in the Tower until he resigned the crown.[28] In the two English chronicles most favourable to Richard there is evidence of a change of allegiance at some point after 1399. The Kirkstall chronicler, who applauded Richard's self-assertion in 1397, seems to have either revised his views or become more circumspect in 1399.[29] In the Dieulacres chronicle there is a change in authorship and political tone in 1400. The second chronicler protests that his predecessor 'had condemned actions which ought to be commended, and commended actions which ought to be condemned'. He adds that he knew it for certain, 'because I was present on many of these occasions and saw for myself'.[30]

From Capgrave onwards, historians have tended to regard the chronicles of 1399 as either pro-Ricardian or pro-Lancastrian.[31] This sort of categorization is somewhat misleading. The French sources, for example, cannot be regarded as uniformly pro-Ricardian. Jean Creton and the author of *Traison et Mort* were favourably disposed to Richard, and sought to inspire their French patrons to take up arms on his behalf. Creton was with the king in the last months of the reign, and was powerfully affected by the personal tragedy that he witnessed. His account of the king's actions at Conway is scarcely flattering. He reports that Richard surrendered to the earl of Northumberland on false promises, but at the same presents him as assuring his friends that his surrender was entirely tactical, and that when the opportunity came he would flay his enemies alive.[32] The author of *Traison et Mort*, who was in London during the summer of 1399, clearly testifies to Richard's unpopularity in the capital.[33] Froissart, though out of touch in 1399, probably knew the English political scene well, and while his account of events is wildly inaccurate his overall assessment of the king and the forces which brought about his overthrow is not so very different from the English sources. He found much to condemn in Richard, and is unqualified in his praise for Henry.

In a similar fashion no English chronicle should be dismissed as merely Lancastrian propaganda. It was later alleged that John of Gaunt sought to tamper with monastic chronicles in order to provide support for a Lancastrian succession.[34] If he did so, he was singularly unsuccessful, and what is remarkable about 1399 is how little Bolingbroke achieved in terms of rewriting history. It is true that the 'Record and Process' was widely circulated, but the chroniclers seem to have been under no compulsion to publicize it. In any case it was parliament itself which petitioned that the 'horrible causes' for which Richard had been deposed 'be declared through England in every shire' so 'that the realm be not slandered' for the deposition.[35] A large portion of the narrative was eminently creditworthy, and could be authenticated by the hundreds of lords, knights and burgesses who had participated in the deposition. The description of Richard's surrender and voluntary abdication had to be taken on trust, and probably raised eyebrows in some quarters. Yet it may well have been generally and genuinely accepted as a formalized and economical account of what had been a messy process, full of twists and turns. It had the character, and the reassuring neatness, of a legal fiction.

There is ample evidence of criticism of Richard before his deposition. The king himself was aware of the slanders against his person, and required the sheriffs to take a special oath to arrest immediately anyone speaking ill of him.[36] It is odd therefore to regard all criticism of Richard after 1399 as somehow Lancastrian. John Gower, the author of *Richard the Redeless* and Adam Usk all wrote in the wake of the revolution, yet all appear to have been giving voice to sentiments formed years earlier. Gower claimed that he began writing his *Tripartite Chronicle* in September 1397, and there is good reason to believe it.[37] The author of *Richard the Redeless* was still working on his poem in 1400, but its inspiration can be dated back to 1398, if not earlier. Usk cannot be regarded as a Lancastrian apologist. His factional loyalties, if any, lay with the house of Mortimer. All three writers showed some independence of mind. Even Gower, a long-time enthusiast for Henry, did not find that eulogy came all that easily to him.[38] If the author of *Richard the Redeless* also wrote *Mum and the Sothsegger*, as seems likely, he was soon directing some of his criticisms of Richard against Henry IV. Adam Usk moved even more decidedly from being an admirer of Henry to joining a conspiracy against him. Though he was fairly guarded in what he wrote, he incorporated into his chronicle a letter of admonition addressed to Henry by his confessor in 1401.[39]

The English chronicles reflect not so much Lancastrian propaganda as a significant, if shifting, body of public opinion. The French sources seem in no doubt that Richard had lost the affection of the people. It is true that the author of *Traison et Mort* presents Henry as stirring people against Richard by false rumours and seducing them to his cause by false promises. Propaganda of this sort doubtless played some role in the events of 1399. For the most part, though, Henry had neither the power nor the need to impose on the realm a 'Lancastrian' view of Richard or the revolution. Almost all the major chronicles, including that of Thomas Walsingham, present accounts of men challenging his legitimacy and criticizing his rule. The continuator of the *Eulogium* records an episode in 1402 in which a Franciscan master of theology told the new king to his face that if Richard were alive he was the true king, and if he were dead then Henry forfeited whatever title he had to the throne on account of his regicide.[40] A marked feature of much of this criticism is an acknowledgement of the jubilation with which Henry had been received by the populace when he first returned to England. According to Henry's confessor in 1401, the people had risen up on his first arrival 'as the sons of Israel did to meet Christ on Palm Sunday, crying out to heaven for you, their anointed king, as if you were a second Christ'.[41]

★ ★ ★

An account of Richard II's rule in the 1390s and the events of the revolution of 1399 cannot be based on the narrative sources alone. Many historians have heeded G.O.

Sayles's call to turn from the chroniclers with all their problems 'to the best evidence of all, that of the public records, to evidence that is first-hand or can be reasonably accepted as authentic'.[42] The government records for Richard's reign are indeed voluminous, and remain imperfectly quarried. Then there are the records of the church, other corporations and private families. The major advances in understanding Ricardian politics over the last few decades have come from work in the archives.[43] While there seems little prospect of discovering new chronicles, the archives retain some capacity for surprise. A roll of evidences relating to a dispute over the manor of Ladbroke in Warwickshire was found to include a memorandum detailing Bolingbroke's march through the Midlands in July 1399.[44] An inventory of jewels, mistakenly filed among records relating to Henry VI, turned out to be from the late 1390s. Forty membranes long, itemizing eleven crowns, gold plate, silverware, jewellery and other precious artefacts, it attests the lost splendour of Richard's collection.[45] An item taken from the public records by Sir Robert Cotton in the seventeenth century now appears to be a copy of a letter patent by which Edward III in 1376 sought to settle the royal succession in the male line. It has very considerable implications for an understanding of the politics of Richard's reign.[46]

Archival work over the past decades has tested the chronicle evidence, and sometimes found it wanting. What is remarkable, though, is how often it has won new respect for the chronicles. Almost all the arbitrary measures attributed to Richard in the late 1390s can be evidenced from the public records.[47] Thomas Walsingham is often portrayed as so prejudiced against Richard that nothing he says to his detriment can be believed unless it has been independently confirmed. Yet he was often well informed. He alone reports the visit of the archdeacon of Cologne to Richard in the summer of 1397 and Richard's interest in seeking election to the Holy Roman Empire.[48] It would be easy to dismiss the report as an invention designed to present Richard as consumed by vain ambition. However, the archdeacon of Cologne's visit to England, and a return embassy to Germany on 21 July, are well documented in the public records. The intent of the return embassy can be inferred from an order to the treasurer to pay £405 for Richard's gifts to four members of the electoral college – the archbishops of Cologne and Trier, the dukes of Bavaria and Saxony – and a number of other German lords 'for the honour of us and our realm'.[49] Richard's imperial ambitions were certainly taken seriously in Rome.[50]

Happily, the chronicles have retained their champions.[51] There have been new editions of several major chronicles of Richard's reign and important reassessments of other narrative sources.[52] For all their limitations and silences, the chronicles of the revolution of 1399 provide most guidance with respect to the motives of the actors, the perceptions of the time, and what meanings were being attached to events. John Gower's *Tripartite Chronicle* might be partisan and weak on detail, but it provides valuable insights into how one man viewed the last years of Richard's reign. An obvious point to note is that Gower and other English chroniclers had some sense of the background to the crises unfolding around them. As a close observer of public affairs for at least two decades, Gower could not see it as other than the culmination of events over the whole reign. Adam Usk was still a student in the late 1380s, but he saw the baronial army ride in triumph through Oxford after the defeat of Richard's forces at Radcot Bridge in December 1387.[53]

Thomas Walsingham had a longer acquaintanceship with the chief actors, and an even better understanding of English politics. Even Froissart, in retirement and out of touch, is a guide who is far from sure, but should never be wholly ignored.

In addition to chronicles and records, the historian of Richard II needs to attend to the material remains of his reign. Since he spent lavishly on his own account as well as contributing to the building funds of Westminster abbey and other churches, it is a pity that so little survives to bear direct witness to his personal style and aesthetic sense.[54] After Queen Anne's death in 1394 he ordered the destruction of his favourite palace at Sheen.[55] A remarkable entry in the exchequer issue rolls reveals that a model of a new palace to be built on the opposite bank of the Thames was prepared for him by Henry Yevele and Hugh Herland. This palace, apparently on the site of Syon House, never materialised.[56] Happily, Westminster Hall survives as testimony to Richard's architectural ambition. In Westminster abbey there is the great portrait of Richard enthroned and the double tomb in St Edward the Confessor's Chapel. Above all, there is the Wilton Diptych, the exquisite, intensely private representation of Richard, supported by his three saintly sponsors, receiving a banner from the Christ Child and Virgin Mary. In recent times a great deal of progress has been made in the analysis of the painting and its iconography.[57] It now seems tolerably certain that it was painted for Richard in 1395–6. It is a haunting, mysterious image and can never be wholly explained in historical terms. At the very least it should caution historians against too simple-minded an assessment of the world of Richard II.

★   ★   ★

This study of Richard II and the revolution of 1399 seeks to draw on the full range of English sources for the late 1390s. It also makes some attempt, though, to see the events in England in a European framework. Though born in Bordeaux, Richard spent little time on the continent. Yet he shared the interests and tastes of other European princes, and followed their fortunes in a spirit of solidarity as well as emulation. Even Giangaleazzo Visconti in Milan seems to have caught his attention. A detailed account of Giangaleazzo's coup against his uncle Bernabó in 1385 appears in the Westminster Chronicle following an account of Richard's troubled relations with John of Gaunt.[58] Giangaleazzo's incorporation of the imperial eagle in his coat-of-arms in January 1395[59] may have encouraged Richard, later in the year, to incorporate St Edward the Confessor's arms with his own. Richard saw some affinity with Charles VI of France, who had also come to the throne as a child. Charles's declaration of his majority in 1388 was perhaps as much an inspiration for Richard's self-assertion in 1389 as French court pageantry and the tournaments at Paris were for Richard's Smithfield tournament in 1390. Events in France materially impinged on Richard's plans and actions throughout his reign, but in the 1390s, both before and after the marriage, relations between the two courts were close and amicable. The writings of Pierre Salmon, an attendant on Queen Isabelle, make it clear that Richard was greatly concerned by Charles's illness, which he attributed to malign forces at the French court. Richard's reflections on Charles's pitiable condition probably heightened his suspicion and anxiety about plots against himself.[60]

The Wilton diptych, exterior. (© National Gallery)

At the same time a study of the revolution of 1399 must set the last years of Richard's reign in a deeper historical context. It cannot begin as Jean Creton began in the spirit of adventure in May 1399, even though Richard's departure to Ireland set the scene for his overthrow. It cannot begin as the anonymous author of *Traison et Mort* began, with Richard's 'discovery' of a conspiracy against him in 1397, even though that precipitated the final crisis of Richard's reign. An assessment of the politics of Richard's 'tyranny' needs to be grounded in an appreciation of the politics of at least the previous decade. In 1397–8 Richard was consciously turning the tables on the men who had opposed him in 1387, and systematically reversing the political settlement of 1388. Given the centrality of the king, his personality, his view of his office and his political style, it is necessary to follow the threads back to Richard's formative years. Indeed there may be grounds for adopting, with Jean Froissart and Adam Usk, an even longer historical perspective. Richard and his opponents, like Froissart, looked back to the reign of Edward II, and their reading of the past shaped their response to events in their own day.[61] Similarly, a number of major participants in the drama may, like Adam Usk, have had both an awareness of the more distant British past and a concern to seek in it the workings of Providence.

It is, after all, Richard himself who has this historical sense. It is he who in 1397 sought revenge on the men who had humiliated him and destroyed his friends. It was he who actively campaigned for the canonization of Edward II. He was interested in his royal forebears, associating himself particularly with the cults of Edward the Confessor and other royal saints. Adam Usk records a memorable scene which he himself witnessed in the Tower of London. Richard, then a captive, discoursed mournfully on the fickleness of England, how it had seen so many kings and other great men exiled, slain or destroyed, and how the country 'never ceases to be riven and worn down by dissensions and strife and internecine hatreds'. According to Usk, Richard then recounted the names of sufferers from the earliest habitation of the kingdom.[62] In seeking an understanding of the character of the leading actor in the dramatic events of the late 1390s it is doubly necessary to adopt a historical perspective. Richard had a personal history, but it was a personal history that involved serious reflection on the past.

CHAPTER TWO

PRINCE OF DESTINY

Effigy of Edward, the Black Prince. (Reproduced by kind permission of Heraldry Today, from J.H. & R.V. Pinches, The Royal Heraldry of England, *1974)*

From his earliest years Richard of Bordeaux was imbued with a powerful sense of personal destiny. He had not been born to the purple. His father was Edward, prince of Wales, the eldest son and heir apparent to Edward III, but Richard was the prince's second son. Edward of Angoulême, Richard's elder brother, died around 1371, and cannot have been more than a shadowy memory. Still, Richard recalled him with pious affection twenty years later, taking pains to have his body brought home to England and reinterred in the Dominican friary at King's Langley, Edward II's foundation and the burial-place of the latter's favourite, Piers Gaveston. Some of the circumstances of Richard's birth were not wholly propitious. He was born in Bordeaux in Aquitaine. Royal and noble births outside the country had been the subject of special legislation, and seem often to have fed rumours about true paternity. He may have been born a little prematurely. Fearing that he might not survive, the midwives performed a hurried lay baptism, naming him John, an inauspicious name in the English royal family. In other respects, though, his birth could be seen as portentous. He was born in 1367 on 6 January, Epiphany, the Feast of Kings. It was claimed, too, that three kings attended his formal christening at St Andrew's cathedral, when he was renamed Richard. The king of Majorca raised him from the font.[1]

Froissart was at Bordeaux at the time of the birth. He recalled that Sir Richard Pontchardon, marshal of Aquitaine, came to him and said: 'Froissart, write that it may be remembered, my lady the princess is brought to bed of a fine son: he is born on Twelfth Day, the son of a king's son, and shall be king himself.'[2] From about four years of age, Richard was the sole surviving son of the prince of Wales. If he ever had much in the way of a childhood, it faded with his father's rapidly deteriorating health and subsequent death in the summer of 1376. In June Richard visited his formidable father on his deathbed, and heard some of the provisions of his will, not least the curse that was laid on him if he failed to honour its terms.[3] Richard's introduction to public life came precipitately amid the personal bereavement, the clamour of the Good Parliament, and the bitterness of politics in Edward III's last year. He was doubtless made aware that his succession to his grandfather, who was also very ill, was by no means a foregone conclusion. There were rumours that his eldest uncle, John of Gaunt, duke of Lancaster, might seize the throne. One of the prince's last acts was to ask Lancaster and his other brothers to take an oath to protect his widow and maintain the rights of his son. Within a week of the prince's death, the commons, concerned about this very issue, petitioned to have Richard presented in parliament. On 25 June Simon Sudbury, archbishop of Canterbury, brought the boy before parliament. Speaking on the king's behalf, the archbishop declared that although the prince of Wales had been called to God, 'nevertheless the prince was as if present and not in any way absent, because he had left behind him such a noble and fine son, who is his exact image and true likeness'. Richard stood before them in majestic miniature. Momentarily appeased, the commons demanded that he be immediately created prince of Wales, but the lords demurred, feeling that demand to be too peremptory.[4]

The succession was clearly an issue in the summer and autumn of 1376. Even if Richard's status as heir to the throne was not in doubt, there was discussion about the overall line of succession. Edward III had five sons who survived to manhood: the two elder sons had now predeceased him. Edward, prince of Wales, was represented by a sole son, Richard. Lionel of Antwerp, duke of Clarence, who died in 1368, was represented by a daughter, Philippa, wife of Edmund Mortimer, earl of March. A crucial issue, which would persist until 1399 and beyond, was whether, in the event of Richard's death without heirs of his body, the succession should pass to the heir general (that is, the line of Clarence), or to the heir male (that is, the line of John of Gaunt). It was Gaunt's eagerness to have the matter resolved in his favour which further raised the political temperature at this time. Shortly after the prince of Wales's funeral, there seems to have been a family conference at Havering atte Bower. Edward III, who himself was grievously ill, made his last testament, and declared his will that the crown be entailed in the male line. Whether or not Edward's declaration was generally known, Gaunt's ambitions were widely suspected. He was already acting as the power behind the throne, and rumour had it that on his father's death he would waste little time in doing away with his nephew.[5]

For the moment Richard was exalted and adored. On 20 November Edward III formally

The seal of Edmund Mortimer, third earl of March. (Reproduced by kind permission of Heraldry Today, from J.H. & R.V. Pinches, The Royal Heraldry of England, 1974)

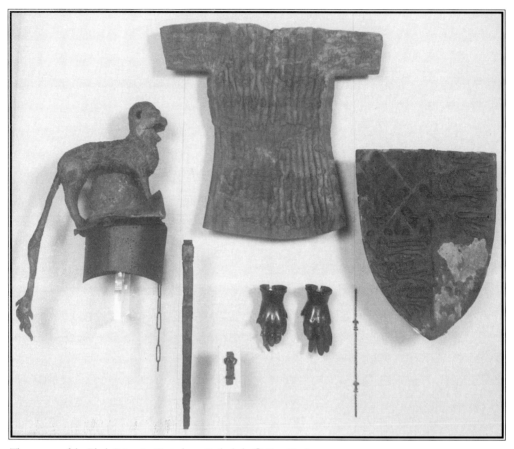

The armour of the Black Prince in Canterbury Cathedral. (© Ben May)

invested him as prince of Wales, duke of Cornwall and earl of Chester, as his father had been before him, and required his sons and the other magnates all to 'swear to uphold and maintain him, as their only lawful lord and undoubted sovereign'. On Christmas Day he made his grandson sit down with him at his table, in great state, above his sons, indicating that Richard should be seen as next heir to the throne.[6] The Christmas festivities, which stretched from the nativity of Christ through the New Year to his own birthday, were always special to Richard. The celebrations of 1376–7 were deliriously so. Early in the new year he sat in the old king's place at the opening of parliament. In the opening speech Adam Houghton, chancellor and bishop of St David's, announced that the king had advanced Richard to be prince of Wales. He then explained to the members how they should honour the prince, as the wise men did to Christ, 'by presenting gold in token of riches and renown; and myrrh in token of his honourable sceptre: since even the pagans were used to throw money at the approach of their princes'. He declared that the prince should be embraced in their hearts 'even as Simeon embraced Christ', because their eyes had now seen that for which their hearts had longed. He explained how they should obey him 'as the vicar and legate of God, that they might see the true peace of Israel, namely here in England, the inheritance of God'.[7]

Richard was the darling of the Londoners. On the evening of Sunday 1 February, some 130 of the leading citizens, 'disguised, as for a mummery', rode by torchlight, to the accompaniment of trumpets, sackbuts, cornets and other minstrelsy, from Newgate through Cheapside and so over the Bridge through Southwark, till they came to Kennington near Lambeth, where his mother the princess of Wales, his uncles, and other lords and ladies were waiting. Leading the cavalcade, riding in pairs, were forty-eight citizens dressed like squires, and another forty-eight dressed like knights, wearing masks on their faces. Then came one richly arrayed like an emperor; and some distance after him another attired in pontificals, representing the pope, with twenty-four cardinals attending him. In the rear there were eight men strangely attired and with black vizards, as if they were the ambassadors of foreign potentates. At Kennington they dismounted in the courtyard and entered the great hall, and the royal party came out from the chamber to receive their salutations. By throwing dice on the table, the mummers 'signified their desire to play with the young prince', and when he accepted their offer, 'they so obligingly contrived the dice, that the prince always won, whether he cast at them, or they at him'. After losing considerable sums, they set on the table three treasures, one after another, namely a gold bowl, a gold cup, and a gold ring, all of which the prince won at three throws. Following the dice-play there was further splendid entertainment, with the most 'exquisite music' and dancing in which the prince and the lords danced on the one part and the mummers on the other. The evening concluded with wine and spices, and the mummers departed in the order in which they came.[8]

On a number of occasions over the next few months Richard found himself the focus of heartfelt protestations of love and loyalty. In the St George's Day celebrations at Windsor in April 1377 he was invested as a Knight of the Garter, sharing this honour, somewhat ironically, with the two agents of his nemesis, his youngest uncle Thomas of Woodstock and his cousin Henry of Bolingbroke. The truce with France was about to expire, and it was assumed that the young prince would soon have the opportunity for combat experience. A large expeditionary force was being assembled. The joint leaders were to be the ten-year-old prince and his uncle, John of Gaunt. The expedition was cancelled when news came of the king's sharp decline and death on 21 June. For the second time in less than a year Richard donned black, and followed the royal cortège through the streets of the capital. He was now not only chief mourner but also the new king. This time the procession ended among the royal tombs in St Edward the Confessor's chapel in Westminster abbey. It was here that he would come when his destiny was fulfilled.

★   ★   ★

Westminster abbey was more brightly decked out for the coronation on 16 July. It was a time for great celebration. The last coronation had been over fifty years ago, and that had been a somewhat makeshift affair. People now thronged to the capital from all corners of the realm, and the streets and abbey itself were packed. There was a great deal

The coronation of a king. (© Dean & Chapter of Westminster)

to be organized. There were worries about protocol, procedure and the regalia, and Richard had to be carefully coached. In the event there were several minor slips, which were later recalled as auguries of misfortune. After the ceremony, instead of proceeding to the vestry to disrobe, Richard was raised aloft by Sir Simon Burley and carried, in his full regalia, through the milling crowds to the palace. In the process he lost in the press one of the ceremonial slippers, reputedly dating back to the time of Alfred the Great.[9]

The ritual itself was awe-inspiring and transformative. After Richard had prostrated himself before the high altar he received like obeisance from the archbishops and bishops. He then took the coronation oath to protect Holy Church and to maintain the laws and customs of the realm. He was then ceremoniously divested of his clothes and anointed with chrism. His old self, even before it had achieved adult self-awareness, was washed away, and he was transformed to a higher plane. He assumed, in the manner of a priest, a sacral quality which could never be effaced. If he had been catechized as to the ceremony and its significance, as he must have been, he would have heard the words of the psalmist:

> Look down, Omnipotent God, with serene eyes on this most glorious king. Grant him to be a most mighty protector of the fatherland, and a comforter of churches and holy monasteries with the greatest piety of royal munificence, and to be the mightiest of kings, triumphing over his enemies so as to crush rebels and heathen nations; and may he be very terrible to his enemies with the utmost strength of royal potency. Also may he be generous and lovable and pious to the magnates and the outstanding leaders and the faithful men of his realm, that he may be feared and loved by all. Also may kings come forth from his loins through successions of future times to rule this whole realm. And after glorious and happy times in this present life, may he be worthy to have eternal joys in perpetual blessedness.[10]

Finally, he was crowned by the archbishop of Canterbury, invested with ring, sceptre and orb, and ceremoniously enthroned.

The coronation of the young king symbolized the coming of a new age, but once it was over the old realities resurfaced. Richard was a minor, and it would be some years before he could be thought ready to assume executive power. All the tensions of Edward III's last years remained, still unresolved. John of Gaunt remained the most powerful man in the land, but he was the object of much hatred and suspicion. For many people, the 'continual' council which was appointed to govern in the king's name served only to mask Gaunt's role behind the scenes. England was again at war with France. Largely futile expeditions by the king's uncles placed a heavy burden of taxation on the people, while the French harried the south coast, and briefly occupied the Isle of Wight. There was rancour within the church. The long sojourn of the popes at Avignon had diminished their reputation in England. John Wycliffe, an Oxford philosopher who was recruited by Gaunt to argue against papal claims, began to develop a radical and subversive body of teachings about the true church and the sacraments. His emphasis on a preaching ministry and Bible reading, and his attack on clerical wealth and privilege, guaranteed the appeal of his heresy to the laity. Gregory XI, who had restored the papacy to Rome, issued bulls condemning Wycliffitism (or Lollardy as it was increasingly known), and urged the king and the English prelates to take action.[11] Faced with the most formidable challenge to its teaching for several generations, the church found its capacity for action and its moral authority further diminished by the Great Schism. On Gregory's death in 1378 the cardinals in Rome hurriedly elected the Italian Urban VI as his successor. A group of French cardinals challenged the validity of the election and, with the support of the king of France, elected 'Clement VII'. Latin Christendom was soon divided into two allegiances, with rival popes in Rome and Avignon. The dramatic advance of the Turks through south-east Europe made the division seem especially deplorable. From the outset, Richard's reign was set against a backcloth of unprecedented crisis in England and in the Christian world at large.

Over the next few years Richard was inducted into his kingly office. At first it was a largely passive role. He was the icon of monarchy, the visible representation of order and justice. His first appearance on the public stage, when he stilled the clamour in parliament in 1376, set the pattern. After his coronation in the summer of 1377 he had some space for recreation and the resumption of his formal education, but the ceremonial round continued, the more necessary in view of the deep political rancour in the kingdom. His first parliament in October 1377 saw changes in the composition of the 'continual council' elected by the magnates after the coronation. By the time of his second parliament the following year, if not before, Richard was learning some hard political lessons. The fact that the parliament was not held in Westminster is significant. London was increasingly restive, and the court had earned the censure of the church through its complicity in a breach of sanctuary and a murder in Westminster abbey. The selection of Gloucester as the venue may have been a political statement. It was the burial-place of Edward II, around whose tomb a cult had improbably developed. Lodged in Gloucester abbey, Richard would have learned more about the deposition and murder of his great-grandfather in 1327. Then, or soon thereafter, Richard formed a resolve to seek Edward's canonization as a royal martyr.[12]

At the beginning of 1380 Richard entered his fourteenth year, traditionally regarded as the age of majority for kings. It was observed in the parliament of 1380, albeit erroneously, that Edward III had taken power at this very age, another evocation of the events fifty years before. The period of 'continual councils' came to an end, but the political problems persisted, and perhaps increased in intensity. A combination of economic and social pressures, religious and political unrest, and above all a novel and noxious form of taxation led to the Great Revolt in the summer of 1381. Armies of peasants and labourers gathered in Kent and Essex and marched on the capital to present their grievances to the king. The rebels proved discriminating in their targets. John of Gaunt, who was held most responsible for the kingdom's ills, was on a mission in Scotland, but his splendid palace in the city was razed to the ground. The chancellor (Simon Sudbury, archbishop of Canterbury), the treasurer and the keeper of the privy seal were executed as traitors to the realm. Richard showed a great deal of courage in riding out to parley with the insurgents. Indeed his display of bravura, and his tactical concessions, at Mile End and Smithfield saved the day.

For Richard, the revolt confirmed his sense of the sanctity of his person and the potency of his office. The rebels held him inviolate, and looked to him to chastise the greedy and factious nobility, and to root out corruption in church and state. The people were calling on him to exercise his God-given authority to govern the land for the common good. Yet it must have shown him all too vividly the fragility of government and the social order. Acts of rebellion could not be condoned. Once the rebels returned to their homes, the authorities went on the offensive. Richard himself toured Essex and Hertfordshire, receiving the submission of the men of the region and presiding over the trials of the more notable rebels. The counties had to compound heavily for their complicity.[13] The young king gained first-hand experience of less principled forms of statecraft. He saw the tactical advantage that could be gained from making promises he did not mean to keep, and the power that could be exercised over men who had submitted themselves to his grace.

Richard began to emancipate himself from conciliar control. By all accounts he showed considerable initiative during the revolt, and in so far as he took counsel it was from among his own immediate entourage of knights and clerks. By the end of the summer of 1381 the size and influence of the royal household was becoming a matter of political concern. Prominent among this circle of favoured advisers was Sir Simon Burley, vice-chamberlain of the household. Though overseas at the time of the rebellion, he had played a significant role in Richard's education and was perhaps his chief political adviser. Richard also relied greatly on his confessor, Thomas Rushook. The Michaelmas parliament, badly shaken by the rebellion, had every reason to promote unity among the governing class. To this end an olive branch was held out to John of Gaunt, whose considerable power was now harnessed to buttress the fragile order. Yet the parliament also instituted a commission to reform the royal household. Rushook was instructed to leave the court. The wings of the young king were being clipped just as he was showing inclination and capacity to fly.

In effect the minority was to continue. Over the winter of 1381/2 Gaunt seemed dominant. It was he who met Richard's bride Anne of Bohemia at Dover and escorted her to Leeds castle where she spent Christmas. The marriage took place on 20 January, and two days later she was crowned by Archbishop Courtenay.[14] A month later the aldermen and leading citizens of London rode out to the king and queen at Kennington to have their charters confirmed. In a not so veiled reference to Gaunt, they petitioned that 'they might have only one king, declaring that they wished to be the subjects of one man alone'.[15] The problem was that Gaunt was not alone in feeling that the king

Anne of Bohemia and Richard II, as depicted on a lost altar-piece in the English College of Rome. (S. Petrasancta, Tesserae Gentilitiae, 1638)

was unfit to govern. In 1384 the earl of Arundel claimed that the kingdom was in danger of destruction on account of the lack of prudent government, and Richard was almost certainly right in regarding it as a personal affront.[16] William Courtenay, the new archbishop of Canterbury, likewise reproved Richard for his insolence and lack of control, and narrowly avoided physical injury from the angry young king.[17] At the very least Richard had many of the defects of character associated with adolescence. Even the friendliest chroniclers present him as arrogant and petulant, lazy and dissolute. The general refrain was that he disdained the counsels of the men of weight and experience in the realm and followed the advice of young fops.

The more the king was subject to criticism and constraint the more dependent, politically and emotionally, he became on an inner circle of courtiers. The most notable and notorious was Robert de Vere, the young earl of Oxford, but the group included men of age and experience as well as younger favourites. They had a clear interest in inflaming rather than assuaging Richard's suspicious and hostile impulses towards his uncles and others who regarded themselves as his 'natural counsellors'. Their *bête noire* was John of Gaunt,

The seal of Anne of Bohemia. (Reproduced by kind permission of Heraldry Today, from J.H. & R.V. Pinches, The Royal Heraldry of England, 1974)

who was widely assumed to be angling for his nephew's throne. Even as late as 1384, in a sensational episode at the parliament at Salisbury, Gaunt had to defend himself against an accusation that he was plotting to murder and supplant the king. His accuser was a Carmelite friar associated with de Vere.[18] In his turn Gaunt accused the courtiers of conspiring to frame him. Fearing assassination, early in 1385 he came into the king's presence with a breast-plate under his gown.[19] Other magnates had reason to resent the favourites who, if not actively poisoning the king's mind towards them, were scorning their counsels and ridiculing their endeavours. Walsingham records a telling scene in which the king and his companions mocked the martial exploits of Thomas of Woodstock and the earl of Arundel.[20]

In 1385 Richard turned eighteen and was eager to win his spurs. A number of military failures had discredited the foreign policies of the magnates, and a truce with France provided the opportunity to settle scores with Scotland. In June writs of summons went out to all the king's tenants in what proved to be the last summons of the English feudal levy. The host that assembled at York was probably the largest raised on English soil for many generations.[21] At the head of what was termed an 'imperial' army, Richard advanced into the heart of the northern kingdom, sacking Melrose abbey and reaching Edinburgh. Froissart's narrative of the campaign, which is somewhat at variance from the historical record, may well reflect the terms in which the young king presented his plans and achievements to a foreign audience. In this account he progressed to Dunfermline, staying in the abbey where the kings of Scotland were traditionally buried, and briefly laid siege to Stirling castle. He was gratified to be told that he had done more than his father and grandfather had ever done, and may have derived some satisfaction from avenging in some wise his great-grandfather's humiliation at Bannockburn by Stirling. In his account Froissart had Edward I and Arthur of Britain very much in mind, noting, somewhat inconsequentially, that Carlisle was a favourite residence of King Arthur 'on account of the fine woods which surround it, and for the grand adventures of arms which had happened near it'.[22]

The expedition was costly and fruitless, but Richard returned to England with his confidence enhanced. On his way south he briefly paused at Stamford, where his mother, Joan of Kent, had recently died, but pressed on to Westminster to lay his standard at the shrine of St Edward the Confessor. At the head of his 'imperial' army, he had felt enabled to create a whole series of new titles, and in the parliament which met at Michaelmas he sought to have them confirmed. The new creations themselves represented a new compact within the royal family. The king's younger uncles joined John of Gaunt on the top tier of the peerage: Edmund of Langley became duke of York, and Thomas of Woodstock became duke of Gloucester. The king's friends were likewise honoured. While Sir Simon Burley's nomination to the peerage was not confirmed, Sir Michael de la Pole was raised to the earldom of Suffolk.[23] Most remarkable was the promotion of Robert de Vere to the marquisate of Dublin, giving him a dignity hitherto unknown in England and precedence over all the other earls.[24] It was a remarkable promotion, bearing comparison only with Edward II's creation of Gaveston as earl of Cornwall.

One consequence of the new creations was to end the unique eminence of the house of Lancaster. Richard now seems to have taken an even more significant step. According to the continuator of the *Eulogium Historiarum*, he named in parliament Roger Mortimer as his heir.[25] This testimony has often been questioned. Yet in the light of the evidence of Edward III's entail, Richard's nomination of Mortimer appears plausible, even necessary.[26] Given his suspicions of Gaunt, Richard had a strong personal motive to name his innocuous young cousin as heir to the throne. As Richard approached his majority, the old king's declaration can scarcely have had any force.[27] In any case, it is hard to explain, other than in terms of a new statement from the throne, a new set of assumptions about the succession in England. Some time in the late 1380s, for example, the monk of Westminster asserted, in matter of fact terms, that if the king died without children the crown would pass by hereditary right to the Mortimers.[28]

A new settlement at this time fits well, too, with an apparent release of tension in the relations between the king and Gaunt. Gaunt was ready to cut his losses in England. The Portuguese victory at Aljubarrota in August 1385 provided an opportunity for Gaunt to renew his bid for the crown of Castile.[29] It was an ambition that the king was willing to support. At a meeting of a great council in March 1386 Richard had his uncle publicly acknowledged as king of Castile, and seated him for the first time on his right-hand side. At Easter he presented his uncle and his wife with gold crowns, and accorded them royal honours.[30] When Gaunt left for Spain in July 1386, it might have been assumed that the shadow over Richard's reign was passing, but events proved otherwise. Gaunt's immense power and authority, and, ironically, his unpopularity, both added ballast to the ship of state and served to take the edge off other animosities and concerns. His departure seems to have upset the balance of power in the kingdom, and set the scene for a major political crisis.

★ ★ ★

In the mid-1380s Richard was a young prince with a distinctive character and style. He was of moderate height, but his golden hair and light beard gave him a distinctly regal air. His face was round and well formed, if a little soft and feminine. Clearly he was reputed to be handsome, and was likened to Troilus or Absalom.[31] He was extravagantly splendid in dress and his sartorial elegance was matched by his delicacy of manner. He installed a bath-house at his palace at Sheen, and – in what seems an unprecedented affectation – had pieces of linen cut to use as handkerchiefs.[32] His effeteness and self-indulgence remained the focus of concern. The monk of Evesham described him as a great carouser, staying up until midnight or even passing the whole night in drinking and other debauchery.[33] At a Christmas feast in 1386 he allegedly allowed Suffolk to recline at table dressed not in the normal noble attire but in a toga.[34] Richard was as indulgent to his friends and servants as to himself. Robert de Vere was his chief favourite and, allegedly, his evil genius. It was believed that Richard planned to make him king of Ireland, and there were rumours of 'obscene familiarity' between them.[35] The atmosphere at court appeared to his critics decadent and lascivious. There were sexual scandals, notably de Vere's repudiation of his wife, a granddaughter of Edward III, for one of the queen's Bohemian ladies-in-waiting. Walsingham wrote witheringly of the courtiers as 'more knights of Venus than of Bellona, worthier in chamber than in field, sharper in tongue than in lance'.[36]

Detail from the Wilton Diptych showing Richard II kneeling. (© National Gallery)

This picture of the court is manifestly partial. Richard was physically robust, and capable of exertion and endurance. His lack of ardour for the war in France cannot simply be attributed to his indolence. By the mid–1380s he must have recognized the realities of the military situation and the high cost of maintaining the war effort. The king came to suspect that the chief beneficiaries of the conflict were the nobles who were able to build up their retinues at public expense. He was perhaps encouraged in this view by Leo de Lusignan, titular king of Armenia, who came to England at Christmas 1385 as an unofficial peace-maker. In this analysis the kings of England and France had much to gain by making common cause.[37] In 1386 Richard was prepared to talk about invoking French military aid against his domestic opponents. Leo probably offered Richard the even more intoxicating vision of the kings of England and France restoring peace and unity to Christendom and leading a crusading offensive against the Turks. Richard was greatly taken with Leo, and granted him an annual pension of 1,000 marks. The magnates regarded him as a sponger and a spy, and prevented his return to England in 1386.[38]

Richard's courtiers cannot simply be dismissed as knaves and fools. Suffolk and Burley may have been arrogant and grasping, but they were men of experience and ability. De Vere was clearly no fop; he was of distinguished lineage, and showed some vigour in arms and tournaments.[39] As he grew in years, Richard naturally sought greater freedom in the disposal of patronage. He wanted to reward his friends, and he needed to build up his own following. As chancellor, Suffolk accommodated him, making grants on the authentication of Richard's signet seal. The royal household was resuming its role as the engine of policy, and Richard recognized the absolute necessity of building up his own power-base, military and political. The expedition to Scotland, when the king's contingent was overshadowed by Gaunt's massive retinue, reinforced this message. From this time onwards Richard seems to have drawn into his entourage a number of knights and soldiers, not least from his own palatinate of Chester.[40] When in 1385 parliament petitioned for the reform of the king's household and restraint in royal patronage, Richard responded, in effect, that it was his own business.

There was a positive side to Richard's promotion of the 'arts of love' rather than the 'arts of war'. In the mid-1380s the court was culturally effervescent. Geoffrey Chaucer was in the royal service, and wrote *Troilus and Criseyde* with a court audience in mind. Thomas Usk, recorder of London, was closely associated with the court party and wrote his *Testament of Love* some time before his execution in 1388. In his cultural patronage, Richard had objectives other than mere diversion, and he certainly has claims to be regarded as England's 'Sun-King'. As early as 1385 the Westminster chronicler noted his 'lust for glory and eagerness to have from everyone the deference properly due to his kingship'.[41] Patricia Eberle has argued that he consciously developed a style of regal magnificence to buttress his monarchy.[42] Emulating the kings of France, he made extensive use of sun-imagery, and in 1387 he distributed 'sun-badges' to all who would support him in arms.[43] He was clearly concerned with the theatre of power. In 1385 the king and his council commissioned a series of thirteen sculptured kings to adorn the old Westminster Hall, a number indicating the kings of England from St Edward to Richard himself.[44] The king and his advisers were likewise much involved in the commemoration of Edward III and the Black Prince.[45] A ship arrived at Poole in 1386 'laden with marble for the tomb of Edward III at Westminster'. The epitaph on the Purbeck marble tomb presented him as the flower and model of kings who had achieved his jubilee, an unvanquished leopard, a Maccabeus in wars.[46]

Richard gave much thought to his regality. From as early as 1383 he showed himself jealous of his prerogatives, and in a succession of acts reserved his rights as king. He took an informed interest in the traditions of his kingship, commissioning works of history, and especially his regalia. The Westminster chronicle records two occasions in

Westminster kings, engraving by John Carter, late eighteenth century. (Author's collection)

1385 when he visited the abbey, seemingly on impulse and at night, once to show the king of Armenia the royal insignia used at his coronation.[47] He sought to harness to his kingship the prestige and power of royal saints. He made St Edward the Confessor his special patron, and sought to harness his spiritual power to his kingship. In a memorable grant of Queenborough castle to de Vere in 1385 he invoked the curse of God, St Edward and himself on anyone who dared seek to revoke it.[48] In January 1386 Richard granted de Vere, for as long as he held the lordship of Ireland, the right to bear the arms of St Edmund King and Martyr.[49] He clearly gave much thought to the burden of recent English history, seeing his predicament very much in terms of that of his great-grandfather. John Bacon, who was sent to Urban VI to seek Edward's canonization, died in Italy, and was subsequently accorded a full requiem mass in Westminster abbey, with Richard present in the choir on both days.[50] The critics of the court increasingly had to recognize that they were dealing with a king who had a decidedly exalted view of his office. He was not only promoting the

Tomb effigy of Edward III. (© Dean & Chapter of Westminster)

cult of English kingship, but was also seemingly drawn to Roman concepts of princely power.[51]

★　★　★

The crisis came in the parliament of October 1386. The commons launched a forceful attack on the government and petitioned for the dismissal of the chancellor, the treasurer and other ministers. Richard retired in dudgeon to Eltham and declared that he would not sack even a scullery boy at their request. On the 13th, the feast of St Edward the Confessor, he gave further evidence of his *hauteur* by granting Robert de Vere the grand title of duke of Ireland with vice-regal powers.[52]

The stand-off between the king and his parliament was only broken when the duke of Gloucester and Thomas Arundel, bishop of Ely, went to Eltham to treat with the king on parliament's behalf. According to Henry Knighton, Bishop Arundel outlined parliament's role in the provision of justice, righting wrongs, giving counsel and granting supply, and explained that if the king continued to absent himself it would disband. Richard replied that he knew well enough that the commons intended to resist him, and that he considered the better course to turn to the king of France for aid, 'better to submit ourselves to him than to our subjects'. Bishop Arundel firmly reminded Richard of the military achievements of his grandfather and father, the sacrifices of the people, and how the realm was on the point of ruin through misrule. In conclusion, he pointed out the existence of 'an ancient law, which not long since, lamentably, had to be invoked, which provides that if the king, upon some evil counsel, or from wilfulness and contempt' alienated himself from his people, 'and will not be governed and guided by the laws of the land', or follow 'the wholesome counsel' of the magnates, 'then it would be lawful with the common assent and agreement of the people of the realm to put down the king from the royal seat, and raise another of the royal lineage in his place'.[53]

The allusion to the deposition of Edward II produced the desired reaction. Richard returned to parliament. On 23 October he dismissed his chancellor, the earl of Suffolk, and appointed Bishop Arundel in his place. The commons then impeached Suffolk on seven articles relating to dereliction of duty and misappropriation of funds, and committed him to prison in Windsor castle. On 19 November a 'great and continual council' was established. Its membership included Archbishops Courtenay of Canterbury and Neville of York, Bishops Wykeham of Winchester, Arundel of Ely and Gilbert of Hereford, the abbot of Waltham, the dukes of York and Gloucester, the earl of Arundel, Lord Cobham, Sir Richard Scrope, Sir John Devereux and John Waltham. Its term was a full twelve months, and it was to govern in the king's name. Richard refused to consider a further petition that the principal officers of state, the members of the new council and the steward of the king's household should be 'ordained and established' in parliament, and that the term of the 'continual council' should run until the next parliament.[54]

Richard soon showed his contempt for the new 'continual council'. He secured the release of Suffolk and showed him great honour over Christmas. In February 1387 he left Westminster and withdrew into the provinces. Over the spring and summer the officers of the realm, concerned to maintain the legality of their proceedings, found themselves seeking out the king in the Midlands and the Welsh marches, and having to present their business to a disdainful king surrounded by their political enemies. On occasion Richard held court in great state. On 29 June the king and queen attended Richard Scrope's installation as bishop of Lichfield. The witnesses included the archbishops of York and Dublin, the bishop of Chichester, the dukes of Ireland and York, the earl of Suffolk, Lords Basset, Beaumont and Zouche, Simon Burley, John Beauchamp, John Golafre and other knights. The king held a great feast in the bishop's palace, 'then the king's palace', to which he invited all the clergy and leading citizens of Lichfield.[55] In the course of his perambulations he sought to build up a military following, retaining gentlemen and yeomen with gold badges in the form of a sun and with silver crowns.[56] One recruiting agent was arrested in East Anglia.[57] Presumably the king had most freedom of action and success in his earldom of Chester, where he spent some weeks, and where de Vere, recently appointed justiciar of Chester, began to build up a powerful establishment.

The king continually sought means to exalt his regal authority and undermine the status of the 'continual council'.[58] The councils he convened at Shrewsbury around 21 August and at Nottingham on 25 August provided the ideological and legal basis for a royalist counter-offensive. Summoning to his presence Sir Robert Tresilian, chief justice of the king's bench, and his fellow judges, he put to them ten questions relating to his regality and prerogative in the light of recent parliamentary initiatives. The judges were asked whether 'the statute and ordinance and commission made and promulgated' in the last parliament was derogatory to the king's regality, whether the king had control over the business of parliament and the right to dissolve it when he pleased, whether the lords and commons could impeach and remove the king's ministers against his will, and whether the judgement against Suffolk was erroneous. In each case the judges found clearly in favour of the crown. Even more ominously, he asked how those people should be punished who procured the offending commission, or moved in parliament for the tabling of the statute by which judgement had been passed on Edward II, or put pressure on the king to consent to the commission or any like commission, or hindered the king from exercising his prerogative. In each case the judges, while falling short of declaring any of the offences to be treason, found that the offenders should suffer capital punishment as traitors, unless the king wished to grant them grace.[59]

The ten questions, however they originated, attest to a clear ideological dimension to royalist thinking at this time. The judges' answers, however obtained, provided a firm legal basis for a royalist revanche. In truth they dramatically raised the stakes by their allusion, however veiled, to the crime of treason. Since the troubled reign of Edward II, when 'sentences of treasons were given and executed in the heat of reprisals or of civil war and with little or no attempt to conform to recognised legal procedure', bringing 'the greatest families in England under a cloud of forfeiture and disgrace', increasing restraint had been exercised with respect to allegations of treason, and indeed the scope of treason had been carefully circumscribed by statute in 1352.[60] In the impeachment of Suffolk in 1386, as in the impeachment of Edward III's ministers in 1376, the 'cry of treason' was not heard in parliament. The punishments were accordingly moderate 'and the fatal craving for reprisals was not roused'. According to Clarke, it was Richard himself who now broke the 'tacit bargain' achieved in 1352 by extracting from the judges new treasons, the chief of which 'was impeding the king in the exercise of his prerogative, a definition stretched by further questions to cover the whole policy of the baronial opposition' in what was manifestly 'a plot to destroy the commission councillors as traitors'.[61]

The king had the questions and responses set in writing, sealed by the judges and witnessed by two archbishops, four bishops and other courtiers, but otherwise showed no inclination to publicize them. His plan was to allow the commission to run its course, and from a position of power and unimpeachable legal authority restore his regality and punish the leading traitors. By late October the king was in the environs of the capital, but his opponents were preparing to meet like with like. Gloucester and other leading members of the 'continual council' had ample reason to be suspicious of the king's intentions. Alerted by the archbishop of Dublin to the proceedings at Nottingham, Gloucester took an oath before an assembly of magnates in London that he 'had never intended to infringe prerogative'.[62] Overall, he and his allies had little option but to prepare themselves for the worst, seeing 'their lives and heritages threatened by interpretations of the law made expressly to destroy them'.[63]

On 10 November the king entered London to the cheers of the crowd. He had for some time been working through the agency of Sir Nicholas Brembre to consolidate support in the city, and earlier in autumn had secured an oath from the city fathers 'to support him against anyone who proposed or talked treason'.[64] Once established at Westminster, the king summoned Gloucester and the earl of Arundel to his presence. They refused to come before him while he was surrounded by their sworn enemies. Along with the earl of Warwick, they mustered their forces at Harringey Park. Heartened by the support they received from the gentry and the commons, they made a powerful bid for the support of the city of London. They named Archbishop Neville, the duke of Ireland, the earl of Suffolk, Sir Robert Tresilian and Nicholas Brembre as 'traitors' in that they had carried off the king to distant parts, advised him 'to do various things to the disinheritance and dismemberment of his crown', and turned him against 'the lords of his council, so that some of them were in fear and peril of their lives'.[65] Alarmed by the military build-up, Richard sought to buy time, and authorised the duke of York and Archbishop Courtenay to negotiate a meeting.

On 17 November Gloucester, Arundel and Warwick rode to Westminster accompanied by three hundred men-at-arms. The king awaited them on the raised marble chair at the end of Westminster Hall, flanked by the recently erected statues of his royal ancestors. Bowing low three times, the three lords approached the throne in full armour.[66] They had already advertised their intention to hoist the king's counsellors on their own petard, and charge them with the crime of accroaching royal power, which fell within the newly expanded definition of treason. They used the ancient form of indictment known as the appeal, by which they offered to prove by personal combat the treason of Archbishop Neville, the duke of Ireland, the earl of Suffolk, Tresilian and Brembre. Richard, who must have been furious at this assault to his royal dignity, kept his nerve. He referred the appeal to a parliament to be held in the new year, and showed some cordiality towards the lords before dismissing them.

It soon became apparent that parliament's role would be merely to endorse a military verdict. The king retired to the security of Windsor castle while de Vere headed for

Chester to raise an army. Archbishop Neville withdrew to Calais, where his brother commanded the garrison, perhaps in the hope of enlisting foreign support, while Burley stationed himself at Dover. London remained critical. A proclamation was issued in the city that no one defame the five appealed of treason or any member of the king's household, and Brembre worked to secure financial and military support in the city. Wisely refusing a royal summons to Westminster, the three lords maintained themselves in arms, selecting Huntingdon as their operational headquarters. Their appeals for assistance met with considerable success. Two younger peers of the blood royal, Henry of Bolingbroke, earl of Derby, the eldest son of John of Gaunt, and Thomas Mowbray, earl of Nottingham, a former royal favourite, joined their ranks. According to Capgrave, the five lords were popularly known as the 'lords of the field', perhaps to distinguish them from their opponents whom they associated not with the battlefield but the bedchamber.[67] The host likewise included Sir Thomas Mortimer, who, as the uncle of the young earl of March, represented the Mortimer interest, as well as many lords, knights and gentlemen from the eastern counties.

In the mean time de Vere, with the assistance of Sir Thomas Molyneux, constable of Chester castle, raised a substantial army in Cheshire and neighbouring counties. By the middle of December de Vere was advancing southwards, and the confederate lords recognized the absolute necessity of defeating his army before Richard placed himself at its head. Perhaps seeking to maintain the axis linking Calais, Dover, London and Windsor, Richard remained in the capital, increasingly furious at the city's failure to provide assistance. In a series of well-conceived and well-executed movements, the confederates cornered de Vere's army near Radcot Bridge in Oxfordshire. In a short but savage encounter on 20 December the Cheshire men were put to flight. De Vere secured his escape by forcing his horse to swim the river, while Sir Thomas Molyneux was slain by Mortimer.[68] De Vere fled overseas, basing himself at Louvain, though he spent some time at the French court in Paris.

From the Tower of London Richard made a last bid to hold out against his adversaries. Gloucester, Arundel and Warwick, along with Bolingbroke and Mowbray, were admitted into London on 27 December, and demanded that the king surrender to them. The five 'lords of the field' had previously ruled out the option of deposition. The recourse to arms and the capture of de Vere's baggage, perhaps including evidence of treasonable dealings with France, seems to have hardened their attitudes. Nothing is known for certain of what happened behind the thick curtain of stone over Christmas 1387, but by the end of December Richard had seemingly surrendered to the inevitable. According to the well-informed, but generally discreet, Westminster chronicle, the lords threatened to depose him. They pointed out to him that 'his heir was unquestionably of full age and for the profit and salvation of the kingdom would gladly consent' to rule according to their advice. Presumably they had in mind one of the king's uncles or Henry of Bolingbroke, who had turned twenty-one earlier in the year.[69] According to the Whalley chronicle, Richard was actually deposed for three days, and reinstated following a dispute between Gloucester and Bolingbroke as to the succession.[70] Ten years later Gloucester made a confession of treason which is probably closest to the truth. Gloucester confessed that he and his colleagues sought advice about renouncing their allegiance, and 'for two or three days' were resolved on his deposition.[71]

CHAPTER THREE

REGAL DILIGENCE

At the beginning of 1388 Richard II was at the lowest ebb of his fortunes. On the feast of Epiphany, he turned twenty-one, but, unlike the lowliest of his subjects, he was not even master of his own house. True enough, he had escaped with his life and his crown. Even under threat of deposition in the Tower of London he may have succeeded in exploiting the rivalry between Gloucester and Derby.[1] When parliament opened on 3 February Richard was firmly seated on his throne. The Lords Appellant marched into the hall, arm in arm, but then knelt humbly before the king. They declared that 'they had never countenanced, devised, or meditated the death of the king by any means, secret or open'.[2] Through the chancellor, Richard assured his uncle that since he was of royal stock and close in lineage to the king he could not be suspected of such things.[3]

None the less Richard was largely powerless to resist the proceedings which destroyed his friends and counsellors, and set up another commission to have governance of him. The parliament has been aptly dubbed the Merciless Parliament. The Lords Appellant formally presented an appeal of treason running to thirty-nine articles against Archbishop Neville, the duke of Ireland, the earl of Suffolk, Sir Robert Tresilian and Nicholas Brembre. The first article declared that the five traitors, 'seeing the tenderness of the age of our lord the king and the innocence of his royal person, caused him to apprehend as truth' many false insinuations, turned the king's mind against 'his loyal lords', and bound him by oath to be governed by them, thus accroaching to themselves royal power and stripping him of his sovereignty. The other articles, arranged more or less chronologically, included a proposal to create de Vere king of Ireland, and concluded with his raising an army in Cheshire and accroachment of royal power by displaying the king's banner.[4] An appeal of treason was also lodged against four chamber knights, Sir Simon Burley, Sir John Beauchamp, Sir John Salisbury, and Sir James Berners. One of the articles alleged that they had proposed and taken steps to seek, in return for the cession of Calais, French military assistance against the lords of the commission.[5]

There was some concern about this manner of proceeding. A panel of judges and doctors of civil law deliberated on the matter, and advised that the appeal was not in conformity with the processes of either common or civil law. The lords considered this advice, but then declared, allegedly with the king's assent, that 'in so high a crime' as was alleged, touching on both the king and the kingdom, perpetrated by peers of the realm among others, 'the process will not be taken anywhere except to parliament, nor judged by any other law except the law and court of parliament, and that it pertains to the lords of parliament and to their franchise and liberty from ancient custom of parliament, to be judges in such a case, and to judge such a case, with the assent of the king'.[6]

With Archbishop Neville, de Vere and de la Pole abroad, and Tresilian in hiding, it was Nicholas Brembre who alone faced the wrath of the lords and commons.[7] On 17 February the former mayor of London denied his guilt, and gamely declared his readiness to prove his innocence in armed combat. Parliament ruled against this manner of proceeding, but that did not prevent some three hundred lords, knights and squires throwing down their gauntlets in response.[8] There was further drama on the 19th when Tresilian was discovered in sanctuary at Westminster. The lords led a mob to drag him from the abbey precincts. He was informed that he had been appealed of treason, and that his non-appearance had been taken as an admission of guilt. He was dispatched to be drawn from the Tower of London and hanged at Tyburn. Brembre, who allegedly aspired to the title of duke of Troy, followed him on the 20th.[9]

Early in March parliament continued its attack on the more notorious of Richard's advisers and agents in 1387. Tresilian's six fellow-judges and Thomas Rushook, bishop of Chichester, were adjudged guilty of treason, but on the petition of Archbishop Courtenay their sentence was commuted to exile in Ireland. John Blake and Thomas Usk, under-sheriff of London and the author of *Testament of Love*, were less fortunate, and suffered the full penalties for their treason. The proceedings continued on 12 March with the impeachment of the four accused knights of the king's chamber, namely Sir Simon Burley, Sir John Beauchamp, Sir John Salisbury and Sir James Berners, and of four royal clerks, namely Richard Medford, Nicholas Slake, Richard Clifford and John Lincoln.[10] Prior to the adjournment for Easter, it was resolved that all the lords and commons should swear an oath to keep the peace, and 'to live and die' with the five lords 'against everyone', saving their allegiance to the crown. It was further ordained that the sheriffs and the leading gentry in the shires, and the magistrates of towns, should likewise take the oath.[11]

Over the Easter recess passions died down a little. Gloucester himself rode out to Shenley to stand as godfather to Thomas, the son of Sir John Montagu, later earl of Salisbury.[12] When parliament resumed on 13 April and the lords came to consider the fate of Burley and other knights there was less unanimity of purpose. Richard lobbied hard. In a meeting in the bath-house behind the White Hall he implored the earl of Arundel to show mercy. Queen Anne went down on her knees to pray for his life. The duke of York declared in parliament that he would prove Burley's loyalty in personal combat, and engaged in a sharp exchange with his brother Gloucester. It was to no avail. Gloucester and Arundel pressed on, though in the end it was to cost them dear. The only mitigation allowed to Burley was that he should be beheaded rather than hanged. His execution on 5 May, and those of Beauchamp, Salisbury and Berners on the 12th, brought the blood-letting to an end.[13]

Many lords may have felt the purge had gone too far. Late in 1387 Lord Basset had declared that he would not fight for the king if it meant fighting for de Vere, but he had probably not envisioned such a blood-letting. The duke of York emerged as a force for moderation.[14] Such men may have been eager to believe that Richard had learned his lesson, and that with his former counsellors condemned and in exile all would be well. The views of John of Gaunt may have been important. Given his stalwart support for Richard on his return to England in 1389, it is likely that he took a dim view of events. Sir John Holland, who returned from Spain in early April, doubtless communicated

Gaunt's views. As Richard's half-brother and Gaunt's son-in-law, he was well placed to assist in defusing tensions. On 2 June, in one of the parliament's few bipartisan acts, he was elevated to the earldom of Huntingdon, and he and his wife were endowed with lands worth 2,000 marks.[15]

In the last days of the session parliament reflected on the audacity of its proceedings and took steps to secure its decisions. In accepting jurisdiction of the appeals of treason, in authorizing new procedures and a new definition of treason, the lords had implicitly claimed jurisdictional sovereignty for parliament.[16] In the final session parliament sought to perpetuate its judgements by declaring that anyone seeking to reverse or annul its decision 'should be adjudged and executed as traitor and enemy of the king and kingdom'. It then declared that its processes and judgements should not be 'held as an example or precedent' in the future, and that the law relating to treason should remain as defined by statute prior to this session. The lords and commons repeated the solemn oath that they had taken at the end of the first session in March to maintain the parliament's statutes and judgements, and writs were sent out to the sheriffs to require all freeholders in their counties to make the same oath.[17] In a ceremony at Westminster abbey, Richard, seated on the throne before the high altar, renewed his coronation oath and received the homage of the lords. The thirteen bishops present then fulminated sentences of excommunication against any who thereafter broke their oath or sought to rouse the king's anger against the lords.[18]

★ ★ ★

In seeking to re-establish his position Richard looked for support from the church hierarchy. It is true that the king's allies in the episcopate had been eliminated in the upheavals of 1387–8. Archbishop Neville had fled overseas, while Bishop Rushook of Chichester had been exiled. Archbishop Courtenay, who had long been a stern critic, may have inclined at first to the view that Richard was getting his just deserts. In the spring of 1388 the Lords Appellant secured from a compliant pope the translation of Neville and Rushook from their dioceses, and the promotion of churchmen supportive of the new order. Bishop Arundel of Ely, a prominent member of the commission in 1386, was promoted to the see of York. Yet the scale of the factional triumph, and the use of papal provisions to effect a series of politically motivated translations, may have tipped the balance back a little in Richard's favour. Archbishop Courtenay and Bishop Wykeham of Winchester, a veteran in the royal service, were inclined to respond positively to signs that the king had mended his ways.

Richard showed studied reverence for the church. Even at the lowest ebb of his fortunes he turned to good effect his role as protector of the liberties of the English church. An issue exquisite to his purpose arose from the breach of sanctuary involved in Tresilian's arrest. The monks of Westminster protested against the violation of their privileges, and Richard was happy to take up their case. On 18 April he organized a meeting with Bishops Arundel and Wykeham at Kennington, and had the abbey's charters read out to them. Bishop Arundel found himself in the embarrassing position of having to justify breaches of sanctuary, and incurred ridicule by raising the issue of whether a regicide could be accorded this privilege. Richard would have none of such casuistry, and won plaudits from the monks of Westminster for his reverence for the church. The Westminster chronicler waxed lyrical about his vigorous championship of the liberties of the church, and how on many occasions, 'but for him and him alone, she might have lost her privileges'.[19]

The church was ideologically predisposed to strong monarchy. Its position was never so vulnerable as in times of rebellion and civil strife, especially given the widespread lay hostility to its wealth and privileges. The upheavals of 1387–8 seem to have provided fertile ground for religious dissent. In 1387 Peter Patteshull, a renegade friar, raised a storm in London through his denunciations of his former brethren. The cry went up, 'Let's finish off the murderers, burn the sodomites and hang the traitors to the king and England', and bills were affixed to the doors of St Paul's.[20] In 1388 Thomas Wimbledon gave a memorable sermon at St Paul's Cross in London on the obligations of stewardship. In a not so veiled reference to the king, he referred to Rehoboam, who had dismissed the counsellors of his father Solomon and taken advice only from young favourites. He issued warnings about the coming Apocalypse, noting authorities that dated it to fourteen hundred years after the birth of Christ, 'the which number of years is now fulfilled not fully twelve year and an half lacking'.[21]

It was the challenge of heresy which above all inclined the leaders of the English church to support the reconstruction of royal authority. The teaching of John Wycliffe had been formally condemned, and his Oxford following dispersed, but there were still many active Lollard preachers, some under the protection of powerful patrons. Richard's stand against heresy in the spring of 1388 may have impressed the bishops even more than his defence of the privileges of Westminster. Thus he intervened to support the abbot of Osney in disciplining a 'Lollard' squire who would not pay tithes.[22] He presumably approved the orders of 23 May to seize all Wycliffite books and writings, and to imprison at his pleasure persons holding to their wicked opinions.[23] Richard's championship of orthodoxy appears to have been a major factor in the improvement of relations between the king and Thomas Arundel, who placed the extirpation of heresy at the forefront of his concerns.

Even the episcopal translations provided Richard with an opportunity to bind new and old prelates more firmly to the crown. In September the king met parliament at Cambridge. On the 3rd, at Barnwell Priory near Cambridge, John Waltham, bishop of Salisbury, did fealty to 'our most serene prince in Christ' Richard, and received the temporalities of his see in the presence of the steward of the household and other lords. On Sunday 20 September he was consecrated at the hands of Archbishop Courtenay in the presence of the king, bishops and nobles.[24] The two ceremonies were repeated for the other prelates. The witness-list to Waltham's homage includes Thomas, archbishop of York, Walter, bishop of Durham and Ralph, bishop of Bath and Wells, specifically noting their translations from Ely, Bath and Wells, and Salisbury respectively. The new concord was commemorated by a pair of bosses, one of Richard and the other of Archbishop Arundel, on the roof of the new porch at Sutton parish church near Ely.

★ ★ ★

Over the summer of 1388 Richard's position strengthened markedly. The king took heart from increasing disillusionment with the Appellant regime. Scottish incursions across the border, one of which ended in a Scottish victory at Otterburn in August, added to the discontent. The earl of Arundel's naval operations proved costly and achieved nothing, and occasioned adverse comment. In the Cambridge Parliament Richard showed himself an astute politician. The commons were much exercised by the issue of public order, especially the lawlessness associated with royal and aristocratic retaining. They complained that men wearing the badges of their lords became so arrogant and bold that they did not hesitate to rob, extort and make it impossible for ordinary people to find justice. The magnates would do more than promise to discipline their own retainers. In a dramatic move, Richard offered, for the sake of peace and by way of example to others, to give up his own badges. His offer was well calculated to affirm his readiness to take the lead in restoring order, and to embarrass the lords, who predictably remained obdurate. Richard then nimbly brokered an agreement by which the lords and commons agreed to shelve the issue until the next parliament.[25]

The Cambridge Parliament marked an important stage in the re-establishment of Richard's personal authority. During the summer a number of the knights and clerks who had been expelled from the court, or were bound over to appear at the next parliament, reappeared at the king's side. Richard Medford, the king's secretary, Sir John Clanvowe, Sir John Golafre and Sir Thomas Blount were among their number.[26] There were no further proceedings against the king's friends, though it may have been fortunate in this respect that Sir Thomas Trivet, who had counselled the king to extreme measures in November 1387, died in a riding accident during the session. One of the last acts of the parliament was to set at liberty the knights and clerks of the royal household still under sentence. On his return to Westminster, Richard presented at the shrine of St Edward the Confessor, perhaps as an act of thanksgiving, a gold ring set with a priceless ruby.[27]

In late November ambassadors were sent to France to negotiate a truce or final peace. While formally an act of the Appellant regime, the move clearly had Richard's support and was a concession of failure by Gloucester, who had stalled on the issue for most of the year. Gaunt's views were clearly a factor, too. Notwithstanding his appointment by the Appellants as lieutenant of Aquitaine, he had declined to fall in with their foreign policy and military plans. There were still some in the summer of 1388 who doubted that Gaunt would ever come back to England, but by the autumn it became increasingly sensible to work on the assumption of his return.[28] Gaunt relinquished his claims to the crown of Castile and moved to Bordeaux, where he arranged the marriage of his daughter to the king of Castile. Gaunt had been greatly changed by his experiences in Spain. Of particular moment to the king was Gaunt's evident conversion to the cause of peace with France. The Westminster chronicler refers to a mission to him in Bordeaux of a French knight 'who, while he was in the Holy Land, was bidden in a vision to visit all the Christian inhabitants of Europe, urging them to abandon their wars altogether and to return to the unity of peace'.[29] Gaunt was drawn to the idea of a general peace in Christendom as preparation for a crusade. It was a vision he and his nephew would increasingly share.

★ ★ ★

By spring 1389 Richard felt ready to assert himself. On 3 May he formally declared his majority at a great council at Westminster. He observed that he was of an age when 'the meanest heir in the kingdom' was entitled to enjoy his inheritance, and declared his resolve to take personal responsibility for the government of the realm.[30] He recalled that for twelve years he and his kingdom had been ruled by others, and that during this time his people had been continuously taxed. He made a pledge to work tirelessly for the well-being of the people and the prosperity of his realm. He reconstituted his household and administration. He appointed Bishop Wykeham of Winchester and Bishop Brantingham of Exeter, both veterans in the royal service, as chancellor and treasurer, and secured the resignation of the judges appointed by the Appellants. He selected a new council, which included Archbishop Courtenay and the earl of Northumberland, but pointedly excluded Gloucester and Arundel.[31] It must have been especially satisfying for Richard to assume personal direction of the peace process with France, securing the first of a series of truces that would continue for the rest of his reign.

Richard's assertion of his rights was entirely fitting. No one doubted the king's responsibility to exercise his will in the government of the realm. The rule of the 'continual council' was an aberration necessitated by Richard's youth and adolescent folly. Even if the Lords Appellant had been less self-serving and more successful in their foreign policy, they could not have offered the leadership and stability required. The issue of public order was especially pressing. The Appellants were too beholden to their supporters to offer firm and even-handed justice. Richard declared that it was his intent 'to provide greater tranquillity to the realm and a more ample provision of justice than it had hitherto enjoyed'.[32] More to the point, his government took action, sending out judicial commissions into various trouble-spots. On 15 July new commissions of the peace were appointed in all counties. They were smaller in size and more professional in composition than their predecessors, and, in a remarkable innovation, no lords were named to them. When new sheriffs were appointed in November, the king was actively involved, and an effort was made to select men of weight and standing in their communities. The novel requirement that they be sworn into office before the king and council was intended to underline the king's personal interest in how they conducted themselves. As Storey observed, Richard was showing 'his awareness that an appeal to the defence of law and order might win a political dividend'.[33]

It was a time for new beginnings. Richard was able to attribute the problems of the time to the weakness of the crown, and offered a vision of peace and order which was deeply seductive. In the first version of *Confessio Amantis*, John Gower reflected the newly positive mood. Alluding to the recent troubles in the kingdom, he pointed out that God had kept Richard and his estate safe, and likened 'my worthy prince' to the sun which has been masked by cloud:

> But hou so that it trowble in their,
> The sonne is evere briht and feir,
> Withinne himself and noght empeired:
> Althogh the weder be despeired,
> The hed planete is not to wite.

Initial R showing Richard II and Anne of Bohemia, from a charter of Richard II to Shrewsbury. (Shrewsbury Museums)

Gower praised the king for mixing justice with mercy, and setting aside thoughts of vengeance. He commended his efforts to promote love and accord, 'not only here at home' but also overseas. In seeking peace Richard was choosing the way of Christ. In showing Christian virtue he would, with God's aid, restore harmony and stability to the realm.[34]

Still, the mood remained one of only cautious optimism. In July the arrest was ordered of certain people in the Forest of Dean who had allegedly 'blasphemed' the king's person.[35] By the autumn it was a matter of mounting concern that Richard remained unreconciled with Gloucester and Arundel, despite overtures from them. Proceedings against usurpations of royal rights and asset-stripping of crown lands may have caused disquiet in the southern counties. Meanwhile the king was showing that he had not lost the habit of playing favourites. The rising stars were his half-brother John Holland, earl of Huntingdon, and his childhood friend Thomas Mowbray, now seemingly restored fully to favour. In October there was a debate in council over Mowbray's terms as warden of the East March. Bishop Wykeham headed conciliar opposition to the king's indulgence towards Mowbray. An irate Richard stormed out of the meeting, but the council held firm.[36]

In the autumn of 1389 England awaited the return of John of Gaunt. After an absence of almost three-and-a-half years, he landed at Plymouth on 19 November. His costly and largely futile adventurism in Spain had been a sobering experience.[37] From Plymouth he immediately made his way to Reading where the king had convened a council. Richard rode out to welcome him on the road and gave him the kiss of peace. In a remarkable gesture he took Gaunt's 'SS' livery collar to wear to signify 'the good love heartfully felt between them'.[38] At the council meeting on 10 December Gaunt formally reconciled Richard with the Lords Appellant. At Richard's urging, Gaunt himself then dropped an old grudge he bore against the earl of Northumberland, 'thereby setting others an example of how, by laying their bitterness aside, they might live in peace and quiet'.[39] The royal party moved to Woodstock for Christmas. The festive cheer turned to tragedy, however, when the young earl of Pembroke was accidentally slain in a tournament on New Year's eve.[40]

In mid-January Richard returned to Westminster to meet the first parliament of his majority. The proceedings began with the new regime seeking and receiving parliamentary endorsement. On 20 January the chancellor, treasurer and all the lords of the council sought to be discharged from their offices, and then asked that anyone who had complaint of them should make declaration in parliament. On the next day the commons declared that they saw no fault in them, and the lords agreed that they had served the realm loyally and well. Richard then restored the ministers to their offices, and reappointed his council, adding to its membership Gaunt and Gloucester. The charade was complete when he announced that parliamentary approval was not to be regarded as a precedent, and that it remained his prerogative to appoint and dismiss ministers at his pleasure.[41]

Parliament attended to a range of business. For the commons public order remained the major concern. Given Gaunt's presence there can have been little hope of making headway on the issue of aristocratic retaining, but there was a move to prevent lords securing pardons for retainers convicted of murder and other serious crimes. In the final week of parliament the king appointed new household officers, namely the earl of Huntingdon as chief chamberlain of England for life, and Sir Thomas Percy as under-chamberlain. At the same time he proved munificent to two princes of the blood. He raised to the peerage his cousin Edward, the eldest son of the duke of York, as earl of Rutland. Above all, he indulged Gaunt with two grants of breathtaking generosity. On 16 February he elevated the duchy of Lancaster to a palatinate, and vested it on Gaunt in tail male. Then, on 2 March, he nominated Gaunt duke of Guyenne for life, and in effect transferred the government of Aquitaine to his charge.[42]

★   ★   ★

Despite the promise of a new start, Richard remained very much on probation. The crown in some degree remained in commission. The council established in May 1389 had some of the flavour of a council of national unity. It was prepared to make a stand against the king, and it regarded itself as in some wise accountable to parliament. Gaunt's return broke through the impasse created by political division and continuing reservations about Richard. According to Walsingham, Gaunt had returned from Spain a changed man. But England, too, had changed. His immense power and prestige made him the natural coping-stone of the new order, to which all three royal uncles now lent their collective weight. The nature of the new regime is well expressed in the remarkable council ordinance of March 1390 that 'no gift or grant that may be turned for the diminution of the king's profit shall be passed without the advice of the council and the assent of the dukes of Guyenne, York, and Gloucester and of the chancellor, or any two of them'.[43] It can be seen, too, in the burying of any proposal to limit aristocratic retaining. In late April the council issued an ordinance which, so far from addressing the commons' concerns, simply made the grant of liveries to retainers the monopoly of secular lords.[44]

In 1390 Richard was content to accept the new political order. Given his own isolation and his vulnerability in 1387–8, his welcome of his uncle may have been heartfelt, and his assumption of Gaunt's livery no empty gesture. Richard recognized that it might be some time before he could fully re-establish his regality, and that he needed the support, perhaps even the guidance, of his immensely powerful and experienced uncle. Over the winter of 1389–90 it became evident, too, that there was a meeting of minds on a number of issues. The most obvious area of agreement was with respect to the war with France. Gaunt had his own interests in a settlement with France, but he knew the horrors of war better than most, and seems to have been a genuine convert to the cause of peace. From early 1390 he represented Richard in a series of diplomatic negotiations, and largely bore the political costs of a foreign policy which was far from popular. While Gaunt remained a self-interested and ambitious dynast, he seems to have shared his nephew's high view of his regality. If there was an understanding between the two men that, should Richard fail to have issue the succession would pass to Gaunt's line, it would make even more comprehensible Gaunt's unflinching loyalty through the 1390s.

The new accord between Richard and Gaunt is strikingly evident in the summer of 1390 when Gaunt entertained the king and queen, the dukes of York and Gloucester,

The seal of Thomas Holland, earl of Kent.
(Reproduced by kind permission of Heraldry
Today, from J.H. & R.V. Pinches, The Royal
Heraldry of England, *1974)*

the earls of Arundel and Huntingdon, and a host of other bishops, lords and ladies at Leicester castle. The royal party arrived on 24 July to a splendid reception, and over the next few days the gaiety continued with hunting and other diversions. An incident from a council meeting at this time provides rare insight into the character and views of the king and his uncle. Gaunt sought a royal pardon for John Northampton, his factional ally in the city of London. Richard answered that he did not think it was in his power 'to do that now'. Gaunt replied that he could do that and more: 'God forbid that your power should be so cramped that you could not extend grace to your liege subjects when the circumstances call for such action.' Richard hesitated for a moment, and then said: 'If I can do what you say, there are others who have suffered great hardship; so that I know what to do for my friends who are now overseas.'[45]

The political reality was that effective government depended on a partnership between crown and nobility. As the senior prince of the blood and the greatest territorial magnate in the realm, Gaunt was vital to this partnership. His pivotal position is well illustrated in the account of the abbot of Crowland's dispute with the earl of Kent, the king's elder half-brother, who was seeking to extend the bounds of his fenland manor of Deeping. After vain attempts to negotiate with Kent, the abbot sought the aid of the house of Lancaster, which had its own interest in maintaining the fenland boundaries. In 1388 Henry of Bolingbroke obtained Kent's agreement to hold the matter over until Gaunt's return, and early in 1390 Gaunt assisted the men of Crowland in securing a royal commission to settle the boundaries.[46] When later in the year the abbot of Crowland came to parliament to lay complaints against Kent, however, he found Gaunt less helpful. For the first time the abbot appealed directly to Richard, declaring that he would no longer be able to support the obligations of the royal foundation 'unless the royal clemency should deign speedily to provide him with opportune assistance'. Richard referred the abbot's bill to Gaunt, asking him to present it to the council 'in order that they might secure peace and quietness, such as the law of the land and justice demand'. A day was appointed for a hearing in the new year. In the mean time the abbot had to be content with a letter to Kent's officers to desist from harassing the abbot and his men.[47]

★ ★ ★

Richard remained very much the ceremonial monarch, and continued to cultivate the liturgical and ideological elements of his kingship. In May 1389 he had his great crown transported to King's Langley.[48] He presumably staged a solemn crown-wearing to mark the declaration of his majority. Such crown-wearings were fairly regularly held during the remainder of his reign. He may even have given thought to a full repetition of his coronation. In 1389 he took steps to make good the ceremonial slipper which he had lost at his coronation twelve years earlier. A new pair, made from red velvet and adorned with fleurs-de-lis set with pearls, were dispatched to Rome for papal blessing. On 28 October he gave Westminster abbey a fine set of vestments, including a chasuble bearing his and the queen's coats-of-arms with the figures of the Virgin Mary, St Edward the Confessor and St Edmund on the one side, and of the Virgin Mary, John the Baptist and an abbess on the other.[49] On 10 March 1390 he presented to the abbey the new slippers to keep with the other regalia.[50]

The death of Urban VI in October 1389 provided an opportunity to apply pressure to the Roman curia. When news arrived in December of the election of Boniface IX, the earl of Northumberland persuaded the king's council not to recognize him immediately.[51] Given the circumstances of the schism, the English government could claim to be acting in the interests of Christian unity. More material concerns were paramount. Richard resented the manner in which papal provisions had been used to transform the episcopate in 1388, and one of the concerns of the commons in 1390 was the reissue of the Statute of Provisors. The parliamentary initiative was followed up at a great council in May when the king dispatched to Rome a firm letter in which he recalled 'the hardship suffered by the English church through the abusive extension of provisions and reservations, and imposition of taxes by the Holy See', and recounted how in the recent parliament, 'the magnates and the community of the realm have petitioned the king for the strict enforcement of the statutes dealing with these abuses'. In conclusion Richard asked the pope to bring a speedy remedy to this intolerable state of affairs.[52]

Richard was a formidable advocate of the rights of the English crown. Some time around 1389 he was presented with a handsome volume of English statutes. In one of the initials Richard is depicted seated on the throne receiving the work from a kneeling clerk. The volume contains a wide range of statutes, including Magna Carta, the Articles on the Charters, and the Ordinances of 1311. From one point of view the collection seems designed to remind the king of the legal restraints on the English crown. Yet there is some reason to suppose that it was commissioned by him, and served as a template for his own ideological response. There is a particular focus on the reign of Edward II. His identification with his great-grandfather 'is hinted at in the appearance of the royal arms in the margin against his name'. According to Saul, the treatise 'represented a stage in the fashioning of a more assertive, more legalistic, style of governance'. It both 'bore witness to the fullness that royal authority achieved in law' and 'indicated what had been lost and still needed to be recovered'. It was, in Saul's words, 'a kind of manifesto for the reassertion of royal power'.[53]

Richard was in no position to rehabilitate Edward II politically, but he had publicly associated himself with the cult at Gloucester as early as 1383, and had sent an embassy to Rome to press for Edward's canonization in 1385. Pope Urban had instructed Bishop Braybrooke of London to inquire into the miracles reported at Edward's tomb, but the project languished during the political upheavals of 1387–8.[54] It should be noted that there was an equally vigorous cult centred on Thomas of Lancaster at Pontefract, and that it was rumoured in 1390 that Thomas had finally achieved sainthood.[55] Richard's visit to Gloucester in late June, immediately prior to joining Gaunt's hunting party at Leicester, had a real political charge. He was accompanied by Archbishop Courtenay, Bishop Braybrooke and other churchmen and canon lawyers. It is not clear what was achieved. The party would either have commissioned or inspected progress on the production of a book describing Edward's miracles for dispatch to Rome. It was probably on a subsequent visit that Richard authorized the adornment of Edward's shrine with his new badge of the white hart.

In the cultivation of his regal image, Richard was by no means neglectful of pageantry and chivalric display.[56] Following the declaration of the truce with England a group of French knights had staged a splendid tournament at St Inglevert near Calais early in 1390. In response, a tournament 'with unrebated lances' had been organized in England in May. Richard hosted a feast at the end of the contest, rewarding a number of Scottish knights who had distinguished themselves. The event was especially remembered in Scotland, where there took root a highly positive image of Richard and his court in full flower.[57] In conscious emulation of the French court, which had set new standards of pageantry with the ceremonial entry into Paris of Charles VI's wife Isabelle of Bavaria in 1389, Richard set about the organization of a magnificent display of regal pomp and chivalric prowess in the capital itself.[58] The Smithfield tournament was well publicized, and no cost was spared in its preparation.[59] It was attended in October by a number of foreign dignitaries, notably his brother-in-law Waleran of Luxembourg, count of St Pol and William of Bavaria, count of Ostrevant. Richard himself figured prominently in the festivities, and displayed, for the first time, his new badge of the white hart. According to one account, he actually took out the honours on one of the days.[60]

The tournament had been timed to conclude on the eve of the most important feast in Richard's calendar, the translation of St Edward the Confessor. The king then played the leading role in a ceremonial of a different sort. Accompanied by his entire chapel, he attended prime, vespers and compline at Westminster abbey, and was present for matins at midnight and joined the procession the following day. At high mass he sat with his chapel in the choir, wearing his crown. Shortly after mass began the queen, likewise crowned, entered the choir and took her place on the north side.[61] In the evening the king held a great feast at Kennington, at which he again wore a crown.[62] The court then withdrew to Windsor where the king lavishly entertained his guests and formally invested Ostrevant as a knight of the Garter.[63] The king was back at Westminster to meet parliament on 12 November. On the vigil of the feast of St Edmund King and Martyr he attended vespers and midnight matins in the abbey, and on the day itself, 20 November, he was present at the procession and high mass.[64]

Richard's interest in the traditions of English kingship was intellectual as well as liturgical. Richard of Cirencester's *Speculum historiale de gestis regum Angliae* was one of a number of works produced for his edification. While it may have been started earlier in his reign, the bulk of it was written in the late 1380s. The *Speculum* itself refers, and indeed defers, to another book entitled the *Liber Regius*. This work, an elaborate history of the kings of England written by a monk of Bury St Edmunds, is no longer extant. Corpus Christi, Cambridge, MS. 251, though, is a related text. It is a history of the kings of England from Brutus to Richard II, compiled at the request of Richard in the fourteenth year of his reign, that is 1390/1. The general history is much abbreviated and customized to serve as a frame for an extended narrative of the life of St Edmund, King and Martyr.[65]

After spending Christmas at Eltham, the king and queen set off on a western progress, paying a further visit to Gloucester in mid-March and spending Easter at Bristol.[66] It was apparently at Bristol that he was presented with a remarkable illuminated manuscript which comprised a miscellany of items clearly to his taste. One item is the *Liber Judiciorum*, a treatise on geomancy. It is dated March 1391, presumably the end of the month.[67] It had been compiled 'at the special request of our most excellent lord Richard, the most noble king of the realms of England and France, who governs by exalting men learned in both the laws as well as men-at-arms; and indeed through very long and arduous acquaintance with astronomy has not declined to taste the sweetness of the fruit of the subtle sciences for the prudent government of himself and his people'.[68] Facing it is an illuminated portrait, subsequently defaced, of Richard himself.

The most substantial item is the *De quadripartita speculum regis specie libellum*, a short version of the *Secreta secretorum*. Its dedication represents Richard as 'the most powerful of princes' who 'by a kind of marvel of intellect and insight, not maintained for show but genuine, is seen to excel the subjects of his own realm and his contemporaries'. It describes itself as a compilation of 'certain counsels, sentences and precepts of wise men, most necessary for both a king and his realm, that his wisdom might shine forth the more, and all his subjects glory in his intellect and bless his rule, and thus become obedient to him in all things'. The later chapters are apparently original and particularly relevant to Richard. Chapter 6, for example, asks whether 'anything more gravely afflicts the hearts of earthly princes than the disobedience of subjects' or 'anything is seen to more greatly incite kings to impose pain and vengeance on their lieges?' The response is: 'Nothing certainly, and quite right, because on account of disobedience many have perished.' Chapter 9, which discusses a king's need for good counsel, offers the advice that prior to appointing lords to his council, a king should first infiltrate their households to discover what they say in secret about him. Chapter 10 advises that a king should recruit into his household knights, squires and yeomen of the kingdom who are attentive to his excellence, discreet and willing to withstand bodily peril on his behalf.[69]

Perhaps modelling himself on Charles V of France, Richard aspired to present himself as a wise prince. He certainly had a range of bookish interests. Geoffrey Chaucer, who served as clerk of the king's works between 1389 and 1391, was not the only poet associated with his court at this time.[70] John Gower offers a vignette about meeting Richard on the Thames, and being asked to write 'some new thing'. The *Confessio Amantis*, written 'for Richard's sake', was a work of high seriousness. Richard's interest in antiquities and history is reflected in the work of monks at Westminster, Bury St Edmunds and, presumably, Gloucester. His commissions attest to a concern to set down and order customs and precedents. He encouraged the setting down of the order of battle during the Scottish expedition in 1385; a tract on the 'order and form of battle within the lists', itself an English adaptation of French usage, was presented to him around 1390; and a treatise on heraldry was written for Queen Anne some time in the early 1390s.[71] Richard's interests were surprisingly diverse, and included medicine, astronomy and the occult sciences. The celebrated 'Form of Cury' was compiled by Richard's chef 'on the advice of masters of physic and philosophy for the health of the household', and a treatise on urine was translated into 'the mother tongue for the comprehension of laymen and for their governance' at the request of King Richard and Queen Anne.[72] The astrological items in Bodley MS. 581 give some credit to the report that after his deposition a scroll containing magical writings was discovered among his possessions.[73]

The authorship of most of these works is unknown, and there must have been many writers apart from Chaucer whose records in the royal service give no indication of their literary activities. The author of the *Speculum* describes himself, somewhat obscurely, as a servant in the king's treasury in Ireland.[74] After 1389 Richard had no shortage of learned clerks committed to the restoration of royal authority. Edmund Stafford, the new keeper of the privy seal, was a doctor of canon and civil law. An important recruit to the royal service was John Waltham, bishop of Salisbury. One of the most accomplished administrators of his age, he was appointed treasurer on 2 May, and may well have become the king's chief mentor.[75] There were also the king's confessors. Thomas Rushook, who was regarded as a noxious influence by Richard's critics in the 1380s, died in exile in Ireland. His successors, the Dominicans Alexander Bache and John Burghill, perhaps played a role in the development of Richard's ideas.[76] Another notable Dominican was John Deeping, who regularly preached before the king on special feast days.[77] Then there were several monks, notably Tideman of Winchcombe and Walter Baldock, who were close to the king. Tideman served as Richard's physician, but had a reputation, too, for arcane learning and magic.[78] Baldock was used in a number of diplomatic missions. Finally, there were the members of the chapel royal, who necessarily played a central role in the liturgical elaboration of Richard's kingship. John Boor, who became dean of the chapel early in 1389, was in all likelihood the 'grand historiographer' of the kings of Britain known to Jean de Montreuil in the 1390s.[79]

★ ★ ★

In the spring of 1391 there was great distress in the land. The harvest of 1390 had been poor, and by the end of the winter it was clear that there was dearth throughout the realm. The crisis was most evident in the city of London. Only the action of Adam Bamme, mayor of London, in making £400 available to purchase and stockpile corn for the summer prevented mass starvation. In pastoral regions the misery was compounded by a collapse in the market for wool. During the summer, too, the plague raged in western and northern England.[80] The arrival of the new harvest brought some relief, but the country must have remained on edge. It is not hard to imagine discontent in some quarters at the expenditure of the king's court. Richard himself was growing restive at his own lack of means. The splendours of the Smithfield tournament seem to have been financed by credit. In 1391 all the aldermen generously contributed to relieve the city's poor, but there were no loans to the crown.[81]

Richard found himself frustrated on other counts. While England waited for the harvest, he waited on news from France. Earlier in the year it had been agreed that peace-talks would culminate in a meeting between the kings of England and France on 24 June 1392.[82] Alarmed by French plans to mount an Italian expedition, Richard proposed bringing forward the meeting to the summer of 1391. In June he received letters from Boniface IX asking him not to make peace with France while it threatened war in the peninsula.[83] Richard's diplomacy had already helped to dissuade Charles VI from invading Italy. In late August Richard moved to Canterbury to be on hand to meet the French king. He ordered his bishops to solicit prayers and processions for himself, the state of the church, and the peace and tranquillity of the realm. On 1 September Bishop Waltham of Salisbury offered participants an indulgence of 40 days.[84] The French emissaries finally found the king at Eltham in late September, and an agreement was reached for a meeting between the royal uncles at Amiens in the new year.

Parliament was opened in November 1391 by Archbishop Arundel, who had been appointed chancellor the previous month. The king sought supply, and stressed the considerable costs incurred in diplomacy. The commons reluctantly granted a subsidy. It also passed a law that all property held in trust for religious institutions, and not amortized before Michaelmas the following year, should fall in to the crown. Henry Knighton regarded it as an 'ungodly' statute against the church and the clergy.[85] It none the less had the support of Archbishop Arundel and Bishop Waltham. As another monastic chronicler observed, the chancellor and the treasurer 'had by Michaelmas accumulated untold sums of money to fill the royal treasury to overflowing'.[86]

For the abbot of Crowland the main issue was his dispute with the earl of Kent. He thrice fell to his knees before the king, and once he had secured the king's attention declared: 'I fly alone for refuge to the throne of your majesty, confessing that you are my king, and the founder of my church, which now stands at the point of ruin.'[87] In fact the earl of Kent was allowed to present his bill against Crowland first. He did so standing 'erect before the king', with the earls of March, Arundel, Salisbury, Huntingdon and Northumberland alongside him. Happily for the abbot, Kent's claims impinged on the interests of the house of Lancaster. Gaunt immediately rose to his feet, promptly followed by his brother the duke of York, and their sons the earls of Derby and Rutland. He declared that since the matters concerned him and his freehold, it behoved him to stand up for his just rights for as long as he lived, and after his death he expected his son to do likewise. The chancellor responded that, considering the exalted station of their persons, the king wished to avoid public discord, and intended to take the disputes into his royal power and arbitration. The abbot was then assured that whatever award was made on Gaunt's behalf would extend to him as well.[88]

On the last day of parliament, 2 December, there was a final piece of political theatre. The commons petitioned that Richard 'be as free in his regality, liberty and royal dignity in his time as his noble progenitors, formerly kings of England, were in their time, notwithstanding any statute or ordinance made before this time to the contrary, and especially in the time of Edward II'. They further requested that 'if any statute was made in the time of Edward in derogation of the liberty and freedom of the crown, that it shall be annulled and of no force'. The lords joined them in this petition, though with what enthusiasm it is hard to say. It is perhaps significant that the duke of Gloucester was absent from the assembly. He had sought leave to go to Prussia on crusade earlier in the autumn. The specific reference to Edward II makes it tolerably certain that the petition was instigated by the king himself. In response Richard thanked the commons for 'the great tenderness and affection that they had to the salvation of his honour and estate, and because their prayers and requests seemed to him honest and reasonable, he agreed and assented fully to them'.[89]

★ ★ ★

The king spent Christmas 1391 at King's Langley.[90] There were disturbances in London. A strict curfew had been imposed in November, and on 23 December the king instructed the mayor and sheriffs to prevent assemblies as he had heard 'that the city was infested with armed peace-breakers'. Some of the unrest was political in nature. William Mildenhall of London appeared before chancery in December 'accused of having concealed the fact that his father, Peter, had spoken disrespectfully' of the king saying that 'he was unfit to govern and should stay in his latrine'.[91] The parliamentary petition, and Gloucester's absence overseas, may well have raised anxieties in some circles. It was rumoured that Richard was on the point of reversing the judgements of 1388, and recalling Archbishop Neville and the duke of Ireland. There is some evidence that Neville at least was making an approach to return in December 1391.[92]

In a great council in February the king and the magnates thrashed out a new settlement. The duke of Gloucester, who had returned to England prematurely after narrowly escaping shipwreck, may have taken the lead in insisting that the king should still the rumours by declaring permanent the banishment of the men condemned in the parliament of 1388. When Richard promised not to reopen old sores, all the lords 'expressed their deep gratitude'. Richard was accorded 'full power to rule his kingdom as he pleased for all time to come', and the lords renewed their oaths to assist him against all enemies.[93] For his part, Gloucester was given a grant of the lordship of Ireland for three years, with any conquests from the 'wild Irish' passing to himself and his male heirs in perpetuity. According to Goodman, there was then a remarkable reaffirmation of peace and concord among the lords, and a repudiation of 'the violence associated with unlawful maintenance'.[94]

In early March John of Gaunt set out at the head of a splendid retinue for the peace conference at Amiens. Richard's grant to him of the duchy of Aquitaine in 1390 added room for manoeuvre on the vexed issue of the feudal status of the province. The English were willing to concede that the duke might do homage to the king of France, provided no services were demanded, while the French were ready to make territorial concessions so long as Aquitaine was detached from the English crown.[95] The proposition that Gaunt's life-grant should be converted into a grant to him and his heirs was actively pursued by the French, raising concern among Richard's subjects. In England there was a feeling that Gaunt might be acting solely in his own interest, especially given the concessions, such as the return of Cherbourg and Brest and possibly Calais, that might well be made. At the same time the men of Aquitaine were indicating their reluctance to accept as their duke anyone other than the king of England or his eldest son.[96]

The conference at Amiens proceeded in a stately and amicable fashion, working out a series of proposals which could provide the basis for a satisfactory settlement. The royal dukes 'parted convinced of each other's good faith and optimistic about the chances of peace'.[97] Gaunt knew that in this respect at least he had the confidence of his king. The problem was that the peace proposals seem not to have been popular in the wider community. At a great council at Stamford on 25 May there was considerable opposition from the knights of the shire, and veiled attacks on Gaunt for what was seen to be a sell-out of the national interest.[98] The hawks found a powerful ally in William, duke of Guelders. Finding himself dangerously isolated by the Anglo-French rapprochement, he had written a remarkable letter to Richard seeking to flatter and cajole him into a more belligerent stance against France. He noted that Providence 'had preserved unharmed into the years of your discretion' his hereditary rights, but observed that 'whatsoever violence may oppose them, a regal diligence should shield its rights with military power'. He stressed the military prowess and fame of 'that great-hearted people of the west' and 'the matchless historic worth' of its magnanimous king. In May he came to England in person to play on the jingoistic instincts of the lords and knights in the council.[99] Richard gave him a hearing, and entertained him well, but seems not to have been deflected from his commitment to peace.

★   ★   ★

Instead Richard was exercising his 'regal diligence' in his own realm and it was the city of London which experienced the full weight of the king's determination to be master in his own house. He clearly regarded the turbulence in London as an affront to his regality, and the disturbances in the city over the winter of 1391/2 provided the justification for a crackdown. Prior to Christmas he ordered John Hende, the new mayor, to prohibit assemblies, and claimed that he had heard that the city 'was infested with armed peace-breakers'. In January he felt the need to instruct the city officials to prevent conventicles in which Londoners 'disputed heretically and subverted the Catholic faith', declaring that 'it is the king's will that within the bounds of his power shall bud forth no heresies or errors to infect the people'.[100] There was an incident involving a member of the household of Bishop Waltham, treasurer of England. When he commandeered some bread in Fleet Street, an angry crowd gathered. Waltham's man took refuge in the bishop's inn, and the crowd threatened to burn down the house. Mayor Hende arrived just in time and persuaded the Londoners to disperse. The incident, duly reported to Bishop Waltham and Archbishop Arundel, may have played into the king's hands.[101]

On 13 May Richard ordered the removal of the court of common pleas from Westminster to York, and made known in no uncertain terms his displeasure with the city of London.[102] Richard went north, spending ten days in his northern capital in early June.[103] Sensing the danger, Mayor Hende instructed his aldermen on the 17th to require all inhabitants of their wards 'to take a fresh oath of allegiance for the better preservation of the peace'.[104] A fortnight later the king dispatched from Stamford a writ written in terms 'so fearsome and utterly hair-raising as to cause the ears of whosoever heard it to tingle'.[105] It instructed the mayor, sheriffs and aldermen, along with twenty-four other citizens, to appear before the king and his council at Nottingham on 25 June, under pain of forfeiture of life and limb. They were to have full power to answer on behalf of the city what was laid before them, the city's privileges notwithstanding.[106]

In proceeding against London, Richard had the support of his chief ministers and the magnates who gathered around him at Stamford, Rockingham and Nottingham.[107] Yet it is clear that his actions were fired by a deep personal animosity dating back to the winter of 1387/8. The city had then not only signally failed him in his hour of need, but had seemed to revel in the destruction of his friends and allies. To compound their fault, the Londoners had shown no alacrity to make amends. The city had assisted the new regime with a corporate loan in 1389, and with a number of loans from private individuals in 1390, but in 1391 there had been no loans at all, and when in 1392 there had been an attempt to raise funds the king's agents had met with a direct rebuff.[108] Of course, it may be that some Londoners had reservations about the king and his financial needs. Bearing in mind Nicholas Brembre's fate, even Richard's most ardent admirers in the city might have been chary of too close an association with the court.

While the Londoners sweated, the king took his recreation in the forests and chases of the north Midlands, accompanied by his cousin the earl of Rutland and the duke of Guelders.[109] The great council at Nottingham was well attended by the magnates of the realm. Lancaster, York and Gloucester and their sons all seem to have been present.[110] A number of grants and settlements attest a concern for solidarity within the ruling house. On 25 June the king granted Gloucester the reversion of lands worth £200 per year in part satisfaction of the £1,000 granted him on his promotion to his dukedom, and resettled on Huntingdon in tail male the grant first made on his elevation to the peerage.[111] On 30 June licence was granted for a new guild in Coventry which would support nine chaplains to celebrate divine service for the good estate of king and queen, the king's uncles, and their children.[112]

The Londoners entered the portals of Nottingham castle on 25 June in greatest trepidation. The king and council wasted little time in announcing the removal from office of Mayor Hende and the two sheriffs, and ordering their imprisonment, alleging defects in their commission and administration. Taking the city into his own hands, the king appointed Sir Edward Dallingridge as warden, and appointed two new sheriffs. Setting out from Nottingham on 29 June Dallingridge arrived at the Guildhall in London on 1 July at 9 a.m., when his commission was proclaimed, and he was sworn into office.[113] The king likewise instituted a powerful commission including the dukes of York and Gloucester, two earls, three household knights and three judges, to investigate defects in the city's administration.[114] Sessions were held at Aylesbury on 10 July, and at Eton on the 18th, when the mayor and sheriffs from 1389–90 were also interrogated. On 22 July the commission found defects in the administration of both mayoralties, declared the city's liberties forfeit to the crown, and imposed a fine of 3,000 marks.[115] At a great council at Windsor the king confirmed the judgement, appointed Sir Baldwin Raddington to replace Dallingridge, whom the king allegedly thought 'too gentle and tender unto the Londoners', reappointed the two new sheriffs, and named eighteen new aldermen. The city was ordered to pay a corporate fine of £100,000, and its entire disposable income was taken into the king's hands to pay this sum.[116]

The scene was now set for the formal submission of London. On 21 August the king and queen came from Kennington to Southwark and entered the city across London Bridge. The warden and aldermen met them at the gate, presented the king with the sword and keys of the city, the first time that this act of symbolical submission was recorded.[117] The royal couple were also presented with fine horses and images of the Trinity and St Anne. To music and cheers of the crowd the pair rode along Cheapside, all decked with gold cloth and bright bunting. Wine flowed from the conduits. A mock castle rose up in the middle of the street, surrounded by artificial clouds. An angelic-looking boy and maiden hovered on invisible pulleys, and presented the couple with gold goblets and twin crowns. Entering St Paul's, the king and queen paid their respects at the shrine of St Erkenwald, and passed out along Ludgate. At Temple Bar they were confronted by a scene of St John the Baptist in the wilderness surrounded by wild beasts. Richard was greatly moved by the sight of the Baptist pointing to the lamb of God. The Londoners, who had already given horses, images of the Trinity and St Anne, goblets and crowns, now presented two exquisitely wrought panels of the crucifixion to serve as altar-pieces. Prior to moving on to a great feast at Westminster Hall, Queen Anne promised to intercede with the king on the city's behalf. With Richard sitting in state on the marble throne, she went down on her knees, pointing out to him that never in the history of Britain, even in Arthur's time, was a king so honoured. Richard reminded the city of its responsibilities, and indicated his readiness to be gracious, restoring the city's liberties symbolically with the return of the keys and sword.[118]

The restoration of the city of London to the king's grace was a slow process and was only achieved at considerable cost. On 17 September the king made it known that the city might elect two sheriffs on the feast of St Matthew, the 21st, according to custom. On the 19th he pardoned the two groups of mayors and aldermen, remitted the corporate fine of £100,000 and restored the liberties of the city, though only 'until the king shall otherwise ordain'.[119] The price of the king's grace seems to have been £10,000.[120] A new mayor was elected on 13 October, and a fortnight later Raddington handed the keeping of the city over to him. Meanwhile arrangements were made for the return of the court of common pleas to London.[121] The Londoners continued to feel the need to buy favour. On 22 October they waited on the royal dukes at Holborn and gave them two silver gilt basins each, with £400 for Lancaster, and £200 each for York and Gloucester.[122] The raising of £10,000 and recouping of the costs of gifts and entertainment placed a heavy burden on the city over the winter of 1392/3.[123]

Meanwhile the king returned to his capital, this time not as a conqueror but as a pilgrim. On 11 October he walked barefoot in procession with the monks of Westminster, and repeated the observances of two years earlier. On the 12th, along with his chapel, he entered the choir of the abbey at vespers, when the bishop of London celebrated mass. On the feast of St Edward the Confessor he began by attending matins, joined the procession during the day, and again attended high mass. Afterwards he passed into the abbot's hall, 'where with the utmost magnificence, the lords and the ladies then at court, as well as the whole convent, or the greater part of it, were brilliantly and elegantly entertained'.[124] In the abbey Richard sat crowned in the top stall on the south side of the choir, with the queen opposite him on the north side.[125] Around this time he commissioned a massive portrait of himself, which was affixed to the back of his choir stall to assure his continuing symbolic presence in the capital.

★　★　★

On the day before Richard entered London like a conquering prince, he was presenting himself as a peace-maker in Christendom. On 20 August he wrote to Charles VI from

Reconstruction of the medieval appearance of St Edward the Confessor's shrine. (British Architectural Library, RIBA, London)

Kennington, advising him of his intention, pursuant to earlier agreements, to send Gaunt to negotiate a final peace. In another letter on the 22nd, the day after his triumph, he wrote again to the French court, referring to letters recently brought by Robert the Hermit.[126] Robert le Mennot, nicknamed 'the Hermit,' was a Norman knight who had undergone a conversion experience in the Holy Land, and had returned to western Europe an ardent apostle for peace. His visit to England was the first of a series of missions in which he exhorted Richard to translate the truce into a firm peace, which in turn would make possible the healing of the schism and ensure Christian unity in the face of the Turk. According to his reports to Philippe de Mézières, his colleague and mentor, Robert found the English king eager for this glorious enterprise. Robert the Hermit almost certainly flattered Richard by the form and content of his address. With the city of London abject before him and an exalted role in Christendom pressed on him, it must have been a heady time for a king not known for self-effacement.

The exhilaration of the moment soon passed. Robert the Hermit's mission must have been rapidly followed by highly distressing news from France. Campaigning on the Breton border in August, Charles VI became suddenly and inexplicably deranged, slaying five men in his frenzy before he could be brought under restraint. The peace process between England and France, and all that might flow from it, was back on hold. Richard and the queen spent the remainder of the year in their palaces around London, visiting in turn Sheen, Langley and Eltham, where they spent Christmas.[127] The Londoners were again required to dig deep into their pockets. Their Christmas gift for a prince who had everything was a dromedary[128] but there can have been little festive cheer. Shortly before Christmas Richard learned of the deaths of two people very dear to him. Robert de Vere, his former favourite, died in a hunting accident near Louvain on 22 November and Isabella, duchess of York, his favourite aunt, died at Langley on 23 December.[129] Isabella had made Richard her chief heir so that he might provide for her second son Richard, the king's godson.[130] Richard took time to attend her funeral at Langley on 14 January before hastening south to meet parliament at Winchester.[131]

From 20 January 1393 Richard was based for three weeks in the old capital of his Anglo-Saxon forebears.[132] Charles VI had made what appeared to be a good recovery in late 1392, and the main business of parliament was the approval of the peace proposals, the appointment of Lancaster and Gloucester as the chief negotiators, and the grant of a subsidy to meet the costs of the conference. Parliament seems to have been generally compliant. The Statute of Provisors was discussed, and the king was given freedom to moderate it in negotiation with the pope. A petition expressing concern about papal proceedings against bishops executing royal orders with respect to appointments to the church prompted the so-called Statute of Praemunire. This act imposed penalties on persons seeking, receiving or implementing papal bulls against the king, his crown and regality, but it was not as all-encompassing in conception as was later believed. Still, it contained the resounding statement that the English crown 'hath been so free at all times, that it hath been in no earthly subjection, but immediately subject to God in all things touching the regality of the same crown, and to none other'. It can be seen as reflecting Richard's general concern with his regality and imperial power.[133] The commons likewise repeated their refrain that the king was as free in his royal liberty as his progenitors. It was later claimed that he 'subtly procured' this petition at Winchester, and used it to justify acts in contravention of the law.[134]

Richard was gathering around him a new inner circle of counsellors and friends. Bishop Waltham, bishop of Salisbury, was appointed treasurer in 1391, and rapidly became a dominant figure in the formulation and execution of royal policy.[135] The death of Sir John Devereux, steward of the household, on 22 February provided the king with an opportunity to appoint a man untainted by association with the commission of 1386. He promoted Sir Thomas Percy to the stewardship, and drew Sir William Scrope, Gaunt's seneschal of Aquitaine, into his service as king's chamberlain.[136] A new favourite was John, Lord Beaumont. He was granted an annuity of £100, and subsequently appointed constable of Dover castle and warden of the Cinque Ports.[137] Bishop Waltham died in 1395 and Beaumont in 1396, but Percy and Scrope were to be prominent in the assertion of royal power in the late 1390s.

On 5 March the dukes of Lancaster and Gloucester crossed to Calais to treat with an equally illustrious French delegation headed by the dukes of Berry and Burgundy. Both sides were prepared to give significant ground in respect of their earlier positions, and the negotiations proceeded in a positive fashion. For the first time the allies of each side were to be included in the settlement. England showed its good faith by agreeing in advance to return Cherbourg, while France was willing to accept the status quo with respect to Calais. Aquitaine remained the main problem. Both sides were ready to discuss a settlement involving French territorial concessions in return for English recognition of French sovereignty. It was widely assumed that such a settlement could be more easily achieved if the duchy of Aquitaine were granted to John of Gaunt and his heirs, and in some measure alienated from the English crown.

It is a measure of the success of the negotiations that reports of them prompted a hostile reaction in parts of England. Rumours of a dishonourable peace spread across the country, prompting disturbances in Yorkshire and a rising in Cheshire, where service in the French wars had long been a way of life for the gentry and yeomanry. The focus of the hostility was the king's uncles, especially Gaunt, who was felt to be selling out English interests to consolidate his own position in Aquitaine. The Cheshire rising was led by Sir Thomas Talbot, a Lancashire soldier who had fallen foul of Gaunt and his affinity. Given that the palatinate of Chester had provided the manpower for de Vere's campaign in December 1387, there were ominous undercurrents. The Cheshire men were fiercely loyal to Richard as earl of Chester, and probably believed that he would welcome support to free himself from the control of his uncles. It is instructive that the king himself had to dissociate himself from the rebellion, issuing letters to declare that he was in no way seeking the destruction of the magnates.[138]

News of the rising briefly interrupted the negotiations. Lancaster and Gloucester returned to England and headed north to secure the pacification of the affected areas. None the less the settlement was all but complete, and when the two dukes returned to Calais in May 1393 it was very much to put the final touches to it. On 16 June the four dukes agreed to a provisional treaty which held the promise of a comprehensive, lasting settlement. Even this accord, though, fell short of what had been within their sights a month earlier, when it was hoped, in Palmer's words, 'to crown the meeting of the four dukes with an interview between the two kings'. It certainly seems that such an interview was planned. Richard accompanied his uncles as far as Canterbury, where he remained for a fortnight. Charles VI was at Abbeville, likewise close at hand for a meeting near Calais. A royal conference would presumably have converted the provisional treaty into a definitive peace and set the scene for Anglo-French cooperation in healing the Schism and confounding the infidel.[139]

However, the conference did not take place. All that was achieved was an extension of the truce, which was proclaimed in England on 26 June. By this time Richard was back at Sheen and making plans to spend the summer hunting. He doubtless hoped to continue the negotiations in the autumn. The glorious vision of peace remained in prospect. The truth was that Charles VI had suffered a further mental breakdown. While at Abbeville he had begun to behave strangely, and to exhibit all the signs of mental derangement. The French court hurriedly returned to Paris. This second psychotic episode would last until January 1394. It put on hold the peace process for some nine months.[140]

★ ★ ★

By 1393 Richard had fully established himself as king. Limits had been set to his exercise of royal patronage in 1390, and there were concerns about the direction of his rule over the winter of 1391/2. Early in 1392, though, he secured recognition from the magnates of his 'full power to rule his kingdom', and for some time he had been finding scope to assert his royal status, authority and power.[141] He cultivated his regal image, and sought to project an elevated concept of his crown. He began to require new forms of address. Parliamentary petitions started to address him as 'very excellent, redoubtable and powerful prince' and refer to his 'highness and royal majesty'.[142] He expanded the royal household and built up an armed retinue. Over the summer and autumn of 1393 he staged an awesome display of princely power and majesty at the expense of the city of London. To consolidate his power and to live royally, Richard needed funds. His policy of peace with France brought savings, but diplomacy was costly, too. Richard and his advisers sought to accustom parliament and convocation to the idea of peace-time subsidies, and were inventive, and not a little ruthless, in securing new sources of revenue. A key figure in the task of financial reconstruction was John Waltham, bishop of Salisbury, whose organizational skills had first been acknowledged and rewarded by the Appellants. Waltham's industry and ingenuity helped increase crown income, while his household served as a training ground for the new royal service.[143]

Richard owed a great deal to the talented group of clerks, knights and even poets who had responded to the promise of a new start in 1389 with an eagerness that was instinctual in an age when kings were expected to rule as well as reign, and when the crown was a natural focus of loyalty and the fount of honour. Still, Richard deserves some credit for the reconstruction of royal authority. The vicissitudes of the 1380s clearly encouraged him to reflect on human affairs, and to cultivate the craft of kingship.[144] Though he was no scholar, Richard had a sharp and lively mind. He understood the psychology of power and the importance of stage-management and image-making. He outwardly honoured his royal kinsmen, especially John of Gaunt, and gave scope to their ambitions – but he implicated them, too, in unpopular policies.

Brass of John Waltham, bishop of Salisbury, 1395.
(© Dean & Chapter of Westminster)

He was likewise able to secure the collaboration and win the respect of two of his most formidable critics in the 1380s, the two archbishops William Courtenay and Thomas Arundel. None the less Richard's regal assertion seems to have rekindled doubts in some quarters about his fitness to rule for the common good. In dated reworkings of the *Confessio Amantis*, John Gower shows increasing coolness towards the king. By mid-1391 he had replaced the prayer for Richard II with a prayer for the state of England. Late in 1392 or early in 1393 he excised the reference to Richard in the prologue and introduced a new section on the responsibilities of kingship. Likewise in changes to his *Vox Clamantis* in the early 1390s, the state of England is depicted in darker hues, and the ills of the realm are attributed less to evil counsellors taking advantage of the king's youthful innocence and more to the king himself.[145]

If in 1393 Richard looked back with any satisfaction, it was only at the recent past and with only qualified satisfaction. He had neither forgiven nor forgotten the destruction of his friends in 1387–8. His sense of grievance on this score is apparent in the grim humour with which he responded to Gaunt's request in 1390 for a pardon for John of Northampton, and in the rumours in the winter of 1391/2 that he was planning to recall Archbishop Neville and the duke of Ireland. While the king outwardly accorded the duke of Gloucester respect and honour, offering him in 1391 the sort of role in Ireland that he had first conceived for de Vere, he may secretly have sought to undermine him. In 1392 Gloucester was assembling a formidable expeditionary force, and there was much talk about what he might achieve in Ireland, when his commission was suddenly superseded. It is hard to know what to make of Richard's relations with Henry of Bolingbroke, who was absent from England for long periods in 1390–1 and 1392–3. Richard may not have wholly forgiven him for his role at Radcot Bridge, and may have had good reason to envy his personal good fortune and public reputation. Each year in the late 1380s and early 1390s brought news of another son for Henry and his wife, another triumph in tournament or crusade, and another instance of his popular esteem.

In time Richard would turn the tables on his opponents in 1387–8, and exact retribution in kind. His determination to re-establish his authority as king went beyond a desire for revenge, and a compulsion to have the judgements of 1388 reversed. By 1385, if not earlier, Richard was reflecting on the history of the English monarchy, and showing considerable interest in the reign of Edward II. For him, the events of the late 1380s were merely the most recent episode in a miserable tale of rebellion and regicide, and it was his duty to restore the crown in all its majesty and power. His opponents drew their own lessons from history, threatening him with the fate of his great-grandfather, and perhaps seeking inspiration in the career of Thomas, earl of Lancaster, whose opposition to Edward had led to his execution at Pontefract in 1322. Richard's campaign for the canonization of Edward II, which was to continue through the 1390s, was no mere whim. It was part of a sustained campaign to rebuild the foundations of royal power, to renew and exalt his kingly office, and to prepare himself for the mission that he believed Providence had vouchsafed for him.

CHAPTER FOUR

PRINCE OF PEACE

In 1393 Richard appeared formidable. He was twenty-six years old, and the very image of a splendid king. His golden hair, comely proportions, and magnificent attire struck all who saw him. Richard of Maidstone wrote flatteringly that in beauty he had no equal among kings, but the king's critics wrote in similar terms.[1] Richard was a man of intelligence, fine discrimination and charm, who presided over a court of some refinement and splendour. Though he presented himself as a prince of peace, he staged magnificent tournaments, and enjoyed some success in re-establishing the English royal court as the fount of chivalric honour. He was conventionally pious, an informed champion of the traditions and liberties of the English church, and cultivated the liturgical dimensions of his kingship. In the projection of his regal image Richard drew heavily on English tradition, but sought inspiration in the forms and styles of the French and imperial courts. To his subjects Richard must have seemed alarmingly original. The great portrait in Westminster abbey, probably painted in the early 1390s, is especially striking. Richard is seated in majesty, crowned, and with sceptre and orb. Its larger-than-life size and the Christ-like pose make it an impressive icon of kingship. The fact that it is also a true portrait makes it breathtakingly audacious, even vainglorious.[2]

Given his birth and heritage, Richard had reason to regard himself as a prince marked for some high destiny. His sense of some, albeit obscure, providential role is apparent in a depiction of Richard and Anne kneeling before the Virgin Mary in

Richard II enthroned, c. 1395. (© Dean & Chapter of Westminster)

a lost altar-piece in Rome. Richard is shown presenting the Virgin Mary 'the globe or pattern of England' and the panel is inscribed: 'This is your dowry, O holy Virgin'.[3] It is not hard to imagine the general outline of his sense of mission. No one in the 1380s could fail to be conscious of the manner in which the war with France had divided and weakened Christendom. From at least 1385, when Leo of Armenia visited his court, Richard was regularly approached with schemes for peace and collaboration between England and France in healing the schism and countering the Turkish offensive in south-east Europe. Richard saw some solution to his domestic problems in the same source. He probably did not need Philippe de Mézières to tell him that war taxation impoverished the country and weakened the crown, and was clearly drawn to the idea of seeking French assistance against his rebellious subjects. Domestic disobedience stood in the way of a larger and more constructive role in Christendom.

For all the promise of the early 1390s, the future looked full of uncertainties. At times in the 1380s, not least in December 1387, Richard may have feared for his own life. He remained all too aware of the fates of some of his predecessors as kings of England and of some contemporary European princes. In 1392 he would have been troubled by Charles VI's mental collapse. Apart from the sheer wretchedness of his condition, which had the French king begging his courtiers to put him out of his misery, there were the rumours that his illness had been brought about by poison or sorcery. Richard knew about the frailty of human life. Archbishop Neville and Robert de Vere had both died in exile in 1392, and Queen Anne was to follow in 1394. Richard himself seems to have had health concerns. At some stage he was under treatment for a stone in his urinary tract.[4] Above all, there was the issue of the succession. Though he had been married for over a decade, he remained childless. In the late 1380s his lack of issue must have added barbs to the charges of puerility and indulgence of male condition. By the early 1390s Richard may have settled his mind to his childlessness. It has been hypothesized that the couple aspired to celibacy in marriage, a mode of piety which was currently fashionable in courtly circles.[5] Perhaps Queen Anne, like her saintly namesake, the mother of the Virgin Mary, remained hopeful to the end. Whatever the case, Richard's lack of issue added to the uncertainties of the times. Richard sought to turn his childlessness to political advantage. His nomination of Roger Mortimer as his heir in the mid-1380s served as an effective foil to the ambition of John of Gaunt, while in the crisis of 1387–8 it may have suited his purposes to encourage Bolingbroke's expectations. Gaunt's solid support for Richard from 1389 onwards may reflect some understanding that Richard, if he remained childless, would nominate Gaunt or Bolingbroke as his heir. By 1393 there was urgent need for clarification. Roger Mortimer was approaching his majority, but receiving few signs of royal favour. Richard showed most affection to the sons of the duke of York: Edward, earl of Rutland, and Richard, his godson. It is hard to escape the impression that he was more interested in widening rather than narrowing the sphere of speculation.

★ ★ ★

For the moment Richard basked in his kingly office. Closely following the progress of the negotiations in Calais in May 1393, he planned a stately progress to Canterbury, both to accompany his uncles on their return to the conference table, and to be on hand

Canterbury cathedral nave, looking east. (English Heritage © Crown Copyright NMR)

if a meeting with Charles VI could be arranged. He set off from Sheen on the 20th. A large company of lords and prelates joined him in London. Crossing London Bridge, they would have passed under a portal newly set with stone images of the king and queen, and with shields bearing the arms of the king, queen and St Edward the Confessor. The work had been undertaken at the king's express command. Since the first payment for it had been made only ten days earlier, it is likely that it had been set in hand for this occasion.[6]

The king was based at St Augustine's abbey, Canterbury, from 23 May to 11 June. While his hopes for a meeting with the king of France were disappointed, he had much to occupy him in Canterbury, the site of so many shrines and his father's burial-place. His sojourn included Whitsuntide, the feast of St Augustine of Canterbury, Trinity Sunday and the anniversary of his father's death. On Whitsunday and the next day, the feast of St Augustine, the king processed into church and 'sat crowned in his glory'. His mind moved predictably from St Augustine to Ethelbert of Kent, England's first Christian king. According to the abbey chronicler, the king instructed the convent to honour the festival of King Ethelbert with daily worship.[7] On Trinity Sunday Richard attended mass at the conventual church of Holy Trinity, hearing a sermon by the Dominican friar Thomas Witheley.[8] The next day, his father's anniversary, he provided at his tomb in the cathedral one hundred torches of wax at a cost of £14.[9] During his time in Canterbury, he presumably inspected the work on the new nave in the cathedral. At some stage he contributed £1,000 to the fabric.[10]

On his return to the capital, Richard presided at two other ceremonies of royal commemoration. News had come to England of the death of the Empress Elizabeth, Queen Anne's mother. On 12 June there was a requiem mass in St Paul's cathedral, and Richard ordered the construction of a 'very unusual imperial shrine, the like of which had nowhere been seen before'.[11] On 21 June there were the customary observances to mark the anniversary of Edward III's death. The king attended a mass at Windsor, while his uncles, who had recently returned from Calais, made their observances at Westminster. Five days earlier they had set their seals to a draft treaty which might have proved the basis for a final peace settlement. Given the turn of events in France, this treaty was not ratified, and all that could be announced on 26 June was a further extension of the truce.

In July Richard set off on an extended tour of the dioceses of Winchester and Salisbury.[12] He was the guest of Bishop Wykeham at Winchester, and entertained at Wolvesey Palace. He attended to the building work at Winchester College, where he is commemorated almost as a 'second founder' in a 'masterly portrait bust on the southern label-stop of the east window of the chapel'.[13] At the beginning of August, Richard spent ten days at Corfe castle in Dorset, doubtless enjoying the beauty of the site, relishing the opportunities for hunting and inspecting the fine marble quarried at Purbeck. He held a requiem mass in the chapel of Corfe castle on the anniversary of the death of his mother, the princess of Wales.[14] Richard was conscious, as well, of the historical associations of the place. The Anglo-Saxon king known as St Edward the Martyr was assassinated at Corfe, and was buried at nearby Shaftesbury. The train of Richard's thought is well evidenced in his response to Archbishop Courtenay, who had sent him news of a miracle performed on a foreign pilgrim at the shrine of St Thomas of Canterbury. In his reply, dated at Corfe on 7 August, Richard offered thanks to 'the High Sovereign Worker of Miracles Who has deigned to work this miracle in our days, and upon a foreigner, as though for the purpose of spreading to strange and distant countries the glorious fame of His very martyr'. He then expressed his 'very complete hope that in our and your time our noble and holy predecessors will be more glorified than they have been for a long time', and explained that this was the more necessary in that 'our faith and belief have more enemies than they ever had time out of mind'.[15] That he had St Edward the Martyr in mind is evident both from the king's presence at Corfe and his requirement a year later that Christ Church, Canterbury, celebrate St Edward's two feast days.

In mid-August the king and his party were guests of Bishop Waltham of Salisbury, and stayed for a time, too, in the Franciscan friary in Salisbury.[16] On the feast of the Assumption of the Virgin Mary, Richard and Anne wore their crowns and other regalia in the conventual church.[17] From late August until the middle of September the royal household was based at Beaulieu abbey.[18] Tideman Winchcombe, who had been granted the keeping of Beaulieu during a vacancy, acted as host. A monk of dubious repute, Tideman had gained purchase on the king's affections through his knowledge of medicine and the occult sciences, and had recently been elected, on the king's urging, bishop of Llandaff.[19] The main occupation of the royal party at this time was hunting in the New Forest. On 22 August the king and queen, accompanied by Bishop Waltham, the earls of March and Rutland, Sir Thomas Percy steward of the household, Sir Henry Percy and others, visited Titchfield abbey. They were formally received at the gates of the convent and escorted into the church with bells ringing and solemn chant. The party stayed overnight. Though Sir Henry Percy paid for the dinner, the abbot contributed twelve pike.[20]

Richard spent the autumn at Windsor, and in November was briefly based at King's Langley with its adjacent Dominican friary. Earlier in the summer he had complained to the pope about Dominicans who did not properly perform their office. The pope's response dated 15 October must have arrived around this time.[21] The king moved to Westminster for Christmas. Some 1,000 marks, half the proceeds of the sale of the jewels of the duchess of York, was paid into the king's chamber for expenditure over the Christmas season.[22] The citizens of London paid court with appropriate pageantry. Some 'engaged in merry-making of various kinds' and 'some rendered assorted choruses and songs'. The centrepiece of their pageantry was a 'mock-ship crammed with spices and other gifts' which were presented to the royal couple and other dignitaries.[23]

The king remained in the environs of Westminster to meet parliament in late January 1394. It was almost certainly during this sojourn in the capital that Richard finalized plans for his long-cherished scheme to remodel Westminster Hall. The old hall, which dated back to the Norman Conquest, was barely adequate for the functions it served, and doubtless had unfortunate memories for the king as the site of so many humiliations in the late 1380s. Richard clearly wanted to create an architectural space which would provide an appropriately magnificent setting for the exercise of his royal authority. The project now set in train involved the removal of the Norman pillars and the blocking of the Romanesque windows, the heightening and refacing of the walls, and the introduction of traceried windows in the new Perpendicular style. A prominent feature was a string-course running below the sill with carvings of the king's white hart badge. Covering the vast space, without any supporting pillars, was a magnificent timber roof, which combined 'the latest technological developments of hammer beams and arched-braced construction'.[24]

The parliament of January 1394 proved a tumultuous session, with Gaunt's peace proposals being subject to sustained criticism. The commons were willing to consider terms which included simple homage and a modified form of French sovereignty over Aquitaine, but they refused to countenance any settlement which involved the king of England performing liege homage to the king of France.[25] The focus of their anger was John of Gaunt. He was regarded as the architect and beneficiary of a foreign policy that was in disinherison of the crown. Gloucester, it was alleged, had been won over to Gaunt's way of thinking by the promise of lands. The earl of Arundel made a strikingly intemperate attack on Gaunt. He complained of Gaunt's arrogance in council and his over-familiarity with the king. He remarked how they walked arm in arm and sported each other's badges and livery.[26] Richard intervened to defend his uncle, doubtless relishing his statesmanlike role as Gaunt took the heat, Gloucester remained hopelessly compromised and Arundel rashly went out on a limb.[27] Arundel was forced to apologize to Gaunt. Through the good offices of Archbishop Arundel, he subsequently obtained a royal pardon for all treasons and other offences.[28]

The issue of the succession may have been raised in this session. According to John Harding, Gaunt petitioned in parliament to have himself acknowledged as heir apparent. The lords demanded to know who dared to suggest that the king would have no issue, adding that 'he is young and able to have children'.[29] The continuator of the *Eulogium Historiarum* states that Gaunt asked to have Henry of Bolingbroke nominated as heir to the throne on the grounds of his descent through his mother from Edmund 'Crouchback', earl of Lancaster, son of Henry III. According to this account, the earl of March countered by pressing his own claim, and Richard silenced both parties.[30] Neither chronicler dates the episode, and there are difficulties with the evidence. It is impossible to believe that Gaunt invoked the legend that Edmund 'Crouchback' was Henry III's eldest son. Such a claim would have impugned Richard's own title. Perhaps all that Gaunt did was to stress Bolingbroke's double descent from the royal line. The issue of the succession was certainly material to the matters at hand, not least Gaunt's standing in the realm and in Aquitaine. The earl of March was now approaching manhood.[31] Meanwhile the king drew attention to his own childlessness in a grant to another nobleman of royal descent. In January 1394 he granted Thomas Mowbray the right to use the leopard crest, differenced with a silver crown, which was by right the crest of the king's eldest son 'if we had begotten the same'.[32]

After the parliament Gaunt, nothing abashed, returned to the conference table. Gloucester, who may have taken Arundel's harsh words to heart, stayed at home. Gaunt was accompanied this time by the duke of York and by Mr Ralph Selby, an experienced clerk and diplomat, who later became a monk at Westminster. Gaunt had to retract his former position, and offer terms that were bound to be unacceptable to the French. Palmer has argued that the negotiations, lasting over two months, focused on the more radical solution of detaching Aquitaine from the English crown, and that some secret compact was achieved.[33] All that was definitely achieved was the announcement on

27 May of a further extension of the truce of Leulinghen, first proclaimed in 1389, until Michaelmas 1398.[34] If there was a secret peace, which seems on balance unlikely, it was certainly wrecked by the revolt which broke out in Aquitaine in the spring of 1394. From the outset the city of Bordeaux and a number of Gascon lords had opposed the grant to Gaunt, fearing the alienation of Aquitaine from the English crown. They were led to believe, seemingly by Richard himself, that the grant had not been made on his wishes. On 6 April the archbishop of Bordeaux, four prelates, fifteen barons, and representatives of the gentry and the third estate took a solemn oath to be governed henceforth only by the king of England, and to stand together in a Union. The king did not clarify his position until early September when he reaffirmed his grant of the duchy of Aquitaine. At the end of the year Gaunt set out in force to restore his duchy to obedience.[35]

★　★　★

Over the summer of 1394 the court was in mourning. On Whitsunday, 7 June, Queen Anne died at the palace of Sheen. In the days which followed Richard wrote to her brother Wenceslas, king of the Romans, and to other princes advising them of the death of his 'much loved companion'. At the same time letters were sent across the land instructing various prelates and lords to join the procession that would take the queen's body from Sheen to Westminster for the funeral on 3 August.[36] The prior of Worcester, who received a letter from the king, received almost simultaneously a second letter, dated 8 June, from John of Gaunt, announcing the funeral of his second wife Constance at Leicester on 5 July.[37] The summer certainly took a heavy toll on the female members of the royal family. The countess of Derby, Henry of Bolingbroke's wife, died in childbirth in early July, around the time of her mother-in-law's funeral.[38]

Richard was grief-stricken. He made a vow not to enter for a year any building, except a church, where he had stayed with the queen, and subsequently ordered the destruction of Sheen.[39] He set in train arrangements for a magnificent funeral. It was an elaborate affair. Orders were sent to Flanders for hundreds of wax torches. The cortège moved by stages from Sheen to St Paul's in London and then to Westminster abbey. The service was conducted by Archbishop Arundel who, according to an early tradition, gave as an example of Queen Anne's piety the fact that, though a foreigner, she had a book of the gospels in English, which she had first submitted for his approval.[40] The ceremony was marred, however, by a scandalous incident involving the king. Enraged by the earl of Arundel's late arrival and moves to leave early, Richard seized a cane from an attendant and struck Arundel such a blow on the head that he fell to the ground at the king's feet, his blood polluting the holy place. According to Walsingham, Richard would have killed him if he not been restrained. The service was so long delayed, both by the altercation itself and by the purification of the church which it necessitated, that it was night time before it was completed.[41]

In planning his wife's funeral Richard gave thought to his own. Over the summer he settled on the notion of a double-tomb in the heart of the chapel of St Edward the Confessor at Westminster abbey. A site was made available by the removal to the chapel of St John the Baptist of the remains of several grandchildren of Edward I. Richard was

The double-tomb of Richard II and Anne of Bohemia, commissioned in 1395, in the ambulatory of Westminster abbey.
(© Dean & Chapter of Westminster)

clearly concerned to create a grand and splendid monument. According to Steene, it was to be set high, as high as the tomb of Edward III, 'well out of the reach of the sacrilegious fingers of their subjects'.[42] The tomb commission, like the crosses commissioned by Edward I for Queen Eleanor, expressed, in Binski's words, 'a certain poetry of grief, and also exemplified the clerical habit of early tomb commission born of childless celibacy'.[43] Shortly after the funeral, the king granted the abbey an annuity of £200 from the exchequer to provide anniversaries for himself and the late Queen Anne.[44] The proposed weekly and yearly masses replicated Edward I's commemoration of Queen Eleanor a hundred years earlier.[45]

The contracts for the tomb were drawn up while the king was in Ireland, but the design had been approved earlier. On 1 April 1395 Henry Yevele, the king's master mason, and Stephen Lote entered a contract to produce the double-tomb, the first of its type in Westminster, in marble according to the model tendered by them and approved by the king. The tomb-chest was to have twelve niches for images, six on each side, with gilt metal shields in foils, and was to be completed by Michaelmas 1397 at a cost of £250. Nicholas Broker and Godfrey Prest, coppersmiths of London, likewise undertook to make, according to agreed patterns, lifelike images of the king and queen in gilt copper. They were to be lying on their backs, crowned, with their right hands joined, and their left hands holding sceptres, with an orb surmounted by a cross between them.[46]

★   ★   ★

After the funeral Richard headed westwards to south Wales and, still in his mourning clothes, crossed to Ireland. The expedition to Ireland was timely. The lordship was clearly in dire straits. Large parts of the island acknowledged neither the king of England nor the pope in Rome. For some time the administration in Dublin had been appealing for the king to come in person or at least to send a lieutenant with adequate power and prestige. Richard was informed that in Edward III's time the lordship of Ireland had realized a handsome revenue for the crown, but it had now become a drain on English resources. Richard was clearly keen to restore English rule in the colony and reduce the 'wild Irish' to obedience. There were plans for major expeditions in 1385–6 and 1391–2 under the command of Robert de Vere and Thomas of Woodstock respectively. Both commanders were given vice-regal powers in the lordship. Allegedly Richard even wished de Vere to have a crown. The king's cancellation of Gloucester's expedition in 1392 made the more necessary an expedition by the king in person. Still, even in the spring of 1394, the king may have been considering a number of options. It was his bereavement that made up his mind. A little over a week after the queen's death, on 16 June, he finally announced his intention of going to Ireland in person.[47]

Over the summer preparations proceeded apace for a large and well-equipped force. At the heart of the host was the king's own household and retinue. The leaders of the main contingents were for the most part magnates who were close to the court: the earls of Rutland, Nottingham and Huntingdon, Thomas Holland, the son of the earl of Kent, Lord Beaumont, Sir Thomas Percy, Sir Thomas Despenser and Sir William Scrope. The young earl of March may perhaps still be regarded as a member of this group. He had been in the king's entourage in the previous summer, and sent ahead to Ireland as the king's lieutenant. The expedition must have appeared an ideal opportunity for March to consolidate his position in Richard's affection and esteem.[48] The exception to this rule was the duke of Gloucester, who followed later and may have been a reluctant expeditioner. Richard may have particularly demanded his participation. Gloucester's proposed expedition of 1392 had raised great expectations, and his involvement in 1394 provided some guarantee that no invidious comparisons would be drawn. At the same time Richard wished England to be secure in his absence. His anxieties on this score provide some context for the extraordinary letter dated at Pontefract on 25 August, in which the dukes of Lancaster, York and Gloucester and the earl of Rutland wrote to the king protesting their loyalty against insinuations to the contrary.[49]

The main body of the army, and the ships to transport it, took some while to assemble at Milford Haven in south-west Wales. During August the king and his household crossed southern England in easy stages, reaching Hereford at the end of the month. For the best part of September the king was in south Wales, spending time in Cardiff and Carmarthen, and perhaps visiting the shrine at St David's.[50] He was accompanied at various times by the duke of York and other magnates and officials who would remain behind. Bishop

The standard of Richard II. (Reproduced by kind permission of Heraldry Today, from J.H. & R.V. Pinches, The Royal Heraldry of England, *1974)*

Waltham was especially active on the king's behalf. On 31 August he instituted processions and prayers in his diocese for the success of the king's expedition. He spent most of September at Bristol commandeering shipping and then travelled to Pembrokeshire for final consultations with Richard prior to his crossing to Ireland.[51]

The king set sail on 30 September, and disembarked at Waterford on 2 October. According to a Gaelic account, the king of England 'came to Ireland with an immense force, including English and Welsh, and such a fleet did not come to Ireland since the Norse fleets came'.[52] No king of England had visited Ireland since King John, and with some five hundred ships engaged as transport the armada must have appeared awesome. Richard's intention, as he explained to the duke of Burgundy earlier in the summer, was 'the punishment of our rebels there and to establish good government and just rule over our faithful lieges'.[53] His immediate target was Art MacMurrough, self-styled king of Leinster, whose power-base lay in the hills of County Carlow, south-west of Dublin. The plan was to mount a naval blockade along the coast, and to starve him into submission through the establishment of a string of forts or 'wards' around his territory.[54]

Richard lingered in Waterford for over a fortnight. According to Froissart, Richard used for the first time St Edward the Confessor's arms, and claims that he did so on account of the Irish people's respect for the royal saint.[55] It may well have been on 13 October, the feast day itself, that he revealed his secret weapon. Meanwhile royal writs, dated the 16th, were sent to the bishops in England ordering prayers, processions and masses for the good estate of the king, the church, the kingdom of England, and the land of Ireland, and for the success of the expedition.[56] Bishop Fordham of Ely explained to his clergy that Richard had gone to Ireland for 'the prosperous and happy government' of Ireland and for the 'castigation' of the disobedient and rebellious.[57] Bishop Waltham's prayers were that the king's enemies 'might be confounded, justice preserved, and perpetual peace established'.[58]

Setting out on 19 October, the king soon achieved results through his massive deployment of arms. While the noose tightened around MacMurrough's stronghold, the English harried the Irish by setting fire to their villages and rounding up their cattle.[59]

On one occasion the earl of Nottingham came close to capturing MacMurrough and his wife, and seized their personal baggage, including a seal inscribed 'Arthur MacMurrough, by grace of God king of Leinster'. By the 28th MacMurrough, O'Byrne, O'Toole and O'Nolan were suing for terms, and the latter three joined Richard's entourage.[60] A parliament was held in Dublin in December, and a great court was planned for Christmas. Pains were taken to transport to Ireland the accoutrements of the king's chapel.[61] At Dublin over Christmas Richard presided over a distinguished gathering of English noblemen and bishops, the Anglo-Irish establishment, and a number of Gaelic chieftains. According to Froissart, four Irish 'kings' served him at his table. The statement cannot be taken literally, but several Irish 'kings' sent their sons to Richard to be knighted and instructed in chivalry.

Early in the new year, there were further successes both in Leinster and in Ulster, where the formidable O'Neill held sway. On 7 January MacMurrough agreed to lead all Leinster 'to the true obedience, use and disposition of the king', and the next day Richard wrote exuberantly that O'Neill and other Irish rebels were about to 'submit, recognize their offences, and receive for them whatsoever we will devise'.[62] Moving north to Drogheda, Richard received the submission of the elder O'Neill on behalf of himself and his son around the 19th. In the following month Brien O'Brien, self-styled prince of Thomond, made clear his readiness to submit to Richard, performing homage to the king in Dublin on 1 March, and leading his men in an act of submission in the countryside three days later.[63]

The submissions of the Irish chieftains followed some of the conventions of traditional vassalage. The vassal went down on his knees, his hands in the posture of prayer, before the king, and swore to become his liegeman, to be faithful to him and to render him assistance against his worldly enemies; to be obedient to his laws and respond to his summonses. The gravity of their oath was underlined by the large sums they undertook to pay to the pope if they broke their word. The old notion of feudal allegiance, as Johnston observes, was being transformed into the harder, more modern concept of allegiance, the obedience of a subject to a ruler.[64] Thus Donnchadh O'Byrne on 18 February swore to serve and obey the king as his liege lord, 'with every kind of submission, service, obedience and fealty, and to keep his laws, commands and precepts, and continually to obey them without complaint'.[65] O'Brien likewise sought the king's pardon for not making his submission immediately on the king's arrival, and promised to make amends 'if he had sinned in any regard against the king's most noble lordship'.[66]

In Ireland, Richard assumed the role of a 'high king'. His commitment was to the notion of Ireland 'as one lordship, with its inhabitants being in theory all liege subjects, and in practice either rebel or loyal, whatever their racial distinction'.[67] In his dealings with the Gaelic 'kings' he was in some measure conciliatory. Provided that due submission and surrender was made, he was willing to acknowledge their special status and endorse their claims to land and lordship. Yet in the stress on obedience, and in the language of subjection and exaltation, there was a hard ideological edge. In Ireland Richard was able to give his ideas about princely power full expression, and they were of a decidedly authoritarian kind. He was also able to indulge his passion for displays of regal authority. On 1 May three former Irish rebels, including Turloch O'Conor Dom of Connacht, came on board the king's ship *The Trinity*, under sail at Waterford, and threw themselves down on the deck before Richard in a show of obeisance. Believing that 'they should not leave without some gift or honour', Richard knighted them, 'and, as token of that order, admitted them to the kiss of peace and granted each of them a sword'.[68] As he set sail for England, Richard may well have been concluding that the Irish had something to teach the English in terms of the honour shown to kings.

★ ★ ★

Richard remained in Ireland for seven months. While the expedition achieved its most signal successes in the first six months, he stayed on to consolidate his achievement and savour the fruits of his victory. He may even have gained some wry satisfaction from the consternation and inconvenience his absence was causing in England. Archbishop Arundel for example had to cross over to Ireland twice, while Gloucester was sent back across the Irish Sea to report to parliament his nephew's latest triumphs and seek further supply. There was a request from parliament for his early return, which referred to the Scots' failure to observe the truce and other great, unspecified matters.[69] According to Walsingham, the most urgent issue was the resurgence of heresy. An unknown group of Lollards had drawn up a manifesto of twelve articles, and distributed it at Westminster during the sitting of parliament. A number of knights in the king's service were believed to be giving countenance to the heretics. It may well have been this issue that prompted Archbishop Arundel to brave the Irish Sea a second time to urge the early return of the king.

The posting of a Lollard manifesto in Westminster Hall prompted Roger Dymock, a Dominican friar, to write a comprehensive refutation of it: *Liber contra XII Errores et Hereses Lollardorum*. Addressed to that 'most glorious and awe-some prince' Richard, it was presumably presented to him on his return from Ireland. Stressing the power given by God to kings and their role in the defence of the faith, Dymock presents heresy as the highest form of treason. He sets Richard in a long line of princes who had maintained the faith and hammered the enemies of God. Beginning with David and Solomon, he includes Alexander the Great, Julius Caesar and Octavian, and concludes with Charle-magne, Arthur of Britain, and the two Edwards 'who had made the crown of the English shine more brightly'.[70] The presentation copy, Cambridge, Trinity Hall MS. 17, has as its frontispiece an image of Richard sitting on a throne holding a sceptre, and two white

Presentation copy of Roger Dymock's Liber contra XII Errores et Hereses Lollardorum. *(Reproduced by permission of the Master and Fellows of Trinity Hall, Cambridge)*

harts with gold antlers, gorged with gold crowns. In later folios there are initials of St John the Baptist holding a lamb and preaching, and of a pope and an emperor, each with a triple crown, supporting a small church.[71] In September Pope Boniface himself wrote to Richard and the English archbishops urging them to take action against the Lollards 'who call themselves the poor men of the treasure of Christ' who have attacked the Mother Church and affirmed 'certain erroneous, detestable and heretical articles', and their lay adherents and protectors.[72]

Richard did not need any prompting from the pope. Back in 1392 he had written to the mayor of London that 'it is the king's will that within the bounds of his power shall bud forth no heresies or errors to infect the people'.[73] Shortly after his return from Ireland in May, there was a well-publicized crackdown on Lollards in high places. John Claydon was arrested and examined by the king's council, and was sent under guard to Conway castle. On 16 July William James, fellow of Merton, was arrested at Bristol, and two days later Richard ordered the chancellor of Oxford to expel all Lollards from the university, especially Robert Lechlade, a colleague of James. Over the summer a number of Lollards, including the Oxford dons, were imprisoned in Beaumaris castle.[74] Sir Richard Stury, a household knight and royal counsellor, was brought before the king at Eltham in August, and required to renounce association with Lollards.[75] Later in the month John Croft of Croft, Herefordshire, another Lollard sympathizer in the king's retinue, appeared before the king at Windsor. He revoked all he might have said contrary to the Catholic faith, and swore that he would not read or own Lollard scriptures, or preach or hear new doctrine. Richard forwarded to the bishop of Hereford a copy of the renunciation, witnessed by John Boor, dean of the chapel. The bishop summoned Croft to appear before him, but Croft initially declined, feeling his oath to the king was sufficient.[76]

In his Latin epitaph, Richard is represented as pious, munificent to the church and the hammer of heretics. In the long period of mourning following the queen's death, he was perhaps especially given to pious exercises and good works. In addition to his support of the fabric at Westminster abbey and Canterbury cathedral, he granted 100 marks for work at York Minster in July 1395.[77] He continued to promote the cults of royal saints. In the spring of 1395 the book of the miracles of Edward II seems to have been finally dispatched to Rome.[78] In early July he made a concession to Christ Church, Canterbury, on condition that the convent celebrate both feasts of St Edward King and Martyr, praying on each day 'for our health and the prosperity of our realm' and for his late queen.[79] In terms of his private devotions, Richard had a long-standing association with the Dominican Order. His confessors and many of the court preachers were Dominican friars. In the summer of 1395 he sought permission from the pope to have divine office celebrated at court according to the Dominican usage. The papal response noted that Richard himself was accustomed to read the daily hours in this form. Bede Jarrett believed that Richard was a Dominican tertiary.[80]

For his role in support of the church Richard seemingly won the gratitude of the bishops. A measure of his success in harnessing the spiritual, intellectual and material resources of the English church is the constructive relationship he came to enjoy with the two proud prelates who had censured him in the 1380s. Archbishop Courtenay kept his new-found faith in Richard until his death in 1396, while Archbishop Arundel kept on trying to believe in him until the time of his brother's execution and his own exile.

Some time early in 1397 Arundel wrote to Richard offering wholehearted support for his efforts on behalf of the church. Writing from Launde priory in Leicestershire, Richard thanked the archbishop for what he took to be a 'blank charter' and enthused 'the more our Lord Almighty shall strengthen us with his honour and power, the more we intend to strive and labour to show honour to our Holy Mother Church, and to cherish and strengthen our faith as aforesaid'.[81]

★ ★ ★

During his sojourn in Ireland a steady stream of messengers kept Richard well briefed on the diplomatic front. The issue of the schism remained intractable. The best hope for Christendom had lain since 1389 in the increasingly amicable relationship between the French and English courts. Queen Anne's death introduced a new element of uncertainty. It was assumed that Richard would remarry, and early in 1395 a match with Yolande of Aragon seemed in prospect. An Anglo-Aragonese alliance, however, posed a threat to peace, and threatened to entrench rather than repair the division of Christendom. In March English ambassadors set out for Barcelona by way of Paris. On learning of the English mission, the French court sent an urgent embassy to Richard in Ireland.[82] A French counter-offer may have been what Richard wanted from the outset. The Aragonese negotiations lost momentum, and a match between Richard and a daughter of Charles VI rapidly became the major focus of diplomatic interest, not only in England and France, but throughout Christendom.

The French court was certainly keen on the alliance, and may have taken the initiative. On 15 May Charles VI wrote to Richard with great warmth and enthusiasm. The letter congratulated him 'on his bloodless victories in Ireland', and then presented to him a scheme involving a final peace between England and France, the healing of the schism, and a united offensive against the Turks.[83] The letter, though, cannot have been the first adumbration of the scheme. Proponents of peace between France and England had been linking peace with Christian unity and a crusade for some time. King Leo of Armenia may well have converted Richard to this way of thinking in 1385. Robert the Hermit proselytized tirelessly for this cause, acting as an intermediary between the French court and Richard in the summer of 1392 and then twice in May 1395. Philippe de Mézières, former chancellor of the king of Cyprus, chamberlain of the kings of France and tertiary at the Celestine convent in Paris, gave the scheme intellectual weight and strategic focus. Charles VI's letter echoes, in summary form, Philippe de Mézières' *Letter to Richard II*, which was indeed written on Charles's behalf. If, as it would seem, the treatise accompanied the king's letter, the particular proposal of marriage must have been weeks, if not months, old.

Richard was all too aware of the portentous significance of a French marriage, and can scarcely have been passive in this process. De Mézières himself said that 'for some years past' he had been kept informed by Robert the Hermit concerning Richard's own 'lofty purpose'.[84] The main impediment to a marriage alliance in 1395 was the lack of a suitable match. In all likelihood Richard made it plain that he would settle for no one less than a king's daughter, and it may have required some delicate negotiation before it became clear that he was willing to discuss marriage to a five-year-old princess. After all,

Richard was approaching thirty, and was still childless. There could be no hope of issue from the marriage for seven or more years. Richard's readiness to consider Isabelle of France must have been known to de Mézières when he embarked on his treatise. While he marshals arguments in favour of a marriage that would prove the occasion of peace and unity rather than discord and war, he is at his most specific and original in handling issues relating to Richard's childlessness and Isabelle's age. He draws examples from the Bible and history as to great men who lived chastely in marriage, waited for their wives to reach maturity, and won great fame despite their lack of posterity.[85] It is unlikely that Mézières would have engaged so directly with such sensitive matters unless he knew that Richard was inclined to be responsive.

Richard's answer to Charles's letter was more restrained, but none the less very positive. For his own private reasons Richard may have been happy with the prospect of a child-bride, but he recognized the advantages to be derived from appearing the more hesitant party. On his return from Ireland he took counsel, and by the beginning of July was ready to negotiate. On 8 July 1395 he appointed the archbishop of Dublin, the bishop of St David's, the earls of Rutland and Nottingham, Lord Beaumont and Sir William Scrope as his ambassadors, and gave them their instructions. One set of instructions related to the marriage itself, and requested a dowry of two million francs, that is 500,000 marks. The second set related to terms for a final peace, which were pitched extravagantly high. They were to demand that the duchy of Aquitaine be held without homage; that Normandy, and Anjou and Maine be granted to the first two sons of Richard and Isabelle; and that, if it were established that Scotland belonged to the English crown, and another son needed an appanage, the king of France would assist in its conquest.[86] The French were predictably reluctant to negotiate on such terms, but were correspondingly more inclined to be generous with the dowry. By autumn negotiations were proceeding in earnest.

The prospects of a firm peace between England and France brought new vigour to moves to end the schism. In the years since 1378 a growing body of concerned scholars had addressed the theoretical and practical issues of the unification and reform of the church. The university of Paris led the discussion, identifying three possible paths, the ways of 'cession', 'compromise' or 'council', all of which might or might not involve some degree of compulsion on one or both parties. In the course of 1395 the Parisian masters committed themselves to the way of cession, according to which both popes would renounce their claims. They won some degree of support from the French court, and sought to lobby the English universities to this end. Armed with a letter addressed to 'all Christ's faithful during the schism', a deputation from Paris approached Richard at the end of August seeking to confer with colleagues from Oxford. Richard kept the deputation at Westminster, perhaps fearing that their appearance in Oxford might provoke some disturbance. He none the less forwarded the letter, and allowed the abbot of Mont St Michel to present the French case.[87] At the same time Richard set a number of English canonists and theologians to work on the topic. The author of one treatise claims that he wrote in response to 'edicts' lately sent out by 'our most Christian and most pious king that those who received talents of learning entrusted to them by the Lord, should inquire studiously about suitable, likely and honest methods by which the flock of the Lord, now dispersed by the error of schism, could be brought back to the care of one just shepherd'.[88] Richard's major theoretician was Nicholas Fackenham, the Augustinian Provincial. He undertook, on the king's behalf, a full 'determination' of the options. Given the seriousness of the crisis in Christendom, he was prepared to concede that it might prove necessary to force even the rightful pope to resign. In this case it should be done on the authority of a general council convened by the popes, or if they refused by the prelates from the two obediences. If the prelates failed to act then the emperor and princes should take the lead. Fackenham accorded Richard and Charles VI special roles in view of the wealth and power of their kingdoms and the reputation of their clergy and universities. Fackenham completed his determination on 5 November, and it was to inform English attitudes for over a decade.[89]

★ ★ ★

Richard was at a crossroads of his life in the summer of 1395. His response to the death of Queen Anne had been melodramatic. In his refusal to enter for twelve months any building, other than a church, where he had spent time with her, he seems to have been as good as his word. His time in south Wales and Ireland were new experiences for him, and he did not return to England until a few weeks before the anniversary of the queen's death. His bereavement prompted him to contemplate his own mortality. While in Ireland he not only approved work on the double-tomb under construction at Westminster abbey, but also ordered the destruction of Sheen and was presented with a model for a new palace to take its place at Isleworth.[90] On his return from Ireland, he presumably inspected progress on his works at Westminster, not least his tomb. If, as seems likely, he was consulted about an epitaph, he was giving serious thought to the direction of his life and how he would be viewed by posterity.

With respect to marriage, Richard may not have been personally inclined to remarry at all. The nature of his sexuality can only be a matter for conjecture. He dearly loved Queen Anne, and enjoyed the company of ladies at court. At the same time he had intense feelings for a number of male friends, notably Robert de Vere. One of Richard's concerns in the autumn of 1395 was the return to England of the embalmed body of his former favourite. Some time in November, perhaps on the third anniversary of de Vere's death, he attended his reburial at Earls Colne. In an extravagant gesture of affection, he had the casket opened, gazed at his face, and placed on his fingers precious gold rings.[91] It may be significant that no one ever claimed, even after his death, to be Richard's child. The problem may well have been medical, but it is possible that in its last years at least his marriage with Anne was chaste. De Mézières acknowledges the possibility that Richard might wish to commit himself to celibacy. Richard's increasing identification with St Edward the Confessor points in this direction. For some time he had been using St Edward's coat-of-arms along with his own, and in Ireland had campaigned under the saint's banner. In the autumn of 1395 he took the remarkable step of formally impaling the arms with his own, and ordered the production of a whole new set of silverware with this heraldic device. In all likelihood he announced the new coat-of-arms – which represented nothing less than a heraldic marriage between Richard and the royal saint – on 13 October, the feast of St Edward the Confessor. The first recorded use of his new seal is a few days later.[92]

In the circumstances Richard's readiness to take a five-year-old child in marriage is a little less remarkable. While in the negotiations and in the contract itself attention was

Philippe de Mézières presents his letter to Richard II. (The British Library, Roy.20.B.VI)

paid to the possibility of children, it is hard to imagine that Richard contemplated issue from the union. The match commended itself for a range of reasons, hardheaded as well as idealistic. Richard was interested in the substantial dowry, and in French military assistance in the case of rebellion.[93] He doubtless appreciated the providential fittingness of the proposed new marriage between Plantagenet and Valois. It was the French view that the misfortunes of the generations had flowed from Edward II's marriage to another Isabelle of France. In his *Letter to Richard II*, de Mézières refers to this marriage 'then thought a fortunate one', and reflects on 'the deadly thorns resulting from that union, which have been active for sixty years in such a cursed way that the beautiful lilies, from whom you spring, have been horribly trampled under foot and have largely become withered and spoiled, and the greater part of Christendom has been disturbed and led astray, and without much lasting profit to you from such evil'.[94] Richard would have concurred with this general analysis, not least with respect to the bitter legacy of Edward II's reign, and endorsed de Mézières's point that when kings go to war they become serfs to their own subjects.[95] Richard's marriage to the second Isabelle of France would remove the burden of war, add significantly to Richard's coffers, and strengthen his position with respect to his own subjects. In setting the scene for peace and unity within Christendom it gave Richard the glittering prospect of some higher destiny.

Richard was almost certainly drawn to the grand vision elaborated by de Mézières. The truce of 1389 had already prompted English and French nobles to cooperate in crusading ventures. In 1395 there was talk of a crusade led by the dukes of Lancaster and Burgundy, which might clear the way for an advance on Jerusalem by the kings of England and France. Richard's experience in Ireland, campaigning under the banner of St Edward the Confessor, encouraged a sense of his capacity for 'the holy passage'. His Irish expedition was represented as the more glorious in that it involved little shedding of blood. De Mézières may have been echoing Richard's own publicity when he praised him for his success 'in bringing under his lordship, without bloodshed, a race of people as savage and uncivilized as the Irish, who live with the wild creatures in the mountains'. He concluded that 'these events, so great, so marvellous, and so unheard of in times past, brought about so gloriously by divine grace in so short a time' were sure testimony to the workings of God's grace and demonstrated Richard's ardour 'for the peace of his Christian brothers, for the union of the Church, and finally, for the enterprise of the holy passage'.[96]

It all seemed very portentous. Over the summer of 1395 an old prophecy circulated in England 'to the terror and alarm of many people' which predicted unfavourable conjunction of the stars in autumn, bringing eclipses and fearful signs in the sky, fierce winds, landslides and other calamities, which would involve many deaths, including that of a great emperor.[97] Premonitions of natural disaster were nourished by well-founded concern about the general state of affairs in Christendom. It all seemed a sorry tale of moral decline, corruption, lawlessness, rebellion, heresy and the schism. God was chastising mankind for their sins. The signs of divine wrath, clear enough in the west, were even more evident in the east. Each year more Christians in south-east Europe were brought under the Turkish yoke. It seemed that the world, as the fourteenth century after the birth of Christ drew to its close, was going rapidly to perdition. Thomas Wimbledon cannot have been the only preacher who spoke of the apocalypse.

A time of millenarian anxiety was also one of millenarian expectation. It would have been odd if Richard did not examine his own position in the light of the fears and hopes of the age. There were many people in 1395 eager to cast him in a crucial role as the hammer of heretics, the restorer of Christian unity and the champion of Christendom. In his determination on the schism, Nicholas Fackenham emphasized that Richard and Charles VI had a special duty to take the lead in calling a general council of the church and, if need be, forcing the two popes to resign. In a similar vein de Mézières urged the two kings not 'to await the summons of the world, for God has long chosen you for this work and has especially trusted you with it'. He continued: 'Grasp the reins and, fully armoured with virtue and great humility, seated on your horse, that is, on your royal power, one after the other leap triumphantly into the gulf, and so redeem Christian folk from death and bring real healing, without fear or favour, to the great evil which rises continually from it, and this without lending an ear to those churchmen who wish to rule and whose rule, in the words of the prophet, is not of God.'[98]

Richard's sense of providential mission was nourished by a tradition of prophecy which linked English history with its British and Arthurian past. Richard's expeditions against Scotland in 1385 and Ireland in 1394–5 seem to have carried with them some ideological freight. According to Geoffrey of Monmouth's *History of Britain*, King

Arthur had launched his glorious career in Christendom with the conquest of Ireland, and a number of prophecies specifically linked Ireland with some future English king who would win back the Holy Land. *The Verses of Gildas* relate to 'our king now ruling', who is further identified by reference to his marriage to the daughter of the king of France. They predict an astonishing career which would begin with the conquest of Ireland undertaken after a grave crisis. This king would then go on to defeat the Scots, suppress rebellion in Gascony, and on his return home would honour the lords who sought his grace, but exile the malcontents. He would then conquer France, march through Spain and north Africa, subdue Egypt and advance triumphantly on Babylon. After the recovery of the Holy Land, and after the Pope had thrice offered to crown him, he would finally accept coronation as the Emperor of the world.[99]

This prophecy was written in Edward II's time, but given Richard's identification with his great-grandfather and the similarity of their circumstances it may well have had some currency in the 1390s. Indeed the existence of this sort of fantasy in England in 1395 can be documented by reference to a letter-book or formulary composed at this time. A remarkable series of model letters begins with one dated 13 October 1395, the feast of St Edward. The first letter is fairly prosaic. The king seeks information from the duke of Lancaster about the condition of Ireland. In his reply, Gaunt assures the king of the loyalty of the Irish and then reports a victory over the Scots who had invaded the island. In a third letter to an earl, his nephew, presumably the earl of Rutland, Gaunt announces a major expedition, involving auxiliaries from Ireland, against the king of the Scots. The nephew in turn responds with news of his father, presumably the duke of York, who was 'in the parts of Babylon' with a very fine company. He reports that the army had torched the land around Alexandria and won a great victory in an open field near Cairo. Many Saracens had been slain, and the Sultan of Babylon had been taken prisoner, 'to the great honour of our lord liege the king' and 'all the chivalry of England'.[100]

It was above all, perhaps, the vision elaborated by Philippe de Mézières that was especially beguiling to Richard. De Mézières continually associates Richard with the 'British' tradition. He addresses him as king of Great Britain as well as king of England. At one point he apostrophizes him as 'gentle and thrice noble king of Great Britain, prince of Wales and North Wales, lord of Great Ireland and king of Cornwall'.[101] He likens him, in terms of 'royal and imperial splendour', to Arthur, while Charles VI is likened to Charlemagne.[102] De Mézières depicts them setting out together to conquer Turkey, Egypt and Syria, and assures them that, their conquests complete, they 'will set little store by' their 'western kingdoms which are cold and frozen, and given over to pride, avarice and luxury'.[103] Indeed, he assures Richard, Jesus Christ himself 'will lead you on from strength to strength, from kingdom to kingdom, until you reach the earthly Jerusalem, and, finally, after many a victory and a long and deserving life, will bring you to safe lodging in the heavenly city of Jerusalem triumphant'.[104]

Richard's adoption of the new arms in the autumn of 1395 may have signified a new beginning, a rededication of his life to some new end. According to Walsingham, the act was merely another instance of the king's vanity. Even if he had known Richard's mind, he might still have thought so. Yet it is likely that Richard kept such matters close to his chest. While Charles VI's letter of 15 May had some circulation, it is clear that a great deal of what passed between the French and English courts was not generally known outside the inner circle of Richard's friends and counsellors. De Mézières's letter may have originally been read by him alone. There may have been other works in a similar vein. John de Montreuil, for example, wrote an elaborate Latin epistle to John of Gaunt in 1394 asking him to use his influence with Richard to secure peace and Christian unity. He brought it with him to England in the summer of 1394, and prepared a Latin version while in Scotland in the autumn.[105] Yet neither version is extant in England. A similar point can be made with respect to another project of de Mézières', his promotion for a new crusading order, the Order of the Passion.[106] This order had the sponsorship of both the kings of France and England, and its members included prominent noblemen and knights on both sides of the channel. It may be no coincidence that the three English princes who figure most prominently in the crusading fantasy in the privy seal formulary – Gaunt, York and Rutland – were members of the order.[107] The most active English member was the king's half-brother, the earl of Huntingdon, and his copy of the statutes survives in the Bodleian Library. English sources are otherwise wholly silent about the existence of a knightly order which so caught the imagination of the English court in the 1390s. The only extant text of de Mézières' *De la Chevallerie de la Passion de Jhesu Crist* is a presentation copy to Richard II, but it survived not in England but in Italy.

The most compelling testimony to the grandeur of the king's conception of his role in the mid-1390s is likewise a chance survival.[108] The celebrated Wilton Diptych is a work of haunting beauty and richly evocative. It is surprisingly small, and was designed to open up behind a portable altar. In the centre of the work Richard is depicted in splendid robes kneeling before the Virgin Mary and the Christ child, from whose hands he is receiving a standard with the banner of St George. The king who is on the left-hand panel is supported by St Edward the Confessor, St Edmund King and Martyr, and St John the Baptist. The Virgin and Christ Child on the right panel are attended by eleven angels, all sporting the king's badge of the white hart. On the back of the panel there is a depiction of Richard's new coat-of-arms on the right, and a fine painting of a white hart on the left. The exact date and specific meaning of the diptych are hard to establish. Given the heraldic evidence, it can be no earlier than 1395, and may well have been made then or very soon afterwards. There can be little doubt that it was commissioned personally by the king, and it remained hidden from view until Charles I acquired it by exchange in the 1630s. In terms of its meaning, while the presence of the insignia of the passion indicate some sort of crusading context, it seems not to be a representation of the king specifically making a crusading vow. The banner of St George assuredly represents England, and the revelation of the depiction of a small island on the boss of the standard confirms this reading. The message seems to be that Richard has surrendered his kingdom to the Virgin Mary, and is now receiving it back from her, presumably to perform some higher undertaking.

★　★　★

Richard was based at Windsor in October 1395, while the marriage negotiations increasingly focused on the size of the dowry, which was set at 800,000 francs (200,000

The Wilton diptych, interior. (© National Gallery)

marks), and an extension of the truce. On the 29th the substance of the agreement was ratified by Charles VI at Paris. Richard's movements around this time are a little hard to establish. He spent some time at Abingdon abbey, and attended de Vere's reburial at Earls Colne in November. He spent Christmas at Langley, making an offering at the adoration of the cross in the friary church on the 21st, and attending high mass on Christmas day, on the feast of St John the Evangelist two days later, and on the feast of the deposition of St Edward the Confessor, 5 January.[109] Despite his well-documented devotions, he celebrated Christmas in fine style. Large sums were paid into the chamber in anticipation of the Christmas season, including £933 11s 1d on 16 December.[110] On 30 December he ratified the treaty with France, and on 1 January he provided instructions for his ambassadors with respect to the marriage contract.[111] A surprise visitor at Langley was John of Gaunt, who returned unheralded from Bordeaux. Walsingham claims that the king received him with honour but not warmth, and that Gaunt outraged the court through his marriage early in 1396 to his long-term paramour Catherine Swinford.[112]

For Richard the new year was one of waiting for his plans to bear fruit. The king had no intention of waiting around Westminster, where the remodelling of the hall continued at a frustratingly slow rate. Soon after Epiphany, he set out at a brisk pace for Woodstock, and then crossed to Gloucester, where he presumably visited Edward's shrine. He made an offering at the adoration of the image of the Virgin Mary in Tewkesbury abbey, and attended the installation of Tideman Winchcombe as bishop of Worcester.[113] Still in the first wintry month of the year, he rode through Birmingham to Coventry, where he gave further instructions to his ambassadors on the 26th, and headed north through Leicester to Nottingham, where he spent some weeks.[114] On 2 February, the feast of the purification of the Virgin Mary, he attended high mass in the Carmelite friary, and around the same time was presented by some Hanse merchants with the relics of two of the Holy Innocents.[115]

While Richard lingered in Nottingham, his ambassadors were finalizing in Paris the details of the marriage contract. According to Froissart, the earls of Rutland and Nottingham were lodged at the Croix de Tiroir, and, accompanied by some six hundred horsemen, occupied the whole street and part of an adjoining street. They remained in Paris upwards of three weeks, living entirely at the charge of the king of France.[116] The contracts were signed on 9 and 11 March. A proxy marriage took place on the 12th, with the earl of Nottingham taking Richard's part. Isabelle was thenceforward styled queen of England. Young as she was, she was able to act as queen, being immediately called on to intercede for Peter de Craon who was imprisoned for debt. When the treaties were concluded, the ambassadors returned to Calais and England 'where they were joyfully received by the king, the duke of Lancaster, and the lords attached to the king's person and pleasures'.[117]

Richard was thus a married man when he set off along the Great North Road. The king's household travelled through Doncaster and Pontefract, reaching Tadcaster on 22 March.[118] Richard appears to have taken a side-trip to the shrine of St John of Bridlington.[119] The court was established at York over Easter, from 23 March until 4 April.[120] He was attended by a large contingent of prelates and nobles, including his three uncles.[121] On Maundy Thursday, 30 March, Richard was at the bishop's palace

The negotiations for the marriage of Richard II and Princess Isabelle. (The British Library, Harl. 4380, fol. 62)

giving alms to 102 paupers.[122] On Easter Sunday he made offerings at the adoration of the cross in the archbishop's chapel and in the cathedral, where he heard high mass.[123] Richard granted to the minster the relics of one of the Holy Innocents which were encased in a silver reliquary. His visit and his gift were commemorated by the carving of a white hart on a capital at the entrance to the choir.[124] During April the king retraced his route back through Nottingham and Leicester, spending a week at Langley before moving on to Windsor for the Garter feast on St George's day.[125]

At Windsor on 1 May Richard and the magnates attended to the business of the king's marriage and the peace process. In accordance with the terms agreed by the English proctors in March, a letter was drawn up on 1 May in the names of the dukes of Lancaster, York, Gloucester, and the earls of Derby, Rutland, Huntingdon and Nottingham, the king's 'uncles, brothers and cousins', in which they agreed that in the event of his death they would allow Isabelle to return to France. They presented themselves as 'considering the very great good and advantages that are arranged by means of the marriage for the future in aid of God, not only to the two kings, their realms, lands, lordships and subjects, but also to all Christendom, to the union of Holy Church, and to the confusion of miscreants'.[126]

In early June Richard made his way downriver to Westminster, where he was on 6–8 June.[127] His business in the capital seems to have been mainly liturgical. He attended services on the anniversary of Queen Anne on 7 June, and on the anniversary of his father the day after.[128] He was clearly quite anxious to complete the marriage, sending Sir William Scrope from Havering on 15 June to request that Isabelle be brought to Calais by the beginning of August.[129] In late June and early July he made occasional visits to Westminster, including attendance at the anniversary mass for Edward III on 21 June, but seems to have been based at Havering and Eltham.[130] He was at Eltham when in July he received a visit from Waleran, count de St Pol and Robert the Hermit, who urged him to work for a final peace, perhaps even through a secret agreement.[131] According to Froissart, the king was with Gaunt and his half-brothers, the earls of Kent and Huntingdon. In affirming his eagerness for peace, Richard reported that he had the support of two of his uncles, Lancaster and York, but expressed concern that Gloucester was violently opposed to it, and had the capacity to stir up a rebellion against him.[132]

At the end of July Richard set out in the company of the count of St Pol in the direction of Dover.[133] Archbishop Courtenay had recently died, and on 3 August Richard attended his funeral at Canterbury.[134] The king was at Dover on the 5th, and took ship the next day.[135] Richard remained in Calais from 7 to 22 August.[136] It soon became evident that he would meet neither the French king nor his bride on this occasion. The duke of Burgundy came to Calais to represent the French court, and agreement was reached on a number of points. It was now resolved that both parties should return to seek ratification of the articles preliminary to a meeting between the two kings and the hand-over of Richard's queen later in the year.[137] One issue related to a common approach to the schism. Richard, against the advice of his own clergy, agreed to send an embassy to both popes to press for a settlement, and wrote firm letters to Rome and Avignon fixing the feast of St Mary Magdelene (22 July 1397) as a deadline, after which, if they had not adopted the way of cession, he would use his power to end the schism.[138] In his *De subtractione obedientiae*, Simon de Cramaud noted with satisfaction that the king of England, showing great vision, now adhered to the French approach to healing the schism.[139]

Richard was back at Dover on the 23rd, and took the road through Canterbury, Rochester and Eltham to Windsor where the household was based from 29 August until 21 September.[140] During this time, though, he visited Barking abbey, where on 4 September he made an offering at the shrine of St Alburgie.[141] In Windsor chapel he heard mass for Lord Beaumont on 8 September,[142] and made an offering at the adoration of the Neyt Cross.[143] Since the king and his household were at Windsor on 21 September and at Dartford on the 22nd, they must have travelled by barge down the river.[144] Retracing the route through Rochester and Canterbury the royal household was at Calais at the end of the month.[145] On 27 September 1396 at Dover Archbishop Arundel of York, the chancellor, delivered the great seal to John Scarle, keeper of the rolls.[146]

Richard's exact movements in late September and early October remain unclear. Oblations at a requiem mass in the parish church at Calais for Edward the king's brother on 24 September may indicate a visit ahead of the arrival of his household.[147] Richard may have wished to check on preparations, and may have made several crossings of the Channel in late September and early October. The establishment of his household at Calais a full month prior to the meeting is some testimony to the organization involved. Great purveyances were made in England, and quantities of provisions were likewise purchased and stored in a number of Flemish ports.[148] There is evidence of frenzied fund-raising. On 2 October he acknowledged substantial loans of 500 marks each from Chief Justice Clopton and the abbot of Glastonbury, £100 each from the abbot of Gloucester and the bishop of Bath and Wells, £40 from the abbot of Reading, and £200 from a consortium of Bristol merchants.[149]

★ ★ ★

As the meeting date approached, Richard gathered around him at Calais a most distinguished entourage. It included the dukes and duchesses of Lancaster and Gloucester, other noblemen and their ladies, and several Gaelic chieftains.[150] Many bishops and prominent churchmen were in attendance. Richard was accompanied by his household and chapel, and a large retinue of knights and squires dressed in his livery. A veritable army of clerks, servants and camp-followers must have descended on Calais. The king of France moved more slowly, arriving at St Omer around 17 October. He sent St Pol ahead to discuss the order of proceedings with Richard, while the duke of Burgundy waited on Richard at Calais on the 11th, and offered early hospitality to the English lords and their ladies.[151] In his turn Burgundy, along with the dukes of Berry and Bourbon, was sumptuously entertained at Calais. The French sources record residual scepticism about Gloucester's commitment to the peace and the rumour that Richard had won him over with a promise to raise his son to the peerage as earl of Rochester with an annuity of £2,000.

In the mean time two tent cities had been constructed on the plain near Ardres, midway between Calais and St Omer.[152] In front of the two encampments were the richly decorated pavilions erected for the kings of France and England. On Friday 27 October the two kings proceeded from their lodgings to their pavilions. Richard was dressed in a long red velvet robe, and wore a gold collar given by the French king with his device of the broom plant. His escort wore the livery of his late queen, Anne of Bohemia. From their pavilions the two kings walked towards each other along an avenue created by two lines of French and English knights. Charles VI was supported by Lancaster and Gloucester, and Richard was supported by Berry and Burgundy. As the kings met and embraced, the knights fell to their knees weeping for joy. Charles led Richard to his pavilion, and the four dukes followed. While the kings and the royal dukes conversed amicably, wine and spices were served. The discussions concluded with the formal presentation of gifts, and an announcement that a chapel in honour of the Virgin Mary would be built on the site to commemorate the meeting.[153] The next morning, the feast of Sts Simon and Jude, there were further formalities interrupted by a heavy downpour of rain. The two kings had a four-hour-long conference, and made agreements for mutual assistance, collaboration with respect to the schism, and further

The meeting of Richard II and Princess Isabelle. (The British Library, Harl. 4380, fol. 89)

meetings to secure a final peace. At dinner they were served by the dukes of Berry, Burgundy and Bourbon, the last entertaining them with his drollery. Charles wished that his daughter was of an age to love the thirty-year-old Richard as his wife. She was still a week short of her seventh birthday.[154] Richard insisted that he was well pleased with her age, and that he valued more the king of France's love, and 'that of our subjects, for we shall now be so strongly united that no king in Christendom can any way hurt us'.[155]

On Monday Richard prepared to receive his young queen in his pavilion. Isabelle arrived to great fanfare, riding on a richly caparisoned palfrey. Wearing a gold crown set with jewels, and in a blue gown of traditional cut, she curtsied twice to Richard, who tenderly raised her up and gave her the kiss of peace. Charles kissed his daughter and in presenting her to Richard asked him to cherish her. Richard readily agreed, and spoke warmly on the alliance they had formed in the interests of peace. Given over to the charge of the duchesses of Lancaster and Gloucester and other English noblewomen, Isabelle was carried to Calais on a litter. The next day, All Saints Day, Archbishop Arundel conducted the marriage service in the church of St Nicholas at Calais. According to Froissart, there was a great deal of feasting and celebration, and the heralds and minstrels received great rewards.[156] On Thursday the dukes of Orléans and Bourbon came to Calais to conclude some final business, and the next day returned to the king of France at St Omer. This same morning Richard and Isabelle, after an early mass, embarked for England 'with a favourable wind'.[157]

CHAPTER FIVE

PRINCELY CASTIGATION

At the beginning of 1397 Richard II turned thirty. It was the age at which Christ was traditionally regarded as having begun his ministry, and it was an age held to be specially important for a king. Richard was at the height of his prosperity and prestige. According to Walsingham, England 'seemed to be basking in peace, and the hope was for an entirely prosperous future on account of the magnificence of the king'. Furthermore, England 'had more, as well as more worthy, lords than any other kingdom could boast'.[1] The marriage celebrations of 1396–7 were the occasion of an impressive show of solidarity among the nobles. The position of the royal uncles as pillars of the throne was given visual expression when the dukes of Lancaster and Gloucester paired the dukes of Burgundy and Berry as attendants of the two kings in the 'field of cloth of gold' outside Calais.[2] Richard's marriage to Isabelle of France brought him a massive dowry, a compact with the king of France, and a truce for thirty years. It was agreed that there would be further high level meetings in the new year at which the truce would be converted into a final peace.

Richard had the opportunity to play a leading role in the affairs of Christendom. With regard to the schism, he now committed himself to the view, championed by leading French churchmen, that both popes should resign, or if necessary be forced to resign. Even before the end of the conference, the two kings sent Robert the Hermit first to Avignon and then to Rome to inform the popes of their intention to address them.[3] In a formal agreement dated 5 November the two kings agreed to send in the new year a joint embassy to present the popes with an ultimatum to achieve a settlement by Michaelmas 1397 or forfeit their allegiance.[4] There was agreement, too, to send an Anglo-French mission to Germany to persuade Wenceslas of Bohemia, the emperor-elect, and other German princes to support the 'way of cession'. Even more materially, Richard agreed to cooperate in a French expedition to Italy in the spring. Philippe de Mézières had envisaged this intervention as a means of finding 'some good treaty, without the spilling of Christian blood, whereby the Church of God, bride of Jesus Christ, divided and troubled as it was, might by the mercy of God be reunited under a single and true pope at the behest of the kings of England and France'.[5] An Italian based in Avignon wrote in December that 'it is believed that the king of France, or even the king of England, will come here next April to enforce union on the Church, and will go to Lombardy for this purpose'. Palmer regards the approach to the popes and the expedition as 'two halves of a single plan, a plan designed to secure the unanimous election of a new pope endowed with sufficient power in Italy to guarantee his position'.[6]

Finally, there was the prospect of the chivalry of France and England collaborating in a major crusade. Froissart believed that the two kings agreed to set out in the following summer 'with a great force of men-at-arms and archers to conquer the Holy Land'.[7] The great enterprise had in a sense already begun. Plans had been laid for a crusade in 1395 involving the dukes of Burgundy, Orléans and Lancaster. An expeditionary force under John of Nevers, Burgundy's eldest son, had left for the east via Hungary in the spring of 1396. Though largely a Burgundian force, it had been joined by other prominent French lords, like Enguerrand de Coucy, and included an English contingent under the command of Sir John Beaufort, Gaunt's eldest son by Katherine Swinford. The expedition was designed to serve as the vanguard for a larger force under the command of the royal dukes or of the two kings themselves. By early November lack of news regarding its progress may have been a cause of some anxiety,[8] but it was not until Christmas that reports of the disaster at Nicopolis reached Paris and London. The defeat of the crusading force, the death of many French lords and the captivity of others threw the French court into mourning, and all the plans and hopes invested in the marriage and the peace were thrown into confusion, if not wholly destroyed.[9]

★　★　★

Even as Richard and his queen left Calais for England there were a number of ominous signs. The royal party crossed the Channel on 4 November, and enjoyed a good passage lasting only three hours.[10] Some of the transports were not so fortunate. A storm blew up and wrecked several ships, sending to the bottom of the Channel the stage-props of what had been a veritable 'field of cloth of gold'.[11] After a night at Dover the party proceeded by way of Rochester and Canterbury to Eltham. At each stage the young queen was laden with gifts, including two gold crowns presented to her by the king, one at her entry into Dover castle and another, garnished with precious stones and pearls, at Canterbury.[12] On 23 November the queen made her ceremonial entry into London. A crowd gathered on a bridge to watch her cross from Southwark to Kennington, and in the crush to leave a number of people, including an alderman's wife and a prior from Essex, were killed.[13]

The king spent Christmas near London, the last time he would do so.[14] The tone was one of prodigality. On New Year's Day 1397 Sir William Courcy and his wife, the queen's profligate governess, secured an annuity of £100 for their services.[15] There were rewards, too, for Margery, Lady Moleyns, always a royal favourite at court festivities.[16] The chronicles are fairly reticent about the queen's coronation. The news of the disaster at Nicopolis, which was known in London by 2 January,[17] may have cast a shadow over proceedings. The queen entered London on 3 January and spent the night in the Tower of London. The next day, accompanied by many lords, ladies and damsels, she was taken by way of Cornhill and Cheapside to Westminster where Richard waited to receive her.[18] Twenty ladies led twenty knights, all dressed in red gowns decorated with white harts, in the procession.[19] She was crowned on 5 January, by the archbishop-elect of Canterbury, Thomas Arundel, who officiated by special commission of the chapter of Canterbury.[20] The coronation was followed by tournaments lasting a fortnight during which twenty knights held the field on the queen's behalf against all comers.[21]

The celebrations notwithstanding, it may be that the marriage alliance attracted adverse comment. Richard received an ample dowry, but he had incurred very

The king of France receives
news of the Turkish victory.
(The British Library, Harl.
4380, fol. 98)

considerable expense. According to Thomas Walsingham, the king spent 300,000 marks
at that time, not including 10,000 marks in gifts to the French court.[22] Before his
marriage the king had raised substantial loans, and further financial demands were
expected in the parliament summoned for January 1397.[23] To the costs incurred in
France can be added those associated with the young queen's reception, the Christmas
festivities and the coronation. The great problem was that the terms of the peace with
France were not especially popular. According to Froissart, Gloucester remained
unhappy about England's concessions, and his reservations were probably shared by a
number of magnates.[24] The king could certainly be presented as selling out English
interests. Cherbourg had been restored to the French in 1393, Brest was now to follow
and Calais was rumoured to be next. It was suspected, too, that the king's policy in
relation to the papal schism was too accommodating of the French viewpoint. The
English would need a great deal of persuading that Boniface IX, the pope in Rome, was

not the true pope. To cap it all, the king's commitment to assist the French in Italy must have appeared rash, if not wholly misguided. Still, over the winter, the earls of Rutland and Nottingham began to recruit men at the king's expense to go to Italy, while the earl of Huntingdon advertised his intention to go at his own costs.[25]

Given the political climate in England, Richard must have been aware that it might prove hard to keep his promises to Charles VI. It is difficult to know how straight he was in his dealings with the French court. While both kings shared in the enthusiasm for Christian unity and the crusade, Richard certainly had interests that could scarcely be accommodated within the Anglo-French entente. With respect to Italy, Richard was more interested in increasing his leverage with Boniface than with forcing his resignation, and Richard's later support for Giangaleazzo Visconti, duke of Milan, makes it unlikely that he would have supported French expansionism in Lombardy. It is true that Richard did take steps to send forces to Italy, and that in the event it was the French government which cancelled the expedition. Yet the only plan for English military involvement in Italy to assume any concreteness in 1397 does not seem wholly in accord with French policy. The Roman curia, ostensibly at least, welcomed it. On 1 March Pope Boniface wrote to commend the purpose of the earl of Huntingdon 'to come shortly to Italy and other parts for the extermination of schismatics, rebels, and usurpers of cities and lands of the pope and the Roman Church', and appointed him 'gonfalonier of the Holy Roman Church, vicar in temporals in all provinces, cities, lands, castles and other places in Italy and elsewhere belonging to the pope and the said Church, and captain-general of all men-at-arms fighting in their service'.[26]

Richard may have secretly harboured an ambition that was even less consistent with the Anglo-French entente. A number of diplomatic initiatives in 1396 may reflect the genesis of his campaign to become Holy Roman Emperor. In May 1396 Thomas Merks, bishop of Carlisle, was sent to Cologne and Germany on the king's business, and did not return until late August.[27] He doubtless visited the archbishop of Cologne, who was to prove Richard's main supporter in Germany, Rupert, count palatine of the Rhine, and possibly other members of the electoral college. On 9 September, a fortnight after Merks's return to England, Richard granted Rupert an annuity of £1,000.[28] In the spring of 1397 there was an Anglo-French mission to the diet of Frankfurt, but the English ambassadors may have regarded their main task as being to strengthen Richard's position in the electoral college. Richard's imperial ambitions made it less likely that he would take action to unseat Pope Boniface who, for all his problems, had some capacity to help or hinder them.

★ ★ ★

Parliament opened at Westminster on 22 January. In his opening speech the new chancellor, Bishop Stafford of Exeter, discoursed generally on the well-being of the church and realm. Several days later he informed the commons of the king's commitment to assist the French in Italy, and sought financial aid for the expedition under Rutland and Nottingham. The commons expressed some misgivings, and evaded the issue by referring the matter to the lords, many of whom had still not arrived. Richard wanted to know who had stirred them to oppose 'his honourable purpose'.

The commons denied any conspiracy, and pointed out, as politely as they could, that they should not be obliged to pay for an enterprise that concerned the king rather than the kingdom. Richard went to the commons to explain his policy in person, justifying it in terms of peace and unity, and stressed his intention to be free 'to order his people to go to the support of his friends, and for that purpose to dispose of his goods as and when he pleased'. The commons now urged him to proceed with the expedition, but stressed again that it was a private undertaking. The commons were given time to reconsider the king's request for assistance, but on receiving news from France of the abandonment of the expedition the matter lapsed.[29]

On 1 February the commons delivered an even sharper rebuff to the king by presenting the lords with four points of grievance. The first complaint was that sheriffs and escheators were kept in office beyond their terms. The second related to the government's failure to provide adequately for the defence of the Scottish marches. The third was concerned with the widespread distribution of badges against the terms of the statute. The fourth related to the 'great and excessive cost' of the king's household, and the large number of bishops and ladies maintained within it. The king responded to the first three points, but angrily asserted that criticisms of his household were against his 'regality'. Gaunt was ordered to discover the name of the person whose 'bill' lay behind the petition, and on 3 February the commons produced the author of the bill, Thomas Haxey, and submitted themselves to the king's will. On the 5th the lords resolved that it was treason for anyone to excite the commons to reform anything touching the person, government or 'regality' of the sovereign, and two days later Haxey was brought into the white chamber before king, lords and commons, and adjudged a traitor for his role in the production of the bill.[30] As a cleric, he escaped the ultimate penalty, and was committed to the custody of Archbishop Arundel.

The whole episode is a little mysterious. Haxey was well connected at Westminster, and was in a position to offer an informed critique of royal policy and finances. Serving as the proctor of a number of religious houses, he may have found himself articulating 'country concerns'. He may have been acting on behalf of the 'backroom boys', the experienced royal clerks who found promotion prospects limited by the king's advancement of favoured monks and friars to the episcopate.[31] Yet Haxey, who was a close associate of the late Bishop Waltham,[32] must have known that his bill was dynamite. It could not fail to call to mind the criticisms of Richard's household in the 1380s. It is tempting to see Haxey as the mouthpiece of the magnates who were hostile to the court. Yet the nobleman with whom he was most nearly connected was the earl of Nottingham who was now close to Richard.[33] It is even conceivable that the bill was a ruse engineered by the court to flush out opposition and provide an opportunity for royalist assertion. Richard was capable of this sort of double-game. In 1393 he was suspected of giving countenance to the Cheshire rising, and despite petitions from parliament he never allowed Sir Thomas Talbot, the rebel leader, to be put on trial. On 20 April 1397 he gave Talbot a full pardon, and retained him in his service.[34] In this case, five days later he ratified Haxey's estate in his benefices, and pardoned him a month later.[35]

The events in parliament indicate the resurgence of the tensions which had led to civil strife a decade earlier. Whatever Haxey's own motives in presenting the bill, the

The duke of Gloucester plotting against Richard II. (The British Library, Harl. 4380, fol. 108)

commons registered their disapproval of royal extravagance. They likewise made it clear that they were unwilling to assist the king in his adventuresome foreign policy. In his response Richard professed to believe that some magnate was fomenting opposition. According to Froissart, Gloucester was scarcely able to conceal his distaste for the peace, advocated a reopening of the war early in 1397 to take advantage of the disaster at Nicopolis, and sought to exploit discontents arising from the surrender of Brest. There is no record of opposition in parliament from Gloucester and his former allies, but it may be significant that neither Arundel nor Warwick figure among the lords presenting gifts to the new queen in the winter of 1396/7.[36]

For his part, Richard was experiencing mounting frustration. His initiatives, far from meeting acclaim and support in England, were disavowed in parliament, and probably ridiculed in private. The demeanour of the lords and the actions of the commons strengthened his conviction that there was opposition to surmount in England before he could embark on any grander design. In draft peace proposals with France in 1395 he had included a request for military assistance, if necessary, against his own subjects. What is remarkable is not that the request was dropped in the final agreement, but that it was ever on the table. Froissart's report of Richard's conversation with the count of St Pol in the summer of 1396 is instructive in this light. Richard pointed out Gloucester's hostility to the peace and his capacity for mischief, and expressed concern about the threat of 'a second rebellion' by Gloucester and other lords 'who are, as I know, of his way of thinking'. St Pol advised him to seek to win Gloucester over with fine words and gifts until the marriage was completed, after which 'you will be powerful enough to crush all your enemies or rebellious subjects, as the king of France will at all times be ready to assist you, and this you may securely depend upon'. According to Froissart, Richard was pleased with the advice, and declared that he would follow it.[37]

One act in the parliament in February 1397 served notice that Richard was revisiting the events of ten years earlier. He recalled from exile in Ireland the judges whose advice in 1387 had expanded the scope of treason to cover acts in derogation of his regality. During the spring Richard proceeded with his plans, but prepared the ground for a strike against the men who had humiliated him in 1386–8. He made a special effort to shore up Gaunt's support. On 6 February he announced the legitimation of the Beauforts, Gaunt's children by Katherine Swinford, in parliament. Acting as 'entire emperor of the realm' Richard removed all taint of bastardy, and overrode the laws of inheritance.[38] To set the seal on the event, he raised Sir John Beaufort, a survivor of the disaster at Nicopolis, to the peerage as the earl of Somerset. Richard drew other members of the royal family around him. Gaunt, the duke of York and the earl of Derby accompanied him to Canterbury in late February, while York, Derby and Rutland were with him at Windsor in early March.[39] Later in the month Richard dispatched key members of his entourage on important missions. Rutland and Nottingham joined an Anglo-French embassy to the diet of Frankfurt, while Sir William Scrope was sent to Brittany to receive from the duke of Brittany 120,000 francs, the sum agreed for the return of Brest.[40] The earl of March's appointment as lieutenant of Ireland on a reduced salary and with half the forces represented a temporary scaling back of his commitments in Ireland.[41] Richard was seeking to marshal his resources, and expand his retinue in England. On 1 March he retained Sir Henry Green who, along with Sir William Bagot and Sir John Bushy, would achieve notoriety as an agent of the crown.[42]

★ ★ ★

In contemplating a showdown with his former opponents, Richard felt especially confident of support from senior churchmen. Even Thomas Arundel now appeared very much the king's man. He was the obvious choice to replace Archbishop Courtenay at Canterbury in August 1396, and Richard did not hesitate to postulate him. Early in 1397 the king attended the ceremonies relating to his consecration and installation. He was present on 12 January when Arundel received the cross of Canterbury from Prior Chillenden at the high altar of Westminster abbey, and on 10 February when he received the pallium at the hands of Bishop Wykeham.[43] He travelled to Canterbury to preside at the archbishop's enthronement on the 18th, and processed with him through the city to St Augustine's abbey.[44]

The challenge of heresy, so salient in the 1380s and 1390s, greatly strengthened the bond between Arundel and the king. On his return to London in late February Arundel led convocation in seeking a response 'in defence of the faith' to eighteen points extracted from John Wycliffe's *Trialogus*. William Woodford was enlisted to refute them, and to write up his refutation while staying as the guest of the countess of Norfolk at Framlingham during Lent.[45] There can be no doubting Arundel's sense of mission with respect to the suppression of heresy. Early in Henry IV's reign, he declared to the Lollard William Thorpe that God had called him from exile 'and brought me into this land, for to destroy thee and the false sect that thou art of'.[46] It is probable that a petition by the archbishops of Canterbury and York, seeking the death penalty and forfeiture of goods for convicted heretics, dates from this time.[47] Though Richard did not accede to this request, he was well able to convince the clergy of his commitment to the church and the faith. The high regard for Richard at Canterbury at this time is attested in a remarkable letter sent to him by the archbishop, prior and chapter. It commends him for the restoration of tranquillity to the realm and to the church, and for the erection of a 'wall of defence' against Lollard assault through the 'exaltation of the Catholic faith'. Acknowledging the great expense that the king has incurred in this work, the letter seems to offer him open-ended support. In his response Richard thanks the church of Canterbury for the equivalent of a 'blank charter'.[48]

In the spring of 1397 bishops continued to be prominent in Richard's entourage. In the first week of March he received the homage of three new prelates – Robert Waldby, archbishop of York, Edmund Stafford, bishop of Exeter, and Thomas Merks, bishop of Carlisle – at Windsor castle. The witnesses included the bishops of Salisbury, Chichester, Llandaff and Waterford.[49] While the presence at court of so many prelates was warranted in the circumstances, the flavour of the proceedings may have been spiced by a triumphalist disregard of the carping in the commons. Interestingly, there was an echo in convocation of parliament's concerns about courtly bishops. Bishop Rede of Chichester was a Dominican friar who spent a great deal of time in Richard's entourage, and had taken to wearing, contrary to his order, the red and purple of the episcopal office. On 10 March, hearing reports that Rede had not yet forsaken his bishop's robes, Archbishop Arundel issued a formal reprimand and on the 12th received his submission at Canterbury.[50]

In late March Richard may have been in the Midlands. He returned to Eltham late in April, and established himself at Windsor early in May.[51] He must have been eager for news of his various diplomatic initiatives and indeed the return to England of the lords in whom he placed greatest trust. The earl of Huntingdon seems to have been abroad. Sir William Scrope did not return from his mission to Brittany and France until 16 May.[52] The earls of Rutland and Nottingham did not return from Germany until July. Richard may have felt a little insecure. The final hand-over of Brest doubtless prompted further murmuring against the peace with France. It is instructive that Richard at this time saw fit to pardon and bind to him two swashbuckling desperadoes. On 20 April he pardoned Sir Thomas Talbot for his rebellion in 1393, and on 2 June, at the request of Sir Baldwin Raddington, he pardoned Sir Roger Swinnerton for the murder of Sir John Ipstones, knight of the shire for Staffordshire, in the parliament of 1394.[53]

Little can be learned about the demeanour of the senior Lords Appellant. Gloucester, Arundel and Warwick certainly spent little time at court. They attended parliament in February, though possibly in a fairly half-hearted fashion. They do not appear as witnesses to the peerage creations on 10 February. According to the monk of Evesham, they incurred Richard's wrath at this time by failing to attend a council meeting and claiming infirmity.[54] Gloucester was largely based at Pleshy in Essex, and was apparently ill in spring or early summer. On 5 July he wrote to the prior and convent of Llanthony thanking them for their good wishes and gift of cheese, and reporting that he was now in better health.[55] He was still able to secure royal grants.[56] Arundel had played little part in public life for some years. He was at Westminster during parliament time, taking the opportunity to conduct some private business, but then retired to his castles at Arundel and Reigate. It was Warwick who found himself most immediately vulnerable in the changing political climate. For some time Nottingham had disputed his title to the lordship of Gower. Riding high in the king's favour, Nottingham secured a favourable settlement. On 1 June Warwick made a quitclaim of Swansea castle and the lordship of Gower, and committed himself to pay Nottingham 8,000 marks in instalments over the following five years.[57]

Early in July Richard moved to the capital, basing himself at Eltham and Kennington.[58] The king met with his council, and there was much weighty business to consider. The diplomatic activity of the spring was bearing fruit. Sir William Scrope returned from France in mid-May with the proceeds from the surrender of Brest. The king received a report of the ceremony on 30 May from Rupert of Bavaria, count palatine of the Rhine, who became his vassal at Oppenheim, and a meeting on 16 June between the count palatine and the earls of Rutland and Nottingham and Bishop Merks of Carlisle at Bacharach.[59] Late in June Hugh Hervorst, archdeacon of Cologne, arrived in England and on 7 July, in complementary ceremonies at Westminster and Godesberg, Frederick, archbishop of Cologne, performed homage to Richard in return for an annual pension of £1,000.[60] On 10 July payment was made to an emissary of the duke of Guelders.[61] On the 11th the earls of Rutland and Nottingham returned from their embassy and made their reports to the king.[62] By this stage Richard had gathered around him in London the nobles in whom he placed most trust. The earl of Huntingdon, who may also have been abroad, joined his nephew the earl of Kent at the king's side. It was a time for feasting and celebration. The author of *Traison et Mort* reports a banquet held in Richard's honour by Huntingdon at Coldharbour, his Thames-side palace.[63] In this heady atmosphere Richard decided to act.

★   ★   ★

The coup, when it came, was precipitate. According to Walsingham, the king invited Gloucester, Arundel and Warwick to a feast on 10 July.[64] He likewise sent orders to Ireland that Sir Thomas Mortimer should come before the king.[65] Gloucester wisely excused himself. Arundel, who likewise had every reason to suspect a trap, chose to remain at Reigate castle. Alone among the triumvirate, Warwick responded to the invitation. According to Walsingham, the king acted like Herod of old. To all appearances, he was the genial host, commiserating with Warwick over the loss of

The arrest of the duke of Gloucester. (The British Library, Harl. 4380, fol. 134)

Gower and assuring him of recompense.[66] Once the dinner was over, though, his mood changed abruptly. Warwick was arrested and promptly dispatched to the Tower of London. Measures were then immediately taken to secure Arundel and Gloucester. Archbishop Arundel was prevailed upon to persuade his brother to surrender. Richard allegedly assured the archbishop that the arrest was a temporary measure, for appearance's sake, and swore by St John the Baptist that his brother would come to no harm.[67] Meanwhile the king himself set off to ride through the night at the head of a large company to arrest Gloucester. According to Walsingham, he feared that his uncle would be waiting in strength, and was relieved to learn that there was only a skeleton establishment. On arrival at Pleshy, Richard acted with a hypocritical courtesy, addressing Gloucester as 'fair uncle' and dissimulating his intentions. Powerless to resist, Gloucester was led away, though not to London. It was deemed safer to send him abroad to Calais.[68]

Within a day or so the coup was complete, with Warwick safely in the Tower of London, Arundel on his way to prison on the Isle of Wight, and Gloucester on board ship for Calais. On 13 July the king dispatched letters across the realm to announce their arrests on account of various extortions and oppressions committed by them, and prohibiting, under pain of treason, all assemblies and congregations. The proclamation stated that the arrests had been made on the advice of the earls of Rutland, Kent, Huntingdon, Nottingham, Somerset and Salisbury, Lord Despenser and Sir William

Scrope.[69] On the 15th the king caused a further proclamation to be made reassuring the people that the lords had not been arrested for their actions ten years earlier, but for 'other offences against the king's majesty to be declared in parliament', and informing them that the dukes of Lancaster and York and the earl of Derby had now joined the king's person, and likewise given their assent to the proceedings.[70] On the 18th writs were issued for a parliament to be held at Westminster on Monday 17 September.[71]

In their account of the coup, the French sources report that Richard acted on evidence of a new plot against him. The author of *Traison et Mort* offers a detailed account of a conspiracy involving the three lords, the earls of Derby and Nottingham, Archbishop Arundel, the abbot of St Albans and the prior of Westminster. The plot was directed against the king and the dukes of Lancaster and York, and was sealed by an oath at Arundel castle around 23 July 1396. Since the story of the conspiracy is prefaced by an account of the return of Brest and Gloucester's reactions to it, historians have assumed that the chronicler intended '1397' not '1396' as the date of the conspiracy.[72] They then proceed to impugn the credibility of the story on the basis of their own redating. The three lords were arrested a fortnight before the alleged meeting at Arundel; Nottingham, who allegedly divulged the conspiracy to the king, was abroad until 11 July; and Thomas de la Mare, abbot of St Albans, who was Gloucester's godfather and adviser, died in September 1396.[73]

If the chronicler's dating is restored, a rather different picture emerges. A meeting of the key conspirators at Arundel castle on 23 July is perfectly conceivable. Richard was waiting to cross to Calais to receive his bride, and many lords and bishops were on hand in the southern counties. Indeed at the very time of the alleged conspiracy Richard was at Eltham in the company of the dukes of Lancaster and York, expressing his concerns to the count of St Pol about Gloucester's attitude to the peace and the possibility of a second rebellion.[74] The focus on Brest may be explained in terms of the coincidence in time between the delivery of the town and the arrest of the lords. Of course, the conspiracy itself remains somewhat improbable. Apart from Warwick's confession, no evidence of treason seems to have been brought forward in parliament. What is possible, though, is that in July 1396 Gloucester and other malcontents shared their concerns about Richard and his policies, and that at some stage Nottingham, who was privy to their discussions, reported them to the king.[75]

For some English chroniclers, Richard's coup is explained by reference to his desire to avenge the events of 1386–8. According to the monk of Evesham, Richard called to mind how he had been constrained and coerced in his rule, and 'was filled with an ardent desire to exact revenge for the bitter rebuke he had endured'.[76] Adam Usk reported the popular rumour that the marriage with Isabelle of Valois was arranged so that with French assistance he might 'vent his pent-up hatred on those whom he detested'.[77] In hindsight it is all too apparent that Richard was determined both to reverse the political outcomes of 1386–8 and to exact retribution in kind from the men who had humiliated him. There is no doubt, too, that he looked to the compact with France to strengthen his hand against his own subjects. In the weeks prior to the coup he received 150,000 francs from the duke of Brittany for the delivery of Brest.[78] Of course, Richard's desire for revenge might well have been kindled by fear and suspicion. In 1399 members of parliament believed that certain bishops and friars had told Richard

Arundel town and castle, in 1644, etching by Hollar. (© The British Museum)

that 'they had found by calculation and necromancy' that unless 'certain lords of the realm were put to death' he himself 'should be destroyed'.[79] Richard certainly had an astrologer brought from Paris for private consultations around this time.[80]

In his account of the timing and rationale of the coup, Walsingham focuses more specifically on the embassy from Cologne. He claims that the ambassadors, aware of Richard's 'fickleness and ambition', informed him that he was about to be elected Holy Roman Emperor. Flattered, Richard sent agents to Germany who confirmed that the majority of the seven electors were supportive, but reported that two or three withheld their consent, asking how Richard could govern the empire when he could not even discipline his own subjects. According to Walsingham, it was this intelligence that especially angered Richard and led him to turn against his own subjects.[81] Walsingham links Richard's imperial ambitions with the coup more than once. He allegedly won over Archbishop Arundel to the view that his brother should surrender by saying that any imprisonment would be only temporary to show the Germans that he was master of his own house.[82]

Given his position at St Albans, Walsingham had good reason to explain the coup in terms other than a conspiracy originating with his own former abbot. Yet his story has some substance. There was a great deal of diplomatic activity between England and Germany in the month or so prior to the coup, and Hugh Hervost, provost of Hauten and archdeacon of Cologne, was in England from late June until August.[83] On 21 July Richard dispatched another embassy to Cologne and Germany, and sent gifts of silver white harts and cloth worth £405 'for the honour of us and our realm'. The principal recipients were the archbishops of Cologne and Trier, the duke of Saxony and the count palatine, four of the seven electors of the Holy Roman Empire.[84] He presumably reported to them his actions against Gloucester, Arundel and Warwick. By the end of 1397 Richard's imperial ambitions were certainly well known in Europe.[85]

In seeking an understanding of Richard's actions in July 1397, there are grounds for taking all the chronicle accounts seriously. Richard certainly had in mind the events of a decade earlier, and was determined to punish the men who had humiliated him. Though there may not have been a plot against his throne, he had ample reason to suspect the loyalty of Gloucester and Arundel, and may have genuinely believed that proof of their treason would be forthcoming. Furthermore, while Walsingham's focus on the mission from Cologne may be too narrow, his general point that Richard's coup was the product of frustration and anger at opposition to his rule seems apposite. Furthermore, for all their differences, the accounts have features in common. They reveal a wilful king whose sudden strike against his old opponents caught them by surprise. They present him as acting on the advice of an inner circle of courtiers who by scaremongering, tittle-tattle or flattery encouraged his designs. Walsingham claims that Richard's emissaries presented the response of the German electors in terms calculated to provoke his wrath. Above all the stories concur in presenting a king who felt thwarted and threatened in his own realm.

A number of the interpretative strands can be seen neatly illustrated in a letter by the emperor-elect Wenceslas. Writing from Nuremberg on 24 September, Wenceslas commiserated with Richard with regard to the rebellion against him, and made an offer of assistance.[86] The letter indicates that Richard's coup was seen on the continent as defensive or pre-emptive rather than offensive. It testifies, too, to the fact that Richard's problems with his subjects were known in Germany. Above all, the letter from Wenceslas, whom Richard aspired to displace as emperor, must have served to raise further his bile against the lords who through disobedience and rebellion had brought dishonour on his crown and himself.

Richard had embarked on a very dangerous course. He had secured the persons of Gloucester, Arundel and Warwick, but only by moving quickly and with a degree of trickery. The arrest of the three lords prompted angry demonstrations and unrest in many parts of the realm. The proclamation of 13 July — the first announcement of the arrests — prohibited, on pain of forfeiture and being reckoned a traitor, men from gathering in assemblies or inciting men so to do, save by special command of the king, or letters of the loyalist lords.[87] Two days later orders were sent to the sheriffs to arrest all the followers of the three lords found in arms in London, Middlesex, Essex, Hertfordshire, Surrey, Sussex, Kent, Shropshire, Warwickshire, Leicestershire, Gloucestershire, and Worcestershire.[88] Fear as well as loyalty to their lord may have made some men bold. Rumours that the king was about to punish all who had risen against him a decade earlier would have been all too credible. On 15 July the king sought to head off opposition by having it proclaimed that the lords had been arrested for new not old offences, and that, contrary to rumour, it was not the king's intention to trouble members of their retinues in 1387.[89] Notwithstanding the proclamations, partisans of the imprisoned lords remained at large in the southern counties, disseminating abuse against the king and inciting resistance to his actions. On 28 July the keepers of the peace in Sussex, Surrey, Kent and Essex were commanded to arrest and imprison 'all who by word, deed or craft were stirring against the imprisonment of the disgraced lords, or behaving towards the king otherwise than a true liege should'.[90] Significantly, in the previous week the government had established new commissions of the peace, which better conformed to the new political dispensation, in twelve counties in the south, the west Midlands and East Anglia.[91]

The arrests had thrown the realm into confusion. The three lords had political followings wider than the retinues they had led to Radcot Bridge. According to Walsingham, there was 'public grief' at the arrest of three lords, because everyone had such faith in them, and especially in Gloucester, that they 'considered that while he was hale and hearty the kingdom would be well governed internally and safe externally from foes'.[92] Writing from various perspectives, Jean Froissart, John Gower and the author of *Richard the Redeless* confirm the standing of the 'good duke' in public opinion.[93] The arrests raised in people's minds the spectre of turmoil and civil strife. On 24 July, at the king's request, Archbishop Arundel ordered prayers and processions for the health and peace of the king, the tranquillity of the realm, and the unity of the universal church.[94] According to Walsingham, there were prayers and processions through the land, but they were on behalf of the lords as well as the king, and sought to change the king's heart from hate to love. The king allegedly ordered bishops and other prelates to prohibit them.[95] The countryside remained disturbed through the summer. Even as late as 31 August the abbot of Westminster wrote to the prior to restrain the monks from travelling, and to admonish them to apply themselves, as the evil spirit of the times required, more fervently to prayer and processions 'for the happy expedition and common prosperity of the king and kingdom'.[96]

★ ★ ★

By deferring the whole matter to the next parliament, Richard was playing for time. Over the summer he marshalled his forces. Royal castles were strengthened. The strongholds of the arrested nobles were secured. The earl of Arundel's castles at Arundel, Lewes and Reigate were assigned to the keeping of the earls of Huntingdon and Nottingham and Sir William Arundel, while Warwick castle was committed to the charge of Sir John Clinton.[97] Even as he sought to convince the people that the arrests did not spring from a desire to avenge the events of 1387–8, he was seeking to mobilize, as he had done in November 1387, the military resources of his palatinate of Chester. In a letter of 13 July he ordered the sheriff of Chester to recruit some two thousand archers.[98] A week later the sheriff of Warwickshire was instructed to array men ready to be brought to the king when required, perhaps to provide security as he travelled through the Midlands to Nottingham at the end of July or early August.[99]

Richard likewise sought to amass funds. His main initiative was a large-scale campaign to raise loans from his subjects. Serjeants-at-arms were sent out in wide circuits around the realm armed with letters soliciting loans. In a letter to the prior of Llanthony, dated

23 July, he refers to 'the great necessity' of the time, and asked for the loan of a 'notable sum', which would be repaid at Easter 1398. The actual amount was unspecified, and was presumably a matter of negotiation with the serjeant-at-arms.[100] Llanthony agreed to lend 100 marks, a sum acknowledged on 5 September.[101] By the end of the year the king had secured loans to the total value of around £20,000, including a loan of 10,000 marks by the city of London and 1,000 marks by Bishop Wykeham.[102] The diligence of two serjeants-at-arms, John Drax and Thomas Wodingfield, in securing promises of loans in Lincolnshire, Yorkshire and Durham is attested in a bundle of indentures entered into by towns, religious corporations and individuals. The indentures reveal promises of both loans and gifts. The latter were less common and involved smaller sums, generally £20 or less, but were additional to the £20,000 worth of loans.[103]

In the first critical weeks after the arrests the king operated from the safety of Windsor castle. Despite the crisis, he found time and resources at the end of July to send William Bret, a monk of Gloucester, to Rome to expedite the canonization of Edward II.[104] On 1–2 August he lavished grants on key retainers, including annuities of £100 each to Sir John Bushy and Sir Henry Green, and a gift of 1,000 marks to Sir Nicholas Hawberk. Hawberk's patent was dated at Windsor on 2 August, possibly indicating that the king was still in residence.[105] Shortly afterwards Richard moved to Nottingham, where he had convened a great council.[106] Lancaster and York were both present.[107] Bolingbroke was likewise in attendance. His accounts record that he was lodged for five days in early August at Dale abbey.[108] Given the disturbances in the southern counties, Richard may have felt safe in Nottingham castle. It was a convenient location for the many lords who retired to their northern estates to hunt over the summer. Above all, Richard's choice of Nottingham for this new stage in royalist assertion had symbolic importance. It had been in Nottingham, in August 1387, exactly ten years earlier, that the judges had expanded the definition of treason to cover moves to limit his regality.

On 5 August, St Oswald's day, Richard was seated at the high table in the great hall of Nottingham castle. Eight noblemen came into his presence to make an appeal of treason against Gloucester, Arundel and Warwick. The new Appellants were Edward, earl of Rutland, Thomas Holland, earl of Kent, John Holland, earl of Huntingdon, John Beaufort, earl of Somerset, Thomas Mowbray, earl of Nottingham and earl marshal, John Montagu, earl of Salisbury, Thomas, Lord Despenser and Sir William Scrope. What happened at Nottingham is known only from the testimony of the six Appellants who survived the deposition. Not surprisingly, all then sought to play down their involvement, claiming that they acted out of fear of the king. Only Scrope, who was already dead, was presented as actively complicit in the king's designs. Rutland told the most heart-rending tale. He claimed that he told his uncle and father 'that he had been ordered that day to do something that made him sadder than he had ever been before, but that for fear of death he dared not contravene the king's order'.[109] Kent, Huntingdon, Somerset and Salisbury all denied knowledge of the appeal until they were variously instructed by the king to join their companions outside. At the castle-gate they found Scrope reading out a draft of the appeal and requiring them to append their names.[110] Despenser offered circumstantial detail. During dinner he was sitting at a side-table when he suddenly received an order to go out to the gate-house. Assuming that someone was to be arrested, he went to his room in the keep, donned his hauberk, took up his sword, and ordered six yeomen to accompany him. He claimed to have been the last to join the party of Appellants.[111]

After a week in Nottingham and its environs the king moved back south. On 14 August he was at Lutterworth, the burial-place of the arch-heretic John Wycliffe.[112] A few days later he took up residence at Woodstock, his headquarters for the remainder of the summer. He was attended by the earls of Rutland and Nottingham and Lord Despenser. Plans were laid for the raising of troops prior to the opening of parliament. The king's friends were encouraged to bring large retinues. On 17 August Lord Despenser wrote from Woodstock requesting the prior of Llanthony to contribute five men-at-arms, one lance and sixteen archers to the substantial force he was mustering at Merlow on Tuesday 11 September.[113] On 20 August the king issued a proclamation that all lords, knights, esquires and gentlemen who wore his livery of the white hart, and all yeomen of the crown and other fee'd men, were to assemble, suitably arrayed and armed, at Kingston-upon-Thames at high morn on Saturday, the morrow of Exaltation of Holy Cross.[114] The king continued to place great store on the men of his palatinate of Chester. On the 19th he issued a proclamation forbidding any Cheshire archer from enlisting with any other lord until the royal retinue was 2,300 strong, and on the 20th he retained Sir Robert Legh, sheriff of Cheshire, with an annuity of £40.[115] Richard may have thought hard about the size of the Lancastrian retinue. On 28 August the duke of Lancaster and Henry of Bolingbroke were licensed to bring to Westminster, 'for the comfort of the king', a total of 500 men-at-arms and 1,000 archers.[116]

Thomas of Woodstock, duke of Gloucester, cannot have been far from the king's mind. On 17 August he wrote two letters to Sir William Rickhill, chief justice of the common pleas. One was addressed to the judge at his home and instructed him to go to Calais in the company of Thomas Mowbray, earl of Nottingham, and to do as he commanded. The other was sent to await him at Calais, and instructed him to interview Gloucester and to report under his seal what he should say to him. It is not easy to establish the import of the letters. To add to the obscurity of the affair, the first letter was not delivered until 5 September, some three weeks later, when John Mulsho brought it to the judge's home at Islingham. Roused from his slumber, Rickhill crossed to Calais on the 7th, and received the second letter from Mowbray. He later professed to be astonished that the commission could still be executed as he believed that Gloucester was already dead. On 8 September Rickhill was escorted to the castle and found himself face-to-face with the king's uncle. Gloucester was willing to cooperate, and when Rickhill returned in the evening he handed him a confession that he had earlier dictated to a clerk. Rickhill returned to the castle the next day, but was refused admittance. He returned to England, fearing the worst.[117]

Gloucester's death was reported in England in late August. The earliest reports followed hard on Mowbray's arrival in Calais around 24 August.[118] Mowbray himself was perhaps responsible for the misinformation. According to evidence presented in parliament in 1399, Mowbray was commanded to put Gloucester to death, but resisted the king's orders for some three weeks. His procrastination may explain the delay in the delivery of the first letter to Sir William Rickhill. Mowbray may have hoped that nature would do the executioner's work. Richard wanted an end to the business, but he wanted a full confession of treason first. Rickhill secured a confession, though it was not entirely to the king's liking. Gloucester perished soon afterwards. Foul play was widely suspected, and Mowbray inevitably found himself under suspicion. In conversation with Sir William Bagot in October 1397, Mowbray did not deny his involvement in the murder. He merely insisted that he had been forced to act in the end solely 'for dread of the king and eschewing of his own death'.[119] The evidence that was presented in parliament in 1399 makes it tolerably certain that Richard ordered Gloucester's murder, and that the earl of Rutland was complicit in it. One of the assassins, John Hall, named as his associates servants of the king and Rutland. He informed parliament that Gloucester had been suffocated by a down bedcover.[120]

★ ★ ★

As the date for the opening of parliament approached, tension mounted, not least in and around the capital. The king's raising of an armed retinue and his licensing of the loyalist nobles to bring large companies must have caused great apprehension in the city of London. Even at the best of times, the presence around the city of so many large retinues was likely to prove combustious. According to Walsingham, the king had marshalled his forces as if they were about to go to war against their enemies.[121] Uniquely, the continuator of the *Eulogium Historiarum* claimed that Richard enlisted some French men-at-arms, a notion perhaps encouraged by the arrival of a French embassy in September.[122] The king's Cheshire retinue generated most anxiety. In August 1386, at the time of an invasion scare, Cheshire men had been encamped around London, and had quickly acquired notoriety for violence and rapine.[123] In December 1387 an army recruited in Cheshire had been marching on London under the leadership of de Vere when it had been checked at Radcot Bridge. Now, ten years on, over two thousand men-at-arms and archers from Cheshire converged on the capital. Engaged in Richard's service and wearing his insignia, they were doubtless in arrogant mood.

On Saturday 15 September Richard's retinue gathered at Kingston upon Thames and the king presided over jousts in the meadows.[124] On Sunday the king entered London. According to one chronicle, he rode menacingly through the middle of the city surrounded by five thousand armed men.[125] In the evening the royal party was entertained by Henry of Bolingbroke in his lodgings in Fleet Street.[126] There was a magnificent feast featuring herons, pheasant and doves. Some of the fare came from Baginton in Warwickshire by courtesy of the wife of Sir William Bagot.[127] Exquisite 'subtleties' were prepared. Bolingbroke employed John Prince to create the right ambience, and paid him for painting thirteen curlews, thirteen columbelles and thirteen popinjays in gold, silver and other colours.[128] The king then took up residence at the palace of Westminster, where the various lords in his retinue kept nightly watches in rotation.[129]

The precinct around Westminster Palace had been prepared for the occasion. Four years earlier the king had set in train the reconstruction of the old hall to provide the largest royal space in Christendom. The great hammerbeam roof was still under construction, and the whole complex must have been an immense building site. To accommodate parliament, a grand marquee had been constructed in the yard between the tower and the hall. There remained ample scope for stage-management, and the king's throne was presumably set on a high stage. In alluding to the siting of the king's throne, 'from which he could deliver his judgements', the monk of Evesham presents Richard 'as presiding in greater solemnity than any king of the realm ever had before'.[130] The makeshift quality of the building had other advantages. The Cheshire archers were posted on the scaffolding around, clearly visible to members of the assembly.

On 17 September the chancellor, Bishop Stafford, opened what was soon to be termed the Great Parliament.[131] He preached a sermon on the blessings of monarchy, taking as his theme the words of Ezekiel the prophet: 'there shall be one king for all'. The first requirement of good government, he averred, was that the king be powerful enough to govern. For this reason kings were given 'regalities, prerogatives and several other rights annexed to the crown', which they at their coronation are pledged to maintain. The king wished to be informed if any rights of the crown should be subtracted, and if not remedy should be provided so that the king can be 'made as his ancestors were before him in his liberty and power; and as he should be of right, notwithstanding any ordinance to the contrary'.[132] The second and third requirements of good government were that the laws should be kept and executed justly, and that the realm should be duly obedient to the king and his laws. Ominous stress was laid on parliament's obligation to punish all who had restrained the king's authority, and to provide safeguards against repetition of the offence in the future.[133] Despite the generality of the address, it was all too apparent that reference was being made to the events of 1386–8. The speech concluded with an assurance that the king was disposed to be merciful, and with the proclamation of a pardon to all guilty persons – excepting fifty unnamed persons who would be impeached in the parliament – provided that they sued for their pardons before the feast of St Hillary, 13 January 1398.[134]

In the king's view, parliament's role was to acknowledge that the assaults on his regality had been treasonous, to adjudge his chief protagonists as traitors, and to celebrate the full restoration of his sovereignty. Given the gravity of the proceedings, and the king's clear interest in them, parliament could be expected to be compliant. To make doubly sure, Richard probably instructed the sheriffs to return knights of the shire favourable to his cause. The commons certainly included an unprecedentedly large contingent of household knights and squires. According to the articles of deposition, the commons were likewise intimidated by the king's armed retinue. At the end of the first day of parliament it was announced that no one, save the king's own retainers, should bear weapons in parliament.[135]

On Tuesday the 18th the commons announced the election of Sir John Bushy as their speaker. A Lincolnshire knight, he was an experienced parliamentarian who had served as speaker earlier in the year. According to a report of the parliament, he was 'a man of undoubted discretion and enormous eloquence'. Above all, he was the king's man. Though he had no formal status, he had been a royal counsellor for some time, and had been recently retained in the king's service. He set the tone for the proceedings with slavish forms of address and posture designed to accentuate the distance between the lowly commons and the king's high majesty. According to Walsingham, Bushy 'imputed to the king in his statements not human, but divine honours, finding strange and flattering words hardly suitable for mere mortals; so that whenever he addressed the king, who was seated on his throne, he would extend his arms and supplicate with his hands, as if praying to him, entreating his high, excellent and most praiseworthy majesty that he might deign to concede these or those things'. The 'young' king, he added, 'courting honours and seeking praise, did not stop these words, as he should but rather delighted in them'.[136]

Richard had asked parliament to be informed of assaults on his 'regality'. Bushy reminded him, as if he needed reminding, how in the tenth year of his reign the duke of Gloucester, the earl of Arundel and Thomas Arundel, now archbishop of Canterbury, compelled him 'to concede a commission touching the government and state of your kingdom which was to the prejudice of your regality and majesty, whereby they did you great injury'. Parliament proceeded to revoke and annul the commission and all that flowed from it.[137] With Gloucester in custody in Calais, it was the Arundels who were the immediate focus of the attack. Parliament revoked the royal pardon previously given to the earl. Bushy alleged that the pardon had been 'traitorously obtained'. The allegation brought Archbishop Arundel into the frame. As chancellor of England, he had issued the pardon. The commons believed that he should be adjudged a traitor. The archbishop rose up to protest, but the king stopped him and gave him leave to reply on the morrow.[138]

The final items of the day's business struck an ominous tone. First, it was 'ordained that anyone who should in future be convicted of violating, usurping or undermining the king's regality, should be adjudged a false traitor, and should be sentenced to suffer the appropriate penalty for treason'. Then it was ordained that since parliament would be dealing with capital crimes the consent of the prelates was not required. The bishops and abbots 'sorrowfully withdrew'.[139] The decisions apparently caused a stir among the commons. The Cheshire archers who surrounded the building, believing some dissension had broken out, drew their bows and, to the terror of all, actually unleashed some arrows until the king himself quietened them down.[140] In the gathering dusk the lords and commons returned to their lodgings full of foreboding.

Overnight the king and his counsellors modified their plan with respect to the spiritual lords. While it suited their purpose to eliminate a potential source of principled opposition, and to deny Archbishop Arundel a platform among his colleagues, they saw the value of committing the higher clergy to their proceedings. On Wednesday, parliament was called on to revoke its exclusion of the spiritual lords. The bishops and abbots were then commanded, 'on pain of loss of their temporalities', to appoint a spokesman who would consent on their behalf to all that would be done in parliament.[141] They nominated Sir Thomas Percy, steward of the household, as their proctor. Expressing some disquiet about the exclusion of fifty unnamed persons from the pardon, the commons made representations to have the matter clarified. The king's response was sharp. He declined to name names, and declared that anyone asking him to do so deserved death themselves. He explained, a little speciously, that if he named names the guilty would escape, while their associates, who had nothing to fear, would take needless fright.[142]

On Thursday the 20th there was a lull in the proceedings. Archbishop Arundel made a bid to take his place in parliament but the king ordered him to return to his lodgings. Bushy then laid charges of treason against the archbishop for his role as chancellor in the work of the commission of 1386–7 and in holding the parliament of 1388 to the

Archbishop Arundel.
(Bodleian Library,
University of Oxford. MS
Laud Misc. 165, fol. 5r)

prejudice of the king's regality. On behalf of the commons Bushy petitioned the king to pass sentence on him 'commensurate with such treasonable actions', and asked that in view of his 'untrustworthy and vengeful character' and his capacity for mischief he be committed to prison. Richard declared his intention to consider the charges later. He then took the opportunity to affirm his belief in the innocence of other members of the commission. The duke of York and Bishop Wykeham of Winchester then 'fell weeping on the ground, thanking the king for his kindness'.[143] Over the next few days Richard allegedly met with Archbishop Arundel in private. He pretended to be well-disposed to him, counselling him to be at ease, stay at his place and bide his time, and assuring him that nothing would be moved against him.[144]

On Friday the 21st the earls of Rutland, Huntingdon, Kent, Nottingham, Somerset and Salisbury, Lord Despenser and Sir William Scrope, dressed uniformly in red silk robes banded with white silk with gold lettering, stood before the king.[145] Styling themselves the king's 'foster-children', they presented an appeal of treason against the duke of Gloucester, the earls of Arundel and Warwick, and Sir Thomas Mortimer. Drafted at Nottingham in August, the appeal focused largely on their armed rising against the king at Harringey in 1387.[146] Richard FitzAlan, earl of Arundel, clad in a robe with a scarlet hood, was brought before parliament. Making some play of his status as steward of England, John of Gaunt presided over the trial. After instructing Ralph, Lord Neville, to strip Arundel of his belt and hood, he ordered that the appeal be read aloud.

At first the earl of Arundel refused to respond to the charges, which, in his view, had been framed to secure both his death and the seizure of his lands. Pressed further, he protested that what he had done a decade earlier had been in response to the circumstances of the time, and that he had twice been pardoned by the king for his actions.[147] He insisted that 'he had no desire ever to withdraw himself from the king's grace'. Gaunt broke in: 'That pardon is revoked, traitor.' Arundel denied ever being a traitor, and when asked by Gaunt why then he had sought a pardon he snarled: 'To silence the tongues of my enemies, of whom you are one, and to be sure, when it comes to treason, you are in greater need of a pardon than I am.'[148] Arundel pointed out that the king's ability to pardon offences was his highest prerogative, and that if Gaunt was claiming that the king should not have granted the pardon then he himself was most guilty of treason. Going on the offensive, he drew attention to Gaunt's own past record of actions prejudicial to the crown.[149]

The king cut short the argument, and ordered Arundel to answer the appeal. Arundel replied haughtily, 'I see it clearly now: all those who accuse me of treason, you are all liars. Never was I a traitor. I still claim the benefit of my pardon, which you, within the last six years, when you were of full age and free to act as you wished, granted to me of your own volition.' Bushy reminded Arundel that the pardon had been revoked by the king, the lords, 'and us, the faithful commons'. Arundel rounded on him: 'Where are those faithful commons? I know all about you and your crew, and how you have got here.' He continued: 'The faithful commons of the kingdom are not here. If they were, they would without doubt be on my side, trying to help me from falling into your clutches. They, I know, are grieving greatly for me; while you, I know, have always been false.' Bushy turned Arundel's outburst against him: 'Look, lord king, at how this traitor is trying to stir up dissension between us and the commons who have stayed at home.'[150]

Throughout this time the eight lords who carried the appeal of treason continued to provoke Arundel. According to Walsingham, they behaved abominably, making obscene gestures and prancing around, as if they were stage-villains rather than knights or sober men. The young earl of Kent, who was Arundel's sister's son, behaved most outrageously.[151] Even Henry of Bolingbroke joined the hunt. 'Did you not say to me at Huntingdon, where we first gathered in revolt', he asked Arundel, 'that before doing anything else it would be better to seize the king?' Arundel vehemently denied it, claiming that he never said anything about the king 'except what was to his welfare and honour'. The king had his own question: 'Did you not say to me at the time of your parliament, in the bath-house behind the White Hall, that Sir Simon Burley was for various reasons worthy of death? And I replied that I neither knew nor could discover any reason for his death. And even though my wife, the queen, and I interceded tirelessly on his behalf, yet you and your accomplices, ignoring our pleas, traitorously put him to death?' For the king, it was an open and shut case. He instructed Gaunt to pass sentence.[152]

As steward of England, Gaunt declared his judgement that Arundel was a traitor, and sentenced him to be drawn, hanged, beheaded and quartered, and his lands, both entailed and unentailed, to be forever forfeit.[153] Pressed to acknowledge his guilt and beg for mercy, Arundel proudly submitted his cause to God and indicated his readiness to die to maintain the laws and the welfare of the kingdom.[154] The king softened on only one point. Acknowledging the small consideration that Arundel had shown Burley in 1388, he lifted the penalties of drawing and hanging.[155] Arundel was led on foot, his hands bound behind him, to Tower Hill, where Burley had likewise been executed. It was noted that among the lords who, riding fine steeds, led him through the streets were his son-in-law Mowbray and his nephew the earl of Kent.[156] A company of Cheshire archers deterred the Londoners from attempting a rescue.[157]

Arundel's *via dolorosa* is well documented. On leaving the palace compound, he asked that his bonds be loosened so that he might give alms to the beggars sitting along the roadside. At Charing Cross an Augustinian friar heard his confession, and recited with him the office of the dead.[158] His hands still bound behind his back, he was led through the busy streets, along Cheapside, to Tower Hill, followed by a huge 'crowd of citizens who mourned him as much as they dared'.[159] According to Walsingham, they lamented the fortune of such a noble lord, renowned throughout Christendom and a champion of his country, who was now trussed like a brigand and brought to the most shameful death.[160] Arundel bore himself with patience and dignity. When asked again to acknowledge his treason, he replied that he was no traitor, either in word or deed, and knew not the cause of his ruin except that he could not please the king in the manner he desired. Bullied to break the seal of the confessional, his confessor refused to say anything other than that Arundel had not shown himself to be a traitor. In his turn Arundel rebuked Mowbray and Kent for their lack of gratitude, and warned them that the time would soon come when men would marvel at their misfortune just as now they wondered at his fate. Ready for death, Arundel forgave his executioner, asking him to strike his head off with one blow. He jauntily reassured himself by feeling the sharpness of the sword's edge. According to Froissart, Mowbray tied a band around his father-in-law's eyes.[161] One stroke was indeed sufficient. Arundel's head was struck clean off, leaving his trunk eerily standing for some time, before finally it fell prone on the ground. According to report, it stood unsupported for as long as it took to recite the Lord's Prayer.[162] The Augustinian friars collected his remains, and took them for burial in the choir, near the high altar, of the conventual church in Bread Street.[163]

On Saturday parliament turned its attention to Sir Thomas Mortimer, who had wisely stayed out of the king's reach in Ireland. The king expressed impatience at the earl of March's failure to apprehend him. It was determined that, unless he surrendered within three months, he would share the earl of Arundel's fate. On the same day it was announced that all grants made since 1386 by those who had been or were to be condemned in this parliament should be entirely annulled and revoked.[164] On the Saturday evening Sir John Hawkeston, a Cheshire knight in the king's service, laid an ambush for William Laken who was prosecuting him for various crimes. Hawkeston assaulted Laken, a retainer of Henry of Bolingbroke, as he approached his lord's inn in Fleet Street, and killed him with a thrust from his sword.[165] On Sunday, in counterpoint to the savagery in parliament and mayhem in the streets, the king and the loyal nobles continued their round of festivities. It was Gaunt's turn to act as host, and he held a grand feast in the inn of the bishop of Durham.[166]

On Monday the 24th there was another dramatic moment in parliament when Gloucester was called to stand trial. A writ had been issued to Mowbray to deliver him from custody at Calais and bring him before parliament. Mowbray now announced that he was not able to obey this command because the duke was dead. He elaborated a little, but left unanswered the important questions of when, how and by whose agency. Rumours of Gloucester's death had been in circulation since late August. What the court probably wanted people to believe was that Gloucester, who had been ill earlier in the summer, had confessed to his treason in prison, and then, his soul unburdened, had died a natural death. Many people in parliament must have had their suspicions, but were willing, for a time, to suspend their disbelief. They would have found it much harder to do so had they known that Gloucester, far from having died over a month ago, had been alive and well less than a fortnight earlier, when Sir William Rickhill had crossed to Calais to record his confession.[167]

To a hushed assembly Gloucester's confession was read out. It was in English, and began 'I, Thomas of Woodstock.' The fact that the record on the parliament roll is a slightly edited version of that which survives under Rickhill's seal is some evidence of the document's authenticity. In the full text Gloucester acknowledged that he was the instigator of the commission in 1386; that he and others had taken upon themselves royal powers; that he had come armed into the king's presence and acted against his regality and estate; that he had taken the king's letters and opened them without leave; that he had slandered the king; that he, among others, had sought advice from clerks about giving up their homage; that they had even agreed for a few days to depose the king but then they had renewed their homage 'and put him highly in his estate as ever he was'. He claimed in some mitigation of his offences that he had often acted out of fear of his own life, and did not appreciate then the seriousness of his assault on the king's regality. He pointed out, moreover, that he had already fully acknowledged his guilt, and been accepted back into the king's mercy and grace at Langley.[168]

Gloucester's confession was not entirely to the king's satisfaction. It contained no direct admission of treason, still less an admission of any 'new' treason. In presenting it to parliament it was deemed wise to omit the date, 8 September, which might have fuelled speculation about foul play. There were other significant excisions. Gloucester's reference to the royal pardon he had received was removed. The version presented to parliament likewise omitted Gloucester's moving appeal 'for the passion that God suffered for all mankind, and for the compassion that he had of his mother on the cross, and the pity that he had of Mary Magdelene' that the king would 'accept me unto his mercy and to his grace, as he that hath ever been full of mercy and of grace to all his lieges and to all other that have naught been as nigh unto him as I have been, though I be unworthy'.[169]

The appeal of treason proceeded. With the assent of the king, and with Sir Thomas Percy presiding, the lords judged Gloucester a traitor to the realm, and pronounced the same sentence as had been delivered against the earl of Arundel.[170] The commons meanwhile began proceedings against Lord Cobham, another lord who had been an active member of the commission of 1386, and had been arrested and imprisoned at Donington castle in Leicestershire earlier in the month.[171]

It was also on the Monday that Archbishop Arundel was stripped of his temporalities and banished from the realm. To the last, Richard pretended to be the archbishop's friend, colouring the issues 'with fair speech and glossing words'. Richard allegedly claimed that the sentence had not been his doing, and that he hoped to countermand it. He asked that the archbishop should prepare himself to leave through Southampton, and indicated that he might be able to lift the sentence, giving out that he had done so on the petition of the queen. If the archbishop did leave the country, Richard allegedly continued, he should return 'without fail' the following Easter. Richard showed him a large gold brooch fastened under the hem of his robe, and said that when he sent it to him 'for a token, he should not tarry to come to him'. He assured him that he would keep safe for him the jewels and ornaments of his chapel. Above all, Richard promised that the archbishop would not be deprived of his see, and took an oath to this effect on the cross of St Thomas of Canterbury.[172]

On Tuesday the 25th Richard raised the earldom of Chester to the status of a principality 'on account of the great love and affection' he had for the people of Cheshire. The principality was augmented by the annexation to it of the earl of Arundel's forfeited lands. The men of Arundel's marcher lordships were confirmed in their liberties, provided that the Welsh inhabitants were also allowed to continue to exercise their ancient laws and customs.[173] There was a general territorial reordering in Cheshire and the northern Welsh marches to provide a citadel of royalist power.[174] In the same session the earl of Salisbury petitioned for a writ to proceed against the earl of March for the lordship of Denbigh in Wales. After taking advice, Richard granted this request, perhaps another sign that Mortimer, who was absent from parliament and received no new honours, was outside the charmed circle the king was drawing around himself.[175]

Over the following two days the position of Gloucester's and Arundel's heirs were considered. To suppress lobbying on their behalf, it was declared on Wednesday the 26th that 'anyone who offered help, or counsel or support to the children of those who had been or were to be condemned in this parliament should suffer punishment as a traitor'.[176] On the 27th the king formally announced that the male heirs of the men condemned as traitors, and indeed all their descendants in the male line, 'should be debarred for ever not only from their inheritances, but also from the councils and parliaments of the king'. To reinforce the point, and to confirm all the proceedings thus far, it was decreed that all the lords spiritual and temporal should swear to observe unswervingly all the deeds, ordinances, pronouncements and sentences of the parliament, and support any ecclesiastical censures applied against opponents of this measure, 'saving always the lord king's regality'.[177]

On Friday the 28th Thomas Beauchamp, earl of Warwick, was put on trial. After Arundel's execution he was in no mood for martyrdom. Once the appeal was read, he broke down, weeping profusely, and admitted his guilt. He blamed his involvement on Gloucester, the late abbot of St Albans, and a monk of Westminster, and sobbing begged the king's mercy. Moved by the sorry spectacle, some of his colleagues pleaded on his behalf.[178] According to Froissart, the earl of Salisbury made special efforts for him, claiming that he was an old man, that he had been deceived by Gloucester, and that none of the Beauchamps had ever done treason against the crown.[179] Richard granted him his life, condemning him to imprisonment and the forfeiture of his goods. An annuity of 500 marks was provided for the maintenance of his household.[180]

The king then proceeded to reward his supporters. In distributing new titles, Richard was defining and exalting a new nobility. Since the exile of Robert de Vere, duke of Ireland, the only dukes in England had been the king's three uncles Lancaster, York and Gloucester. Richard now created five new ducal titles. His cousins, Henry earl of Derby and Edward earl of Rutland, became respectively the dukes of Hereford and Albemarle. His nephew Thomas Holland, earl of Kent, became the duke of Surrey; his half-brother John Holland, earl of Huntingdon, became the duke of Exeter; and Thomas Mowbray, earl of Nottingham and earl marshal, became the duke of Norfolk. In an unusual move Margaret of Brotherton, the dowager countess of Norfolk and Mowbray's grandmother, was created duchess of Norfolk in her own right. The new dignity introduced to honour de Vere in 1385 was revived for John Beaufort, earl of Somerset, who became marquis of Dorset. In addition, the king created four new earldoms. Ralph Neville, Thomas Despenser, Thomas Percy and William Scrope became respectively the earls of Westmorland, Gloucester, Worcester and Wiltshire.[181]

There was also a massive redistribution of land to cement the new political order. The scale of the grants made in patents dated 28 September alone was prodigious. The duke of Albemarle was granted the castle and lordship of Clun in the Welsh marches, formerly of the earl of Arundel, together with the duke of Gloucester's castles, lordships and advowsons in Holderness.[182] The duke of Surrey was granted Warwick castle and other Beauchamp lands in Warwickshire to the value of over 1,000 marks per year.[183] The duke of Exeter was granted in tail male the castle and honour of Arundel and other FitzAlan lands, and manors forfeited by the earl of Warwick in Devon and Cornwall.[184] The duke of Norfolk was granted the earl of Arundel's castles and lordships of Lewes in Sussex and Castleacre in Norfolk, and the earl of Warwick's castle and lordship of Hanslope in Buckinghamshire.[185] The marquis of Dorset was granted in tail male other Beauchamp lands in the Midlands; Thomas Despenser, earl of Gloucester was granted in tail male Elmley castle and other lands in Worcestershire; Thomas Percy, earl of Worcester, acquired properties in several counties, including the earl of Warwick's inn in London; William Scrope, earl of Wiltshire, was granted the Beauchamp lordship of Barnard castle in Durham.[186] Three knights were especially well rewarded from the spoils: Sir John Bushy, Sir Henry Green and Sir John Russell.[187]

On Saturday the 29th, with his business for the moment complete, Richard adjourned parliament to meet at Shrewsbury in the New Year. The commons reminded the king that he had exempted some fifty persons from his general pardon, and expressed concern about Bolingbroke and Mowbray and members of their retinues at Radcot Bridge. From the throne the king publicly testified to 'the loyal bearing and good name' of the two lords, and ordained that not only them, but also their retainers 'should, in reputation, name and honour, be known as, held for, and publicly declared among all his liege subjects throughout the realm to be, loyal liegemen'.[188]

Ralph Neville, first earl of Westmorland, and his two wives. (The British Library)

John Gower. (Author's collection)

Finally, on Sunday the 30th, the lords and commons attended high mass at Westminster abbey, and participated in a ceremony which replicated the events at the end of the Merciless Parliament of 1388. In the presence of the king, crowned and enthroned, all the lay lords appeared before the shrine of St Edward the Confessor to swear solemnly to observe, perpetually, the laws and judgements passed in the present parliament, saving only the king's regality, and to hold as traitors anyone seeking their annulment or repeal. The knights of the shire, allegedly at their own request, took the same oath with their right hands raised. Thomas Percy, earl of Worcester, took the oath on behalf of the clergy. As in 1388, the bishops threatened with excommunication all who did not keep their oath to uphold parliament's proceedings.[189]

The king then hosted the feast that traditionally brought the parliamentary session to a close. According to the author of *Traison et Mort*, Richard held 'a great court and gave a sumptuous feast'. At supper there was a call for 'largesse', and the heralds received large gifts from the lords and ladies. He observed, too, that there was dancing and singing, and that the duchess of Exeter received the prize as the best dancer and singer.[190] Across London the retainers of the king and his noble allies doubtless celebrated in their own fashion. John Gower was a gloomy spectator of proceedings from across the river in Southwark. He recorded a song composed in derision of three nobles by their enemies. Gloucester, Arundel and Warwick are identified respectively by their badges of the swan, the horse, and the bear and ragged staff: 'The Swan does not keep its wing forever, nor the Horse its hide; now the Swan is without wings, the Horse is flayed. The Bear, whom biting chains torment, does not bite.' 'During the month of September,' Gower wrote, 'savagery held sway by the sword.' As he watched and reflected, he began to write a passionate indictment of Richard's tyranny.[191]

CHAPTER SIX

TYRANNY

At the end of September 1397 Richard was triumphant. He had made considerable progress towards a systematic reversal of the events of 1386–8. He had destroyed the three men, Gloucester, Arundel and Warwick, who had raised an army against him in December 1387, and who had caused him most anguish and anxiety over the past decade. Archbishop Arundel had likewise been pronounced a traitor, and condemned to exile. Richard had used parliament to honour the noblemen who supported the re-establishment of his authority and were loyal to his person. In a ceremony at Westminster abbey the lords and the commons had bound themselves to uphold the acts and decisions of the parliament. Richard would complete this work when parliament reconvened in February, ten years after the opening of the Merciless Parliament. The decision to reconvene parliament in Shrewsbury was troubling. Given the town's remoteness from the capital and proximity to the principality of Chester, the decision would have been regarded as imperious and menacing. It had some symbolic force. The king had not visited Shrewsbury since his first questioning of the judges in the summer of 1387.

Richard took measures to publicize the acts of the Great Parliament at Westminster. The circulation of a semi-official account of proceedings can be inferred from careful comparison of the accounts of the monk of Evesham and Adam Usk.[1] This original account is no longer extant. It is scarcely surprising that more explicit royalist propaganda has been lost. Ironically it is John Gower, Richard's severest critic, who records the writing of songs hostile to Gloucester, Arundel and Warwick. Part of a chronicle written at Kirkstall near Leeds before 1399, however, captures some of the mood of royalist exultation, and may incorporate the language of a royalist newsletter. The chronicler ends his account of parliament by marvelling at the 'long suffering of the king' and rejoicing at the restoration of his power. Alluding to Richard, and possibly to his sun badge, he writes: 'of late the sun had been hidden in cloud, that is to say the king's majesty concealed by the power of others'. 'Yet, now,' he continues, mixing metaphors to make reference to the king's white hart badge, 'the king in arms bounds on the mountains and leaps over the hills, and tossing the clouds on his horns he shows more brightly the light of the sun.'[2]

At the ceremonies and the feast at the conclusion of parliament Richard was doubtless resplendent. Adding lustre to his crown were seven dukes, five of whom were new creations. The ducal title had been unknown in England prior to Edward III's reign, and hitherto there had been no more than four English dukes at any one time. According to Walsingham, the people spoke derisively of the 'duketti'.[3] Richard seems to have regarded his new creations as part of a new aristocratic order. He accorded them all the privilege of incorporating in their arms the arms of St Edward the Confessor. On Monday 1 October Richard was present at an event which accorded well with his vision of a new aristocratic order and revivified kingship. It was the reinterment at Whitefriars in London of Lord John Mowbray, who had been killed by the Turks outside Constantinople in 1368. A martyr to the Christian faith, he was described as 'catholicus', and his tomb at Galata, and subsequently at Rhodes, was visited by English pilgrims. For Thomas Mowbray, duke of Norfolk, the reburial was the climax of several years' work. The ceremony was probably attended by all the new nobles. Henry of Bolingbroke's wardrobe accounts include reference to an offering on the tomb of Lord Mowbray 'whose bones were brought from Rhodes'. Further expenditure by Bolingbroke at a dinner with the king and queen in the refectory at Whitefriars attests the presence of the royal couple.[4]

In the first week of October the king withdrew to Windsor castle, but it would be surprising if he did not return to Westminster to celebrate the feast of St Edward the Confessor. This would have furnished a splendid opportunity for the new dukes to display their new arms and to join the king in the reinauguration of his kingship. Richard would have 'rendered humble and devout thanksgiving', as he expressed it in a letter to Albert of Bavaria, count of Holland, 'to the highest observer of human minds, in whose hands are not only the hearts but the bodies of kings and princes', who has until now protected 'our royal throne and person since the very cradle from the hands of all enemies, and especially those of household and intimacy, whose contrivances are notoriously more destructive than any plague'.[5] He might, too, have rededicated himself to some grand role in Christendom. In letters written to Rome in late September Richard appears to have impressed Pope Boniface with the seriousness of his intent with respect to the Holy Roman Empire.[6] On 22 July Richard sent an envoy to Paris and Constantinople, and in October he received at his court Theodore Cantacuzene, the uncle of the Byzantine emperor Manuel II, soliciting aid against the Turk.[7]

If Richard was in expansive mood, he was aware of the problems surrounding him. If his letter to Albert of Bavaria is any guide, his mood was as much grim satisfaction as exultation. After thanking God for his protection, he reported 'how since his tender years nobles and members of the royal household' had 'traitorously conspired to disinherit our crown and usurp our royal power' leaving him 'hardly anything beyond the royal name'. He continued that 'though our royal clemency indulged these traitors with time enough to change their hearts and show the fruits of repentance, so deeply rooted in evil seemed their obstinacy that by the just judgement of God our avenging severity has been meted out to the destruction and ruin of their persons'. Through God's providence, 'we have brought together the right hands of our power, bruising these confessed and convicted traitors and, threshing them out even to the husks, we have adjudged them to natural or civil death, so bringing to our subjects a peace which, by the grace of God, may last forever'. Given the heinousness of the crimes, Richard added that he had 'caused their punishment to be perpetuated upon their heirs' who must 'be forever shut off from reaching the height of any dignity or privilege, that posterity may learn what it is to offend the royal majesty, established at howsoever tender years; for he is a child of death, who offends the king'.[8]

★ ★ ★

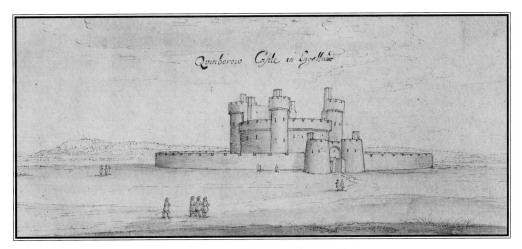

Queenborough Castle, engraving by Wenceslas Hollar. (© The British Museum)

Through October the king continued to thresh out the traitors 'even to the husks'. The process of spoliation, already well advanced, became more systematic. On 3 October commissioners were appointed in southern and midland counties to survey the lands of Gloucester, Arundel, Warwick and Archbishop Arundel, and to seize all accounts and writings going back to 1386–7. They were to enquire into all chattels from 18 July in the case of the three lords, and from 25 September in the archbishop's case. They were to appoint stewards to administer and account for the property, who on taking an oath to the king, would be retained at his charges.[9] In addition to the grants of lordships in tail male to the new dukes, Richard continued to make grants of lands, offices and goods to members of his retinue. He seems to have shown most personal interest in the jewels and plate, incorporating much of the loot into the royal collection. In the spring of 1398 he engaged a number of clerks to prepare an inventory of the jewels of Gloucester and Arundel, along with the jewels of the late queen, for safe-keeping in his treasury at Westminster abbey.[10]

There were less palatable loose ends. The king still had to deal with the earl of Warwick and Archbishop Arundel. Warwick presented the least problem, though his wife proved importunate. On 12 October Warwick was taken under armed escort from Queenborough castle to Chester for passage to the Isle of Man. The escort to Chester comprised 60 men-at-arms and 100 archers under the command of William Scrope, earl of Wiltshire, and the passage to Man was overseen by Sir Stephen Scrope with 40 men-at-arms and 60 archers.[11] With regard to Archbishop Arundel, Richard had given him six weeks' grace to leave the realm. His continued presence was doubtless unsettling. Prior to his departure he allegedly preached a sermon castigating the pride and extravagance of the court. According to Adam Usk, he went into exile on the feast of St Edward the Confessor. This may be the date he left London, since he was at Canterbury several days later.[12] Richard continued to affect to be the archbishop's

Brass of Eleanor, duchess of Gloucester, Westminster Abbey. (© Dean & Chapter of Westminster)

friend. Though he had already written to Rome to secure Arundel's translation from Canterbury and his replacement by Roger Walden, he encouraged Arundel to believe that he would soon be recalled. On 23 November he even wrote to the men of Ghent to thank them for their hospitality to the archbishop. When he discovered that Arundel had gone to plead his cause in Rome, however, Richard became positively venomous. He informed Pope Boniface that Arundel had been the instigator of all the plots against him, and insisted that he should never be allowed to return to England.[13]

The bodies of Gloucester and the earl of Arundel presented even greater problems than the persons of their allies. According to Walsingham, the king was haunted by the earl of Arundel's ghost. A cult had developed around his tomb. It was claimed that his head and body had been miraculously reconstituted, and there were reports of other miracles. The king's anxieties led in early October to a bizarre commission to the dukes of Lancaster, Albemarle, Surrey and Norfolk and the earl of Northumberland, to make an inspection of the corpse. The lords arrived in the middle of the night, startling the friars, and ordered the exhumation of the body. They found the head and body stitched together with thread. Richard ordered the friars to rebury the earl, pave over the grave, and leave it unmarked. He also ordered the exile of six or seven friars, associates of Dr Thomas Ashbourne, the earl's confessor.[14] On one point Arundel continued to haunt the king. His letters of pardon remained at large, and in February proclamation was made that if anyone knew their whereabouts they should be returned to the king in person for cancellation.[15]

Then there was the body of his uncle, Thomas of Woodstock, still unburied in Calais. The son of Edward III had to be shown some honour in death. Richard ordered prayers for his soul on 9 October, and nine days later he instructed Richard Maudeleyn to deliver his corpse to the duchess of Gloucester for burial at Westminster abbey.[16] The king then changed his mind. Fearing the development of an oppositionist cult in Westminster itself, he ordered burial at Bermondsey Priory.[17] The secret death of Gloucester may have proved even more destabilizing than the public execution of Arundel. John of Gaunt and Edmund of Langley must have been especially disturbed by reports of their brother's murder, and according to Froissart were bold enough to blame the king.[18] Thomas Mowbray, duke of Norfolk, was in an even more unenviable position. As Sir William Bagot informed him in a conversation in Savoy Street in October, he was popularly regarded as Gloucester's murderer. Mowbray denied the allegation with great oaths. He claimed that he resisted the king's commands for three weeks, that in the end he acted only through fear, that the king had sent his own men to do the deed, and that Albemarle was the king's chief counsellor.[19]

★ ★ ★

The atmosphere remained tense through October. Based at Windsor castle, Richard gathered around him his noble allies and took steps to expand his permanent retinue. He looked especially to the men of his new principality of Chester. From late August he granted a growing number of Cheshire knights and squires the livery of the white hart, and from mid-September he began to engage scores of Cheshire yeomen as archers of the crown at sixpence a day and with 'bouche of court'. On 1 October alone twenty-five archers received patents recording the terms of their engagement. Richard established a bodyguard of Cheshire archers, some 300 strong, which was divided into seven 'watches'.[20] The king's Cheshire retinue, however, was much more extensive. Within twelve months he had some 750 Cheshire men, including 10 knights and 97 squires, on his pay-roll at an annual cost of over £5,000.[21] Prominent members of Richard's Cheshire affinity were Sir John Stanley, controller of the wardrobe, Sir Richard Cradock, a chamber knight, John Macclesfield, keeper of the great wardrobe, and Peter Legh of Lyme, evidently a royal favourite. Given that the king's entourage included members of almost every Cheshire family of note, it may well have provided the primary audience for *Sir Gawain and the Green Knight* and other courtly verse written in the Cheshire dialect in the late fourteenth century.[22]

Contemporaries viewed the building up of the Cheshire retinue with dismay. The Kenilworth chronicler complained that Richard was overly familiar with the guardsmen, conversing with them 'in the mother tongue'. He attributed to them a curious lullaby: 'Dycun, slep sicury quile we wake, and dreed nouȝt quile we lyve sestow: ffor ȝif thow haddest weddet Perkyn douȝter of Lye [the daughter of Peter Legh] thow mun halde a love day with any man in Chester schire in ffaith.'[23] According to Walsingham, Richard formed the bodyguard on account of the nightmares he experienced after Arundel's execution.[24] The Dieulacres chronicler describes them as standing outside his chamber armed with huge battleaxes.[25] The Cheshire retinue rapidly acquired a reputation for arrogance and rapine. According to Adam Usk, 'wherever the king went, night and day, they stood guard over him, armed as if for war, committing adulteries, murders and countless other crimes'. The king showed the guardsmen such inordinate favour that, in Adam Usk's words, 'he would not listen to anyone who complained about them; indeed he regarded such people with loathing'. For Usk, as for the author of *Richard the Redeless*, they were the chief cause of the king's ruin.[26]

In building up his retinue, Richard revealed his own sense of insecurity and maintained a threatening stance towards the realm. Fear and menace seem likewise to be linked in what appears to have been a major political crisis in October. According to Froissart, rumours of Gloucester's murder caused dissension in London, and led Gaunt to confront the king and seek assurances as to his government.[27] Froissart's story is plausible, but is not corroborated by English sources. Yet it may be linked with another story indicating a crisis in the relations between the king and his uncle. In conversation with Bolingbroke in December, Thomas Mowbray claimed that there had been a plot to seize or kill Gaunt and Bolingbroke when they came to Windsor in October after the close of the parliament. He alleged that the conspirators were the duke of Surrey, and the earls of Wiltshire, Salisbury and Gloucester, but that their plot had been resisted by the dukes of Albemarle and Exeter, the marquis of Dorset and Mowbray himself who made a sworn compact that 'they would never assent to the ruin of any lord without just and reasonable cause'.[28] It may well be that Gaunt's confrontation of the king prompted a group at court to plan his arrest or assassination, whether as a pre-emptive strike or as a fall-back position if negotiations failed.

According to Mowbray, the four noblemen who plotted against Gaunt and Bolingbroke had as their larger aim the destruction of the house of Lancaster through the reinstatement of the judgements of 1322 against Thomas of Lancaster. It is hard to know what to make of this allegation. It was in all likelihood more loose talk than a firmly conceived plan. Yet there can be no doubt at all that the events of Edward II's reign were in people's minds. During the proceedings against Warwick, the earl of Salisbury made an appeal for clemency on the grounds that Warwick's ancestors had always been loyal to the crown. It was a debatable claim, but it may have served to present Warwick in a more favourable light than the heirs of Thomas of Lancaster and Roger Mortimer. Thomas Despenser had a special interest in the rehabilitation of his grandfather and great-grandfather, Edward II's chief counsellors prior to his deposition. Above all, Richard himself had long brooded on the events of Edward's reign and was actively seeking his canonization. He may have come to believe that the full restoration of royal authority required, symbolically as well as materially, the destruction of the house of Lancaster.[29]

★　★　★

It may be that the immediate crisis resolved itself by the end of October. John of Gaunt retired to Hertford castle, while Henry of Bolingbroke set off westwards to south Wales.[30] Passing through Hereford at the beginning of November he headed for Brecon, the marcher lordship which he held in right of his late wife Mary Bohun. Preparations for his arrival were well underway, and during his week's stay at Brecon local notables such as Sir John Devereux paid court.[31] Henry may have been seeking in this tour to establish himself as the political heir of the duke of Gloucester. On his return to England he spent a few nights, 16–18 November, at Llanthony Priory near Gloucester, a house much patronized by Thomas of Woodstock.[32] Assuming his uncle's mantle, he wrote to the burgesses of Gloucester, with whom the priory was in dispute, informing them that he had taken the priory, which was of 'our foundation', under his protection.[33] Henry remained in contact with the court. Passing through Burford on 19 November, he joined the king at Woodstock later in the day, and travelled with the royal party to Banbury before returning to London.[34]

The court was based at Woodstock in November.[35] Early in the month Richard played host to the Catalan knight Raymond, viscount of Perellós, who was on his way to

St Patrick's Purgatory in Ireland. Seeking to learn the fate of the recently deceased John, king of Aragon, Perellós had secured approval from the pope in Avignon for his venture, and during the autumn had obtained the requisite safe conducts from the kings of France and England. Landing at Dover around All Saints day, he made his way to the king in Oxfordshire. Richard entertained him for ten days before providing him with an armed escort to Chester and a letter of introduction to the earl of March in Ireland. He was not the only knight to set out on this dangerous pilgrimage at this unseasonable time of year. When Perellós arrived at St Patrick's Purgatory he found William sire de Courcy, the husband of Queen Isabelle's governess.[36]

The seal of John Holland, earl of Huntingdon and Duke of Exeter. (Reproduced by kind permission of Heraldry Today, from J.H. & R.V. Pinches, The Royal Heraldry of England, *1974)*

The atmosphere in Richard's court at Woodstock was far from serene. Pierre Salmon, Queen Isabelle's secretary, recalled a disconcerting conversation with the king about Charles VI. Richard insisted that the duke of Orléans had brought about the king's illness through necromancy, and planned to usurp his brother's throne. Richard allegedly promised to reward Salmon lavishly if he were willing to make such a drink for Orléans as would ensure that he never again did harm to the king or anyone else.[37] There seems to have been more intrigue against Gaunt. According to the duke of Exeter in 1399, Sir William Bagot, acting on behalf of the king and Mowbray, called him into the chapel at Woodstock and swore him to secrecy. Claiming that 'we should never have our purpose but after the death' of the duke of Lancaster, he then outlined a plot by which Gaunt would be summoned to a council at Lichfield, put under arrest, and then in 'chance-medley' beheaded. According to his own account, Exeter replied that Richard should summon a council, and if it agreed to the deed, he would too.[38]

From Woodstock the king rode out to Abingdon abbey on 11 November to witness the consecration of Guy Mone as bishop of St David's. The ceremony was performed by Robert Waldby, archbishop of York, assisted by three other bishops, including the chancellor, Edmund Stafford.[39] Later in the month he spent a few days at Banbury castle, where a number of important items of business were transacted.[40] The king continued to add to his retinue. At Abingdon he granted Sir Thomas Talbot an annuity of 100 marks.[41] Richard appears to have involved himself directly in the selection of new sheriffs.[42] Sir Thomas Clanvowe, sheriff of Herefordshire, John Golafre, sheriff of Oxfordshire and Berkshire, and Andrew Newport, sheriff of Cambridgeshire and Huntingdonshire, were among the royal retainers appointed to the shrievalty at this time.[43] It was alleged in 1399 that Richard required his sheriffs to swear a new oath to obey all writs, including writs under the signet seal, and to arrest immediately all who spoke ill of the king. A 'new oath' was certainly devised at this time. Early in the new year a royal clerk was dispatched to administer it to the sheriff of Shropshire.[44]

Meanwhile the screws were turned on the men who had served under Gloucester, Arundel and Warwick in 1387. At the end of September it was arranged that the people excluded from the general pardon would be summoned before a committee of council and required to compound for the king's pardon. The fines were to be placed in a special bag kept by the treasurer.[45] Entire communities felt anxious. The men of Essex and Hertfordshire, who had paid dearly for the king's grace in the aftermath of the Peasants Revolt, indicated their readiness in December to treat for an acquittal of past debts and a pardon for all treasonable offences. The king accepted an offer of £2,000 and in February appointed commissioners to raise the sums. As Barron has shown, while the men of Essex ultimately paid their share and more into the exchequer, no letters of pardon were issued.[46]

Richard was back at Windsor in December. At some stage in the month Henry of Bolingbroke was returning from the court to the capital when Thomas Mowbray caught up with him near Brentford. The conversation they had during the ride was to prove momentous. According to Bolingbroke, Mowbray began by telling him that the two of them were 'on the point of being undone' for 'what was done at Radcot Bridge'. When Bolingbroke pointed out that Richard had pardoned them, Mowbray claimed that the king intended to annul the pardon, and 'would deal with us as he had dealt with others in the past'. Observing that it was a strange and uncertain world, Mowbray revealed details of the plot at court against the house of Lancaster, including the plan to reverse the judgement concerning Thomas of Lancaster, which would result 'in the disinheritance of us and of several others'. Bolingbroke refused to believe that Richard, who had sworn by St Edward 'to be a good lord' to him and the others, would agree to such acts. Mowbray replied that he placed no trust in the king's oaths, and added that the earl of March was to be drawn into the plot. 'If that is the case,' Bolingbroke replied, 'then we can never trust them.' 'Indeed we cannot,' Mowbray concluded, 'for even if they do not succeed with their present plans, they will still be plotting to destroy us in our homes ten years from now.'[47]

Bolingbroke's version of this interchange may be partial. His protestations of faith in Richard certainly seem contrived. According to Froissart, it was Bolingbroke who first spoke indiscreetly to Mowbray.[48] On balance, though, it is most likely that it was Mowbray who took the initiative. At the time of the conversation Mowbray must have felt dangerously isolated. He may have been generally regarded as an instigator of the coup against Gloucester, Arundel and Warwick, and responsible for Gloucester's murder. Yet he may have had reason to believe that Richard was disappointed with him, and to feel insecure at court. The plot against Gaunt, and the plans to 'effect the ruin' of other lords, including himself, must have further unnerved him. His best hope was to win the trust of Bolingbroke, to make him aware of the dangers they both faced, and to cooperate to thwart any moves against them. The subsequent actions of Mowbray and Bolingbroke are generally consistent with Bolingbroke's version of the story. Acting on the advice of his father, and perhaps suspecting that Mowbray was an agent provocateur, Bolingbroke reported the conversation to the king. Mowbray was wholly rattled by the disclosure, and his counter-charges against Bolingbroke appear to be no more than generalized bluster.

★ ★ ★

The king held a great Christmas court at Lichfield.[49] The duke of Albemarle was prominent among the lords in the royal entourage, and administrative business was conducted from Coventry.[50] Henry of Bolingbroke and Thomas Mowbray were among the absentees. Around New Year's Day Bolingbroke left London on a northern tour. His itinerary gave him the opportunity to meet key members of his father's affinity in the north Midlands and Yorkshire. Yet, as he rode northwards, he must have found in the wintry landscape a reflection of his own bleak frame of mind. For a time he was at Pontefract, the burial-place of Thomas of Lancaster. He seems to have visited Beverley, and even Bridlington.[51] Facing a new year full of foreboding, perhaps he felt the need to pray at the shrines of St John of Beverley and St John of Bridlington.

At Lichfield on 10 January Richard received the homage of Roger Walden, the new archbishop of Canterbury.[52] He was still at Lichfield a week later, when he issued a licence to elect a new archbishop of York to replace Waldby who had died shortly after Christmas.[53] Around 22 January he was lodged at the bishop of Lichfield's palace at Great Haywood.[54] It was there that Bolingbroke was summoned into his 'honourable presence' to relate the conversation in which Mowbray 'had slandered the king's person'. Richard, who may already have heard the gist of the tale, required his cousin 'upon his allegiance' to repeat Mowbray's words 'faithfully and exactly' and set them in writing for presentation to parliament.[55] Richard's attitude to the whole affair is hard to read. He knew the truth or otherwise of the alleged slander and he can hardly have welcomed Bolingbroke's public airing of the conversation. Yet he knew that Mowbray would not dare accuse him of bad faith, and would have no option but to call Bolingbroke a liar. For Richard there may have been a delicious irony. Three of the five lords who had opposed his standard at Radcot Bridge had been destroyed, the remaining two would now destroy each other.

On Thursday 24 January the king and his entourage arrived at Lilleshall abbey, where they spent the next two days as guests.[56] According to the abbey chronicle, the company included the king and queen, five dukes, four earls, three bishops and a chamberlain of France. In all likelihood the five dukes were York, Hereford, Albemarle, Surrey and Exeter.[57] Roger Mortimer, earl of March, was probably not a member of this court party. He had been specifically summoned to attend this session at Shrewsbury, and had crossed from Ireland in good time. Yet Adam Usk gives the impression that Mortimer entered Shrewsbury independently of the king's entourage.[58] The chamberlain of France was none other than the viscount of Perellós who had visited the court at Woodstock two months earlier. Beside the hearth after dinner he may have related his adventures beyond the Pale in Ireland, his ordeal and visions at St Patrick's Purgatory, and the Christmas court of 'King O'Neill'.[59]

Banner of Roger Mortimer, fourth earl of March. (Reproduced by kind permission of Heraldry Today, from J.H. & R.V. Pinches, The Royal Heraldry of England, *1974)*

The royal party left Lilleshall for Shrewsbury in the morning of Saturday the 26th. The small country town must have been overwhelmed by the vast concourse of people. While the king had instructed his lords to bring only moderate retinues, the uncertain times may have prompted many lords to have at hand bands of armed supporters. Adam Usk claimed that some 20,000 men wearing the earl of March's livery welcomed him in the streets of Shrewsbury.[60] Above all, the king himself had a huge entourage, vastly augmented by his proximity to his principality of Chester. As well as accommodating men with business in parliament, the town had to provide billets for the king's guardsmen. Thomas Sy, the king's servant, found rooms in Glover's Row for a company commanded by Richard Coningscliffe. The atmosphere in the town was tense. On Sunday a group of townsmen were involved in a fight with the guardsmen, two of whom, Nicholas Vernon and John Moldesdale, were slain.[61]

★ ★ ★

Parliament opened on Monday, 28 January, in Shrewsbury abbey. According to Adam Usk, there was an unprecedented display of 'earthly ostentation'. He claimed that 'the world stood amazed at what might come from such futility, and at the destruction wrought upon the kingdom by this coming together of such a multitude of people all armed as if for war'.[62] In his opening address Bishop Stafford, the chancellor, declared that parliament had been assembled in honour of God and for the protection of all men's rights, and that to achieve such ends there should be only one ruler in the realm, and that his laws must be obeyed. The main business of parliament was clearly to continue the work of the first session in Westminster. A reference to the need to defend the realm indicated that the king also sought financial aid.[63]

On the 29th Sir John Bushy set the submissive tone. Addressing the king on behalf of the commons, he declared that 'the needs and necessary charges of the king and the kingdom' had been demonstrated to him, and advised that 'although the commons were in great poverty' they 'would be ready, like loyal liegemen, to do their duty to the best of their ability'. Acknowledging that many people were in peril on account of past crimes against his royal majesty, he then prayed that the king grant them, for their comfort, a general pardon. The chancellor replied that the king wished firstly to know how they intended to aid him; 'and, once he had been given to understand from their deeds and wishes that he could be beholden to them, he would be minded for his part to grant such a grace and pardon as would give them reason to be beholden to him'.[64]

Richard devoted the next day to a preliminary hearing of Bolingbroke's case against Mowbray. However potentially embarrassing for the court, it served to concentrate the minds of the lords and commons on the implications of treason. Henry presented his account of the conversation with Mowbray, denied any malice in the act, and protested his own innocence.[65] The king appeared to take his part. Mowbray's absence, and a possible ambush on Gaunt on the road to Shrewsbury, told against him.[66] On 30 January Richard stripped Mowbray of the office of marshal of England, and appointed the duke of Surrey in his stead, authorizing him to bear a gold staff ornamented with the king's and Surrey's arms.[67] At the end of the session, Bolingbroke knelt before the king in full parliament, acknowledged the hurt he had done, albeit without evil intent, to the king and his royal estate, and humbly begged his pardon. The king accepted his prayer and confession, and pardoned and granted him his good lordship.[68] On 4 February the sheriffs were ordered to make proclamation that Mowbray should, under pain of his life, appear before the king in person within fifteen days. The proclamation was made in Shrewsbury on the 6th, and at some two hundred other places across the realm over the following month.[69]

In the mean time parliament completed the work of the autumn session. Following on from the nullification of decisions of the parliament of 1386, it turned its attention to the judicial advice received by Richard at Shrewsbury and Nottingham in 1387. The lords and commons, and the current judges, now affirmed that the responses of the judges were 'good law'. It was accordingly resolved that the parliament of 1388 was not a true parliament, and that its acts and judgements were null and void. As Jones observes, 'the last and most grievous stain had now been officially removed from the royal escutcheon'.[70] There were further proceedings against Lord Cobham, who was condemned to life imprisonment on Jersey, and Sir Thomas Mortimer who, in his absence, was likewise adjudged a traitor. One measure appeared significant in the light of the alleged plot to reinstate the verdict of 1322 against Thomas of Lancaster. Thomas Despenser, earl of Gloucester, secured the annulment of the sentences of treason of 1321 and 1327 against his grandfather and great-grandfather, Edward II's chief counsellors.[71]

On Thursday the 31st, Richard was voted a generous grant of one and a half subsidies of a fifteenth and tenth, a level of taxation unknown in peace-time. In addition, he received a grant of wool subsidy for life. This grant was wholly unprecedented, and was accompanied by a petition that the proceeds could be spent wholly at his discretion to reward the new peers and the Cheshire men who had served at Radcot Bridge. In return for the grants, the king issued a general pardon, though he attached conditions which dispelled any illusion of magnanimity. Persons seeking pardons were required to sue out individual pardons, and, in the case of persons who rode against the king in 1387, to do so before the feast of St John the Baptist, 24 June. The king's concession represented little advance on the position at Westminster four months earlier. It was then declared that the pardon would be entirely annulled if in the future parliament sought to withdraw the grant of customs duties for life.[72]

The king deliberately left some matters open and unresolved. On the 31st it was announced that the dispute between Bolingbroke and Mowbray was to be determined by the king on the 'counsel and guidance' of a parliamentary committee. The members were the dukes of Lancaster, York, Albemarle, Surrey and Exeter, the marquis of Dorset, the earls of March, Salisbury, Northumberland and Gloucester, or any six of them, as representatives of the lords; the earls of Worcester and Wiltshire, or either one of them, as proctors for the clergy; and John Bushy, Henry Green, John Russell, Richard Chelmswick, Robert Teye and John Golafre, or any four or three of them, as representatives of the commons.[73] One of the three surviving copies of the parliamentary roll adds, in a new hand, that the committee would deal with 'several other matters'. The doctoring of the parliamentary roll is instructive with respect to the king's approach: he wanted to manipulate rather than eliminate the institution.[74] The king thenceforward had available to him a standing committee of parliament, with some at least of parliament's awesome powers.

The session at Shrewsbury lasted for four days. Given the time of year and the distance involved, it was an arduous journey for little gain for most of the members. The small town of Shrewsbury could have offered little in the way of amenities. The king probably relished the inconvenience inflicted on the knights and burgesses from the south-east. Huddled together in the cramped quarters of Shrewsbury, they must have felt demoralized and vulnerable. It is hard to escape the conclusion that the main purpose of the exercise was to bend the assembly to his will. The author of *Richard the Redeless* almost certainly had this session in mind when he wrote his satire of a parliament whose members were variously apathetic, afraid of or suborned by the king, and failed to protect the interests of their communities.[75] For the knights and burgesses there can have been little inclination to do other than to accede to the king's threats and demands.

Yet there are signs that not all went quite to Richard's satisfaction. The king had some explaining to do to John of Gaunt. He probably found it a nail-biting challenge to prevent Bolingbroke's allegations spilling over into a premature showdown with the house of Lancaster. If he had planned to ensnare the earl of March, as Adam Usk claims, he was likewise disappointed. The townsmen of Shrewsbury allegedly gave March a rapturous welcome 'in the hope that through him they might be delivered from the king's wickedness'.[76] At some stage before 1399, perhaps during this parliamentary session itself, Thomas Prestbury, a monk of Shrewsbury, was arrested for preaching against the king.[77] Above all, Richard must have known that his ascendancy at Shrewsbury was based on fear not consensus. The impression of Richard that the knights of the shire and burgesses took home to their constituencies in February 1398 cannot have been at all positive. As Adam Usk noted, 'in addition to other deeds which were odious to the people, and which threatened their very livelihood, he paid nothing even for his provisions'.[78]

★　★　★

After the dissolution of parliament Richard headed north to his new principality of Chester. He probably spent a night at Holt, a castle confiscated from the earl of Arundel, which he was soon to develop as a major treasury. His officers were dispatched to Chester to organize his reception on 5 February.[79] He spent over a fortnight in the principality, and probably hunted in Delamere forest.[80] According to a continuator of the *Brut*, the king 'loved well' Chester castle and had it 'royally repaired', with white harts set in freestone in niches on the walls.[81] Some £68 was spent on a 'stew' (bathroom) for the king's chamber.[82] He left Chester on the 21st, passing through Holt and Shrawardine to Oswestry, where the parliamentary committee met on 23 February.[83]

Many nobles remained in the royal orbit. After the parliament Gaunt, suffering from a fever, retired to Lilleshall. During his stay he, his wife and several retainers were received into the abbey's confraternity.[84] Bolingbroke was at nearby Prees on the 8th.[85] Father and son remained in contact with Richard, and significantly secured assurances from him regarding the Lancastrian inheritance. On the 20th Richard, 'after mature deliberation', made a release to the dukes of Lancaster and Hereford of all rights and

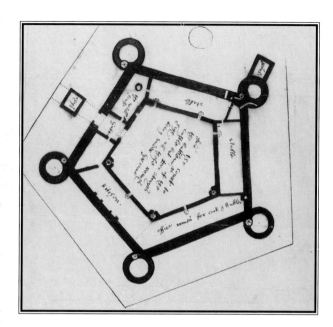

Holt Castle. (The British Library, Harl. 2073, fol. 112)

claims in the castles and lands formerly of Thomas of Lancaster that might fall to the crown by reason of Lancaster's treason against Edward II.[86] They must have raised concerns about plots against them, one of which involved Sir William Bagot. On 3 March Bagot entered a recognizance, a condition of which was that his life would be forfeit, without any other judgement or process, if he were ever to slay the duke of Lancaster, his wife or children.[87]

On 23 February Bolingbroke and Mowbray appeared before the king and the parliamentary committee at Oswestry. It was ordained that their case would be heard at Windsor on 28 April, and Mowbray was committed to custody.[88] The court moved south and was based for some time around Worcester and Gloucester.[89] On 4 March Richard was based at Despenser's manor-house at Hanley by Severn.[90] He granted the duke of Surrey an arras cloth depicting scenes from the history of Guy of Warwick, which had been forfeited by the earl of Warwick.[91] At Worcester Richard took an interest in work on the cathedral cloisters, licensing the convent to retain six masons on the project.[92] While in Gloucester, he checked on progress with respect to the canonization of Edward II. Archbishop Waldby of York may have been engaged in this business when he died suddenly at Gloucester in late December. Richard Scrope, bishop of Lichfield, was currently at Rome promoting the scheme. The issue of Waldby's replacement was especially salient. Around this time Richard was advised of the election at York of Walter Skirlaw, the veteran bishop of Durham.[93] News would soon arrive, however, that Bishop Scrope had been 'provided' to the see by the pope.

The king and his court next moved to Bristol. The chancellor and other officers arrived early in March, and the royal party joined them around the middle of the month. The king's visit was intended to be a major event. Anticipating a great gathering of people, orders were sent on 14 March to the bailiffs of local towns to require all victuallers to bring their corn to market first in Bristol.[94] On the 19th the king held a

Mowbray's challenge to Bolingbroke. (The British Library, Harl. 4380, fol. 141)

meeting of his parliamentary committee, and many nobles, including Bolingbroke, were in attendance. It was decided that, unless other evidence was forthcoming, Bolingbroke's dispute with Mowbray would be settled by a judicial duel.[95] On the 22nd the king was at Bath. In a single day he took into his service five knights and seventeen squires from Lancashire, augmenting his own retinue as he made inroads into his uncle's power-base in the palatinate of Lancaster.[96] At Bristol there were a number of memorable events. A 'theatre' was built for a duel between an English squire and Sir Walter Stewart, a Scots knight of English allegiance.[97] Among the spectators were the dukes of York, Albemarle, Exeter and Hereford, and the duke of Brittany who had recently arrived in England. In an act of great munificence, Richard granted Walter Stewart, the victor, an annuity of 100 marks.[98]

Richard may have hoped that the good folk of Bristol would be suitably impressed by the display of regal magnificence but a poem written by a resident of Bristol would suggest otherwise. *Richard the Redeless* was written in the wake of the revolution of 1399, but the author's views almost certainly had their genesis in 1397–8, if not earlier. The poet wrote feelingly of the king's vast army of retainers, wearing his livery of the white hart, despoiling the country and terrorizing the populace. For every badge that Richard marked with a hart, he claimed, the king lost ten loyal hearts.[99] The poet is especially scathing of the king's evil counsellors, specifically naming Sir John Bushy and Sir Henry Green. On 20 March they were at the heart of affairs at Bristol, counselling the king with respect to a petition submitted to him.[100] The poet may well have witnessed their execution at Bristol by Henry of Bolingbroke and his allies in July 1399.

★   ★   ★

In the spring and summer of 1398 Richard was at his most imperious. He none the less still felt insecure. On 15 March he commissioned Albemarle and Surrey 'to follow and arrest all traitors found in the realm of England, and after they have informed themselves of their treasons and convicted them by their acknowledgement or otherwise, chastise them at discretion according to their deserts'.[101] The following day a proclamation was issued to prohibit persons taking unauthorized letters into or out of the country, and royal officials in the various ports were instructed to prevent letters being taken abroad and to intercept letters to the continent addressed to the magnates of the realm.[102] Richard was still actively pursuing knights and squires who had served in the retinues of Gloucester, Arundel and Warwick. On 3 April a group of knights and squires, including Sir Edward Charlton, Sir Hugh Zouche, Sir Payn Tiptoft, Sir Arnold Savage, Sir Giles Malory, Sir John Trussell and Sir Richard Waldegrave, was ordered, under pain of £200, to be before king and council at Westminster in the quinzaine of Easter 'to declare what shall there be laid before him'.[103]

The king's concerns for his safety were not wholly unfounded. At the end of March there was a popular rebellion in the upper Thames valley. According to the trial record, around 200 men gathered at Cokethorpe in Oxfordshire on the evening of Palm Sunday, 31 March, and plotted to kill the king and nobles. Across the Thames there was a rising of 120 men at Eynsham in Berkshire. The rebels were mainly yeomen and artisans, and the leadership came from Witney and Bampton. The men at Cokethorpe elected Gilbert Vaughan as their captain, and gave him gold spurs as a symbol of authority. The Berkshire men chose Thomas Goldesowe of Witney as their leader. Henry Roper of Bampton showed himself a firebrand and a man of daring. With an axe in one hand and a taper in the other, he called out: 'Arise all men and go with us, or else truly and by God ye shall be dead.' Roper took on the assignment of seeking out the king in Bristol and Gloucestershire and investigating 'his state and governance'. Over the next two days he rode to Burford and elsewhere seeking, according to the indictment, to destroy the king, the nobles and the laws of the realm. He was arrested by local gentry and committed for trial at Oxford.[104]

The rebellion merits taking seriously. Roper's arrest may have led to the collapse of the rebellion but the area remained disaffected. The hostility to the king seems clear.

The focus on finding him and discovering his 'state' suggests that the scheme involved regicide. One of the captains, Thomas Goldesowe of Witney, assumed the name of the heir of the earl of Arundel. The rashness of the enterprise may contain an element of desperation. It can be no coincidence that the rising took place in the very district in which de Vere's army had been checked and put to rout at Radcot Bridge.[105] The earl of Arundel had positioned himself at Witney. Bampton is the nearest village to Radcot Bridge. The men of the district very likely played some role in aiding the 'lords of the field', and harrying and despoiling the royalist army. The king's determination to punish the men in arms against his standard in December 1387, and indeed to reward his loyal Cheshire men, was well known. If the rebels feared reprisals, it may explain the recklessness of their undertaking. In calling on his comrades to rise up or else 'ye shall be dead', Roper may have been issuing not a threat but a warning.

★   ★   ★

Some time in late March the king left Bristol. Henry Roper and his comrades may have planned to ambush him as he passed through Berkshire or Oxfordshire. Richard's movements in the fortnight before and the fortnight after Easter Sunday, 7 April, are in fact wholly obscure. His intention to honour St George's day in customary style at Windsor may have been well advertised, and he was certainly in residence by the 22nd.[106] Over the next few days he was well attended for the Garter feast and associated celebrations.[107] John de Montfort, duke of Brittany, was a special guest and a bed was brought upriver from London for his use.[108] On the feast day itself the king and the duke made the first of a series of agreements that would pave the way for a firm alliance.[109]

On St George's day, too, Richard received communication from an even more illustrious Christian prince, Manuel II, the Byzantine emperor. Richard had sent an embassy to Constantinople in the summer of 1397, and received a visit from the emperor's uncle in autumn. The letter asked Richard for assistance against the Turks. In reply, Richard excused himself from sending an army since it would be impossible to convene parliament, raise an expedition, and have it arrive before the onset of winter. He none the less promised troops in the following year. With regard to financial assistance, he was even less sanguine. Indeed he treated the emperor to an extended account of his problems. 'You know,' he wrote, 'what I believe is notorious enough throughout all quarters of the world, how some of our subject magnates and nobles, while we were yet of tender age and afterwards also, have made many attempts on the prerogative and royal right of our regal state, and have wickedly directed their malevolence even against our person.' He then explained how 'when we could no longer endure their rebellion and wantonness, we collected the might of our prowess, and stretched forth our arm against them our enemies; and at length, by the aid of God's grace, we have by our own valour trodden on the necks of the proud and haughty, and with a strong hand have ground them down, not to the bark only, but even to the root; and have restored to our subjects peace, which they had troubled, and which by God's blessing shall endure forever'. He explained that this work had drained his treasury, and given that 'scarce seven months have passed since these things began' he had not been able to recover his outlay.[110]

The letter is a little disingenuous, but reflects Richard's conviction that the disobedience of his own people stood in the way of his playing a major role in the affairs of Christendom. After all, Richard provided some financial assistance to Constantinople, and may have hoped to do more. Some of his grandiose ambitions remained current. On 23 May he arranged for the archdeacon of Cologne to go to Rome, presumably to enlist papal support for his candidature for the Holy Roman Empire.[111] In September Sigismund of Hungary referred to Richard's ambitions when exhorting the emperor-elect Wenceslas to go immediately to Italy to be crowned by the pope.[112] With respect to the problem of the schism, Richard proved a disappointment to the French. He had no wish to offend Pope Boniface, whose good offices were necessary both to his imperial ambitions and to the consolidation of his authority in England. He knew, too, that it would be difficult to persuade his subjects to adopt the 'way of cession'. The French remained active in the cause of Christian unity. After a futile attempt to secure the collaboration of Wenceslas at a conference at Rheims in March, they began to prepare for unilateral action. At a council in Paris in May 'subtraction of obedience' became official policy. On 27 July Charles VI issued an ordinance withdrawing French allegiance to 'Benedict XIII' at Avignon.[113]

Despite his claim that he had ground down his opponents 'not the bark only, but even to the root', Richard obviously felt that he had work still to do in enforcing obedience to his rule in his own realms. For some time he had been contemplating a second expedition to Ireland. His achievements in 1394–5 had been largely undone by the spring of 1397, when he found himself obliged to scale back the establishment in Ireland and rely on the private resources of the earl of March. There is evidence that at the end of 1397 Richard saw the reduction of Ireland to obedience as a priority second only to the rooting out of opposition in England. An extant indenture between the king and Thomas Percy indicates that a royal expedition was being planned for 1398.[114] The crisis associated with the dispute between Bolingbroke and Mowbray may have led to its cancellation. On 24 April the king confirmed the earl of March as lieutenant for the remaining two years of his contract, and appointed Thomas Cranley, the new archbishop of Dublin, as chancellor of Ireland.[115] Yet the confirmation of March's position was for form only. Richard was grooming his nephew the duke of Surrey for a major role in the lordship, and may have been secretly bent on March's ruin. Richard may well have had in mind as well those prophecies which presented the conquest of Ireland as the first stage in a glorious career of an English king who would assume the imperial mantle and lead Christendom on crusade.[116]

From Windsor, Richard may have made a fleeting visit to London. According to an anonymous letter, he came in the evening with a number of lords, including the dukes of Lancaster and Hereford and the archbishop of Canterbury, and planned to return to Windsor in two days.[117] The correspondent notes that Mowbray was then under arrest in the office of the king's wardrobe in London, and that on the following Monday a judgement was to be made between him and Bolingbroke. The date is given as 'le jour de seinte Marie', but there is reason to assume a scribal error for St Mark's day, 25 April.[118] The order to commit Mowbray to the wardrobe is dated 23 April, while the case was heard on Monday the 29th.[119] The purpose of the king's visit is a mystery. Richard may have wished to confer privately with Mowbray, perhaps to reassure himself

Westminster Hall.
(English Heritage ©
Crown Copyright.
NMR)

as to what might or might not be revealed. Alternatively, he may have wished to inspect progress on Westminster Hall, or to show the duke of Brittany and other foreign guests his regalia and jewel collection.[120]

On Sunday 28 April the dukes of Hereford and Norfolk came before the king at Windsor castle, and the next day judgement was given. The official record is terse. Since 'no proof had been found by which the issue could be decided', it was resolved that the two lords be given a day to do battle.[121] According to *Traison et Mort*, Richard made an effort to reconcile the two lords. Bolingbroke was obdurate. Through his spokesman, he alleged that Mowbray had been 'at the bottom of all the treasons committed' in England for the past eighteen years, including the murder of the duke of Gloucester, and declared his readiness to 'prove the truth of this by his body between any sunrise and sunset'. Mowbray declared his innocence of the charges, stood on his record of loyal service, and likewise demanded justice in the form of a judicial duel. Finally, in the king's presence, Bolingbroke threw down his gage and Mowbray picked it up. With a show of anger Richard declared that he would no longer seek to make peace between the intransigent pair. Sir John Bushy announced that the trial by combat would take place at Coventry on a Monday in August. The date was subsequently set for Monday 16 September.

★　★　★

Richard may have returned briefly to Westminster at the end of April, but during May he headed westwards and northwards. A number of counsellors, including the three chief officers of state and the ubiquitous Sir John Bushy and Sir Henry Green, were engaged in business at Westminster on 30 April.[122] This working council remained in harness in the capital for some time, conducting a range of business and seeking to maintain contact with the peripatetic court. It had to deal with the steady stream of men suing for pardons on account of their association with the Lords Appellant in 1387. To the fore were some of the counsellors themselves: Bushy and Green both secured pardons on 1 May.[123] In May over forty knights and squires, including Sir Leonard Kerdeston, Sir William Calthorpe and Sir John White from Norfolk, obtained pardons for their treason.[124] Most of the supplicants compounded for their pardons, and paid large sums into the treasurer's special bag. Sometimes the fines are recorded, but for the most part they seem to have gone straight into the king's coffers. Even the dead were not immune. The feoffees of the late Sir Edward Dallingridge, an adherent of the Appellants in 1387, had to pay 500 marks 'to the king's use' in order to secure the Dallingridge estates at Bodiam and elsewhere for his son and heir.[125]

There was a broad concern to raise revenue. Some of the loans promised in the autumn of 1397 had been delivered. In April John Drax, serjeant-at-arms, was sent northwards to secure the sums rashly promised by the townsmen of Nottingham, York, Hull, Chesterfield, Lynn and Grantham.[126] The king was in no hurry to repay the loans that he had received. Llanthony priory was due to be repaid 100 marks at Easter. In the event it settled for a royal licence to annex and appropriate two vicarages.[127] On 3 May the duke of Surrey delivered in person the king's endorsement of this request into chancery.[128] It would be interesting to know whether Geoffrey Chaucer was drawn out of semi-retirement to act as the king's agent in business of this sort. On 4 May he was given protection for two years while on 'arduous and urgent affairs of the king in divers parts of England'.[129] In the mean time the king called on the clergy of the province of Canterbury for a grant of taxation. On 17 May convocation voted an unprecedented one and a half 'tenths'.[130] There was resistance to its collection in the archdeaconries of Bedford and Huntingdon in June, and 'resistance and rebellion' in the diocese of Worcester in September.[131]

The rising in Oxfordshire may not have been an isolated occurrence. On 28 April the duke of Surrey and Lord Berkeley were commissioned to deal with malefactors, who had assembled, 'by way of insurrection', in the lordship of Winterbourne and Frampton in Gloucestershire.[132] On 2 May a serjeant-at-arms was dispatched to arrest and bring before the king and council John Aunterous esquire and Ralph Boond of Stamford.[133] Four days later another serjeant-at-arms was sent to haul another four men before the king and council.[134] It may be that not all the cases were politically significant, but it is instructive that on 9 May Albemarle and Surrey were given another commission 'to follow and arrest all traitors wherever found in the realm of England, and when convicted of their treasons by their acknowledgement or otherwise, punish them at discretion according to their demerits'.[135] On 15 May Henry Roper was found guilty of treason at Oxford, and hanged, drawn and quartered. His head was dispatched to Reading, and his quarters to Colchester, Norwich, Northampton and Coventry. On 23 May Richard ordered the sheriffs to repair to their dwelling-places during the coming summer season to ensure that 'no insurrections, riots or unlawful assemblies take place' in their bailiwicks, 'as it is most meet for the king's majesty to take heed to cherish peace between his subjects within his realm, inasmuch as his dignity rests thereupon, being aware of the blessing of peace by reason of the sheriff's personal residence within his bailiwick, and the danger thereto by reason of his absence out of the same, especially during the coming summer'.[136]

The king, for his part, was putting some distance between himself and his capital. He presumably passed through Berkshire and Oxfordshire on his way to the Midlands. He may have seen Roper's head at Reading. Richard often lodged at Reading abbey, and on a recent visit he had noted the poor state of the tomb and effigy of Henry I, who was buried in the convent, and made their repair a condition of the confirmation of its liberties. On 24 May the abbot and convent informed the treasurer that 'the king would be pleased to testify' that they had fulfilled this condition.[137] By this stage Richard had confirmed earlier grants to the Carthusian priory at Coventry, and taken up residence in the bishop's palace at Lichfield.[138] It was at Lichfield on 24 May that he entered into a formal alliance with the duke of Brittany, his guest for the past two months.[139] On the 28th he received the homage of Cecily Fovent, the new abbess of Shaftesbury. Given the antiquity of the abbey and its association with St Edward the Martyr, a royal predecessor, the ceremony may have been especially majestic. The homage was witnessed by the 'magnificent' duke of Surrey, the 'magnificent' earl of Salisbury, and Richard, 'by the grace of God', bishop of Salisbury.[140] The king, who was demanding more exalted forms of address for himself, was extending the principle to his inner circle.

At Lichfield Richard had total freedom of the bishop's palace. On 4 April the see had been declared vacant. Bishop Scrope had been sent on a mission to Rome the previous year, and while at the curia on 27 February had been translated to the archbishopric of York. This exercise of papal power was the occasion of some concern in England. After Archbishop Waldby's death Richard had given the cathedral chapter at York permission to choose a successor, and in March they had duly advised him of the election of Walter Skirlaw. To add to the concern, Scrope's translation had been used, as Archbishop Neville's translation had been used ten years earlier, to achieve wider changes to the episcopate, all of which became known in England at the end of March. Bishop Buckingham of Lincoln was translated to Lichfield for no better reason, it seems, than to make Lincoln available for the provision of Henry Beaufort, Gaunt's son. By early April it became clear that Bishop Buckingham was refusing this transfer, and since Scrope's provision had been accepted Lichfield was declared vacant. Around the end of June Buckingham reluctantly made way for Beaufort at Lincoln, and retired to Christ Church, Canterbury. In the mean time Richard had written to Rome to secure the translation of John Burghill, bishop of Llandaff, to Lichfield.[141]

For Richard, the outcome was satisfactory all round. He may well have supported Scrope for York from the outset. He was well qualified, well connected, and involved in the scheme for the canonization of Edward II. Richard may have welcomed, too, the provision of his cousin Henry Beaufort to the see of Lincoln. It is even conceivable that the king was actually complicit in the series of translations. It would not have been the only occasion when he sought to deploy, for both material advantage and symbolic effect, the tactics used against him in 1388. Of course, it cannot have been his wish to see Bishop Buckingham, an old associate of the earl of Warwick, installed in his favourite cathedral city. Yet Buckingham's refusal to accept the translation, which was so patently designed to dislodge him from Lincoln, might have been reasonably predicted, and was rapidly assumed. His retirement gave Richard a clean sweep. On 2 July he was able to secure the translation of his confessor John Burghill to Lichfield, an unusually rich prize for a Dominican friar.[142]

The papal translations of Scrope and Buckingham gave Richard the opportunity to assert his regalian rights. At a meeting on 17 May the convocation of Canterbury was asked on the king's behalf 'whether the pope was entitled to make such translations of bishops arbitrarily and, if so, then how to impede them'. While they were unhappy about the translations, the clergy were not prepared to dispute their validity, and merely asked the king to write to the pope to exercise restraint.[143] At Lichfield, Richard brooded on their response. According to Walsingham, he appeared to be offended by the clergy's acceptance of papal power to effect arbitrary translations, and 'swore that if the clergy had stood up firmly to the pope over this question, he would have intervened to help them'.[144] On the 27th he sent William Ferriby, who brought letters on the matter from the privy council, back to Westminster to make his wishes known. On 4 June the council agreed that the chief justices would be assembled to declare the law on the king's prerogative with respect to cathedral churches, and to advise how the recent translations might be prejudicial to the king's regality. The judges were to commit their advice to writing, and to send one of their number to report to the king at his next council at Nottingham around the feast of St John the Baptist.[145]

★ ★ ★

From the end of May until late June the king sought recreation in the west and north-west Midlands.[146] Doubtless he relished the opportunities for hunting in the chases north of Lichfield and, later, in the forests of Cheshire. On 30 May he made gifts by name to six of his groom-falconers.[147] In the following weeks he was based in and around his much-favoured principality of Chester.[148] He seems to have been at Macclesfield in eastern Cheshire on 11 June.[149] He was at Holt on the 14th, and in a chamber in the castle, attended by the duke of Surrey, the earl of Wiltshire and Nicholas Slake, dean of Westminster, he received the homage of Thomas Pigot, abbot of St Mary's York.[150] He was in Flintshire when William Ferriby caught up with him on his return from the capital some time in mid-June.[151] Richard was likewise kept well informed by Guy Mone, the treasurer. One letter reported that order had been restored in Oxfordshire, and the neighbouring counties were now tranquil. Another briefed him on the elaborate commemoration of Queen Anne at Westminster abbey on 7 June, the anniversary of her death, in which six bishops, the mayor of London and other prominent citizens participated, and informed him that his father's exequies would take place on the 9th. The same correspondent reported that James Clifford, one of the king's squires, rode armed through London in an affray on the eve of Corpus Christi, 5 June, but happily there was no damage done. He assured the king, in so far as he could tell, that the men of London and the country were in 'good peace, unity and accord'.[152]

Richard returned to Lichfield for a few days prior to crossing to Nottingham for a meeting of council. On 22 June, in the dining hall of the dean of Lichfield's house, Richard Scrope, archbishop of York, performed his homage. Among the *magnifici* witnessing the event were the marquis of Dorset and the earl of Salisbury.[153] Richard doubtless celebrated the Nativity of St John the Baptist, 24 June, with appropriate formality. The Baptist was Richard's special patron, and the feast marked the anniversary of his coronation. He had also nominated the feast day as the deadline by which the men who had served the Appellants in 1387 had to sue for pardons.[154] On the 25th the king showed 'his tender love' to his lieges by extending the deadline until 31 October.[155] Richard gave thought as well to the men who had fought under his standard at Radcot Bridge. The sum of 4,000 marks had been promised in the last parliament for the relief of the Cheshire veterans of this campaign. From Lichfield, Richard wrote to the treasurer to arrange payment by Michaelmas.[156]

As in 1387 and again in August 1397, Nottingham provided the setting for a further round of royalist assertion. The council seems to have been scheduled for 30 June.[157] The business included hearing the judges' advice with respect to the translation of bishops. According to the continuator of the *Eulogium Historiarum*, Richard declared at Nottingham that he could not safely ride around the realm on account of the hatred of the people of London and the neighbouring counties, and that he intended to gather an army to destroy them unless they offered security to him.[158] Richard now appeared to be excluding from the general pardon whole communities as well as individuals. The city of London and sixteen southern counties were required to acknowledge in writing their offence against the king's majesty, submit themselves and their goods to his grace, and appoint proctors to treat with him on their behalf. There survive copies of a group letter of submission from the seventeen communities, and a separate letter from the city of London, naming Archbishop Walden of Canterbury, Bishop Braybroke of London and Richard Whittington as its proctors. Each community seems to have had to pay either £1,000 or 1,000 marks to buy back the king's pleasure.[159]

At Nottingham the constable and marshal of England presided over at least one treason trial. William Aleyn of Ashby by Lutterworth was impeached of certain treasons in the court of chivalry. He confessed and was sentenced to be drawn, hanged and beheaded. On 2 July the sheriff of Leicester was ordered to escort Aleyn from Nottingham, draw him through the middle of Leicester, hang him, and then place his head openly on one of the town gates.[160] The king found time for more pleasurable pursuits. On 4 July he was based at the royal manor of Clipstone, which gave him access to the chase in Sherwood.[161] A week later he was a guest of the duke of Lancaster at Tutbury castle. In the great chamber of the castle on the 12th he received the homage of Henry Beaufort, the new bishop of Lincoln.[162] He may have joined his nephew the duke of Surrey at Warwick castle, where the white hart and Surrey's badge of the white hind had replaced the Beauchamp arms on the portal of the gatehouse. On the 24th Surrey confirmed an endowment in the collegiate church at Warwick which provided prayers for the king and queen as well as himself and his wife.[163]

On 26 July the king and Surrey were together at Leicester when Richard formally appointed his nephew as lieutenant in Ireland for a term of three years beginning 1 September.[164] The decision to replace the earl of March had been taken some time earlier.[165] The formal announcement was made only days before the arrival of the remarkable news that Roger Mortimer, earl of March, had been slain in a skirmish with the Irish on 20 July. His death without an adult heir had immense consequences. It certainly buried any prospect of a Mortimer succession to the throne, though March's claim to be regarded as heir presumptive was probably already discounted in the royal family. He was not among the princes of the blood who agreed to return Queen Isabelle to France in the event of Richard's death, and he was not among the select group elevated to dukedoms and permitted to bear St Edward the Confessor's arms in 1397. March's death simplified the political chessboard and brought the king another windfall. On 1 August Richard granted Queen Isabelle the wardship of all the Mortimer lands, and ten days later leased them, with rents payable to the queen, to the dukes of Albemarle and Exeter and the earl of Wiltshire.[166] The wardship of Mortimer's lands in Ireland was assigned, rent-free, to the duke of Surrey during his lieutenancy.[167]

★ ★ ★

The king now headed back north-westwards. He had arranged a meeting of his council at Shrewsbury in early August, and intended to spend some time in the principality of Chester. Bolingbroke and Mowbray were required to appear before the council at Shrewsbury. Bolingbroke, who had waited on the court at Nottingham, fitted in a visit to London before setting out for the long ride to Shrewsbury.[168] It is unclear what other business, if any, was transacted. Presumably the king continued to receive submissions from the men of the southern counties. Richard crossed into Cheshire, pausing at Holt castle, where large-scale building work was underway.[169] On 8 August he appointed Gaunt hereditary constable of the principality of Chester at Holt castle.[170] A letter under the signet seal, however, is dated 9 August at Macclesfield, the other side of Cheshire.[171] He was the guest of John Macclesfield, keeper of the wardrobe. A chance reference reveals that he was served trout fresh from the Pennine streams.[172] He probably hunted in Macclesfield forest, and saw the countryside described in *Sir Gawain and the Green Knight*. Across the Lancashire border, Gaunt was occupied in a similar fashion. An indenture of 29 August indicates his presence at Ightenhill chase near Whalley.[173] By this stage the king was back in Chester. On the 30th at Chester castle he granted John Macclesfield a licence to crenellate his mansion in Macclesfield.[174] He set out the same day, leaving the principality by way of Nantwich on the 31st, when tapestries were delivered back to the chamberlain of Chester.[175]

The king's progress through September is well documented. On 1 September he was at Newcastle under Lyme in Staffordshire, and on the 4th he received the homage of Bishop Burghill of Lichfield at Great Haywood.[176] By this stage his entourage was growing in size. At Burghill's installation at Lichfield on the 8th the witnesses included the archbishops of Canterbury, York and Dublin, the bishops of Salisbury, Exeter, Hereford and Bangor, the dukes of York, Albemarle, Exeter and Surrey and the earls of Worcester, Salisbury, Wiltshire and Gloucester.[177] As the month progressed the king's host became larger still, as lords and knights from all over England, and indeed from France and further afield, converged on the city of Coventry for the duel between Bolingbroke and Mowbray. Bolingbroke, who had used his father's castle at Kenilworth as his base, established himself in Coventry in a fine house which 'had a handsome wooden pavilion near its gate' to protect his privacy.[178] Mowbray seems also to have been at Coventry. Richard took up residence at Baginton, the seat of Sir William Bagot, not far from Coventry.[179]

The dispute between Bolingbroke and Mowbray was much talked about in England, and may have encouraged division and unrest. In a remarkable move on 23 August Henry Beaufort, bishop of Lincoln, made a public declaration of support for his 'most honorable and dear brother' in his duel with 'a certain adversary' and ordered prayers and processions in his diocese for his brother and the declaration of justice in his cause.[180] On 10 September Albemarle was granted a further commission as constable of England. It recited that people were prosecuting causes 'touching the estate, fame and condition of the king's person and concerning the dignity of his crown royal, by way of appeal and otherwise' more frequently than before, and that the king was resolved not to 'pass over such causes or leave them undetermined, but punish delinquents herein according to their deserts'. Albemarle was commissioned 'to hear all such cases and matters', to proceed with them 'in accordance with the demands of justice and the laws and customs of the court of chivalry', and to make due determination of them.[181]

The duel aroused considerable interest on the continent. Giangaleazzo Visconti, duke of Milan, sent Bolingbroke a suit of fine Milanese armour, while German friends furnished Mowbray with equipment. Bolingbroke's wardrobe accounts reveal gifts to heralds of the king of Portugal, the dukes of Orléans, Burgundy and Guelders.[182] The herald of the duke of Brittany presided over proceedings. Alongside the interest in the chivalric spectacle, there were broader diplomatic concerns. The duke of Milan was seeking an alliance with England, and there were proposals for a match between Bolingbroke and his sister.[183] The French court was especially anxious at the turn of events. England's domestic problems were inherently destabilizing to the Anglo-French accord, especially if Richard used them as an excuse for reneging on commitments, or as a screen for new foreign policy initiatives. Over the summer Charles VI sent a number of emissaries to lobby Richard to follow the French lead with respect to healing the schism, and to urge him to proclaim the extension of the truce which was due to expire at the end of September.[184] Richard proved evasive on the one issue, and agonizingly dilatory on the other. As the date of the duel approached, the French king sent the count of St Pol to persuade Richard not to allow the duel to go ahead.

At daybreak on Monday 16 September the two antagonists, both in their early thirties, prepared themselves for the ordeal. Mowbray called on Richard at Baginton and then returned to Coventry to hear mass at the Carthusian priory. He was armed by a Bohemian squire at his tent near the lists.[185] Bolingbroke, who had made his courtesy call on the king the previous evening, made his preparations in his town-house.[186] The dukes of Albemarle and Surrey, as constable and marshal respectively, organized the lists.

Richard II pronounces sentence of banishment upon Bolingbroke and Mowbray. (The British Library, Harl. 4380, fol. 148)

They and their twenty followers were splendidly attired, each clad in a doublet of red Kendal cloth decorated with silver girdles on which was written 'Honi soit qui mal y pense'. The author of *Traison et Mort*, who provides this information, was almost certainly an eye-witness, and was probably associated with one of the heralds. The protagonists proceeded to the lists with great fanfare and prepared themselves for combat. Suddenly the herald of the duke of Brittany intervened and stopped the duel.

According to the official record, Richard regarded both Bolingbroke and Mowbray as culpable and undeserving of his pity, but wished to avoid the 'great dishonour which would befall one or other of them.' Claiming to act on the advice and by the authority of parliament, he sentenced Bolingbroke to banishment for ten years and Mowbray for life.[187] Mowbray's greater punishment was explained by his confession at Windsor 'to certain civil points' which he had previously denied, 'which points, once admitted, might be the cause of great trouble in the realm'. It was noted as well that Mowbray 'both privately and publicly' opposed the annulment of the acts of the parliament of 1388, and maintained 'the validity of the wicked and unlawful appeals' against the king's friends. Richard had overlooked the opposition at the time, and even rewarded Mowbray with lordships, lands and offices. He now resolved that Mowbray should forfeit all his grants, and that his inheritance should be taken into the king's hands, with the exception of an annual allowance of £1,000, until full satisfaction had been made for his maladministration of Calais.[188] Richard laid down that Bolingbroke and

Mowbray should communicate neither with each other nor with Archbishop Arundel. Bolingbroke was to pass his time in France or Spain, while Mowbray would travel in Germany or cross the Mediterranean on pilgrimage. It was determined that if either party or anyone else attempted to secure for either of them a pardon or a licence to return to England, he or they should incur sentence of treason. Furthermore, it was ordained that all the penalties declared in parliament should extend to the judgements now made.[189]

According to the author of *Traison et Mort*, Richard and the count of St Pol left for Nuneaton on the day after the duel.[190] Bolingbroke was likewise at Nuneaton on 20 September, when he made a further grant to his trusted squire Robert Waterton.[191] On Wednesday the cavalcade arrived at the duke of Lancaster's castle at Leicester, and 'there the two lords who had been banished took their leave of him, on going abroad'.[192] For the aged and ailing Gaunt it must have been a poignant moment. The

Bolingbroke enters Paris. (The British Library, Harl. 4380, fol. 151)

chances of his ever seeing his son again were very slight. According to the author of *Traison et Mort*, the duke of Surrey immediately set out for Ireland with an army of 20,000 men.[193] He was certainly busy making preparations for the expedition and sorting out his affairs. On 18 September he acquired a licence to entail some of his lands, with the dukes of Albemarle and Exeter, the bishop of Exeter and Lord Lovell serving as feoffees.[194] He still appears to have been with the king at Leicester on the 22nd, when he was granted in tail male lands in Warwickshire forfeited by the earl of Warwick, and was given all the earl of March's lordships in Ireland for three years without rent.[195] He did not leave England until October.

From Leicester the king returned to Windsor castle, where Bolingbroke and Mowbray finally took their leave of the court.[196] They proceeded to London to make their final arrangements before going overseas.[197] Mowbray was authorized to leave from any east coast port, and on 29 September serjeants-at-arms were appointed to secure ships for his transport.[198] On 3 October Sir Thomas Grey of Heaton, Sir William Elmham, Sir George Felbridge, Sir Richard Cradock and others were licensed to be of his continuous council while he was abroad in Germany, Bohemia and Hungary.[199] On the same day serjeants-at-arms were dispatched to secure vessels at Dover for Bolingbroke's passage to Calais.[200] He was authorized to take in his company 'no more than 200 persons'.[201] Henry and his companions were granted letters patent of general attorney, to be renewed annually, and granted the right, through his attorneys, 'to sue for livery of any inheritances that may descend to him'.[202]

According to Froissart, thousands of Londoners lined the streets to bid a sorrowful farewell to Bolingbroke. They allegedly declared that 'this country will never be happy until you return'.[203] Richard had reduced Bolingbroke's term of banishment from ten to six years, and as a parting gesture made him a gift of 1,000 marks.[204] Yet the injustice of the sentence was all too apparent, and Richard's malice must have been suspected. In the autumn of 1398, as prominent Londoners escorted Bolingbroke to Dover, it could hardly be claimed that Richard was a full-blown tyrant. He did not exploit the realm merely to satisfy his private desires. Yet none could doubt that Richard was ruling in a highly vindictive and arbitrary manner. If he was not a tyrant, he was acting tyrannically. Twelve months later the Londoners would endorse Bolingbroke's claim that the kingdom was on the point of being 'undone for default of governance and undoing of the good laws'.[205]

CHAPTER SEVEN

FORTUNE'S WHEEL

Richard came to Westminster to celebrate the feast of St Edward the Confessor. It was the first time in twelve months that he had celebrated a major feast day in the capital. It was the occasion of considerable regal pomp and *hauteur*. The continuator of the *Eulogium Historiarum* tells how on solemn feast-days Richard had a throne prepared in his chamber, and presented himself seated in majesty from dinner to vespers. He would talk to no one, but cast his eyes over all, and when he looked at anyone, whatever his rank, he had to fall to his knees before him.[1] Adam Usk had specific memories of the feast of St Edward the Confessor in 1398. It was then that Richard had the decisions of the recent parliament confirmed at Westminster by the papal legate, and indeed by his own authority. It was then that Richard had lost his temper with the countess of Warwick who came to plead with him on behalf of her husband. Threatening to put her to death, he swore that he would dispatch her immediately were it not for the fact she was a woman. Above all, Usk recalled it as the time when Bolingbroke was finally driven into exile.[2]

Over the autumn Richard would have received the submission of London and the sixteen southern counties. In their petitions for the king's grace they acknowledged their great offences, and put their lives and goods at his disposal. The proctors who brought the letters of submission doubtless presented them to the king with appropriate displays of subjection. At the same time individual knights and squires continued to compound for their pardons, adding to the store of money at his personal disposal. Sir Giles Malory and Sir Nicholas Lilling received pardons on 18 October.[3] The king continued to make considerable demands on the exchequer for a number of projects, not least the provision of funds for the duke of Surrey's expedition to Ireland. Large sums were sent to Chester as recompense and reward for the veterans of Radcot Bridge. On 26 October Sir Robert Legh acknowledged receipt of 3,000 marks, deposited it in Chester abbey for temporary safe-keeping, and in the following months began to distribute the sum, with an additional 1,000 marks, among the seven hundreds into which Cheshire was divided.[4] The flow of patronage elsewhere was slowing to a trickle. One new retainer must have raised a few eyebrows. On 15 October Richard took into his service Sir Peter Craon, a French knight notorious for his attempted assassination of the constable of France in 1392, granting him the princely annuity of £500.[5]

Richard appeared all-powerful. It was a little over a year since he had achieved the destruction of Gloucester, Arundel and Warwick, and the exile of Archbishop Arundel. In the previous few months the untimely death of the earl of March had brought the custody of the Mortimer lands to the crown, while the banishment of the duke of Norfolk was accompanied by a punitive mulct. It must have appeared that Richard was bent on the ruin of all who threatened his power. Though he cannot be held responsible for March's death, he seems to have resented him and sought ways to undermine him. According to Froissart, Richard was even more jealous of Henry of Bolingbroke. Bolingbroke's popularity in London was brought home by the size of the crowds which turned out to commiserate with him as he went into exile.[6] Yet if the king was at the height of his fortune in October 1398, the wheel was beginning to turn. In the following year it would lurch violently. Adam Usk's recollection of the feast of St Edward the Confessor was the sharper in that twelve months later, on that very day, Henry of Bolingbroke was crowned at Westminster.

★ ★ ★

Over the autumn Richard remained in contact with the French court. It may be that relations were a little strained. Richard left it until the eleventh hour to proclaim the extension of the truce, and in September he made clear his opposition to a proposed French expedition to Italy. His alliance with the duke of Brittany, his growing friendship with Giangaleazzo Visconti of Milan and his acceptance of Peter de Craon as his vassal may all have seemed unfriendly acts in France. There was still a good deal of courtly interchange. On 18 October Richard made a gift of £20 to a French emissary bringing news to the queen and himself of the birth of another son to the king and queen of France.[7] In late October Richard sent the earl of Salisbury and the bishop of Carlisle to Paris to secure the latest instalment of his wife's dowry.[8] An additional task may have been to subvert the position of Bolingbroke, who had been warmly received by the French court. Richard wanted it known in France that he regarded Bolingbroke as tainted with treason. The earl of Salisbury, though he had no stomach for the work, was eminently qualified for it. He was well regarded in France as a knight and a poet.[9] Salisbury would soon rue the day that he snubbed and slandered Bolingbroke in Paris.

The French remained concerned at Richard's failure to honour his undertakings with respect to healing the schism. At the beginning of November they sent a major embassy headed by Nicholas Paynel, who had visited England earlier in the summer, and including other knights of the households of the king of France, the duke of Orléans and the duke of Bourbon. Richard rewarded them with silver vessels and cloth to the value of over £100.[10] In other respects the embassy was less successful. Richard merely agreed that the French proposals be forwarded to the English universities for their consideration.[11] On 20 November he wrote to Oxford seeking a response before Lent, and observed that he was 'aware of the hurt and peril' caused by the schism, and that worse would happen 'if it be not extirpated by the sagacity of the Catholic princes and other servants of God'.[12] He delayed until the new year before summoning a select council of senior clergy to debate the matter.[13]

Richard had good reason to move slowly along a path which was bound to alienate the Roman curia and provoke opposition in England. In fact he was busy turning to political advantage his standing as Boniface IX's principal supporter.[14] Peter de Bosc, bishop of Dax and papal legate, arrived in England earlier in the summer, and rapidly made himself agreeable at court. At Windsor castle in September he presented the queen with a parrot and distributed spiritual privileges to a number of courtiers.[15] On 13 October he

Richard II gives credentials to the earl of Salisbury, to hinder Bolingbroke's marriage in France. (The British Library, Harl. 4380, fol. 163)

confirmed the acts and judgements of the parliament and parliamentary committee, fulminated against anyone who sought to overturn them, and sent to Rome for the appropriate bulls.[16] Finally, the king and legate negotiated a settlement which gave Richard effective control over appointments to bishoprics. According to the concordat of 25 November, the pope agreed to confirm an election only if and when the king signified his assent. This right of veto brought him all the leverage he needed to refashion the episcopate. The concordat may well indicate, as Davis argues, that Richard was sincere in the belief that 'royal influence over appointments was altogether too insecure'.[17] Yet it remains likely that he was complicit in some of the translations in 1398, and that his expressions of outrage were rather staged. On 16 December the king wrote from Coventry to the archbishops of Canterbury and York ordering a moderation of statute of provisors, on account of the king's affection for the pope and his legate Peter de Bosc.[18]

Meanwhile the king made plans for Christmas at Lichfield. On 11 December payment was made for the filling of a large silver cruet in the shape of a ship for the king's alms.[19] The Christmas celebrations were magnificent, and acquired an almost legendary status. Heralds were sent across the land to proclaim revels and jousts planned for Lichfield.[20] According to the monk of Evesham, the king's entourage was so large that twenty-odd head of cattle, three hundred sheep and innumerable poultry were consumed daily.[21] The guests of honour included the papal legate and Hilario Doria, the son-in-law and ambassador of the Byzantine emperor.[22] Many bishops and lords were present.[23] There was evidence of gift-giving on a grand scale. Richard and the queen received gifts sent by the dukes of Burgundy and Berry.[24] Hunting was almost certainly on the agenda. There were jousts every day, presumably culminating in a great tournament on Twelfth Night, the king's birthday.

The papal legate and Byzantine emissary added lustre and an exotic flavour to the court over Christmas and New Year. Their presence reflected Richard's importance at this stage in the affairs of Christendom. In truth, Richard could offer little in the way of real succour for beleaguered Constantinople. He may have done no more than repeat what he had written to Manuel II earlier in the year. Still, Richard committed himself to raising funds in England to aid Constantinople, and may have promised military aid in the near future. He was sufficiently encouraging to prompt the Byzantine emperor himself to undertake a personal mission to the west a year later.[25] With regard to Anglo-French collaboration to end the schism, Richard continued to play for time, especially given the presence of the papal legate. On 2 January he none the less sent orders to the bishop of Hereford and a number of other prominent clerks to meet at Oxford on Monday after the conversion of St Paul, 27 January, to give counsel regarding the schism.[26]

It was at Lichfield, either at Christmas 1398 or earlier in the year, that Richard had a remarkable conversation with Sir William Bagot. According to Bagot, the king told him that he desired 'to live long enough to see the crown held in such high respect, and obeyed with such lowly humility by all his lieges, as had been the case under previous kings, for he considered that he had been humiliated and disobeyed by both his lords and his commons, so that it might be chronicled forever that with skill and with strength he had recovered his royal dignity and his honourable estate; and should he achieve this, he would renounce his crown on the following day'. He then went on to raise the issue of the succession. Richard allegedly declared his belief that his cousin Albemarle was the best person to succeed him. When asked for his view, Bagot expressed doubts as to whether the people would obey him. Richard then said that he thought that Bagot would support Bolingbroke, but that if he 'became king he would be as great a tyrant to the holy church as ever there was'. Bagot said no more, leaving Richard to add pensively, 'and yet there have been many good confessors among both his ancestors and mine, who never persecuted the holy church'.[27]

Bagot made this statement in a bill to Henry IV's first parliament. His account served the needs of the moment in several respects. It presented Richard contemplating a form of abdication, and acknowledging Bolingbroke's claims as a prince of the blood. It testified to Bagot's good will towards Bolingbroke. Yet it is entirely credible. Bagot was addressing an audience which knew Richard very well. Richard's ambition to enforce obedience and to restore the crown to its former glory was well enough known. His

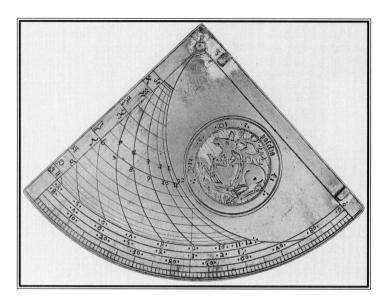

*Horary quadrant of 1399
showing Richard's white hart.
(The British Museum)*

talk about renouncing the crown to one of his cousins was more surprising. Richard, however, may well have conversed in this fashion to a number of people. Such ruminations served to tease and test his inner circle. In any case Richard was presenting himself as a candidate for the Holy Roman Empire, and may have intended, if elected, to renounce his English crown.

The conversation provides an insight into the king's mind as he approached another milestone in his life. At the beginning of 1399 he turned thirty-three, the age at which Christ completed his mission on earth. Richard thought long and hard about his destiny. In the book of wisdom and divination presented to him in 1391 he is presented as a prince who through long 'acquaintance with astronomy has not declined to taste the sweetness of fruit of the subtle sciences for the prudent government of himself and his kingdom'.[28] In 1397 he had a notable French astrologer brought to England for private consultations.[29] Interestingly there survive two horary quadrants bearing his emblem of the white hart, one dated 1398 and one dated 1399.[30] Richard would doubtless have taken some interest in the remarkable comet which had appeared in late November 1398. For eight successive nights, it could be seen in the sky, 'burning with extraordinary intensity, its tail turned towards the west'. The monk of St Denis in Paris, who noted this astronomical wonder, reported that astrologers took it as a sure sign of the death of kings or the imminence of revolutions in 1399.[31]

According to the English chronicles, Richard was very interested in prophecies. He was allegedly encouraged in his arbitrary rule by prophets who told him that he would be raised to the imperial dignity, and that he deserved to be counted the greatest among the princes of the world.[32] He sought to apply to himself the prophecies associated with the holy oil of Canterbury. They record his discovery in the Tower of London of a gold eagle enclosing a stone ampulla of the holy oil which the Virgin Mary had given to St Thomas of Canterbury. It was written that all who wore the eagle around their neck would achieve victory and prosperity, and that the oil should be used in the unction of kings, one of whom would reconquer the Holy Land.[33] The chronicles likewise present Richard as being troubled by less favourable prognostications. According to Walsingham, a prophecy which gained some currency over the winter of 1398/9 related to the 'pomp of John' which was to last only two years. Richard increasingly came to believe that the prophecy referred to him, since he had originally been christened John.[34]

The chronicles written after 1399 have an interest in presenting Richard as vain and gullible. It has been claimed that it was the Lancastrian regime which played the key role in harnessing prophecy for propagandist ends.[35] Yet Richard cannot have been oblivious to the prophetic writings which were such a feature of British political culture in times of crisis and upheaval. His character and the vicissitudes of his reign predisposed him to take them seriously. The portion of the Dieulacres chronicle written from a Ricardian perspective begins its account of the reign of Richard 'the most excellent king of all the kings of the world' with a whole series of laudatory prophecies.[36] Given Richard's documented ambitions with regard to the Holy Roman Empire, it would be rash to dismiss Walsingham's claims that he heeded prophecies that presented him in that role. The existence of a tradition of prophecy specifically linking the conquest of Ireland to the accomplishment of a high destiny in Christendom may help to explain his otherwise remarkable decision to leave England at this crucial juncture.[37] For all his other ambitions, obligations and concerns over the winter of 1398/9, Richard proved resolute in his determination to lead a major expedition to Ireland in 1399.

★ ★ ★

The New Year began full of ill omen. The comet which was seen as the harbinger of revolutions in France was accompanied by more mundane portents in England. According to Walsingham, the laurel trees throughout the realm withered and then revived, while a river in Bedfordshire dramatically changed its course, signifying, it was said, division within the land and defection from the king.[38]

At Lichfield the Christmas revels continued until Twelfth Night. Some 20 miles away, in a chamber of his castle at Leicester, John of Gaunt lay on his deathbed. He seems to have taken ill before Christmas. An early tradition has it that Richard visited him. According to Andrew Wyntoun, writing in the 1420s, Richard sought to cheer and console him, but left behind some 'privy bills' which broke Gaunt's spirit when he came to read them.[39] In the 1440s Thomas Gascoigne wrote a rather different account of this last meeting. He claimed that Gaunt showed Richard the ulcerated flesh around his genitals as a warning against lechery.[40] If Richard visited him in New Year, it adds even greater interest to the hitherto unremarked fact that Gaunt's death was prematurely announced. On or shortly after 8 January messengers were paid for taking letters to advise the magnates and clergy of Gaunt's funeral at St Paul's on Thursday before Passion Sunday.[41] Gaunt actually lived for another month, but still died in ample time for the funeral. Perhaps Gaunt had suffered a stroke, and his death was prematurely reported. Richard had an unfortunate habit of anticipating the deaths of his uncles.

The king remained for some time in the Midlands. On 13 January he held a great council at Coventry. It was attended by prelates, barons, knights and commons of the principality of Chester and many other counties.[42] There were certainly several

Interior of St Mary's Hall, Coventry, showing Richard's white hart badge on the ceiling. Engraving by W.F. Taunton in B. Poole, Coventry: Its History and Antiquities *(London, 1870).*

important items of business. The king's proposed expedition to Ireland was doubtless high on the agenda. Within a fortnight privy seal letters were being dispatched spelling out the king's need for horses for the proposed 'voyage'.[43] At the same time the king's relaxation of the statute of provisors was formally approved. A proclamation to this effect was made on the 16th.[44] At Richard's instigation, the council likewise agreed that a 'notable sum' be raised for the relief of the city of Constantinople 'and the support of Christians against the malice and invasion of the miscreants'. Lords were asked to contribute according to their estate by the octave of Candlemas. A surviving letter indicates that 40 marks was the going rate for a bishop.[45]

At the conclusion of the council all the prelates, lords and knights swore to uphold the statutes and judgements of the recent parliament, including the decisions of the parliamentary committee on 16 September.[46] The king ordered the proclamation of this oath in all the counties, cities and boroughs.[47] On 20 January the justices of the peace in Worcestershire were instructed to administer the oath in their bailiwick and to make a return with the names and seals by Easter.[48] On 8 February the bishops were likewise sent a copy of the oath, and asked to administer it to all their clergy and to return a schedule of their names.[49] The bishops did not respond with any great expedition. Bishop Wykeham of Winchester did not act until 14 May, while the only surviving return, from Bishop Medford of Salisbury, is dated 3 June.[50] While the letters of submission by the city of London and the sixteen counties seem to have been returned, copies of the petition and lists of names of the people contributing to the 'Le Plesaunce', that is the composite sum required to win back the king's pleasure, were kept in chancery.[51] The corporate submissions did not remove the requirement for individuals to seek the king's grace. In a general pardon proclaimed on 27 February, Richard continued to exclude men who had been in the company of Gloucester, Arundel and Warwick at Harringey and Radcot Bridge.[52]

As he headed northwards, Richard parted company with his foreign guests. On 20 January Hilario Doria, the Byzantine ambassador, was formally granted licence to leave the kingdom.[53] On 8 February Robert de Boissay, councillor of the king of France, was licensed to take out of the country, duty free, cloth, horns, bottles, two beds and 12,000 pins.[54] The king looked to replenish his coffers by seeking aid from the northern clergy. On 25 January he instructed Archbishop Scrope to summon a convocation at York to grant a subsidy for the defence and safety of the English church and realm and the marches.[55] The king noted that the subsidy voted in Archbishop Waldby's time remained uncollected, and asked for payment before the quindene of Easter, 13 April.[56]

In the mean time John of Gaunt finally passed away. On 3 February he set his seal to the final version of his will, and died, in all likelihood that evening.[57] According to the Kirkstall chronicle, he was 'sadly bereaved on account of the banishment of his eldest son to France'.[58] He made detailed provisions regarding his funeral. He was to be buried in St Paul's by the principal altar next to his first wife Blanche of Lancaster. He ordained that on the first night in London his body should rest at Carmelites in Fleet Street, and that on the morrow, after a requiem mass, it should be taken to St Paul's. He made provision for a blaze of candles: ten for the broken commandments, seven for neglected works of charity and the deadly sins, five for the wounds of Christ and the abused senses, and three for the Trinity. An odd feature of the will was the provision that he should remain above ground, unembalmed, for forty days after his decease.[59] Given that his death had been announced prematurely, it is possible that he feared being buried alive.

Gaunt's body remained at Leicester for most of February. Attended by his widow and his son Henry Beaufort, bishop of Lincoln, it was then transported by easy stages to London. The cortège rested one night at St Albans, and passed through Barnet on the 14th. Gaunt was laid to rest in a splendid tomb in St Paul's cathedral, London, on either the 15th or the 16th, Passion Sunday.[60] He was buried with the 'most solemn exequies in the presence of the king and many dignitaries'.[61] Liveries of black cloth were issued to a number of bishops and clerks, including John Boor, dean of the chapel royal, and to the dukes of Albemarle, Surrey and Exeter, the marquis of Dorset, the earls of Salisbury and Wiltshire, the duchess of Ireland, the marchioness of Dorset, and Ladies Mowbray and Poynings.[62] According to his household accounts, Lord Bardolf paid for his own black robes at the 'interment of the duke of Lancaster'.[63] Peter de Bosc, the papal legate, was probably one of a number of representatives of foreign potentates.[64]

Richard was probably in Cheshire at the time of Gaunt's death.[65] Early in March he headed south through Staffordshire, shadowing his uncle's funeral cortège. Before and after the funeral he was based at King's Langley. It was there, according to Sir William Bagot in 1399, that he took the decision to deny Bolingbroke his inheritance and banish him for life. He allegedly declared that he would sooner restore the heirs of Gloucester, Arundel and Warwick than allow Bolingbroke to return to England. According to his own account, Bagot immediately sent a message by Roger Smart to Bolingbroke in France, advising him that the king 'was his full enemy and that he should help himself with manhood'.[66] Given that Bolingbroke was in a position to corroborate this statement, Bagot must be adjudged creditworthy on this point. It is more difficult to know what to make of Bagot's statement that Albemarle told Bushy and Green that he would happily give £20,000 to see Bolingbroke dead, not because he feared him personally, but because of the trouble and strife he would bring on the realm. Albemarle was quick to deny this allegation in parliament in 1399.[67]

On 18 March Richard convened a council at Westminster to confirm his decision with respect to Bolingbroke. The chancellor informed the assembly that Bolingbroke had petitioned to seek livery of his inheritance, through his attorneys, as was allowed in the letters patent granted to him. The chancellor explained that the letters had been granted inadvertently, and that after careful consideration they had been found to be inconsistent with the judgements given at Coventry. For this reason, he announced, the king and the parliamentary committee had resolved to revoke and annul them. The council appears to have discussed the matter, and it was resolved that similar letters patent granted to Mowbray should likewise be revoked and annulled.[68] At the end of the session eighteen prelates, sixteen peers and four commoners again swore a solemn oath on the cross of Canterbury to uphold all the acts and judgements of the parliament of 1397–8 and of the committee acting in its name, including the decisions just taken.[69]

It cannot be claimed that Richard acted precipitately. Given the premature announcement of Gaunt's funeral, he had several months to settle on a course of action. According to Froissart, he reported Gaunt's death to Charles VI of France 'with a sort of joy', and it may be that for him it was an event long awaited and desired.[70] For Walsingham, the decision to deny Bolingbroke his inheritance was proof that Richard 'vehemently hated' his cousin and 'first exiled him not on account of the dissensions, discord and disturbances that could truly arise' between Bolingbroke and Mowbray and their retinues 'as he craftily pretended', but so that he could get his hands on his ample possessions.[71] In the spring of 1399 Richard took steps to apportion the sequestered Lancastrian lands among his key supporters. He granted the honours of Leicester, Pontefract and Bolingbroke to the duke of Albemarle; the honours of Lancaster and Tutbury and the lordship of Kenilworth to the duke of Surrey; the Lancastrian lordships in Wales to the duke of Exeter; and the lordship of Pickering to the earl of Wiltshire. Yet the grants were made only until Bolingbroke 'or his heir, shall have sued the same out of the king's hands according to the law of the land'.[72] Furthermore, Bolingbroke was left undisturbed in the possession of the lands he held by right of his late wife, and was allowed to continue to draw an annuity from the exchequer. Richard's ultimate plans with respect to the house of Lancaster remain obscure, though they must have included some diminution of its inordinate wealth and power. He may have thought in terms of admitting, when he came of age, Henry of Monmouth, Bolingbroke's son, to the core of his patrimony.

The annulment of Mowbray's letters patent on 18 March proved singularly opportune. On the 24th Margaret, duchess of Norfolk, died at Framlingham castle at around eighty years of age. The daughter of Thomas of Brotherton, son of Edward I, and twice widowed, she was the richest woman in the realm. The Brotherton inheritance and the dower lands from her marriages brought her a yearly income of around £3,000.[73] Her royal blood and landed wealth had been acknowledged in 1397 when she had been created a duchess in her own right. Thomas Mowbray was her grandson and principal heir, and at the time of his banishment his expectancies as well as his lands had been granted by the king to two bishops, Sir John Bushy and Sir Henry Green. They gained immediate custody of the duchess's lands in England and Wales, and on 4 April granted Framlingham castle to Sir Simon Felbridge, the king's standard-bearer.[74]

The sequestrations of the Lancastrian and Mowbray lands added enormously to the king's wealth and potential for patronage. There is ample evidence to support the testimony of the chroniclers that Richard was accumulating vast wealth, not least the forty membrane inventory of his crowns, jewels and plate that was compiled from earlier lists around 1399.[75] Over the winter of 1398/9 he seems to have been salting away huge sums of money. His principal treasury was Holt castle, and there are records of wagon-loads of treasure being sent to this remote fastness in the new principality of Chester.[76] According to Walsingham, 'though he abounded in riches beyond all his predecessors', he 'none the less continued to busy himself amassing money, caring not at all by what title he

The brass of Sir Simon Felbridge and wife, 1416. (Society of Antiquaries)

could acquire it from the hands of his subjects'.[77] Walsingham recalled Lent 1399 as a time when, preparing for his expedition to Ireland, Richard extorted money, horses and wagons, seized grain, meat and fish, paying nothing, and 'as much as he unjustly garnered his people's goods, so much he justly incurred their hatred'.[78] There is documentation of Richard's requests for horses and other equipment from religious houses, though they were clearly not always successful. A letter to the prior of Worcester seeking a horse received a most evasive reply. The prior of Rochester, who was asked to provide a wagon for the transport of the king's chapel to Ireland, was likewise unobliging.[79]

During Lent Richard prepared himself spiritually for his great undertaking in Ireland. He declared his intention of making a pilgrimage to the shrine of St Thomas at Canterbury. He made a point of expressing his lack of confidence in the Londoners and the men of Kent. Despite Archbishop Walden's assurances, he took with him his Cheshire guardsmen. The pilgrimage probably took place in Easter week.[80] The archbishop entertained him regally at Canterbury, while the corporation records attest gifts of wine to his bodyguard.[81] Meanwhile William Norham, a holy man from Northumberland, made his way south to rebuke the king and archbishop. Securing an audience with Archbishop Walden he urged him to surrender the see, and to advise the king to amend his life, to recall the exiles and reinstate the disinherited lords. The archbishop imprisoned him, and then brought him before the king. According to the *Eulogium*, Richard asked him to prove his closeness to God by walking on water. The hermit replied that he could not perform miracles, but stoutly declared that unless his warnings were heeded 'such dire news will shortly occur with you as you have never read nor seen'. The king committed him to the Tower of London.[82]

Prior to leaving for Ireland, Richard showed some interest in stamping his authority on his capital. He ordered the yeomen of the livery of the crown to gather in London on the Wednesday after Easter.[83] In Easter week, too, he had proclaimed at St Paul's and St Mary Spital papal bulls ratifying the excommunication of all who sought the repeal of the statutes and judgements of the recent parliament.[84] According to the *Eulogium*, it was on Richard's return from Canterbury that he went to the Tower of London to select his regalia for transport to Ireland and found the gold eagle containing the holy oil of Canterbury. Richard took it from the treasury, and thenceforward wore it around his neck.[85] As he assembled men and munitions for the expedition to Ireland, and organized the packing of his regalia, he may have felt that he was in sight of securing his goals in England. All the five magnates who had fought against the royal banner in December 1387 were dead or ruined. Gaunt, who had cast a long shadow over his reign, had gone the way of all flesh. Richard must have relished the powerful visual statements of his regality in Westminster: the remodelled Westminster Hall, whose great hammerbeam roof was now all but complete; the grand portrait of himself seated in majesty in Westminster abbey, an icon of his kingship during his absence from the capital; and the grand double-tomb resplendent in St Edward's chapel, whither in the end he would come.

Yet it was not a time for exultation. Richard saw a future full of uncertainty. According to Walsingham, he reflected gloomily on the dangers that he faced in Ireland and the unrest that he left behind in England.[86] The extraordinary will to which he set his seal at Westminster on 16 April is full of anxiety and apprehension. In the preamble he wrote how 'for some time since our tender age submitted our neck by the mercy of the supreme king to the burden of the government of the English'. He expressed his desire for 'a royal burial in the church of St Peter at Westminster among our ancestors kings of England of famous memory', but made provision, too, in case by misfortune 'our body should be snatched from the sight of men by hurricanes or tempests of the sea' or 'we should pay the debt of nature' in distant lands. He asked to be laid to rest with his crown and sceptre, and with a precious ring on his finger. Among his legatees, he showed special favour to the dukes of Surrey, Exeter and Albemarle, and the earl of Wiltshire. He bequeathed Surrey 10,000 marks, Exeter 3,000 marks, and Albemarle and Wiltshire 2,000 marks. In a remarkable passage he willed all his crowns and other valuables to his successor, whom he did not name, on the condition that he fulfilled the terms of his will. Setting aside £20,000 for the debts of his household, he bequeathed the residue of gold to his successor, but only as long as he confirmed and firmly observed the acts of his recent parliament and parliamentary committee, including the decisions of 18 March. If his successor were unwilling to do so, then the residue was to go to Surrey, Exeter, Albemarle and Wiltshire 'for the sustaining and defence' of these acts, to the death if need be.[87] It was a 'will extremely prejudicial to the realm, as was said by those who saw it'.[88]

★　★　★

Some days later Richard left his capital for the last time as king, and moved to Windsor. According to Froissart, a grand tournament had been scheduled for St George's day, with forty knights and forty squires dressed in green holding the field. The tournament was allegedly poorly attended.[89] Still, there were quite a number of nobles and courtiers at Windsor. On 24 April the duke of Albemarle, the earl of Westmorland, Lord Furnival, and Richard Holme took the oath taken by the council on 18 March.[90] It was at Windsor that Richard bade farewell to his young queen. According to the author of *Traison et Mort*, it was a tender scene. They walked hand in hand through the castle courtyard; Richard promised her that she should join him in Ireland later; he kissed her dozens of times, lifting her from the ground before bidding her his final adieu.[91] Even with his young bride, Richard showed himself dissembling and a little cruel. Concerned about the prodigality of Lady Courcy, the queen's governess, he arranged with the earl of Wiltshire that once he had left for Ireland he would write instructing him to pay her debts and send her back to France.[92] Lady Courcy was indeed dismissed, and the queen left largely friendless in England. Richard's responsibility for the decision was unknown to the parties involved.[93]

Richard was soon heading westwards. A letter under the signet seal was dated at Osney abbey on 30 April.[94] His progress seems to have been quite leisurely. He spent time at centres like Cardiff and Carmarthen, and was able to take advantage of the well-stocked wine-cellars at the Lancastrian castle at Kidwelly.[95] The preparations for the expedition were well advanced. On 14 April Richard Kays, serjeant-at-arms, and John Newbold, clerk, had been sent from London to commandeer ships and conduct them to Chester and Bristol as well as to Haverford, from where the king would make his crossing. Kays collected twenty-nine ships, mainly from the West Country, and conducted them to Chester to carry 576 horses to the duke of Surrey in Dublin.

Newbold arrested some fifty-six ships for the main expedition.[96] In the mean time Dublin castle was being put in a state of readiness for the royal visit.[97]

The king led a host, which if not especially large was socially distinguished. The duke of Surrey, who was already in Ireland, commanded the largest company, with 160 men-at-arms and 800 archers. The dukes of Albemarle and Exeter each led 140 men-at-arms and 500 and 600 archers respectively. The earls of Gloucester, Salisbury and Worcester each brought retinues of 35 men-at-arms and 100 archers.[98] The king was accompanied, too, by a number of churchmen, including the abbot of Westminster, and a number of the lesser lords, such as Lord Bardolf who is known to have purchased armour for the expedition.[99] The king's Cheshire guardsmen were likewise much in evidence. A number of foreign knights arrived to join what promised to be a momentous campaign. Peter de Craon, who crossed to Paris on the king's secret business in February, was back in the king's company in May.[100] In the company of an unnamed French knight, Jean Creton set out from Paris at the end of April eager for adventure. When he arrived in London he found 'many a knight taking his departure from the city'.[101]

Richard left England in a state of unrest and anxiety. Prior to his departure he appointed his uncle Edmund of Langley, duke of York, as keeper of the realm, but left the day-to-day business of government largely in the hands of a privy council consisting of William Scrope, earl of Wiltshire, Bushy, Green and Bagot.[102] As a conciliatory gesture, he had authorized the return to London and the sixteen counties of their letters of submission, but in their place seemingly asked for 'blank charters' from their various proctors. Richard remained fearful of treason and betrayal. Even the Cheshire men were not above suspicion. At Cardiff on 8 May he required Sir Robert Legh, sheriff of Cheshire, along with Sir Ralph Radcliffe, sheriff of Lancashire, to take a special oath of loyalty, to inform him immediately of any slanders against him, to resist with all their power any rebellion, and to quit the realm rather than assent to anything to the dishonour of the king or realm.[103] For surety he took to Ireland the sons and heirs of Thomas of Woodstock and Henry of Bolingbroke. He likewise carried to Ireland, without the consent of the community of the realm, the crowns and regalia of England as well as other treasures and relics normally kept safely at Westminster.[104]

The rumour-mill ran riot. It was alleged that Richard had required many churchmen to accompany him so that he could form a parliament. The 'blank charters' might then be used to secure acquiescence in its decisions. It was rumoured that the sale of Calais was under negotiation, and that Richard was planning to crown the duke of Surrey as king of Ireland.[105] It was said that Richard would never again regard England with favour, but would remain in Ireland or Wales expending and wasting English resources from these places. Any lord who opposed the king's plans or in whom the people had confidence would be summoned to Dublin or elsewhere and be attainted. The earl of Wiltshire would take all escheats to farm for three years. Any lord who was not in the king's company and favour was safe neither 'in substance nor in life' as there was always someone poorer eager to make false accusations, 'while tyrants ruled'.[106] It is easy to dismiss the rumours as preposterous. The problem was that Richard's actions over the previous two years made some of them appear all too credible.

★ ★ ★

Richard's ships setting sail for Ireland. (The British Library, Harl. 1319)

The king set sail for Ireland around 29 May, the feast of Corpus Christi, and probably arrived at Waterford on Sunday 1 June.[107] Thenceforward Jean Creton, the French squire who had crossed to England seeking adventure a month earlier, is the only guide to the king's activities in Ireland. Though his account is somewhat problematic, not least in its chronology, it is none the less full of interesting circumstantial detail. He records coming in sight of the Tower of Waterford, and the wretched Irish porters, dressed in rags, wading in the water to their waists to unload the ships, and the welcome accorded by the merchant community. He relates that the king made Kilkenny his headquarters, pausing in the hope that Albemarle would bring up the rest of the army.[108] The royal host set out on the vigil of St John the Baptist, that is 23 June. They advanced directly against MacMurrough, seeking out their quarry in the woods and 'haulx deserts'. They sought to smoke out the Irish by setting fires which consumed forest and settlement alike. In the mean time the king's host established a base camp, raising tents adorned with standards and pennons. Richard knighted Henry of Monmouth, Bolingbroke's son, and eight or ten other young noblemen.[109]

Creton likewise provides some insight into the mood of the royal host. At first the prospects looked bright. The expeditionary force under the duke of Surrey had made some progress, perhaps largely under the direction of the redoubtable Janico Dartasso.[110] The king may have felt that Ireland lay open to conquest. A number of Irish chieftains, including MacMurrough's uncle, came into camp, with halters round their necks, 'naked and barefoot, like criminals ready to be put to death', and threw themselves on the king's mercy. Richard may have written exuberantly back to England about the imminent subjection of the Irish. According to Walsingham, Richard, by crushing the Irish, 'became great in his own eyes'.[111] Despite the bravura, though, Creton felt some unease. He wrote that 'melancholy, uneasiness, and care' chose 'my heart for their abode', and he could not explain why.[112] His record of his feelings were perhaps coloured by hindsight. Albemarle's failure to make a rendezvous was seen as ominous in retrospect. Yet he may well have been picking up on the anxieties of the king and others in the royal host.

The expedition was in any case proving less than glorious. Deep in enemy territory, the king's position was far from enviable. MacMurrough remained defiant, and was able to harry the English in guerrilla-style operations. The king's army, which had laid waste the land around it, was running perilously short of provisions. According to Creton, there were many knights and squires 'who did not eat a morsel for five days together'. The king had no option but to return to the coast to seek supplies. There was an unseemly riot as the famished soldiers scrambled to gorge themselves on the food and wine brought down from Dublin.[113] Fortunately MacMurrough indicated his readiness to discuss terms. Amid much fanfare the earl of Gloucester set out to parley with him in a secluded glen. MacMurrough was unwilling to offer satisfaction for the earl of March's death and other crimes, and no agreement was achieved. On hearing the outcome, the king 'grew pale with anger' and swore 'in great wrath by St Edward, that, no, never would he depart from Ireland, till, alive or dead, he had him in his power'.[114]

Richard now proceeded to Dublin, and was soon joined by Albemarle with a well-equipped force. He continued to dispatch forces against MacMurrough, and put a bounty of 100 marks on his head. According to Creton, the king remained in the city, well provisioned, for a fortnight, but this time-frame is overly generous. If the king's offensive began only on 23 June, the king can scarcely have been in Dublin before the beginning of July. By the middle of month Richard must have begun to receive reports of Henry of Bolingbroke's return to England. By 17 July the arduous process of finding shipping to take the royal host back across the Irish Sea had begun in earnest.[115]

★ ★ ★

Henry of Bolingbroke had spent his life waiting. The eldest son of John of Gaunt, he was born in April 1366, making him almost a year senior to Richard.[116] Edward III's entail of the crown indicates some measure of agreement within the royal family that in the event of Richard's death without issue the house of Lancaster would succeed. In 1387 Henry had joined Gloucester, Arundel and Warwick in the attack on the court party, and in the winter of 1387/8 may have been primarily concerned to safeguard his own position in the line of succession. From 1389 Gaunt probably lived in hope that Richard would designate either himself or his son as heir to the throne. Bolingbroke seems not to have felt entirely secure in his relationship with Richard. In the early 1390s he sought opportunities to absent himself from the kingdom, and to seek honourable employment elsewhere. To add to the difficulties of his position, he may have become the focus of the hopes of sections of the community disaffected with the Ricardian regime. In autumn 1397 he did not join the king's friends in the appeal of treason against Gloucester, Arundel and Warwick, though he did join in Arundel's prosecution. He was created duke of Hereford, but received few other rewards. While he professed to disbelieve Mowbray's allegations in December 1397, he must have been all too aware of the parlousness of his position.

Henry may have accepted his exile with some equanimity. It allowed him to retire with some honour from the royal court and the kingdom, but saved his rights as a prince of the blood and heir to the duchy of Lancaster. He saw opportunities to advance his standing through military service in Europe, alliances with French noblemen, and perhaps a new marriage. At first he was well received in Paris, where he established himself at the Hôtel de Clisson. He soon found that the king's animus followed him abroad. Negotiations for a marriage with the daughter of Jean, duke of Berry, were broken off on account of pressure from England. The French court joined him mourning Gaunt's death, but when news arrived that he was to be denied his patrimony and banished for life, he found it impossible to shake off the taint of treason.

The stages by which Henry resolved upon and planned a descent on England are uncertain. He was in regular contact with members of the Lancastrian affinity and well-wishers in England. Even as he learnt of the king's decision to banish him for life, Sir William Bagot was exhorting him to look to his interests.[117] His half-brother John Beaufort, marquis of Dorset, likewise perhaps encouraged him to challenge for his rights. At some stage Henry made contact with Henry Percy, earl of Northumberland, and Ralph Neville, earl of Westmorland. Both lords joined him in arms soon after his landing. Their motivation is a little hard to establish. They may have resented the advancement of the king's favourites to positions of influence in the northern marches.[118] They doubtless felt solidarity with a nobleman who had been unjustly disinherited. Westmorland was Bolingbroke's brother-in-law. Northumberland, who had considerable experience in government, may have made his stand on principle. According to Froissart, he was openly expressing his disaffection with Richard early in 1399. There is more than a hint of an association between Northumberland and the northern hermit who during Lent rebuked Archbishop Walden and the king.[119] Still, throwing their lot in with Henry was a massive gamble for the two northern lords. It is some indication of the mounting hostility to Richard's regime.

Of critical importance to the enterprise was Henry's alliance with Archbishop Arundel, and his nephew Thomas FitzAlan, the son of the earl of Arundel. The archbishop had preceded Henry into exile. Early in 1398 he visited Rome and Florence, winning the friendship of the humanist scholar Coluccio Salutati, chancellor of Florence.[120] He later took up residence at Utrecht, where he was joined by his nephew who escaped from the duke of Exeter's custody at Reigate castle.[121] As fellow-exiles, the FitzAlans and Henry might have appeared natural allies. Yet the FitzAlans had little cause to love the house of Lancaster. Gaunt and the earl of Arundel had quarrelled bitterly in 1394, and both Gaunt and Bolingbroke had hounded him in parliament in 1397. It was related that on the night he died at Leicester, Gaunt appeared before Archbishop Arundel in his chamber at Utrecht, his spirit in torment on account of the injustice he had done to the Arundels. The archbishop called on God to forgive him, remit his sins and give him peace, and promised to celebrate masses and pray for him.[122] The tale may indicate that it was not until after Gaunt's death that the exiles made

Archbishop Arundel visits Bolingbroke in France. (The British Library, Harl. 4380, fol. 170)

common cause. The alliance between the heirs of the earl of Arundel and the duke of Lancaster, once forged, was a formidable one. Above all, Archbishop Arundel, a former chancellor of the realm and primate of England, was able to add administrative weight and moral force to the insurgency.

In planning his descent on England, Henry could expect no assistance from the French court. Charles VI had cause to be disappointed in Richard, but he and the duke of Burgundy placed a high premium on the truce and the alliance with England. They were unlikely to support Henry in his designs, and might even seek to detain him. It was fortunate for Henry that the plague kept Burgundy away from Paris over the summer, and left the field free for the intrigues of the duke of Orléans. Over the spring Orléans and Henry became close. In May the duchess of Orléans presented Henry with a gold buckle set with rubies, pearls and a sapphire.[123] On 17 June Orléans and Henry,

Bolingbroke takes leave of the king of France. (The British Library, Harl. 4380, fol. 172b)

styling himself duke of Lancaster, entered into a formal treaty of friendship, promising to assist each other, saving their allegiances to the kings of France and England.[124] It was a reckless act on the Frenchman's part. Henry was about to depart for England, and Orléans must have encouraged his enterprise. He may even have offered assistance.[125] Of course, it does not follow that he countenanced Richard's deposition. In the aftermath of the revolution, Orléans was loud in denouncing Henry's bad faith, though Henry was equally firm in alleging Orléans's complicity.[126]

According to the monk of St Denis, Henry acted without the knowledge of the French court. When he took his leave he professed to be going to Spain. Instead he headed for Boulogne, whither his English allies had gathered ships for his transport. The monk, however, is a little disingenuous. He cannot resist reporting that, on the advice of the duke of Berry, Henry visited the abbey of St Denis prior to his departure. The abbot, who seems to have been all too aware of Henry's real destination, raised with him his concern that their priory at Deerhurst in Gloucestershire had been given over to lay hands. Henry promised to assist in the matter, and indeed, as the monk reports, he was as good as his word.[127] A great deal of the obscurity about the descent on England is attributable to Henry's concern to retain the element of surprise, and not to embarrass his hosts. Froissart's account of Henry's going to the duke of Brittany and securing support for the expedition may derive from a piece of deliberate misinformation.[128] It must be remembered, too, that the French accounts of the event are coloured by a concern to deny French complicity not so much in Henry's return to seek his inheritance but in his subsequent seizure of the crown.

★ ★ ★

Henry moved with considerable speed. He was still in Paris with the duke of Orléans on 17 June, but within a week he must have been embarking from Boulogne. By the 28th the duke of York had received intelligence of the assembly of enemy forces in Picardy, some of whom were about to attack Calais and some about to invade the country. Crossing the Channel, Henry's ships touched the southern coast at a number of points, perhaps deliberately seeking to throw the keeper of the realm and the council off their guard. A small company may have been put ashore to establish a beach-head at Pevensey, where Sir John Pelham now garrisoned the castle in Henry's name.[129] Either by prior plan, or by virtue of the prevailing winds, the ships headed northwards, perhaps probing the defences along the East Anglian coastline. In a number of parts of England members of the Lancastrian affinity may have begun to mobilize. Dunstanburgh castle on the Northumbrian coast was held for Henry from 1 July, while Kenilworth castle in the West Midlands appears to have been taken by Henry's agents on 2 July.[130]

Henry made landfall on the northern mouth of the Humber near Ravenspur around 4 July.[131] A hermitage was established on the site, and a large stone cross was raised to commemorate the landfall.[132] His company was very small, perhaps no more than a hundred or so strong.[133] The only men of name were Archbishop Arundel, the young earl of Arundel, and a dozen or so knights and squires, including Sir Thomas Erpingham, Sir Thomas Rempston and John Norbury. While Henry's arrival was allegedly marked by a miracle at the tomb of St John of Beverley, he seems to have been refused admittance to Hull.[134] It is significant that Henry decided to head northwards to the Lancastrian stronghold at Pickering rather than strike boldly westwards. He needed a secure base from which to rally his forces and to make contact with his northern allies. He went by way of Bridlington, perhaps by ship, visiting the shrine of St John of Bridlington.[135] The honour of Pickering had been granted to the earl of Wiltshire, but his officers surrendered the castle readily enough. Henry remained there for two days, recuperating, and then crossed the Vale of York to Knaresborough castle, whose surrender he secured, with a little more difficulty, around 9 July.[136]

Henry now advanced boldly south to Pontefract. He had chosen Pontefract, a Lancastrian stronghold athwart the Great North Road, as a meeting-point for the men from the 'north parts' of the duchy of Lancaster. The massive capacity of the Lancastrian military and political machine under John of Gaunt was well enough known. In the summer of 1399 the issue was whether it could be effectively mobilized by his son. At Pontefract, the cult centre of Thomas of Lancaster, Henry had his answer. The Lancastrian machine was delivering. Soon after his arrival Henry had been joined by Robert Waterton with several hundred men from the forest of Knaresborough. At Pontefract, according to the Kirkstall chronicler, 'a great multitude of knights and squires came to him'. They came from Lancashire, Staffordshire, Derbyshire and Lincolnshire as well as Yorkshire. 'Some came of their own volition,' the Kirkstall chronicler adds, 'and some by fear of future events.'[137]

In the mean time Henry was in touch with a wider circle of allies and well-wishers. He may have met Northumberland and his son and namesake, better known as Harry 'Hotspur', at Bridlington.[138] He must certainly have been in touch with Northumberland, Westmorland and other northern lords, as he crossed north Yorkshire. There is some evidence that at Knaresborough he made contact with Archbishop Scrope of York.[139] Doncaster was the rendezvous for this wider coalition. The earls of Northumberland and Westmorland, William, Lord Willoughby, Ralph, Lord Greystoke, and William, Lord Roos, all now brought in their retinues. Harry 'Hotspur', reputedly 'the best knight in England', was especially prominent in Henry's host.[140] According to the Kirkstall chronicle, Henry had some 30,000 stout men under his command at Doncaster.[141]

How Henry presented his cause at this stage is a matter of considerable interest. It was claimed by the Percies that he had sworn oaths to them at Bridlington and Doncaster that he sought only his inheritance and had no designs on the crown.[142] There is little reason to doubt that Henry swore oaths of this sort, and he may well have sworn them in good conscience. Yet it would be absurd to think that the men in rebellion with him were risking their lives simply to restore the duchy of Lancaster to its rightful heir. The presence of the dispossessed Archbishop Arundel and the disinherited earl of Arundel made it abundantly clear that the movement had wider aims. There is reference to a further oath, sworn at Knaresborough, in which Henry promised that the church and people would be free of tenths and other imposts during his lifetime.[143] In any case it appears that the oath sworn at the Carmelite friary at Doncaster went beyond Henry's private cause. According to Harding's chronicle, Henry swore to put the king 'in governance', to reform his household, to dismiss the Cheshire men, and limit taxation to what was deemed necessary by parliament.[144] Archbishop Scrope's manifesto likewise indicates that Henry offered himself more generally as a champion of justice and liberties.[145] In October 1399 he was hailed as a new Maccabeus, the biblical freedom-fighter.[146] Interestingly, in a letter written to Henry in 1403, Northumberland calls himself Mattathias, presenting himself as a sort of father-figure to the new king.[147]

Henry and Archbishop Arundel sent out large numbers of letters to individuals and corporations.[148] The bursar of Selby abbey recorded a payment to Thomas Wright of Rothwell who brought a letter from Henry of Lancaster at this time.[149] Regrettably not a single letter seems to have survived in any archive. The author of *Traison et Mort* reports that Henry's letters were full of 'artful fabrications'. Thus he wrote to various lords that Richard had made a secret treaty with France to surrender Calais and other bases in return for a large annual pension. In a letter to the city of London he allegedly claimed that Richard plotted to 'domineer more greatly and mightily, over the kingdom of England than any of his predecessors had done', and that he planned to strike down all who opposed him, and impose whatever taxes pleased him.[150] Henry doubtless saw advantages in scaremongering, but it is doubtful if his letters were so specific. In all likelihood the French chronicler has larded pithy statements about Richard's misrule with tavern tittle-tattle. His key point is that the people were seduced into regarding Henry as their champion. Once it became known, he wrote, that Henry had arrived to save the realm 'there was no good mother's son who did not go to the duke and offer him both his services and his goods; and in less than six days he had so great a number of people, both of nobles and others, that they were innumerable'.[151] This is striking testimony, from a witness ill-disposed to Henry, to the popularity, however misguided, of Henry's movement.

★ ★ ★

Given Richard's absence in Ireland, a great deal hinged on the capacity and resolve of his agents in England, not least the enigmatic keeper of the realm, Edmund Langley, duke of York.[152] The government had timely intelligence of Henry's plans and took appropriate measures. At first they may have taken care to attend to the southern defences, and the author of *Traison et Mort* reports that York and the marquis of Dorset initially set out towards the West Country. They each led 100 men-at-arms and 200 archers.[153] The decision of 28 June to order a general muster at Ware in Hertfordshire may indicate that a more northerly landing was anticipated.[154] As news arrived of the activities of Lancastrian agents, it must have been hard for York and his council to discern Henry's overall strategy. On 3 July it was learned that Pevensey castle, a potential beach-head on the southern coast, was in rebel hands. York appointed Lord Poynings and others to join the sheriff of Sussex in recapturing it.[155] By the 4th the full dimensions of the crisis must have been apparent. A messenger was paid to go to the king in Ireland, and letters were sent to the northern prelates and the earls of Northumberland and Westmorland to make proclamations on the king's behalf.[156]

A few days later York and the members of the privy council moved to St Albans. Mobilization was now well advanced. The energetic response of Bishop Despenser of Norwich, the earl of Suffolk and Sir William Elmham may have served to contain Lancastrian recruitment in East Anglia. Among the men assembling at Ware were Lord Ferrers of Chartley with ten men-at-arms and fifty archers, and some ten sheriffs with an average of a hundred men each. Altogether, York succeeded in raising a large force, though probably less than the 16,000 claimed by the Crowland chronicler.[157] Over 3,000 men claimed wages for their service, but the records reveal that some of them served only for a few days, and many had returned to their homes prior to York's meeting with Henry.[158]

On 7 July York instructed the sheriff of Nottingham to safeguard Nottingham castle.[159] The focus had now shifted decidedly to the north, and reports of the landing at Ravenspur would soon be spreading south. On the 8th Bishop Fordham of Ely issued orders for prayers for peace and tranquillity in the realm.[160] On the 10th York instructed the lords responsible for watch and ward at Rockingham castle to make provision for its defence.[161] The abbot of Peterborough made shift to respond. On 15 July Brother Thomas Fannel, one squire and twenty archers, along with one of the abbot's wagons loaded with victuals, went to Rockingham to serve under William Burdon, lieutenant of Richard Sydrak, janitor of the castle.[162] There is no evidence that York used his influence in south Yorkshire to hinder the rebel advance.[163] It was at York's manor at Doncaster that a largely Lancastrian insurgency became a more broadly based rebellion.

Over the following week the news of Henry's arrival and some of his propaganda spread through southern England. London seems to have been restive, and York felt it necessary on 18 July to order the mayor of London to proclaim that no one should give, sell or hire armour or weapons to anyone other than true lieges of the king, who will stand with him against his enemies in defence of the realm.[164] On the 19th Bishop Wykeham of Winchester issued an indult which might well have been penned by Archbishop Arundel himself. He ordered prayers throughout his diocese that 'the Father of Mercies shall in his compassion lead the king and direct him in the ways of his commandments, and deign to keep the state of the church, the king, the kingdom and its nobles safe, prosperous and tranquil'.[165] It may still have been hard for Bolingbroke's letters to penetrate to the far south of England. Loyalist forces were still active in Sussex on the 25th, and Sir John Pelham, who was holding Pevensey for Bolingbroke, had only recently received communication from his 'dearest and best beloved of all his earthly lords' at Pontefract.[166]

After collecting the forces at Ware, York briefly moved north to Bedford, but then crossed westwards towards Oxford. Seeking to maintain lines of communication with the king in Ireland, Scrope, Bushy, Green, Bagot and Russell headed directly to Bristol. York was still at Oxford on 20 July.[167] Within a few days he was pulling back in the face of the rapid advance through the Midlands of the insurgent forces. York must have been aware that the regime was crumbling, and may already have resolved to throw in his lot with Henry. Adam Usk, who was probably based at Canterbury, records how quickly events moved. On receiving news of the return of the exiles, Archbishop Walden's servants moved quickly to secure their master's ill-gotten gains. Loading the household goods confiscated from Archbishop Arundel into six carts, they sought to hide them away in Saltwood castle. The marquis of Dorset, whose loyalty to the new regime was clearly in doubt, intervened to keep them safe for Arundel.[168] Adam Usk himself was soon making his way to Bristol to join his former master in the insurgency.

★　★　★

By the end of the second week of July Henry had crossed the Trent into the Midlands, his forces fanning out to secure adequate supplies and fodder for horses.[169] His course seems to have been set south-westwards to Bristol. His aim may have been to draw York away from London, and break his lines of communication with the king and the principality of Chester. This line of advance likewise allowed Henry to seek provisions and reinforcement in the Lancastrian lordships of the north Midlands. By 20 July he was at Leicester, a major centre of Lancastrian influence. Philip Repton, abbot of Leicester, had already rallied to his standard, and many local men followed his lead. On 23 July Henry's army advanced from Leicester to Coventry, and the next day arrived at Warwick. Perhaps with the assistance of men loyal to the Beauchamps, Henry's men removed the badges of the white hart and the white hind that the duke of Surrey had had carved on the castle gatehouse.[170] It may be that Henry stayed at the Lancastrian castle at Kenilworth, where Roger Smart had awaited his arrival with a small garrison.[171]

Henry's host continued to grow. There was large-scale mobilization in the Midlands. Even in the royal borough of Nottingham ordinary townsmen were caught up in the enthusiasm. John Ward, barber, and two other men with cases pending in the borough court in August were certified as being in the service of the duke of Lancaster for the 'general utility of the king and kingdom'.[172] In towns like Leicester, with its strong Lancastrian associations, and Warwick, where the townsfolk looked to a restoration of

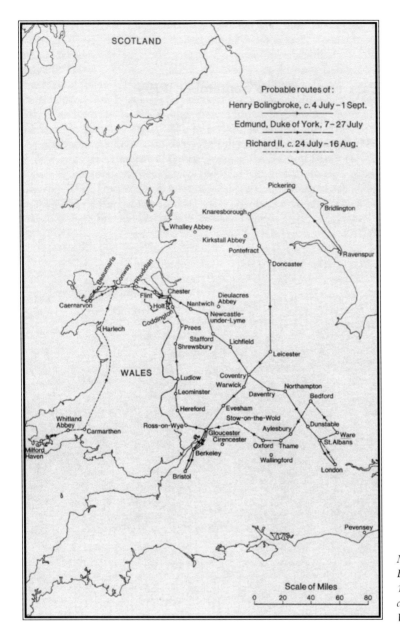

Map showing Henry of Bolingbroke's movements in 1399. (Reproduced by courtesy of Chris Given-Wilson)

the Beauchamps, it is easy to imagine large numbers of ordinary people rising on Henry's behalf. According to Adam Usk, Henry raised some 100,000 men, and this figure may not be too far off the mark at the height of the mobilization at Bristol.[173] The sheer scale of the movement threatened to prove an embarrassment. The author of *Traison et Mort* claims that so vast was his army that 'he was obliged to dismiss the greater part, for his people could not find them means of subsistence'.[174] After Richard's surrender, Henry twice made reference, in orders sent to the sheriffs and justices of the peace, to the large numbers of people rallying to him, and the chaos that had ensued.[175]

Above all, of course, it is the chronicles and the literary sources which present a picture of a triumphal progress. Henry was a popular figure, and he had plenty of well-wishers. More striking is the manner in which he was presented as the champion of the people and the saviour of the realm. A number of writers busily reworked ancient prophecies to see him as the eaglet of whom Merlin spoke, or the greyhound that featured in the prophecies of John of Bridlington. The latter allusion gave rise to a striking image that neither Adam Usk nor the author of *Richard the Redeless* felt able to resist. Henry was the greyhound who put to flight all the harts, the men who wore Richard's livery of the white hart.[176] Of course, Usk and the anonymous poet may be regarded as hostile to Richard. Yet each proved critics of Henry, too. What is significant is that in their criticisms of Henry IV, they explicitly attest to the high hopes vested in him at the time of his arrival. In a letter of admonition to the new king, and included by Usk in his narrative in 1401, it was stated that in 1399 all the people were clapping their hands and praising God, 'crying out to heaven for you, their anointed king, as if you were a second Christ, "Blessed is he that cometh in the name of the Lord!", our king of England' in the hope of a happy reign.[177] In his manifesto against Henry IV, Archbishop Scrope likewise states that the people acclaimed him in this fashion. Jean Creton, another hostile witness, claims that Archbishop Arundel rallied the people by preaching indulgences to all who joined the host.[178]

From Kenilworth Henry skirted the Cotswolds to Berkeley, where on 27 July he met his uncle, the duke of York, before the high altar in the church. According to Walsingham, York had already expressed his belief that his nephew's cause was just.[179] He neither wished, nor had the military capacity, to resist him. It is not known what Bolingbroke said about his aims. No one ever claimed that Bolingbroke swore an oath at Berkeley disclaiming any ambition other than the restoration of his inheritance. York knew that he as well as Bolingbroke had crossed their Rubicon. Bishop Despenser, Sir William Elmham, Sir Walter Burley, Lawrence Drew, John Golafre and other loyalists were arrested.[180] On the 28th the combined forces marched on Bristol, and demanded its surrender. Sir Peter Courtenay, the constable of Bristol castle, was a huge man, inordinately jealous of his honour, and one of the most distinguished knights of his generation. A king's knight, he might have been expected to hold firm. It was proclaimed that anyone who wished to depart would be allowed to do so unharmed. In response, many men poured out of the castle gate, and some even let themselves down by ropes from the windows.[181] After no more than a token show of resistance Courtenay surrendered the castle and handed over Richard's hated counsellors, Scrope, Bushy and Green, to Henry of Lancaster. Bagot had already crossed over to Ireland, while Russell, feigning madness, slipped away.[182]

★ ★ ★

Reports of the invasion threat presumably reached Richard in Ireland early in the first week of July, and news of Bolingbroke's landing presumably followed some time in the second week.[183] The king was in no position to make a rapid response. His forces, and the ships required for transport, still had to be assembled. An account of the expenses of John Lowick, receiver of the king's chamber, states that the king and his army left

Dublin on 17 July.[184] This statement may only indicate the beginnings of the movement of men and material from Dublin. Richard was still in Ireland when he resolved to send a force under the earl of Salisbury to Chester to secure the principality. Salisbury's commission as 'governor of the principality of Chester and of the part of North Wales' is dated 19 July.[185] Richard presumably had the option of crossing to Chester in advance of his main army but he seems to have chosen instead to marshal his forces at Waterford and cross to south Wales. According to Creton, Richard was delayed in Ireland by false counsel. Since Creton left Ireland in the company of Salisbury, his account of events after the 19th is necessarily second-hand. From his perspective, anxiously counting the days until the king's arrival at Conway, the delay must have seemed inordinate.[186] In fact Richard probably arrived in Milford Haven around the 24th.[187]

After landing, Richard's first priority would have been to establish contact with his council in England, to learn the news about Henry of Lancaster, and to marshal men and resources. Creton states that the duke of Albemarle was sent eastwards to raise troops. Thomas Despenser, earl of Gloucester, was likewise sent into Glamorgan to raise troops in his lordship, while there was some mobilization in the lordship of Usk.[188] On 29 July the king's agents made contact at Whiteland abbey with a clerk sent from Westminster. Richard Maudeleyn, the king's clerk and royal favourite, and John Serle, a valet of the chamber, received from him 1,000 marks for the king's use.[189] The tidings he brought cannot have been good. By the 30th Richard, who may have been based at Lawaden castle near Carmarthen,[190] must have learned that Bolingbroke was making himself master of the kingdom, and that the duke of York had all but capitulated.

Even before he learnt of the fall of Bristol, Richard took the fateful decision to leave his army and ride across Wales to join the earl of Salisbury at Chester. In a sense he was adopting the course that he might have taken almost a fortnight earlier. In Dublin, though, he had no means of knowing how rapidly his position in England would deteriorate. It would then have seemed sound strategy to mass his forces in south Wales for an advance into southern England. Henry's rapid advance towards the Severn, and his imminent capture of Bristol, made the king's position in south Wales hopeless. His only option was to put himself at the head of the army that Salisbury had raised at Chester as soon as possible. Leaving his forces in south Wales under the command of the duke of Albemarle and the earl of Worcester, he set out at night in great haste with a small company, including the dukes of Exeter and Surrey, the earl of Gloucester, the bishops of St David's, Carlisle and Lincoln, a number of other knights and clerks, and some of the Cheshire guardsmen. Fearing capture, Richard allegedly disguised himself as a Franciscan friar.[191]

It took several days for Richard and his company to cross Wales. They presumably followed the coast as far as Harlech, where they may have spent a night.[192] According to Creton, they arrived at Conway at day-break.[193] They were met by the earl of Salisbury, but the reunion was far from joyous.[194] Salisbury told Richard that he had raised some 40,000 men from Cheshire and Wales, and had kept them in the field for a fortnight.[195] Alarmed by the king's absence and news of Bolingbroke's progress, the men had begun to desert, some returning to their homes, others joining the rebellion.[196] Richard had relinquished one army to find that he had already lost the other. He may have instructed Albemarle and Worcester to marshal the forces in south Wales and then lead them north. If he did so, it cannot have been with much optimism. His precipitate departure was bound to destroy what was left of the army's morale. According to Creton, Albemarle and Worcester proved faithless, and disbanded the army. The men deserted taking with them the king's belongings, including 'robes, jewels, fine gold, and pure silver, many a good horse of foreign breed, many a rich and sparkling precious stone, many a good mantle, and whole ermine, good cloth of gold, and stuff of foreign pattern'.[197]

The capture of Bristol marked a new stage in the insurgency. From the outset the rebellion had aims broader than the restoration of the duchy of Lancaster to its rightful heir. It sought the reinstatement of Archbishop Arundel to Canterbury and his nephew to the earldom of Arundel. The destruction of Richard's insignia at Warwick castle signalled a readiness to champion other lords who had suffered injustice. The capitulation of the keeper of the realm at Berkeley implied some transfer of the 'rule' of England to Henry and his colleagues. At Bristol another step was taken. Scrope, Bushy and Green were summarily tried and executed as traitors. Some store was placed on Henry's status as steward of England. According to traditions, some in writing, dating back to the early fourteenth century, the steward had the responsibility and power to act for the security of the realm, even against the king himself. The rhetoric of reform, justice and the public good had already been heard. According to the continuator of the *Eulogium Historiarum*, Henry wrote to the Londoners professing his resolve to restore the realm to due governance and its former liberty.[198] The rhetoric was now translated into action. Richard's chief counsellors were to be treated as traitors. Forfeitures were anticipated. On 31 July Henry promised to grant John Norbury the goods, in the event of their being declared forfeit, of John Lowick, a Ricardian clerk.[199] There were fewer confiscations in 1399 than might have been anticipated. While Henry did not claim England by right of conquest, he did seize Scrope's kingdom of Man, granting it to his chief supporter, the earl of Northumberland.

Henry and his confederates did not linger in Bristol. Crossing the Severn at Gloucester, they advanced to Ross-on-Wye, doubtless moving quickly to block any loyalist probes into the southern marcher lordships. According to Adam

The south prospect of part of Bristol Castle. From S. Seyer, Memoirs Historical and Topographical of Bristol and its Neighborhood *(Bristol 1821)*.

Usk, Richard's niece Lady Charlton sought to organize some resistance in the lordship of Usk, and Usk himself played a key role in persuading the men to return to their homes and in the recruitment of Sir Edward Charlton into Henry's service.[200] The rebel host advanced northwards rapidly. On 2 August Henry reached Hereford, where he was joined by the bishop of Hereford and Sir Edmund Mortimer.[201] In a clear usurpation of royal authority he granted Northumberland, under the duchy of Lancaster seal, the wardenship of the West March.[202] He spent the night of the 2nd in the bishop's palace, the night of the 3rd at Leominster priory, and the night of the 4th at Ludlow castle, where there was liberal consumption of the king's wine.[203] The next day he pressed on to Shrewsbury, where he paused for a couple of days marshalling his forces and perhaps waiting on intelligence of the king's movements before the final assault on Richard's principality of Chester.

At Shrewsbury, around 5 or 6 August, Henry learned of the disintegration of the king's forces in south Wales. Large numbers of men had straggled back through central Wales, some laden with booty from the king's wagons. In the winding and narrow ravines, they were fair game for local bandits. According to Creton, the Welsh 'pitied the very great wrong and outrage that the English did to the king' and constantly harried them, divesting them of their ill-gotten gains. Several hundred were stripped of their goods, and sent to Henry of Lancaster in their doublets, with nothing but a staff in their hands, and nothing on their feet.[204] Even noblemen suffered in this fashion. Lords Scales and Bardolf, who had been robbed while crossing Wales, submitted to Henry at Shrewsbury.[205] The most remarkable defector was Richard's greyhound. According to Adam Usk, the dog had found its way to Richard after the death of its first master, Richard's half-brother the earl of Kent, and for two years it had been Richard's constant companion, ever at his side, stern and lion-like. After Richard's abandonment of his army in south Wales, the dog made its own way from Carmarthen to Shrewsbury. As Usk watched, it found Henry in the abbey and 'crouched obediently' before him 'with a look of the purest pleasure on his face'. Needless to say, when the greyhound was subsequently brought to the captive Richard, it no longer recognized him.[206]

Henry's rapid advance northwards from Bristol convinced the Cheshire men that resistance was useless. They had good cause for apprehension. The king's invidious favour and their own depredations had made them prime targets of the insurgents. As the earl of Salisbury withdrew to Conway, the principality prepared itself for the storm, with leading Ricardians finding bolt-holes and everyone hiding their valuables. A group of county notables met together and decided to sue for terms. On 5 August a delegation was sent to Shrewsbury. It was headed by Sir Robert Legh, sheriff of Cheshire, who had sworn a special oath of loyalty at Cardiff little more than two months earlier. The inner citadel of Ricardian power capitulated without a fight.[207] For his part, Henry proclaimed that the men of Cheshire should be spared, prompting some of his men, denied the prospect of booty, to return to their homes.[208]

On 9 August Henry advanced on Chester, and drew up his forces in warlike array before the walls. The monks of St Werburgh's processed out to meet him, and he entered the city in triumph. Establishing himself at Chester castle, well stocked with Richard's wines, he immediately dispatched forces to take Holt, the king's regional treasury. According to Creton, it was defended by a hundred men and was well able to withstand a long siege. None the less the castle was given up without a fight, and all the treasure, arms and provisions fell into the hands of the rebels.[209] In the mean time, notwithstanding the proclamation, Cheshire was plundered. According to the Dieulacres chronicle, Henry's captains cried 'havoc' and the county was subject to systematic pillage.[210] Even Adam Usk acknowledged the devastation. When he visited Coddington church, hoping to celebrate mass, he 'found nothing there except doors and chests broken open, and everything carried off'. During the next fortnight the insurgents wasted fields, destroyed houses and seized whatever they needed 'no matter where they were found or to whom they belonged'.[211] Henry ordered another execution, seemingly without any trial. Peter Legh of Lyme, one of the king's Cheshire favourites, was beheaded, and his head was set on a stake by the east gate of the city.[212]

★ ★ ★

At Conway Richard was stunned by mounting evidence of treachery and the success of his enemies. Once news arrived of the disbandment of his forces in south Wales, he had no capacity to resist. Unwilling to contemplate flight, he decided to send the duke of Exeter to negotiate with the rebels. The plan was to remind Henry that he had been banished with his father's consent, to urge him to 'take pattern from his father' who was never disloyal 'and hated falsehood', and to indicate the king's readiness to restore his inheritance provided that he sued for pardon. Exeter set off, accompanied by the duke of Surrey, on what proved a hopeless errand.[213] When they arrived at Chester, they were assumed to have come to make their submission. By this stage, it would seem, Albemarle and Worcester had joined the insurgents.[214] Henry listened in silence as Exeter delivered his message, and then insisted that he remain with him. Surrey was likewise taken into custody.[215]

After the departure of the emissaries, Richard and his companions withdrew westwards to Beaumaris and Caernarvon. The castles were not furnished, and the party lay on straw at night. After a few nights, lack of victuals and the other privations prompted them to return to Conway. According to Creton, the king bewailed his fate and cursed 'the hour and the day that ever he had crossed the salt sea into Ireland'. He prayed to the Virgin Mary and God, and expressed the hope that the king of France and other kings would for shame seek to avenge him.[216] He seems to have considered flight overseas. Such a move, though, would have been regarded as tantamount to abdication. In any case Richard believed that he could outwit his opponents.

It was Henry who would control the end-game. Northumberland was sent to Conway to bring Richard in 'by truce or by force'.[217] On the way he secured the surrender of Flint and Rhuddlan castles.[218] Concealing most of his men in a valley, he approached Conway with a small retinue.[219] Northumberland offered Richard Henry's terms. According to Creton, Richard would be governed by the advice of a parliament convened in his name by Henry acting as 'chief judge' of England, and that five named individuals – Exeter, Surrey, Salisbury, the bishop of Carlisle and Maudeleyn – would be committed for trial for treason.[220] The Dieulacres chronicle is more terse, but confirms the key points. The king would present himself without fear and of his own free will before Henry as hereditary steward of England and the estates of the realm.[221]

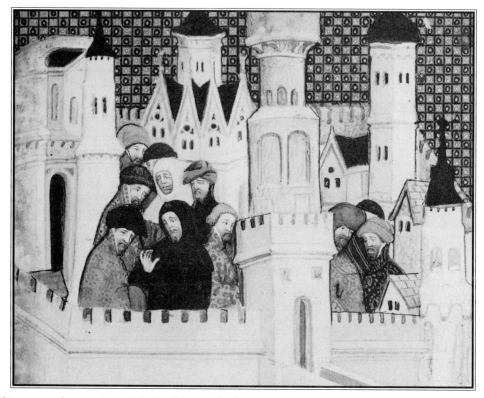

This sequence of pictures shows Richard and the earl of Salisbury at Conway; the dukes of Exeter and Surrey setting off to treat with Henry at Chester; Henry receiving Exeter and Surrey at Chester; and Richard receiving the earl of Northumberland at Conway. (The British Library, Harl. 1319, Illuminations VIII–XI)

The terms were anathema to the king. If accepted, they would have destroyed all that he had achieved in the past decade. He asked Northumberland to withdraw while he took counsel. According to Creton, he declared that he would surely put Henry 'to a bitter death for the outrage and injury that he hath done unto us'. He assured his companions that there would be no parliament because it would be bound to be vindictive against them. What he proposed was a call to arms in Wales. After meeting Henry he would slip away and put himself at the head of the army. He believed that many men, 'sorry at heart for the wrong that they have done unto me', would rally to his cause. 'God, if we trust in him, will aid us.' His opponents, once defeated, would be put to death. 'There are some of them,' he added, 'whom I will flay alive.'[222]

Richard recalled Northumberland and asked him to swear an oath as to the good faith of the terms offered.[223] Once the oath had been taken, Richard agreed to accompany him to Henry. Creton concluded sorrowfully that 'the one had bad intentions, and the other still worse', but felt that the king was less blameworthy in that 'necessity hath no law' and he did not actually make any oath.[224] Setting out from Conway, the king found the size of Northumberland's company ominous, reproved him for acting dishonourably, and declared his wish to return. Northumberland claimed that the large company was necessary considering the state of the country, and insisted that Richard come with him.[225] The party dined at Rhuddlan, and then rode on to Flint. Richard was mortified

This sequence of pictures shows the earl of Northumberland taking an oath to Richard; Richard betrayed by Northumberland; and Richard's meeting with Henry at Flint. (The British Library, Harl. 1319, Illuminations XII–XIV)

to find the castle garrisoned by his enemies, claiming that he had been delivered 'into the hands of wolves'.[226]

From Flint Northumberland sent a messenger to Chester.[227] Henry was overjoyed to learn that the king was in custody, and immediately mustered his men and set out across the Dee.[228] According to Creton, who changed from verse to prose to record events more exactly, Henry came with a massive force, 'marching along the sea shore with great joy and satisfaction' and eager to take the king captive.[229] After hearing mass with his companions, Richard went up on the ramparts of the castle, saw Henry's forces gathering, and railed against Northumberland's perjury.[230] A company broke away from the host and rode up to the castle. Archbishop Arundel was in the van, and Richard would have been dismayed to see Albemarle and Worcester now among his enemies.[231] Richard received this advance party in the keep of the castle, speaking at length with Archbishop Arundel. Creton did not know what was said except that Salisbury had told him that the prelate had comforted the king, and assured him 'that no harm should happen to his person'.[232] According to the continuator of the *Eulogium Historiarum*, the archbishop took the opportunity to upbraid the king for his false dealing and misgovernment.[233]

Henry now approached with a vast army. Creton claimed that he had never seen so many people. The host was 'estimated by many knights and squires at upwards of 100,000 men'. Henry intended to demonstrate not only his overweening military power but also the popular support for his cause. Creton identified the chief captain as Sir Henry Percy junior whom 'they hold to be the best knight in England'.[234] It was agreed that Henry would not enter the castle until after the king had dined. Richard had a last supper with his faithful companions. According to Creton, many men from the rebel host came to gawp at the king 'not for any good will that they bore him, but for the great thirst that they had to ruin him'. They put it abroad that his companions would all have their heads cut off, and the king himself might not escape with his life. When Henry entered the castle, he was 'armed at all points, except his basinet'.[235]

When the king came down to meet him, he bowed very low to the ground, and doffed his bonnet. Richard returned the compliment, and bade his 'fair cousin of Lancaster' welcome. Henry went straight to the point. He had returned to England because it was 'the common report of your people that you have for twenty-two years governed them very badly and very rigorously'. He offered to help Richard 'to govern them better than they have been governed in time past'. Richard answered: 'Fair cousin, since it pleaseth you, it pleaseth us well.' Creton stresses that these were the very words spoken. He heard and understood them very well, and Salisbury repeated them to him in French.[236] Henry made some acknowledgement of the king's companions, but ignored Salisbury, who was filled with dread 'for he saw plainly that the duke mortally hated him'. Henry then called out in a harsh tone, 'Bring out the king's horses.' They brought two poor specimens, one for the king and one for Salisbury. Around two in the afternoon, they set out for Chester.[237]

At Flint Richard, recognizing the hopelessness of his position, surrendered himself to Henry. There is no evidence to support the statement in the 'Record and Process' that he agreed to renounce the crown. It may well be that in public Henry continued to show Richard deference, and claim no more than justice for himself. In private it may

*Richard as Henry's captive.
(The British Library, Harl.
1319, Illuminations XV)*

well have been a different matter. In discussion Richard, Henry and Archbishop
Arundel must have explored a range of possible outcomes. Given his high view of the
kingly office and his rapidly narrowing options, Richard may have sought a solution that
did not involve the fettering of the English crown and a parliamentary bloodbath.
According to Walsingham, Richard expressed a willingness 'to relieve himself of the
burden of government' provided that he be treated honourably and the lives of his
companions spared.[238] It may well be that Richard agreed to renounce the rule of the
kingdom to Henry, and to name him as his heir.

Around 16 August Richard, 'the most excellent king of all the kings of the world',
was escorted back to Chester astride a nag.[239] All wondered at the remarkable
transformation in his fortune. Adam Usk likened Richard to Chosroes, king of the
Persians, 'who fell into the hands of Heraclius, and who at the height of his glory, was
cast down by the wheel of fortune'.[240] There were some who regarded it as the
workings of providence. Creton was accompanied on the road by a knight who told
him how both Merlin and Bede had prophesied 'the taking and ruin of the king', and
how it was written in a book he owned that there 'shall be a king in Albion, who shall
reign for the space of twenty or two and twenty years in great honour and in great
power, and shall be allied and united with those of Gaul; which king shall be undone in
the parts of the north in a triangular place'. The knight identified 'the triangular place'
as Conway because it was 'so laid down by a true and exact measurement' and because
that was where the king was undone.[241]

CHAPTER EIGHT

DEPOSITION

Over the summer of 1399 many people in the Christian world waited on events in England. The monk of St Denis in Paris recalled how the fiery comet in the western skies late in 1398 had been interpreted as a 'harbinger of revolutions' that would bring in its wake 'the horrors of war, rebellion and open treason'. In France there were well-founded concerns that the political crisis in England would bring to power men less disposed to the truce and the alliance. On their return to Paris, Sir William and Lady Courcy caused a great stir, blaming anti-French feeling for Lady Courcy's dismissal from Queen Isabelle's household.[1] The French court had sympathy and regard for Henry of Lancaster, and some princes may have wished him well in his bid to be restored to his inheritance. Learning of the ships assembled at Boulogne, however, the duke of Burgundy took measures to prevent the invasion. Over the following months, as people in France became more aware of the scale and ambition of the rebellion, the duke of Orléans was greatly reproved for his alliance with Henry. Philip of Burgundy posted agents around Calais ready to bring news of developments.[2] Rather recklessly, Master Pietro da Verona crossed to England in August, seeking to retrieve an expensively illuminated Bible which he had sent on commission to Richard. Learning that Richard was a captive, and that the kingdom was in disorder, he returned home, probably reporting on conditions to his main patron, the duke of Berry.[3]

Even as Richard crossed to Ireland, the high edifice of Ricardian kingship was visibly crumbling. The government records indicate a marked slackening of activity in late spring. The king seems to have been encountering a good deal of passive resistance to his policies. Monasteries found excuses not to accede to his requests for horses and wagons; clerical taxes went uncollected; and other orders were executed only slowly. The take-over of the duchy of Lancaster proved easier on paper than on the ground. A great deal of administrative energy was vested in the Irish expedition. Yet Richard was finding the 'yoke of the government of the English' burdensome. It is instructive that one of his few concerns related to the raising of funds for the emperor of Constantinople. In the spring Boniface IX had called for a crusade to relieve the eastern empire, and had offered indulgences to all who contributed to the fund. Collecting boxes were set up in churches in towns across England. Richard advanced 3,000 marks to the fund. On 22 June, in his last extant letter, he explained to the bishop of Chrysopolis how offerings from England would be accumulated in a special coffer in St Paul's in London. As disorder spread across the realm, the papal collector left the country. Accounting for the sums raised proved a financial and diplomatic embarrassment for Richard's successor.[4]

★ ★ ★

Around 16 August Henry's host entered Chester to great fanfare. According to Creton, the fickle populace showed Lancaster great reverence but jeered at the captive king. Richard was immediately lodged in a tower in the outer ward of the castle which he had so recently refurbished and adorned with his white hart badge.[5] Salisbury and the bishop of Carlisle were taken into separate custody. In the evening Henry dined in the great hall, instructing Archbishop Arundel to sit above him, and the dukes of Albemarle and Exeter and the earls of Westmorland, Northumberland and Worcester to sit, all at his table but at some distance below him. According to a continuation of the Brut chronicle, it was then that Worcester, the steward of the household, formally disbanded the king's household, breaking his rod of office, and bidding every man to do his best. In the morning Richard's attendants were replaced. Henry of Monmouth, Henry's son, left Richard with 'a sorrowful heart' for 'he loved him entirely'. Giving him leave to go to his father, Richard said, 'I know well there is one Henry shall do me much harm; and I suppose it is not thou.'[6] Creton states that 'thenceforth we could never see him, unless it were abroad on the journey: and we were forbidden to speak any more to him, or to any of the others'.[7]

Henry was doubtless relieved to find his eldest son well. Orders were sent to bring Humphrey, the duke of Gloucester's son, back from Ireland, and to set free the earl of Warwick. Even more pressing concerns were to secure Richard's treasure and the submission of any Ricardian loyalist still at large. Henry had already taken Holt, Richard's regional treasury. On the 16th he sent two squires to Trim castle in Ireland to take delivery of some £6,544 left in the charge of the duchess of Surrey.[8] He continued to receive the submissions of a number of lords and members of Richard's retinue. Sir John Stanley, Richard's controller of the wardrobe, joined Henry soon after his arrival at Chester. A Cheshire man, he played some role in settling the region, standing as surety for a number of former members of the Cheshire guard. On the 20th he entered a bond that Janico Dartasso, who had been released from close confinement, would not defect.[9] According to Creton, Dartasso was the last man to wear the king's livery, refusing even under the threat of death to remove his white hart badge.[10]

Henry began to rule England in Richard's name, with Archbishop Arundel serving as chancellor and the earls of Northumberland and Westmorland as his chief counsellors. On the 19th he sent out writs in Richard's name for a parliament to be held at Westminster on 30 September.[11] He presumably anticipated presiding over the assembly in his capacity as steward of England. A major task was to restore order to the country. The large-scale mobilization had inevitably brought dislocation and disorder in its wake. All the indications are that the insurgents had lived off the land, and taken the opportunity to settle scores along the way. On the 20th it was acknowledged that 'by colour' of rallying to the duke of Lancaster, who had 'entered the realm to amend the ruling and governing thereof', many crimes had been committed. The sheriffs were instructed to make a proclamation, on pain of death, against unlawful entries and unwarranted seizures of livestock and other goods.[12] Minds needed to be set at rest. Financial accounts reveal Lady Bardolf anxiously seeking news of her husband in Wales, and rewarding a servant of Lord Willoughby who brought word to her that he was with the duke of Lancaster at Chester.[13]

The major issue facing the realm could not be so readily resolved. From the evidence available, there appears to have been no further negotiation between Richard and his captors for over a month. Richard remained king, though a king seemingly now accorded minimal honour. From late July Henry and his colleagues had the 'rule' of the kingdom. Their actions needed to be put on a legal footing. Richard's 'voluntary' surrender to them was taken as their mandate to act in his name, at least until the meeting of parliament. Yet the events of the summer of 1399 seem to have galvanized the nation. It has been claimed that Richard's failure had more to do with his absence in Ireland than with any defects of his rule.[14] It may well be the case that if Richard had been in England Henry's insurgency could have been contained and defeated. Yet Richard had placed a massive strain on the loyalty of a large proportion of his subjects, and it is hard to escape the impression that Henry's insurrection was hugely popular. Many of the men who flocked to his banner must have done so in order to unseat Richard from the throne. The fact that Richard was still hounding the men who had been in arms against his counsellors twelve years earlier made any other settlement with him unthinkable. According to Creton, many people were declaring that Henry would be a worthier king. If Henry had indeed meant the oaths he had sworn, he would find them increasingly hard to honour.

The city of London may have taken the lead in anticipating the outcome. According to *Traison et Mort*, Henry wrote to London from Pontefract, and after the fall of Bristol he seems to have written to them again. The city-fathers had every ground for caution, but their caution should not be confused with contentment. Froissart, while overstating the role of the Londoners in the insurrection, is probably correct in his assumption that Richard was unpopular in the city. When the rumour swept through the city on 11 August that Richard had secretly entered the capital and taken refuge in Westminster abbey, the citizens threw caution to the winds. They rose in arms in what was termed a 'hurling'. At the abbey they found three of Richard's clerks, Archbishop Walden, Nicholas Slake and Ralph Selby, and took them into custody. Slake was committed to Ludgate.[15] Another week would pass before they heard that Richard was in captivity. Given the confusion of chroniclers with dates and places, it is worth noting that news of events at Conway, Flint and Chester would have probably arrived in the very same post. A decision must already have been taken to commit London to the new order. According to Adam Usk, three aldermen and fifty citizens of London came to Henry while he was still at Chester. They recommended their city to him, and, under their common seal, renounced their fealty to Richard.[16]

Henry led his company and the captive king out of Chester on 20 August. At Nantwich he appointed Sir Thomas Erpingham constable of Dover castle and warden of the Cinque Ports.[17] Before he crossed the Cheshire border, there was an incident at Cholmondeston involving some of Richard's former guardsmen.[18] According to Creton, the company was harried by Welshmen on the road as far as Coventry.[19] The journey itself reversed the regional direction of Richard's rule. At Newcastle under Lyme the recently released earl of Warwick joined the company.[20] The first major staging-post was Lichfield, where Richard had held splendid court over the past two Christmases. There was apparently an escape attempt. Richard let himself down at night from the tower where they had lodged him. He was thenceforward guarded by a dozen armed men.[21] According to Creton, who heard the tale from a number of knights and squires, the Londoners petitioned Henry at Lichfield to behead Richard, along with his companions, and bring him no further south. Henry declared that the honourable course was to bring him to London, and to have him judged in parliament.[22]

At each stage Richard was carried closer to his nemesis. After Coventry he was in decidedly enemy territory. The road took him through Daventry, Northampton and Dunstable to St Albans. Through all this time the king, who prided himself on his sartorial elegance, was not permitted to change his clothes.[23] Along the way Henry received expressions of support from a range of individuals and communities. From St Albans on 31 August he wrote to the mayor and community of Salisbury thanking them for letters brought recently by two burgesses indicating their wish 'to be loyal and truly obedient to us'.[24] A few miles from London Henry was met by the mayor and many citizens in their company liveries. They saluted the king first, but showed greater respect to Henry, shouting lustily 'Long live the good duke of Lancaster!' According to Creton, they marvelled at how he had conquered the kingdom in less than a month and praised God for the miracle. Some likened him to Alexander the Great, and claimed that he well deserved to be king.[25] Henry addressed the Londoners, and presented Richard to them. For Creton, he acted like Pontius Pilate in presenting Jesus Christ to the angry crowd of Jews. If Richard were put to death, Henry would hope to be able to say 'I am innocent of this deed.'[26]

Adam Usk likewise presents Henry as proceeding in triumph to London, 'having gloriously, within fifty days, conquered both king and kingdom'.[27] Entering the city of London on 1 September he received a rapturous reception. He made his way to St Paul's where, weeping, he prayed at his father's tomb. He spent a few nights at the bishop of London's palace before taking up residence outside the city at the Priory of St John of Jerusalem in Clerkenwell and at Hertford castle.[28] For Richard, it was his moment of greatest humiliation. The author of *Traison et Mort*, a sympathetic observer, records that he was led through the streets to the Tower of London in a condition that aroused some pity. One boy called out, 'Behold King Richard who has done so much good to the kingdom of England!' It may be that the French observer missed the tone of sarcasm. There could be no doubting the emotion behind the other cry he recorded: 'Now we are all well revenged of this wicked bastard who has governed us so ill!'[29]

It was in the bishop of London's palace that the new regime began to assume a more civilian character. Roger Walden hurried to make his peace with Henry and Archbishop Arundel. He promptly acknowledged Thomas Arundel as the true archbishop and made over to him the Cross of Canterbury, the visible symbol of his office. Walden's actions are the more remarkable in that, as Adam Usk observed, he was still in lawful possession of the see, while Arundel, who had yet to be restored by the pope, held office solely by dint of secular power. Arundel and his servants rapidly set about re-establishing themselves at Lambeth. The palace had been stripped of its ornaments, and Arundel's arms had been replaced by Walden's on all the upholstery. When Adam Usk dined at Lambeth on the Nativity of the Blessed Virgin, 8 September, he saw Walden's arms 'lying under the benches, a laughing-stock, and cast and flung out of window by the servants'.[30]

★ ★ ★

Archbishop Arundel preaching on behalf of Henry of Lancaster in 1399. (The British Library, Harl. 1319, fol. 12r)

In the weeks prior to the opening of parliament Henry, Archbishop Arundel and other key figures wrestled hard with the constitutional and political problems confronting them. Orderly rule was perhaps not an issue in the short term. Formally, Richard was still king, acting on the advice of the magnates to whom he had entrusted the government of the realm. Henry and Arundel clearly led the informal council. Arundel was England's most experienced administrator and senior churchman, and played a key role as acting chancellor in securing the orderly transfer of power.[31] Henry was the senior prince of the blood and, in many people's minds, heir presumptive. His position as steward of England provided some colour of constitutionality. It may have been especially valuable in his dealings with foreign princes like the king of Scotland with whom he seems to have been in correspondence from his first landing. His style remained, however, 'duke of Lancaster, earl of Derby and steward of England', with no special emphasis on the stewardship.[32]

Henry and his allies probably gave thought to formalizing existing arrangements through the establishment of a 'continual council'. Richard would remain king, and Henry would be given the sort of pre-eminence in the council that his father had assumed in 1390. Richard may have expressed a readiness to surrender to Henry the 'rule' of England. There were tactical advantages in his doing so. Yet the events of 1387 and 1397 would have made it all too evident to Henry and Archbishop Arundel that Richard did not regard oaths detracting from his own regality as binding. It was Creton, not some hostile English chronicler, who presents Richard assuring his friends that any concessions he made to Henry would be for show, and that when he was in a position to do so he would flay his enemies alive.[33] There was no option: Richard had to be removed. Henry had reached this conclusion by 10 September, when the use of Richard's regnal year is quietly dropped by Lancastrian clerks.

The problem was how Richard was to be removed. The allies in 1399 looked back to the precedents of 1326–7. The official line, established early in Edward III's reign, was that Edward II had abdicated in favour of his son.[34] In the autumn of 1399 there was some hope that Richard might likewise be persuaded to abdicate. If Sir William Bagot's account of the conversation at Lichfield in 1398 is true, Richard had probably talked to a number of his confidantes about laying down his crown. He may even have canvassed the option, for tactical reasons, with Archbishop Arundel at Flint. Adam Usk gives the impression of genuinely believing Richard's readiness to abdicate.[35] Of course, Richard would need to resign in public, ideally before parliament. Yet Richard was a master of political theatre, and there were dangers in allowing him a platform. The allies may have feared a carefully staged act of self-abnegation even more than a defiant appeal to the loyalty of the people. The wisest course was to have Richard make his renunciation to a smaller group representing the estates of the realm. Once set down in writing it could even be backdated to Richard's first surrender at Conway. This approach, though, was still not without its problems. Richard may have believed that a king could not fully abdicate. Like a priest, he could not renounce his ordination. If he had expressed a willingness to resign, he may well have been talking solely of resigning the 'rule' of the kingdom to another person. Such a resignation could give the new regime no security at all. Ever God's anointed, Richard could repudiate his resignation, and plausibly claim that he had acted under duress. The notion of a voluntary resignation was certainly less plausible in the case of Richard II than in that of Edward II, who ceded the crown to his son and heir. Some among Henry's followers must have regretted that the advice of the Londoners had not been followed at Lichfield, and that Richard had not been slain, perhaps while trying to escape.

The deposition of Richard was another option. Some of the men involved in the revolution of 1399 may have wished to see established or strengthened the principle by which a useless or tyrannical king might be formally set aside. As early as 1386 critics of Richard's governance had asked for the statutes by which Edward II had been tried to be tabled in parliament. They were doubtless aware that, notwithstanding the official line, Edward had indeed been deposed, and only subsequently forced to abdicate. The 'statutes' they had in mind were the 'articles of accusation against Edward II', a copy of which was seemingly then extant in the royal archives.[36] Neither Henry nor Archbishop Arundel can have been entirely relaxed about the notion of the people sitting in judgement on the king. Proceeding cautiously, they set up a panel of senior churchmen and canon lawyers, including Adam Usk, to consider precedents for deposition and to offer advice about the best approach to follow.[37]

The panel focused largely on the precedent of Innocent IV's deposition of Frederick II at the Council of Lyons in 1245.[38] The case showed that monarchs could indeed be deposed for a range of major crimes.[39] Since Richard was tainted with 'perjuries, sacrileges, sodomitical acts, dispossession of his subjects, the reduction of his people to servitude, lack of reason, and incapacity to rule', the panel believed that there were grounds in canon law for setting him aside.[40] According to Caspary, the influence of canon law precedents can be seen in the form and some of the detail of the articles of deposition in 1399.[41] There were a number of difficulties. The deposition of 1245 involved the authority of the pope and a church council. Other canon law precedents and opinions were even less helpful. As Caspary observes, it was impossible to determine from canon law 'whether it was part of the king's right that he should not be deposed'.[42] At the same time no precedent, in either canon law or the common law of England, gave the English people the right to depose a king. Formally, after all, Edward II had abdicated.

What was on order was a combination of both renunciation and deposition. According to Usk, the panel assumed that Richard was prepared to abdicate, but recommended that, 'as a further precaution, he should be deposed by authority of the clergy and people'.[43] While they were uneasy about its revolutionary implications, they recognized that deposition was more conclusive than a mere resignation, which might be subsequently repudiated, and associated the kingdom as a whole in the transfer of authority.[44] Henry and his colleagues seem to have adopted this recommendation. According to Caspary, they 'committed themselves to the proposition that the king had either validly abdicated, or else had been validly deposed; but they refused to commit themselves to either part of this disjunction'. This approach solved the immediate dilemma, but left a major constitutional conundrum. The king was deposed conditionally, 'if anything of his dignity shall remain in him', and it thus remained 'a moot point whether the assembled estates were asserting an absolute right of deposition'.[45] There remained the issue of replacing Richard. In the autumn of 1399 there can have been little real debate among the allies on this score. It is true that in 1403 that the Percies were to champion the claims of Edmund Mortimer, the young earl of March, but it is doubtful that much thought was given to the boy in 1399.[46] In the 1390s Henry may have been widely regarded as the heir presumptive, dutifully awaiting recognition by a jealous king. While he disclaimed an intention to usurp the throne on his arrival in England, the events of the summer confirmed rather than otherwise his fitness for office, and indeed gave his candidacy the appearance of a divine mandate. Of course, in terms of strict hereditary right, the claim of the house of Mortimer remained formally strong. Yet it is worth stressing that the allies in 1399, who may also have considered the claims of the duke of York and his sons,[47] were by no means the first to set it at a discount. Edward III had categorically done so, and, for all his likely nomination of Roger Mortimer as his heir in 1385, Richard showed himself ill-disposed to accord him any honour in his adult years.

The real issue in 1399 was perhaps not so much Henry's claim to be the heir to the throne as his right to replace Richard. The churchmen and canonists who considered Richard's deposition regarded Henry's title in exactly this light. Adam Usk's account of their deliberations is preceded by a reference to the rumour that Richard 'was not born of a father of the royal line, but of a mother given to slippery ways',[48] which may indicate that some consideration was given to impugning his title in this fashion. The fact that Richard had been so publicly acknowledged by his father and his grandfather must have discouraged such a strategy. The panel's interest in an approach by which Richard himself might 'be deprived of his succession to the throne in the direct line' is evident in their consideration of the so-called 'Crouchback' legend. The story ran that Edmund of Lancaster, nicknamed 'Crouchback', was the eldest son of Henry III, but had been displaced in the succession by the future Edward I. If the story could have been shown to be true, it both impugned Richard's title and provided Henry, whose mother was the great grand-daughter and heiress of Edmund 'Crouchback', with a claim that was beyond contention. Henry had already written to the monasteries throughout the land asking them to submit their chronicles for inspection. The experts duly consulted the sources available to them. Usk examined his *Polychronicon*, Nicholas Trivet's *History*, and records of royal births and baptisms kept by the Dominicans in London. The evidence was conclusive: Edward was Henry III's first-born, followed by Edmund and Margaret, queen of Scotland.[49]

In the event, Henry and his advisers settled for a title based on a number of strands. First, Richard should both abdicate and be formally deposed. Henry's title would be hereditary right. His reference to descent from Henry III served at least to suggest a title, based on double descent from the royal stock, to rival that of his predecessor. Henry's title had been tested and affirmed by divine mandate. He had conquered England and was the people's choice. Henry and his advisers, however, had no intention of resting his title either on conquest or popular election. Both courses would have seemed reckless in the extreme. As Chief Justice Thirning warned, a claim based on conquest would threaten the liberties and property of all Englishmen, while a title based on election was doubtless even less palatable to Henry and the other magnates. In this light it is not wholly surprising to find no direct reference to Edward III's settlement of the crown in 1376. If the superiority of Henry's title to Mortimer's had been the immediate issue, it might have been more relevant, but then its validity might be readily challenged by reference to Richard's subsequent nomination of Mortimer. In any case Henry had hopes, too, of presenting himself as Richard's own chosen successor.

★ ★ ★

The main task as the meeting of parliament approached was to secure Richard's agreement to vacate the throne. The strategy appears to have been to break the king's nerve. Imprisoned in the Tower of London, isolated from his friends, invigilated by his enemies, he would have been a prey to all sorts of fears and anxieties. Henry and his advisers doubtless received regular reports of his bearing and mood. Adam of Usk was asked to visit the king for this specific purpose on 21 September. The chronicler noted wryly that it was two years to the day after the beheading of the earl of Arundel. Escorted by Sir William Beauchamp, he was present while Richard dined and reflected on England's record of rebellion and regicide. According to Usk, he began: 'My God, this is a strange and fickle land, which has exiled, slain, destroyed, and ruined so many kings, so many rulers, so many great men, and which never ceases to be riven and worn down by dissensions and strife and internecine hatreds.' He then recounted the names and the histories of those who had suffered such fates, from the first habitation of the

Richard yields the crown to Henry. (The British Library, Harl. 4380, fol. 184b)

kingdom. Observing his sad condition and troubled spirit, the strangers set around him to spy on him, and reflecting on his ancient and wonted glory and on the fickle fortune of the world, Usk admitted to finding himself much moved.[50]

The 'Record and Process' provides a simple account of Richard's renunciation. It states that on Monday, the feast of St Michael, 29 September, at nine o'clock, a deputation of lords and sixteen other notables went to the Tower of London. Northumberland declared that Richard, while still at liberty at Conway, had promised Archbishop Arundel and himself that he was willing to renounce the crown, on account of his insufficiency, and to do so in the best form that could be devised.[51] Richard 'benignly replied that he was willing to give effect to what he had formerly promised'. He asked for an interview with Henry and Archbishop Arundel, and for a copy of the renunciation to consider in the mean time. After dinner the deputation returned with Henry and Archbishop Arundel. Richard spoke apart with them for a while, 'looking from one to the other with a cheerful countenance'. At last he declared he was ready to make the resignation. He read it out distinctly and 'with a cheerful countenance', and signed it.[52] He then added, in his own words, that he wished Henry to succeed him, and asked that his wish be conveyed to the estates of the realm. As a token of his intent, he put his gold signet ring on Henry's finger.[53]

There is evidence that if Richard's resignation was ever willingly given, it was a more protracted process. The 'Manner of King Richard's Renunciation' may have been prepared in the circle of Thomas Chillenden, prior of Christchurch Canterbury, who was a member of the deputation which visited Richard on 29 September.[54] It begins with a meeting on Sunday the 28th, when the king was allegedly first presented with a form of abdication. He asked to be allowed to consider it overnight. The next day, the day on which he allegedly renounced the crown 'with cheerful countenance', Richard declared that he would not resign in any circumstances, and added that 'he would like it explained to him how it was that he could resign the crown, and to whom'.[55] There was an interview between Richard and Henry. Richard offered to resign the crown to him on certain conditions. Henry refused to allow any conditions other than to safeguard the king's endowment of masses at Westminster. A number of other English sources indicate Richard's discomfort with the process. Like the continuator of the *Eulogium Historiarum*, who seems to have known the 'Manner', Walsingham acknowledged that Richard said that he could not renounce his unction or the 'characters' impressed on his soul.[56] The Dieulacres chronicle stated that when Richard gave up the crown he 'placed it on the ground and resigned his right to God'.[57] Even Adam Usk contradicts the 'Record and Process' in one telling particular. He claimed that the lords took the ring from Richard's finger as a token of his deposition, and presented it to Henry in the parliament chamber.[58]

On Tuesday 30 September the lords and a great many people assembled at Westminster Hall. The empty throne, draped in gold cloth, proclaimed the king's absence. Though convened in Richard's name, the assembly did not have the status of a parliament without the king or his representative. For the moment Henry occupied 'his usual and proper place'. According to the 'Record and Process', Archbishop Scrope of York rose to his feet. He slowly read out, first in Latin and then in English, the statement in which Richard resigned the crown on the grounds of his own inadequacies and absolved his subjects of their obedience. Archbishop Arundel then asked the people whether they wished, for the good of the realm, to accept the cession. There was some concern expressed at the proceedings. According to the author of *Traison et Mort*, Bishop Merks of Carlisle expressed the view that Henry was more at fault than Richard, and asked that Richard be brought into the chamber to confirm or not his willingness to resign.[59] The official record omits reference to this protest, but goes on simply to state that the lords thought it expedient to accept the cession, and 'each one singly, and then in common with the people, unanimously and cordially gave his consent'.[60]

After accepting Richard's resignation, the assembly was led to the second part of the strategy. It was declared that, to remove any lingering doubts, a statement should be made of Richard's crimes and acts of misgovernment which, as he himself acknowledged, made him worthy to be deposed.[61] Henry's panel of lawyers had already drafted the articles. According to the 'Record and Process', though, the thirty-three articles were composed and put in writing by authority of the assembly. The bishop of St Asaph then read them out.[62]

The 'articles of deposition' take the form of an indictment of Richard's actions over the whole reign. They are arranged in rough chronological order, and begin by reference to the oath he swore at his coronation and the ways in which he broke his undertakings to rule his people justly. Article 1 relates to his maladministration in the 1380s, the heavy taxes and the feckless patronage which prompted the establishment of the commission of 1386, and how Richard conspired to charge the lords of the commission with high treason. Article 2 refers to his questions to the judges, his intimidation of them, and how 'by colour of their responses' he planned the destruction of Gloucester, Arundel and Warwick, with whom he was indignant because they 'wished the king to be under good rule'. Article 3 records that Richard incited Robert de Vere to raise an army against the lords of the commission in December 1387, causing death and destruction.[63]

With article 4 the indictment moves to the more recent past. Although Richard had pardoned Gloucester, Warwick and Arundel in full parliament, 'and for years acted in a friendly way towards them', he 'carried venom in his heart', and when the opportunity arose he had Gloucester murdered, Arundel beheaded and Warwick imprisoned. To support his evil designs, according to article 5, Richard raised a horde of ruffians from Cheshire, who committed crimes with impunity. The sixth and seventh articles indict the king for related acts of reprisal, all of which involved breaches of faith. Though he announced that he did not intend to proceed against the followers of the three lords, many 'were compelled by fear of death to make fines' and to seek pardons 'as if they were traitors'. Even then, they had to pay further fines and redemptions to save their lives. On this account 'the royal name and estate were brought into great disrepute'.[64] Article 8 concerns Richard's manipulation of parliament. At Shrewsbury he secured the appointment of a standing committee, ostensibly to deal with outstanding petitions. He subsequently used it to proceed with other matters 'at the will of the king, in derogation of the estate of parliament' and establishing a pernicious precedent. To give this committee 'a certain colour and authority', he caused the parliament rolls 'to be deleted and changed'.[65] Article 10 states that though the kingdom should be free from foreign interference Richard petitioned the pope to confirm the statutes of this parliament and issue fulminations against all who presumed to contravene them.[66] Article 19 refers to the king's influence on parliamentary elections. Although the people should be free to choose knights of the shire to present their grievances and sue for remedy in parliament, the king, to facilitate his rash designs, ordered his sheriffs to nominate particular persons favourable to him, whom he could induce, sometimes by threats, sometimes by gifts, to agree to measures prejudicial to the realm and burdensome to the people, not least the grant of the customs on wools for the term of his life. According to articles 13 and 18 he selected as sheriffs men 'who, he knew, would not resist his will', keeping compliant sheriffs in office for longer than their statutory one-year term. Article 20 relates that he required the sheriffs to swear a special oath to obey all his mandates, including orders under his signet seal, and to arrest and imprison anyone speaking in public or in private to the discredit or slander of the king.[67]

Articles 14 and 15 relate to his financial exactions. He took loans from his subjects that he failed to repay, and levied taxes almost every year of his reign. He impoverished his people, and used his income not for the benefit of England but 'for his own ostentation, pomp and vainglory'.[68] Articles 21 and 22 link his concerns to obtain 'a superabundance of riches' and to 'crush the people under his feet'. He induced the men of seventeen counties, in letters under their seals, to make submission to him as traitors, by colour of which he obtained great sums of money conceded by the clergy and people of the shires. Although he sought to appease them by returning to them their letters of submission, he required their proctors to bind themselves and make undertakings to him under their seals on behalf of their counties. Furthermore, he extorted large sums of money from religious houses for his expedition to Ireland.[69]

Article 16 alleges his contempt for the law. He refused to observe and defend the laws and customs of the realm, but wanted to do whatever his whim dictated. Sometimes, when the law was explained to him by judges and other members of his council, or when the requirements of justice were pointed out to him, 'he said expressly, with harsh and determined looks, that the laws were in his own mouth' or 'in his breast, and that he alone could change or establish the laws of his realm'. According to article 17, although the statutes should be binding until repealed by another parliament, the king was unwilling to be bound by them, and so subtly arranged for the commons to petition that 'he might be as free as any of his predecessors were before him', and 'by colour of this petition' he frequently did and ordered many things contrary to statutes, acting expressly and knowingly against his coronation oath.[70] Article 23 claims that he would often suddenly and sharply rebuke members of his council, who were charged to give him advice, 'so that they did not dare to speak the truth about the state of the king and the kingdom'.[71]

Articles 26, 27 and 29 specifically indict the king with breaches of the Magna Carta. Although the lands and goods of all freemen ought not to be seized unless they have been lawfully forfeited, the king declared in the presence of many lords and others of the community of the realm that 'the lives of every one of his lieges and their lands, tenements, goods, and chattels are his at his pleasure, without any forfeiture; which is entirely against the laws and customs of the realm'. At the same time, contrary to Magna Carta, people were accused before the constable and marshal of England and forced to defend themselves by trial by battle.[72] The king likewise hindered lawful processes in ecclesiastical courts by the issue of writs of prohibition.[73]

A number of articles relate to his unjust dealings with Henry of Lancaster and Archbishop Arundel. Articles 9, 11 and 12 report his failure to do justice to Henry of Lancaster, the sentence of banishment, and the revocation of the letters patent allowing him his inheritance.[74] Articles 30 and 33 relate to Richard's trickery in securing the condemnation of Archbishop Arundel in his absence.[75]

Article 28 refers to his attempt to bind the people more firmly to his will. He sent out letters 'to make his lieges take oaths which might be turned to their destruction, and confirm them with their seals'. Article 31 relates to Richard's last will and testament, and the large bequests that he made to his successor and others on condition that they uphold all the acts and judgements of the last parliament and parliamentary committee.[76] According to article 24, the king took the treasures and crown jewels to Ireland without the consent of the estates of the realm. He also falsified the records of the realm.[77] This led on to the broader charge, in article 25, that the king was 'so variable and dissimulating in his words and writings, especially to popes, and rulers outside the realm, that no one could trust him'.[78] Article 32 seems to accuse the king of murder, but curiously subordinates the charge to one of perjury. It claims that although the king, in the presence of the dukes of Lancaster and York at Langley, 'swore on the host that he forgave the duke of Gloucester for all past offences and would never proceed against him for them; yet afterwards he had the duke cruelly murdered for these offences'.[79]

★ ★ ★

This indictment of Richard is partisan, but it is not fiction. The men who drew up the thirty-three articles largely restricted themselves to actions that were notorious. There can have been few among the lords and knights who did not have some first-hand experience of the king's threats and exactions. Government records survive to document many of the charges.[80] The one article that may have been new to the bulk of the audience in Westminster Hall is article 31 which relates to Richard's testamentary provisions. Richard's extant will attests the essential truth of the allegation.[81] In some respects the 'articles of deposition' show great restraint. According to Adam Usk, Henry's legal experts believed Richard was tainted with 'perjuries, sacrileges, sodomitical acts, dispossession of his subjects, the reduction of his people to servitude, lack of reason, and incapacity to rule', but they seem not to have sought to substantiate the charges with lurid detail, fabricated or otherwise. The focus was on what could be presented as public knowledge.

The 'articles of deposition' adopt a surprisingly coherent position. Some of the men involved in drawing up the indictment clearly had an interest in constitutional principles. They made a point of affirming the laws, conventions and expectations which Richard had allegedly broken, flouted or disappointed. They began with a statement of Richard's coronation oath and appealed to the Magna Carta. They assumed the king's obligation to rule within the law, to take counsel from his judges and magnates, and to rule for the common good. They affirmed the special status of parliament in respect of legislation and grants of taxation, and as a forum for seeking redress. They did not seek to challenge the king's regality, or the view that the king should be as free as his royal predecessors. They were most concerned to insist that the king was bound by the laws made in parliament. It is not at all clear whether they believed that Richard was ideologically committed to some contrary position. Their statement that Richard frequently asserted that the laws were in his breast may have been simply designed to present him as undisciplined and petulant, but it may well imply that Richard was thought to subscribe to the Roman law adage that a prince's will has the force of law.

The members of the assembly were asked, 'singly and in common', whether the 'accusations of crime and defaults were sufficient and notorious enough for the deposition of the king'. They were asked to consider, too, the king's own 'confession of inadequacy' in the formal statement of resignation. According to the 'Record and Process', they 'unanimously agreed that there was abundant reason for proceeding to deposition, for the greater security and tranquillity of the realm and the good of the kingdom'. They appointed commissioners to depose Richard 'from all his royal dignity, majesty, and honour, on behalf of, in the name of, and by authority of, all the estates, as has been observed in similar cases by the ancient custom of the realm'. The commissioners were the bishop of St Asaph and the abbot of Glastonbury representing the clergy; the earl of Gloucester and Lord Berkeley representing the nobility; Sir Thomas Erpingham and Sir Thomas Grey representing the knights and commons of southern and northern England respectively; and the judges William Thirning and John Markham. Seated in front of the empty throne, they made a formal record of the judgement. The bishop of St Asaph then recited the sentence of deposition to the wider assembly.[82]

★ ★ ★

Henry now rose to his feet. He humbly made the sign of the cross on his forehead and breast, and began to speak, his voice resonant, in unadorned English: 'In the name of the Father, Son, and Holy Ghost, I, Henry of Lancaster, challenge this realm of England and the crown with all its members and appurtenances, as I am descended by right line of the blood coming from the good lord King Henry III, and through that right that God of his grace has sent me, with the help of my kindred and my friends to recover it; the which realm was on the point of being undone for default of governance and undoing of good laws.'[83] John Norbury, Henry's treasurer, and the earl of Northumberland then asked the spiritual and temporal lords, one by one, whether they would accept Henry as their king. They all gave their assent. Henry may have been embarrassed by this heavy-handed approach. According to the 'Manner of Richard's Renunciation', he begged them to assent with their hearts and not merely with their mouths, adding that he would understand it if some of them had reservations. They all then allegedly assured him of their heartfelt assent. It may have been then that Henry showed the assembly Richard's ring as a token of his predecessor's assent to his succession. The two archbishops and the duke of York kissed Henry's hand and led him to the throne. Kneeling in prayer before it, he was raised up and enthroned to great jubilation. The cheers in the abbey were echoed by the crowd gathered outside.[84]

Archbishop Arundel next preached a sermon loosely based on the text 'A man shall reign over my people' (I Samuel ix, 17). He took the opportunity to contrast Henry's manliness with Richard's childishness. He adverted emotively to Richard's shortcomings as a ruler, his overturning of the laws which he had sworn to maintain, and his responsibility for the death of the duke of Gloucester. Perhaps a little defensively, in view of the recent proceedings, he stressed how Gloucester had been condemned 'without giving him a hearing or the opportunity to reply'. Conversely, he praised Henry, extolled his strength and virtues, and presented him as a man worthy to be king.[85]

Henry gave his thanks to God and the estates of the realm. He restated his claim to the vacant throne, stressing his hereditary right, but assuring his subjects that he had no intention of allowing the status of the realm, the rights of his subjects, or any other law or custom, 'to be in any way affected by his succession in this fashion or by his conquest of the kingdom'.[86] The officers of state were formally recommissioned. Archbishop Arundel announced that the coronation would take place on Monday 13 October, and issued summonses for a new parliament to meet on the 6th.[87] The calling for new elections showed some sense of constitutional propriety. Even if the assembly that was convened in response to Richard's writs of 19 August was a valid parliament, Richard's abdication rendered it defunct. Of course, it was impossible to secure new returns by 6 October. The knights and burgesses who assembled at Westminster Hall on this day were for the most part the men elected in September.[88]

On the following day, Wednesday 1 October, the commissioners came to Richard in the Tower. Chief Justice Thirning acted as their spokesman, and explained to Richard the nature of their commission and that they would be speaking and acting not only for themselves but on behalf 'of all the estates of this land'.[89] After Richard had indicated that he understood, Thirning recounted the various stages of the deposition process, including the king's own abdication, the reading of this renunciation to the estates and people at Westminster, the reading of the thirty-three articles of default of governance, and the declaration of deposition. The commissioners then, as 'proctors of all these estates and people', renounced their homage and fealty 'and all allegiance and all other bonds, charges, and services which belong to it', and declared that none henceforth 'bear you faith, nor do you obedience as to their king'. According to this account, Richard simply answered that 'he looked not thereafter; but that after all this he hoped that his cousin would be a good lord to him'.[90]

According to Adam Usk, the deputation declared its intention to regard him thenceforward not as a king but as Richard of Bordeaux, a simple knight.[91] A Spanish account of Richard's deposition alleges a much more elaborate ceremony of degradation. He was seated in majesty, and then successively stripped of his crown, his sceptre, the orb, his sword and then his throne.[92]

★ ★ ★

Over the next week Henry was preoccupied with plans for the coronation. The date selected was 13 October, the feast of St Edward the Confessor. In all likelihood the timetable was dictated by the opportunity to inaugurate the new dynasty under the auspices of England's most celebrated royal saint. Henry must have been conscious of the challenge he faced in establishing himself symbolically at Westminster. Richard had been a great patron of Westminster abbey. His massive portrait in the choir and splendid double-tomb in St Edward's Chapel marked it out as his royal space. Westminster Hall was more fully a monument to Richard's grand regal vision. There was little that Henry could do with Westminster, though he did move the duke of Gloucester's tomb into the inner sanctum of St Edward's chapel.[93] Richard's portrait was presumably covered over, and other Ricardian images and emblems may have been destroyed. When the time came, Henry would arrange for his own burial in Canterbury cathedral.

Henry met parliament on 6 October, but the proceedings were largely formal. Archbishop Arundel delivered a sermon on the text 'It behoves us to make provision for the kingdom' (I Maccabees, vi, 57). This text may well have been the motto of the revolution. He glossed it to indicate that Henry wished 'to be counselled and governed by the honourable, wise and discreet persons of his realm, and by their common counsel and assent to do the best for the government of himself and of his realm; not wishing to be governed by his own whim, nor by his wilful purpose or singular opinion, but by common advice, counsel and assent'.[94] Given the need to prepare Westminster Hall for the coronation, the parliament was then adjourned until the 14th. The convocation of the clergy of the province of Canterbury, which had assembled at St Paul's on the 7th, was able to continue its business uninterrupted until the 11th. Henry was keen to counteract the perception that he was less favourably disposed to the church than Richard had been. Through the earls of Northumberland and Westmorland and Sir Thomas Erpingham, he affirmed his commitment to the extirpation of heresy, and declared it was not his 'wish or intention' to make 'any exaction of money in his kingdom, except for great necessity of wars' and other unavoidable necessities. He certainly made a great point of not requesting any subsidy from them.[95] Archbishop Arundel played a key role in rallying clerical opinion behind the new regime.[96] On 16 October he proclaimed prayers throughout the province for Henry IV whom God had raised up, like another Maccabeus, for the right government of the people, and attested from his own knowledge Henry's disposition to act in fear of the Almighty and for the safety of the church and the common good.[97]

On 11 October Henry spent the night in the Tower of London, where forty-six young squires, including Henry's three younger sons, the young earls of Arundel and Stafford, and the son and heir of the earl of Warwick, kept vigil. On the following morning he knighted them in Richard's presence, and constituted them as a new order, the Order of the Bath. Henry and the knights then rode through the streets of London to Westminster where they spent the night before the coronation.[98] The coronation itself proceeded with all due solemnity. Four swords were borne before the new king. One 'was sheathed as a token of the augmentation of military honour', two others 'were wrapped in red and bound round with golden bands to represent twofold mercy', and the fourth 'was naked and without a point, the emblem of the execution of justice without rancour'.[99] Henry had the special honour of being the first king to be anointed with the recently rediscovered holy oil of Canterbury. Prior to receiving the crown from Archbishop Arundel, Henry took his coronation oath. Usk observed that he himself heard him 'swear to my lord of Canterbury that he would strive to rule his people with mercy and truthfulness in all matters'.[100]

After the ceremony there was a great feast in Westminster Hall. The festivities were interrupted by the irruption into the hall of a knight in full armour on horseback with two companions, also mounted, one bearing an unsheathed sword and the other a lance. It was Sir Thomas Dymock, who claimed the right to be king's champion by virtue of his mother's tenure of the manor of Scrivelsby, Lincolnshire. He had a herald proclaim in each corner of the hall that, 'if any man should say' that his liege lord 'was not of right crowned king of England, he was ready to prove the contrary with his body, then and there, or when and wheresoever it might please the king'. In 1399 the challenge may have seemed rather less rhetorical than usual. Henry himself broke any tension by interposing, 'If need be, Sir Thomas, I will in mine own person ease thee of this office.'[101]

The date and site of the celebrations led Walsingham and Usk to reflect on the remarkable turn of fortune over the previous year. Usk observed that it was 'on this feast, a year past' that Richard had required Henry to depart the realm, and claimed that Richard had planned on this very day 'to crown his nephew, the earl of Kent, at Dublin, with great worldly pomp, king of Ireland, and had thought to sweep away in destruction many nobles of the realm of England who were to be craftily summoned to that great ceremony, seeking to enrich with their possessions the same earl and other young men whom, as has been said, he had raised up'.[102]

★ ★ ★

On Tuesday 14 October Henry IV met parliament, and received the homage of the lords spiritual and temporal. About two-thirds of the knights of the shire, and over half of all the members, had parliamentary experience. Significantly more members had sat in the parliament of 1388 than in Richard's last parliament.[103] One of the parliament's first acts was to declare the parliament of 1397–8, which it now termed the 'shrewed' parliament, null and void.[104] The commons claimed that the elections in September 1397 had not been free, that proceedings had been overawed by the 'armed force brandished in parliament' by the king's supporters, and that the lords had been coerced to obey the king's will. It was declared that anyone who had been deprived of his rights in this parliament should be immediately restored.[105] Interestingly, the earl of Warwick was excluded from this provision, and reinstated only by the king's special grace. His confession to Richard still rankled among the friends of Gloucester and Arundel.[106] To complete the reversal of Richard's policies, parliament proceeded to reinstate the acts and judgements of the parliament of 1388. The king likewise granted a petition from the commons that the 'blank charters' exacted from London and the sixteen counties should be cancelled and annulled for all time.[107]

On the 15th Archbishop Arundel declared how God, who had sent Henry 'for the recovery and consolation of the realm', had also provided him with 'most honourable and very handsome issue'. He announced that the king intended to create his eldest son prince of Wales, and that he wished him to be accepted as rightful heir to the crown of England. The lords gave their enthusiastic assent.[108] Henry then proceeded to the investiture of the prince by five symbols, namely, by delivery of a golden rod, by a kiss, by a belt, by a ring, and by letters of creation. Later in the session the king further endowed him with the duchy of Aquitaine and the duchy of Lancaster as well as the duchy of Cornwall and earldom of Chester. The advancement of the prince 'by assented proposals to parliament signifies some interest on Henry's part to secure parliamentary endorsement of the new dynasty'.[109]

In the days which followed parliament addressed itself to the issue of the lords who had aided and abetted Richard's misrule. The commons petitioned for the arrest of the lords responsible for their carriage of the appeal against Gloucester, Arundel and Warwick. The dukes of Albemarle, Surrey and Exeter, the marquis of Dorset, and the earls of Salisbury and Gloucester were actually present in the chamber. Lord Cobham spoke at length about the recent troubles, and lamented how the king and his associates had brought dishonour on the realm. He declared that as Richard himself had been deposed and punished for his crimes, so his accomplices should be committed to custody and, if found guilty, punished. He reminded the assembly how the lords, 'glorying in the evils of the time', represented themselves as Richard's 'foster-children', adding sorrowfully 'as the foster-parent is, so shall the foster-children be'. Claiming that he sought not revenge for his own injuries but 'common justice', he declared on his conscience that if his own father were guilty of crimes of this sort, he would not hesitate to say that he should be punished for them.[110]

The debate became very heated. Sir William Bagot, who had been brought back in chains from Ireland, was keen to make himself useful to the new regime. His testimony highlighted Albemarle's prominence in Richard's counsels, and indicated his complicity in Gloucester's murder. John Hall, who was an accessory to Gloucester's murder, confirmed Albemarle's involvement in it.[111] The proceedings degenerated into a series of accusations and counter-accusations among the nobles. Lord FitzWalter challenged

Albemarle, and Lord Morley threw down his gauntlet against Salisbury, who was accused of betraying Gloucester's counsels to Richard. Five of the six were committed to custody, and on the 29th were put on trial. None was able to deny complicity in the appeal, but all claimed that they acted out of fear of the king. The judgement was handed down on 3 November. Albemarle, Surrey and Exeter were stripped of their ducal titles and recent royal grants, and reverted to their titles as earls of Rutland, Kent and Huntingdon. Gloucester lost his comital title, reverting to the title of Lord Despenser.[112] Salisbury was not included in the sentence, but a day was appointed in the new year for his duel with Lord Morley. Merks was deprived of his bishopric of Carlisle.[113] All kept their lives, though only Rutland and Merks would survive the winter. Henry would soon regret the mercy shown to Richard's 'foster-children'.

During the session the commons presented several petitions which reflected their political temper. The recent upheavals had sharpened their concerns about the retinues of magnates, and at their request it was ordained that lords should not distribute badges to anyone other than their household servants.[114] They successfully petitioned to abolish appeals of treason in parliament, and to confirm the point that they were not party to judgements in parliament which were properly the concern of the lords and the king.[115] Rather intemperately, they requested that the king not make any grants, especially of crown property, to unworthy persons. This petition was judged 'unmannerly'. The bishop of St Asaph declared that it encouraged the king 'to be niggardly, and that is a disservice to kingship, which is better served by a generous degree of largesse'. Above all, it involved subjects putting restraint on the king's benevolence. Rather than the king being fettered, 'it is those who submit unreasonable and unmerited requests to him that ought to be punished'.[116]

The parliament concluded on 3 November with several important gestures. The commons noted that though Richard had abused their grant that he be as free in his royal liberty as his progenitors by claiming that he was able to change the laws at his will, they none the less now made the like grant to Henry, trusting in his 'nobility, high discretion and gracious governance'.[117] For his part, in response to a petition to confirm the summary sentences at Bristol against Scrope, Bushy and Green, Henry took the opportunity to state that he had no intention to dispossess anyone 'by way of conquest', and that he held the three knights 'culpable of all the evil that has come to the land'. The commons were allegedly gratified by this 'just judgement', and thanked God for sending 'such a king and governor'.[118]

★   ★   ★

During the session there had been some concern as to what should be done with Richard. On 21 October, while Henry was busy receiving ambassadors from the French court, the commons proposed that Richard should stand trial alongside his cronies for his crimes, and that punishment be 'ordained for him that the realm be not troubled by him' and that the 'horrible causes' of his deposition be publicly proclaimed 'so that the realm be not slandered' for the act.[119] Two days later it was resolved by the lords that Richard should merely 'be kept in safe and secret ward'. The decision was regarded as so momentous that the names of the fifty-four peers and the three knights who assented to it were recorded on the parliament roll. On Monday the 28th Henry himself came before parliament to pronounce the sentence of perpetual imprisonment.[120] The next night Richard was escorted on to a barge in the Thames, and transported, weeping and lamenting that he had ever been born, down river to Gravesend. One of the knights who escorted him reminded him that was how he had treated the earl of Arundel, that is 'with the utmost cruelty at all times'.[121] Some time later he was transported, presumably by boat, to the Lancastrian strongholds in Yorkshire, firstly, it appears, to Pickering and Knaresborough and then to Pontefract, oddly retracing the route of Henry's arrival in England.[122] There was likewise some symbolic statement in the choice of his final prison. Pontefract was the centre of the cult of Thomas of Lancaster, a former steward of England who had led the community of the realm against the tyranny of Edward II.

The usurpation had been accomplished with surprising ease. As prayers went out through the land for the new 'Maccabeus', and as members of parliament returned to their communities with glowing reports of the new king, there must have been some hope of peace and stability. The bulk of the large army which had rallied to Henry had long since returned to their homes. Henry now paid off the smaller retinues that he and his noble allies had kept in service during the parliament.[123] Overall, it is striking how little opposition there seems to have been to the transfer of power. The Percies and Archbishop Scrope subsequently sought to deny their acquiescence in the proceedings, but it is interesting that neither they nor anyone else claimed that the parliament acted under coercion. Throughout the proceedings Henry appears to have been relaxed and genial. He was most tested by the men around him who would have liked to see Richard and his counsellors more severely punished. According to Walsingham, he received a letter threatening insurrection if he did not immediately execute the lords responsible for Gloucester's death.[124]

How well the capital reflected the mood of the kingdom as a whole is more difficult to assess. It is instructive that the sources generally regarded as favourable to Richard, as well as the more overtly Lancastrian pieces, concur in presenting Richard's overthrow as popular. Henry's campaign in the summer of 1399 had been carried along on a wave of popular enthusiasm. It is too simple to characterize the movement simply as a rebellion by disaffected noblemen. Henry had Archbishop Arundel at his side from the outset, and early on may have been able to enlist Archbishop Scrope in his cause. The movement was able to exploit broadly based and deeply felt disaffection with Richard's government, and to present itself as blessed by God and dedicated to the reform of the realm. A hermit immediately set to work building a chapel to mark Henry's arrival at Ravenspur, an act of unauthorized political piety.[125] Henry's reception as he rode through England was likened to the reception given to Jesus Christ when he rode into Jerusalem on Palm Sunday. There were pockets of resistance, and it may be that in other circumstances loyalist forces might have been more effectively mobilized and led.[126] The likelihood is that many of the men who responded to the duke of York's call in July 1399 were doing no more than covering their backs.

In London there is some evidence of 'people power'. On 9 August the citizens went armed to Westminster abbey in search of the king and arrested a number of royal clerks, including Archbishop Walden. Henry and Archbishop Arundel were clearly well received in the capital, and the men of London and the sixteen counties must have felt some sense of liberation as the hated 'blank charters' were annulled and consigned to a great bonfire. Feelings against Richard and his counsellors may well have reached a new intensity as the deposition brought new revelations of their cruelty and rapacity. For the first time men heard 'official' accounts of Gloucester's brutal end. To underline the tragedy, the duchess of Gloucester died, heartbroken, shortly after receiving news of the death of their only son, whom Richard had taken with him to Ireland.[127] There were also the rumours that Richard was planning to sell Calais back to France, and to make the duke of Surrey king of Ireland. It was believed that the king who had already ruined so many magnates was bent on the destruction and despoliation of other noble houses. There were the 'discoveries' among the king's possessions: the vast treasure he had accumulated through the dispossession of his subjects; his priceless collection of jewels and precious objects; splendid gowns of cloth of gold festooned with pearls and other jewels worth 30,000 marks; and occult writings.[128]

★   ★   ★

The most dramatic examples of 'people power' occurred early in 1400. After disbanding his retinue, Henry and his sons took up residence at Windsor for the Christmas festivities. At Westminster the lords who had found themselves so dangerously exposed on account of their prominence in Richard's counsels met together to consider their position. On 17 December a group of conspirators including the earls of Rutland, Huntingdon, Kent and Salisbury, Lord Despenser, Sir Thomas Blount, Roger Walden, Thomas Merks and the abbot of Westminster determined on a plot to capture the new king and the princes at Windsor, and then to liberate and restore Richard. The coup was to take place on Epiphany, Richard's own birthday, and involved infiltration of the castle by the Ricardian lords. The masques and tournaments planned for Twelfth Night provided ideal cover. The plan was to open the gates to men mustered in Richard's name at Kingston-upon-Thames. Richard Maudeleyn, who bore a striking physical resemblance to the former king, would play his part. The coup would be the occasion for risings across the country, coordinated from London by the earl of Huntingdon. However, the plot soon came to the new king's attention. It was allegedly betrayed both by Rutland and by Huntingdon's wife. Henry immediately moved to secure London and raise men from as far afield as the north Midlands.[129] The London trained bands did not fail him as they had failed Richard twelve years earlier.

The earls of Kent and Salisbury briefly occupied Windsor, called on Queen

A roof boss showing Richard's white hart, Dartington Hall, Devon. (© The Dartington Hall Trust)

The decapitation of Richard II's partisans. (The British Library, Harl. 4380, fol. 193b)

Isabelle at Sonning near Reading, and marshalled their forces at Colnbrook. They sent messengers into the western counties with news that Richard was in the field and that Henry had taken refuge in the Tower of London. Ralph Stathum, a Derbyshire squire, had already prepared a small company to ride in support of the earl of Huntingdon. Forty archers were likewise mustered by Huntingdon's agents at Exeter on the 10th.[130] The most significant rising was in Cheshire, where the commanders of Richard's bodyguard were naturally to the fore. Yet the rebellion collapsed even before it really began. The failure of Kent and Salisbury to capture the king and Huntingdon's inability to secure London sealed the fate of the conspiracy. Dismayed by Henry's success in raising men, the rebels fell back westwards to Cirencester, hoping to maintain a line of communication with the loyalists in Cheshire and other western counties. Kent and

Salisbury established themselves in the main inn in Cirencester, while their troops were billeted in the surrounding villages. At dawn, the townsmen took matters into their own hands, surrounded the inn and arrested the two earls. When Kent's chaplain tried to create a diversion by setting fire to the town, the townsmen's fury knew no bounds, and the heads of the two earls were hacked off in the market square. The other lords met a like fate. The earl of Huntingdon, after failing to hold London, fled down river; forced ashore on the Essex coast, he was apprehended and carried across country to Pleshy, where he was executed 'on the very spot where the duke of Gloucester had given himself up to the former king Richard'. Lord Despenser was captured in Cardiff and brought to Bristol, where he too was lynched by angry citizens.[131]

CHAPTER NINE

THE SHADOW OF 1399

It is not known how Richard maintained his spirits over Christmas and the New Year. The failure of the conspiracy scheduled for Epiphany, his birthday, sealed his fate. In mid-January rumours of his death were circulating in the capital, and by the end of the month had reached the French court. On 8 February Henry IV and his council discussed the rumours at a meeting at Eltham. It was agreed that if Richard were alive, as it was officially assumed, he should be kept in strictest security, but that if he were dead, his body should be shown openly so that the people might have certain knowledge of his death.[1] Payments were made, either shortly before or shortly after this meeting, to William Loveney, keeper of the wardrobe, to go on the king's secret business to Pontefract; to a servant of Sir Thomas Swinford coming from Pontefract to certify to the council matters concerning the king's advantage; and to another man sent from London on the council's behalf to the guards and keepers of the body of Richard.[2]

It is possible that Richard died a natural death. News of the failure of the plot may have broken whatever spirit remained in him. Even if he was responsible for no greater cruelty, Swinford must have relished telling Richard about Rutland's betrayal, and the deaths of Kent, Huntingdon, Salisbury and Despenser. Richard would have known that his cause was lost beyond redemption. There was no official version of his death, though it was spread abroad in England that he had refused food.[3] The more sceptical English chroniclers imply that he was helped on the way by the privations imposed on him by his gaoler.[4] The timing of Richard's death was suspiciously convenient to the Lancastrian regime, and allegations of foul play were soon in circulation. The author of *Traison et Mort* offered an account of violent death sufficiently detailed and circumstantial to capture the imagination of later generations. He named Henry's agent as Sir Piers Exton, who allegedly killed Richard with an axe-blow to the head.[5] No one of this name is known, but the name may be a scribal misrendering of Peter Buckton, one of Henry's most loyal Yorkshire retainers. There is no substance to this particular story. When Richard's remains were examined in the nineteenth century, no trace of violence could be detected.[6]

The regime was concerned to put Richard's body on show. On 17 February the sum of 80 marks was issued for the conveyance of the corpse, with his face exposed, from Pontefract to London. It lay for two days at St Paul's cathedral, where Henry attended a requiem mass, paid for a thousand masses for Richard's soul and gave 20 shillings in alms to the poor.[7] It was almost exactly twelve months since Gaunt's body had likewise been brought to the capital. Every encouragement was given to nobles and commoners to view the late king. According to a royal clerk in 1413, Richard was 'seen as dead by thousands upon thousands in the city of London and elsewhere in the realm'.[8] Richard, however, was denied burial with his wife in Westminster abbey. Instead he was taken to Langley, where he was privately buried in the Dominican friary in the presence of the bishop of Lichfield and a few other churchmen. He may have been temporarily accommodated in a tomb prepared for his uncle the duke of York. He was in congenial company: his brother Edward, who had died almost thirty years previously in Bordeaux, and his favourite aunt the duchess of York were buried in the friary. For the next thirteen years Richard of Bordeaux lay in the friary which Edward II had established as a private mausoleum for Piers Gaveston.

★ ★ ★

Richard had contemplated his mortality for some time. In 1394 he commissioned a grand double-tomb for Queen Anne and himself, and cleared a space for it in St Edward the Confessor's Chapel. In 1395–7 he arranged for the burial of several prelates and knights in Westminster abbey as a reward for their loyalty and service to him.[9] In his will in 1399 he alluded wearily to the long years he had borne the burden of governing the English, but showed special concern that his body should be dressed in white satin, in kingly fashion, and that he should be buried with a crown, a sceptre, and a precious ring on his finger.[10] Though he may have given thought to resignation, he could never have reconciled himself to the manner of his overthrow. Richard was jealous of the reputation of the crown and how he would be remembered by future generations. He presumably commissioned the Latin epitaph in which he was presented

Tomb effigy of Richard II, Westminster Abbey. (© Dean & Chapter of Westminster)

as a king who 'supported the church, trod down the mighty and laid low all who damaged his regality'.[11]

Early in 1400 Richard was silenced forever. If he had been given a hearing in parliament, and deigned to justify himself to his subjects, he would have spoken to effect. He was practised in presenting a picture of his reign as a series of acts of disobedience and rebellion, replete with plots against his life and assaults on his regality. He would have recalled, as he did in a letter in 1397, 'how since his tender years nobles and members of the royal household' had 'traitorously conspired to disinherit our crown and usurp our royal power' leaving him 'hardly anything beyond the royal name'. He may have claimed that he 'indulged these traitors with time enough to change their hearts and show the fruits of repentance', but that when they proved obstinate in their evil, he had them put to death as 'confessed and convicted traitors' in order to bring 'to our subjects a peace which, by the grace of God, may last forever'.[12] He might have broadened the frame of reference to present his reign in the context of a longer history of civil strife and regicide in England.[13] He might have concluded with words reportedly spoken at Conway. According to Creton, Richard called God to witness, 'so truly' that he wished 'all mortals, past, present, and to come, could know my thoughts and my desires', that he had ever desired 'to observe justice and righteousness', and had 'followed this righteous course as far as I was able for these three years past, yea, for eight or ten'. If he had been 'most invariable in preserving right', he allegedly declared, 'reason demands it; for a king should be firm and steady both in keeping himself notable for the punishment of the wicked, and for holding to the truth in every place'.[14]

Richard's 'righteous course' was the restoration of royal authority. From the last tumultuous year of Edward III's reign, he was all too aware that the main problem was disobedience. In a speech to parliament in 1383, recalling the Peasants Revolt of 1381, Michael de la Pole, Richard's chancellor, stressed that obedience was 'the foundation of all peace and quiet' in the realm.[15] In the treatise known as the *De quadripartita regis specie* presented to Richard in 1391, disobedience was likewise presented as the major obstacle to good government.[16] In the speech opening parliament in September 1397 Bishop Stafford argued that three things were necessary for good government, the first being that the king must be powerful, the second that the laws should be kept and duly executed, and the third that 'the subjects of the realm should duly obey the king and his laws'.[17] At Lichfield in 1398 Richard allegedly declared his desire to live no longer than 'to see the crown of England in all so high prosperity, and so lowly be obeyed of all his lieges, as it hath been in any other king's time; having consideration how he had been oppressed and disobeyed as well by his lords as by his commons; so that it might be chronicled perpetually that with wit and wisdom and manhood he had recovered his dignity, regality and honourable estate'.[18]

From 1389 Richard was able to call anew on the loyalty of his subjects, and was powerfully assisted in his vision of resurgent monarchy by a number of very able servants. One of the features of this time is a strong working council which, based at Westminster, was attentive to the interests of the crown, not least in the financial sphere. Richard was all too aware that a major source of his political weakness in the 1380s was lack of resources. Though he continued to experience some frustration in securing supply from parliament and convocation in the 1390s, he laid bold claim to the peace dividend and successfully contested the principle that taxation should only be for war. In 1398 he secured from parliament what was then an unprecedented grant of the subsidy on wool for life. Since he had no son, Richard was able to retain in his own hands the principality of Wales, the duchy of Cornwall and the earldom of Chester. He added enormously to his wealth through the spoliation of the Appellants in 1397, the acquisition of the wardship of the Mortimer inheritance in 1398, and securing control of the Lancastrian and the Mowbray lands in 1399. Then there were the windfall gains, most notably the dowry brought by Isabelle of Valois, and the loans and fines exacted from his subjects. By 1399 Richard had amassed great wealth, and it was believed that Richard 'had more riches and treasure than any of his progenitors'.[19]

Richard had the means to reward loyalty on a scale unknown in peace-time. From 1389 he began to increase the size of his household and affinity by retaining knights and squires with grants of annuities.[20] The expansion of the king's retinue had the potential to increase royal authority and maintain order in the localities. As Goodman observes, 'a version of the Ricardian expedient became important as a mainstay in government' in the Yorkist and early Tudor period.[21] For a time Richard was fairly inclusive in the distribution of patronage. His partnership with John of Gaunt involved some integration of the royal and Lancastrian affinities, and provided some breadth and stability to his regime. Yet Richard's anxieties and ambitions set him on a destructive course. From 1397 he was bent on the ruin of a number of magnates, and the advancement in their place of a coterie of noble allies. In recruiting knights and squires he was more concerned with security and power than with good governance, and royal retaining provoked instability as often as harmony in the localities. The core of his retinue was an unruly bodyguard. Richard's policies in the late 1390s opened up a gulf of mistrust between himself and prominent members of the ruling elite, both at Westminster and in the localities. It is true that Richard's new political order was toppled before it had time to put down roots, and that his absence in Ireland allowed Henry's campaign to gain irresistible momentum.[22] The overwhelming impression, though, is that in 1399 Richard had forfeited the loyalty of large sections of political society. If he had triumphed over Henry, he would have demonstrated little more than that his subjects had finally learned the lesson that 'he is a child of death, who offends the king'.[23]

Richard had more success in the projection of a regal image. He had a taste for finery and show. He spent extravagantly on clothes, and had an insatiable passion for jewellery. He patronized poets and scholars, and it may be that the extant evidence does less than justice to the scale of his commissions. He impressed contemporaries as a builder, especially through his remodelling of Westminster Hall. He understood the importance of regal magnificence. In a treatise dedicated to him Roger Dymock argued that displays of magnificence were necessary for a king, and that the preservation of peace required 'an abundance of riches'.[24] In the cultivation of his image Richard drew on the traditions of English kingship, commissioning treatises on the regalia, promoting the cults of royal saints, and staging crown-wearings. He reflected hard on the 'matter of Britain', and had a broad view of his realms. His thinking in this respect seems rooted in the Plantagenet empire rather than anticipating the modern nation-state. Yet Richard had a taste for fashion, not only in clothes and other accessories, but also in ideas. In his commission to Gower he asked for 'some new thing'. He saw himself in the mirror of

A crown of thorns between the crowns of England and France. (The British Library, Roy.20.B.VI, fol. 1v)

contemporary Christendom. A number of his initiatives may have been inspired by reports of rulers of an earlier generation, like the Emperor Charles IV and Charles V of France, or by rivalry with contemporaries like Charles VI of France or even Giangaleazzo Visconti. He was conscious of Roman conceptions of princely power, and the more positive role assigned to princes in Roman law. Richard's awareness of the distance between the theory and practice of English kingship led him to reflect on statecraft in ways which, though ancient, anticipate the Renaissance. He regarded it as the duty of the prince to read the times – past, present and future – and aspire to the princely virtue of prudence.

Above all, Richard had an ambition that transcended his rule in England. Throughout the 1390s there are signs that he was drawn to a larger destiny in Christendom. At the simplest level, there was the notion that peace with France was both a requirement of restoring the fortunes of the English crown and a precondition of peace and unity in England. At the highest level, it may have involved ambitions for a role of leadership in Christendom, perhaps in the recovery of the Holy Land. It is impossible to know how serious he was in the larger concerns. They may have been the stuff of occasional fantasy rather than a sustained secret design. They were probably not public knowledge, though the wider political community may have had some sense of what were flatteringly termed his 'honourable purposes'.[25] It does seem likely, though, that the sirens of this larger destiny shaped his policy and may have heightened his frustration and anger with opposition at home.

★　★　★

In the spring of 1400, as Christendom entered a year with apocalyptic associations, England had to come to terms with the overthrow of a king who had reigned for the best part of a generation. As a mere child he had been crowned, as the author of *Richard the Redeless* observed, 'with a crown that no king under heaven, as I believe, could have bought better, so full was it filled with virtuous stones, with costly pearls to punish wrongs, and with red rubies to judge what is right'.[26] At the beginning of his account of Richard's reign the Dieulacres chronicler hailed him as 'the most excellent king of all the kings of the world'.[27] Even Walsingham acknowledged that Richard's magnificence was regarded as a grounds for optimism in England at the beginning of 1397.[28] In 1399 Creton acknowledged Richard's 'power, possessions and grandeur'.[29]

The overthrow of Richard thus appeared a wondrous event. To many people, Henry's conquest of the kingdom in fifty days seemed a miracle ordained by God. A number of chroniclers sought to make sense of it by reference to the rich tradition of political prophecy in England and Wales. The Lancastrian knight who accompanied Jean Creton to Chester asserted that Richard's overthrow had been plainly foretold by Merlin and Bede.[30] Few commentators could resist presenting the events of 1399 as a revolution in the wheel of fortune. After relating Richard's death, Adam Usk bade him farewell and apostrophized him: 'although you were as liberal as Solomon, as fair as Absalom, as grand as Ahaseurus, and as outstanding a builder as the great Belinus, nevertheless you too were cast down, at the height of your glory, by the wheel of fortune'.[31] A clerk by the name of Ferriby was prompted to reflect more generally on the mutability of fortune: 'In our times the God of Majesty hath in thunder decreed – which we have not only heard, but seen – that the most famous princes of this world, resplendent in apparel as in countenance, glorious in the circumstances of their birth, well-secured by treaties, high-seated on their thrones, while they thought themselves firmly established on the pinnacle of happiness which they had gained, have fallen instantly with an unexpected rush from the summit of prosperity into the abyss of wretchedness.'[32] Creton hailed fortune 'as mistress puissant and proud, most changeable and impetuous' since 'she hath entirely stripped a powerful Christian king of all that he had'. She makes one king, and unmakes another; 'her working is a downright dream'.[33]

In their accounts of Richard's downfall, a number of contemporaries saw elements of tragedy. For the French chroniclers the revolution was a sorry tale of treason and betrayal. Interestingly Jean Creton reserves his animus not for Henry, for whom he has some regard, but for Richard's false friends, most notably Albemarle.[34] In other respects, the French writers show some sense of the dilemmas which prompted otherwise honourable men to commit shameful acts. The author of *Traison et Mort* does not censure the noblemen who failed to make a stand against Henry as he crossed England in the summer of 1399.[35] This sense of tragedy is not wholly lacking in the English sources. The author of *Richard the Redeless* speaks more in sorrow than anger, while Usk shows some personal sympathy with the king. Most writers lay some of the blame on Richard's advisers and servants. Ferriby believed that Richard was undone by 'the misleading deceit of a flattering household'.[36] According to *Richard the Redeless*, it was the arrogance and greed of the king's counsellors and the lawlessness of his retainers, that destroyed the bonds of love that ought to bind subjects to the ruler.

For most English commentators it was Richard himself who was ultimately responsible for his own downfall. It was he who surrounded himself with flatterers and refused to heed good counsel. As in the 1380s, so in the late 1390s, Richard was likened to Rehoboam who lost the kingdom of Israel because he followed the advice of young men.[37] Addressing the estates of the realm in 1399 Archbishop Arundel specifically contrasted Henry's manliness with Richard's childishness. Since Richard was in his thirties, and his counsellors were mainly men in their prime, it is a curious line of attack. There is a sense in which criticism of Richard's youthful folly is a harking back to the debates of the 1380s. Yet it still had some resonance. Richard was childless, a condition he shared with several of his closest confidants.[38] In 1396 he shed some of the obligations of manhood through his marriage to a child. The eight lords who laid the appeal against Gloucester, Arundel and Warwick in the parliament of 1397 are described by Walsingham as gesticulating and prancing around 'as if they were stage-villains rather than knights or sober men'. The young earl of Kent was especially singled out for his outrageous behaviour.[39] Soon to be created duke of Surrey, and set for a vice-regal role in Ireland, it may be that he was gaining in the late 1390s the sort of notoriety associated with De Vere a decade earlier. Above all, Richard disdained the advice of wise old heads. By 1397 a number of loyal servants of the crown may have wished to disassociate themselves from the Ricardian regime.[40] It has been well observed how totally Richard seems to have alienated Lord Scrope of Bolton and Lord Cobham, two of the most experienced and venerable lords of the late fourteenth century.[41]

There was clearly concern about aspects of Richard's character. Walsingham usefully identifies some of them. In describing the events of 1397 he wrote that 'the entire kingdom was thrown suddenly and unexpectedly into confusion' by Richard's *levitas, astutia, and insolentia.*[42] *Levitas* (fecklessness or irresponsibility) is a characteristic commonly associated with immaturity. The king's *insolentia* (arrogance) is likewise well attested. It is the allegation of *astutia* (cunning) that is most striking. It is the negative counterpart of *prudentia*, the princely virtue on which Richard most prided himself.[43] It can be argued that it was his *astutia* that above all led to his overthrow. By all accounts Richard acted in a manner towards his opponents which was chilling in its cynicism. Though he pardoned Gloucester, Arundel and Warwick for their offences in 1387–8 and 'for years acted in a friendly way towards them', he suddenly set out to destroy them in the summer of 1397.[44] He deceived Archbishop Arundel. He 'craftily' advised him not to defend himself in parliament, and assured him that he would defend his interests. After Arundel had been condemned in his absence, Richard assured him that his sentence was only for form, that he would remain archbishop, and that he should soon be recalled from exile.[45] He treated Henry of Bolingbroke in like manner, exiling him for no good cause, and then revoking the letters of attorney granted to him to safeguard his inheritance.[46] Richard's bearing and behaviour made it easy to believe that he was seeking to destroy the house of Lancaster by securing the reversal of the judgements of Edward II's reign.[47]

Amid the general indictment of the king's actions in the deposition articles, bad faith is a constant refrain. He broke his coronation oath and sought to subvert the commission established to reform his government. He pardoned his opponents, but 'carried venom in his heart, and when the opportunity came' moved to destroy them.[48] In 1397 he announced that he did not intend to proceed against the followers of the appellant lords, but then many were compelled to compound for their pardons 'as if they were traitors'. On account of such practices, it was alleged, 'the royal name and estate were brought into great disrepute'.[49] Richard manipulated parliament by interfering with elections, threatening members, and securing the appointment of a standing committee to complete business at his 'will', in 'derogation of the estate of parliament, and a great damage to the whole realm'. He caused the parliament rolls to be deleted and altered for his own ends, and falsified other records.[50]

Above all, there was the issue of truth. No one dared to 'speak the truth about the state of the king and the kingdom'.[51] The king was 'so variable and feigning in his

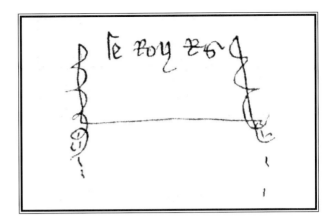

The sign manual of Richard II from Cronicque de la traison et mort, *ed. B. Williams (London 1846).*

words and writing, and also contrary to himself', especially in writing to the pope and other foreign princes, but also to his own subjects, that no one could trust him. His reputation for untruth and inconstancy was so notorious that 'it turned not only to the slander of his own person, but also of all the realm'.[52] The king was felt to be at the centre of the web of intrigue and deceit which came to enmesh the realm. In October 1399 Lord Cobham declared in parliament that 'with such a king, such dukes, and such rulers, the condition of the English people had sunk lower even than that of heathen peoples, who, although infidels to the Christian faith and thus erroneous in their beliefs, nevertheless speak the truth, acknowledge the truth, and act according to the truth'. The English, he continued, 'although they are Christians and should therefore profess the truth and act accordingly, nevertheless, for fear of the loss of their worldly goods, or of being ruined through exile, or even of death – which may befall even the constant – never dare to speak or act according to the truth under such rulers'.[53]

The nature of Richard's achievement and the grandeur of his vision in some sense underline the magnitude of his political failure. The crisis in English kingship was largely a personal one. As the movement around Henry of Lancaster gathered momentum, there was broad agreement that the main task was to bring Richard under constraint in the manner of 1386, or to force him to resign. The first stage in this process was to summon a parliament at which Richard's counsellors would be brought to trial. It may be that Richard himself gave some hope that he would resign the crown, perhaps after formally nominating Henry as his successor. After all, in the summer of 1399 he was presented with compelling evidence of the verdict of both God and the people against him.[54] Yet Henry and Archbishop Arundel cannot have been at all confident of Richard's readiness to accept the verdict. Their experience of him, stretching back over a dozen or so years, and their negotiations with him in the six weeks after his surrender at Flint, must have confirmed their belief that a settlement with him was impossible.

It is tempting to assume that Henry sought the crown from the outset, and to see his accession as an opportunistic seizure of power. McFarlane presents a picture of Henry cutting the ground from under the feet of men who sought some more radical settlement or who wished to replace Richard with Mortimer: 'those who were opposed to deposition were answered by an abdication; those who looked for the removal of Richard in favour of the earl of March were answered by a tumultuous acclamation of Henry IV'.[55] This conclusion needs a little modification. The real option in 1399 was some arrangement whereby Richard reigned while Henry ruled. Once that was found to be impossible, the combination of an abdication and a deposition appeared the overwhelmingly logical course. With regard to the succession to the throne, Henry's title looked stronger in 1399 than most historians have allowed. He was the nearest male heir, and in the late 1390s he may have appeared to many people as the heir presumptive, as his father had at the beginning of Richard's reign.[56] Henry's triumphal progress through England must have confirmed his mandate. God had blessed his cause, and he was the people's champion. When Henry challenged for the crown, his case must have appeared unanswerable.

To regard the events of 1399 merely as a coup seems inadequate. Henry did not march on London and have himself acclaimed before confronting Richard. It is true that he and his allies began to assume responsibility for the government of the realm at the end of the month, but only after York, the keeper of the realm, had thrown in his lot with them. The intention throughout seems to have been to involve the wider political community to ensure an orderly transfer of power, and it is likely that the steps taken to depose Richard and elevate Henry were taken after a fair amount of consultation and compromise. Inevitably there was trial and error, and indeed opportunism, in the process, but what is remarkable is the attention to precedent and legal forms. Once Richard's resignation nullified the parliament summoned in his name, Henry and his allies went through the formalities of summoning a new parliament. Of course, it was not possible to observe all the legal proprieties. Richard was not allowed to make an appearance before the assembly, and presumably that was in part because he could not be trusted to renounce his throne in public. The real point is that there was no legal way to put on trial and depose the king. It probably seemed wisest to proceed, as in 1326–7, on the fiction of an empty throne. Given that no better solution was found in 1688–9, the men of 1399 do not deserve the condescension of posterity.

Ideas as well as interests were at play in 1399.[57] On his arrival in England Henry caught the popular imagination as the righter of wrongs, the stuff of chivalric romance. He was likewise acclaimed as the instrument of God's justice, another Judas Maccabeus.[58] He also held an office which resonated in the English political tradition. In times of crisis, arising from the king's death in battle, his incapacity or his tyranny, it was the role of the great hereditary officers of the realm – the constable, steward or marshal – to take over the reins of power and summon parliament. In his capacity as steward of England, Henry was able to mobilize not merely a faction but a broad segment of the political nation to strive for 'the general utility of the king and kingdom'.[59] Creton recognized this dimension to the movement when he referred to the rebels' demand for a parliament in which Henry would be 'chief judge'.[60] In 1399 there were many people who believed that the rebellion was legitimate, and that Henry had not only the right but the obligation to bring Richard under restraint, and if necessary to seek the consent of the estates of the realm to his deposition.

The men who drew up the 'articles of deposition' sought primarily to demonstrate Richard's unworthiness to be king, but they were by no means unaware of the larger principles. They made a point of affirming the laws, conventions and expectations which Richard had allegedly broken, flouted or disappointed. They began with a statement of Richard's coronation oath and appealed to the Magna Carta. They assumed the king's obligation to rule within the law, to take counsel from his judges and magnates, and to rule for the common good. They affirmed the special status of parliament in respect of legislation and grants of taxation, and as a forum for seeking redress. They did not seek to limit the king's freedom, but stressed that the royal prerogative did not allow him to flout the laws made in parliament. The allegation that Richard asserted that the laws were in his breast or his mouth is especially significant. Superficially it provides another instance of the king's lack of discipline, petulance and folly. Yet it also reflects a concern to reject a conception of princely power which was held to be repugnant to the English political tradition. For many people the principal significance of 1399 lay in its reaffirmation of the principle that the king was subject to the law, and not, as in Roman law, the source of law. In 1401 Philip Repton regarded Richard as the prime example of a king punished by God for disregarding the laws. Princes who scorn the law, he asserted, 'shall be confounded – of which we have seen a striking example, as in a mirror, during these last two years in the case of King Richard, an image which will forever be indelibly impressed upon the memory of the whole world and of future ages'.[61]

The men of 1399 did not propound any new constitutional doctrine. There was no claim that parliament could depose the king or that it could confer the crown on another. There was no explicit repudiation of Richard's conception of monarchy. Instead there was a broad political consensus that the king had a right to rule, and that his prerogatives should remain intact. The commons probably needed little urging to petition in parliament that Henry should be as free in his regality as his ancestors. Yet in assessing the achievement of 1399 it is possible to be too literal-minded. On 19 August, after a successful rebellion in which the king was taken prisoner, a parliament was summoned to address weighty matters relating to the king and kingdom. Assembling on 30 September the lords and commons confronted and out-stared the empty throne. As representatives of the estates of the realm, they received Richard's abdication, set about a process of deposition, heard Henry's challenge for the throne, and acclaimed him as king. When the lords and commons reconvened as Henry's first parliament, they continued to concern themselves with weighty and contentious matters. While the commons requested that Henry should be as free as his ancestors, their reference to Richard's abuse of a like request seemed to imply that it was in some measure provisional. If Henry did not owe his crown to parliament, he certainly sought to secure parliamentary endorsement of the new dynasty.[62]

In the late nineteenth century Bishop Stubbs saw 1399 as a major landmark in the constitutional development of England. The tendency of twentieth-century scholarship has been to diminish its importance. The reaction has generally been a healthy one. It is misleading to read back into Richard's reign anachronistic dichotomies between 'absolutism' and 'constitutionalism'. Richard was not deposed by parliament; Henry was not elected by parliament; and there was no 'Lancastrian constitution'. An assessment of the significance of the events of 1399 must acknowledge the real continuities that give the period between the fourteenth and the seventeenth centuries a clear identity as an age of 'mixed monarchy'.[63] At the same time it must avoid the simple view that the expansion of the political nation, so marked a feature of the fourteenth century, necessarily diminished the role of the king. As Gerald Harriss has observed, 'as political society grew, so it needed the monarchy more, not less: to distribute patronage and power, to regulate and harmonize its tensions, and to provide a sense of direction and identity'.[64]

None the less there are grounds for believing that the overthrow of Richard marks a crucial episode in the longer term development of the English state. The high level of participation in the events, and the generally public nature of the proceedings, reflected in some wise the growth in size, complexity and ambition of the political nation. The whole experience was deeply educative. It contributed materially to the development of a sense of 'commonwealth' and the entrenchment of 'a system of government in which crown and subjects shared responsibility' in England.[65] Above all, key elements of a 'constitutional' tradition were affirmed by a newly enlarged ruling class. Richard's deposition represented an early and significant reverse to the trend which over the next three centuries would largely destroy 'mixed monarchy' on the European mainland. In the 1460s Sir John Fortescue had Richard pre-eminently in mind when he wrote that certain kings of England were drawn to the Roman law, especially the maxim 'that what pleases the prince has the force of law', which seemed to give them the authority to 'change laws at their pleasure, make new ones, inflict punishments, and impose burdens on their subjects, and also determine suits of parties at their own will and when they wish'.[66] Fortescue's conviction that the kings of England were obliged to rule 'politically' as well as a 'regally' was well founded. Richard would have had it otherwise.

The events of 1399 seem more than a coup, but it is a moot point whether they merit the epithet of 'revolution'. It is instructive to compare the overthrow of Richard II, which has traditionally been termed a 'revolution', with that of Edward II, which is typically seen more in terms of a baronial rebellion and a coup. It could be argued that the events of 1326–7 were more radical, and that the only reason 1399 is accorded greater significance is the fact that Richard's deposition was accompanied by a usurpation and dynastic discontinuity. Yet it can be argued that the fact that the struggles of the late fourteenth century were played out between actors mindful of the events of Edward II's time adds enormously to the significance of what Richard sought to achieve and what his subjects succeeded in resisting. The issues were both weightier, and involved a larger political nation in 1399 than in 1327. Of course, the events of 1399 fall short of current understandings of 'revolution'. Yet it must be borne in mind that the original paradigm of a political revolution was not the French Revolution of 1789, but the Glorious Revolution of 1688–9. It is in this idiom that the use of the term seems not only valid but wholly appropriate. Indeed it was in the aftermath of the revolution of 1688–9, and in recognition of the precedents of 1399, that the events surrounding Richard's deposition and Henry's accession were first styled a 'revolution'.[67]

★ ★ ★

Henry IV ascended the throne amid popular rejoicing. The easy suppression of the rising of 1400 attests continuing popular support for his cause. Over the years which followed, however, Henry found himself increasingly embattled. In November 1400 came revelations of a bizarre plot to smear Henry's saddle with a magical ointment that would cause him, before he had ridden ten miles, to swell up and die instantly, 'sitting upright in the saddle'.[68] In March 1402 a Hertfordshire woman alleged that since Henry's usurpation 'there has not been seven days' good and seasonable weather'.[69] The change in mood is difficult to explain. News of Richard's death may have prompted people to reflect on the enormity of what had been done in 1399. There arose a perception that Henry was irremediably tarnished by usurpation and regicide. In relating Richard's fall, Creton and the author of *Traison et Mort* referred several times to the fickleness of the English people. As they followed events from across the Channel, they would have found ample confirmation of this estimate of the English character. God's providence was likewise hard to fathom. As the duke of Orléans warned Henry in 1402: 'God may have dissembled with you, and have set you on a throne, like many other princes, whose reign has ended in confusion.'[70]

Though his accession had been generally supported, Henry found it hard to make the transition from factional leader to king. In the establishment of his regime he depended on his northern allies, and the knights and squires who had rallied to his cause in 1399.[71] He sought to consolidate this support through the distribution of patronage. He granted Northumberland and Harry 'Hotspur' a share of Richard's treasure, and expanded his retinue through grants of annuities. Henry's generosity to his friends led to a call in his first parliament that his largesse should be limited. His retaining prompted even greater concern. In 1399 the commons banned the wearing of lords' badges and even restricted the use of the king's badge to retainers actually attendant on the king.[72] Henry's retainers seem to have become almost as notorious as Richard's. By 1401 many of the grievances which had been directed against Richard were being directed against Henry. Philip Repton, Henry's confessor, wrote a letter admonishing him for his failure to bring law and justice to the land. The letter achieved some circulation, and was included by Adam Usk in his chronicle prior to his departure for Rome early in 1402.[73]

In 1399 Henry promised to 'live of his own'. It was probably assumed that the Lancastrian inheritance, along with the residue of Richard's hoard, would provide cheap government. Henry soon found himself embarrassed financially. The expedition to Scotland, the revolt in Wales and the resumption of hostilities with France made it necessary for him to call on parliament and convocation. His requests were generally met, but rarely with good grace. When in 1401 he asked his second parliament for a subsidy the commons responded by requesting that he first redress their grievances.[74] In the same session the commons unsuccessfully petitioned that the king's chief officers and councillors be named and sworn in parliament. In 1404 the grant of a subsidy was made conditional on the appointment of special treasurers to oversee disbursements. Henry felt constrained to agree to ordain his council in parliament 'for the ease and comfort of his whole realm', and to concede to the council supervision of the expenditure of a grant of taxation.[75] In 1406 Henry insisted that 'kings were not wont to render account', but the commons ordained that he should 'undertake to submit all warrants involving expenditure to the council for its endorsement', and that the councillors should swear to observe articles drawn up 'for their guidance'.[76]

The assertiveness of the commons in Henry's reign, in marked contrast to their subservience in 1397–8, is some testimony to the significance of the revolution of 1399.

It was widely believed that Henry had been raised to the throne on the basis of a covenant with the people. In March 1402 men were arrested for saying that the king had not kept his covenant with the commons in that though he had promised that they would be quit of all taxation other than for war, he had raised funds to enrich his retainers rather than for the common profit of the realm.[77] In May there were reports of preachers alleging that he had not kept the promises that he had made on his arrival in England, at his coronation and to his parliament. Even more remarkably Henry felt it appropriate to issue instructions to the sheriffs and other officials to make proclamation in appropriate places and times that it was, is and always would be his intention to observe and safeguard the public interest and the common good, and the laws and customs of the realm.[78]

Henry continued to face criticism, conspiracy and rebellion. According to the continuator of the *Eulogium Historiarum*, the Franciscans were especially active against him in 1402. William Frisby, a Franciscan friar, disputed with Henry himself, openly challenging his legitimacy. Henry found it impossible to put the circumstances of his accession behind him. At one point he found himself declaring that he did not seize the crown, but was 'properly elected'.[79] Even before the Percies, in alliance with Owain Glyndwr, launched a major rising against him in 1403, Henry had wholly lost the serenity and good humour which carried him through 1399. Though he pardoned a number of the simple folk who spoke against him, he had the friars executed as traitors. His victory over the rebels at the battle of Shrewsbury in 1403 brought him no ease. William Norham, the hermit who had spoken out against Richard, now castigated Henry. While Richard had scoffed and sent him back to prison, Henry had him put to death.[80] In May 1405 Archbishop Scrope of York joined the earl of Northumberland in insurrection. He allegedly urged Henry to make amends for his acts of perjury in 1399, and sought the restoration of the crown to the rightful line of descent.[81] Archbishop Scrope fell into the hands of the earl of Westmorland, and the rising was crushed. Despite Archbishop Arundel's pleas for clemency, Henry ordered Scrope's execution as a traitor. Over the winter of 1405/6 Henry fell ill, and he was dogged by poor health for the remainder of his reign. It was alleged that his illness was leprosy, and that his condition was God's punishment for Scrope's martyrdom.[82]

Inevitably Henry's reign saw a scaling back of Richard's conception of the English monarchy. Henry was an intelligent, studious man.[83] He was a distinguished musician in his own right, and was well served by a number of English poets. Yet there was little scope for regal magnificence, and his court seems to have been poorly attended.[84] Henry failed to maintain the carapace of regality that Richard had so carefully assembled. He could not draw as readily as his predecessor had done on the support of the church. Henry had a reputation for anti-clericalism, and his household included men who scoffed in church and advocated disendowment. In 1401 the price of clerical support for the Lancastrian regime was the passing of a series of measures against heresy, including the institution of the death penalty for obdurate heretics.[85] Either through choice or necessity Henry left undeveloped the sacral dimension of his kingship. Although he had been the first king to be consecrated with the holy oil of St Thomas of Canterbury, Henry appears not to have continued Richard's practice of regular crown-wearings. Perhaps he did not want to repeat the experience of 1399. According to Adam Usk, as a

Henry IV, as he appears in the initial of a Duchy of Lancaster charter. (Public Record Office)

result of his anointing 'his head was so infected with lice that his hair fell out, and for several months he had to keep his head covered'.[86]

Henry did not enjoy his kingship. The blithe chivalric hero of the 1390s became in the next decade the archetypal 'leper king'. The French worked hard to make England appear a pariah state. At the time of the revolution of 1399, it had been assumed in France that Henry's accession marked the triumph of the war-party in England. When he heard the news the duke of Berry wrote that it boded ill for France because Henry would govern 'by the voice of the commons of England' and they would demand war.[87] Henry in fact sought peace, and strove hard to win acceptance among the princes of Europe.[88] Yet in a sense the French were right. The failure of Richard's grand conception of monarchy made inevitable a reversion to the 'war state'. It was on campaign that kings of England could most readily mobilize the resources of the realm and enhance the prestige of the crown. It was in the successful prosecution of war that the solidarity of the ruling elite, so indispensable to public order, was most economically achieved. Yet it was a dangerous course, and ultimately a gamble. Henry IV was content to survive and pass on his crown to his eldest son. It would be Henry V who would test his kingship and affirm England's corporate unity by launching an invasion of France.

★　★　★

The regal image of Richard retained a hold on the imagination of his contemporaries. It is ironic that while Henry had to bear the opprobrium of regicide, he also had to contend with persistent rumours that Richard was still alive. The conspirators in 1400 had sought to make use of a pseudo-Richard to rally the people, and in February Henry and his council had been wise to arrange for Richard's body to be displayed in London and elsewhere prior to the burial at Langley. By early 1402, however, rumours were spreading through the realm that Richard was 'alive and well' in Scotland. An impostor, Thomas Ward of Trumpington, established himself at the court of Robert III of Scotland and, subsequently, of the duke of Albany.[89] In France the reports were taken very seriously, not least since they bore so materially on the position of Richard's queen, who had been finally returned to France in 1401. Jean Creton found that the news stirred his heart. In 1402 he wrote a letter to Richard in which he wondered how it was that Richard's image came so often 'before the eyes of my heart, for day and night my imaginations are no other than thoughts of you'.[90] Meanwhile in England in 1402 letters from the pseudo-Richard stirred the excitable Franciscans and led a number of others into treasonable activities. The invocation of Richard's name was a potent factor in the Percies' rebellion in 1403. Thousands of men from Cheshire, all wearing Richard's badge of the white hart, rallied to Henry Percy's standard at Lichfield.[91] It may have been this faith in Richard's resurrection that led one chronicler to describe Richard as 'the god of the Cheshire men'.[92]

While Henry's hereditary title was formidable, especially in the exceptional circumstances of 1399, it remained open to challenge. For most of Henry's opponents Richard remained the rightful king. In 1402 William Frisby claimed that if Richard were alive he was the rightful king, and if he were dead then Henry was a regicide. He refused to accept the validity of a resignation achieved by compulsion, or an election when the throne was not vacant.[93] Even in 1405 Archbishop Scrope simply maintained that the crown should be restored to 'the rightful line of descent'. By 1400, however, there is some attention being paid to the claims of the house of Mortimer, and in a letter of 1402 Sir Edmund Mortimer declared his intention to ally with Owain Glyndwr to restore Richard to the throne or, if he was dead, to make his nephew, the young earl of March, 'the right heir to the crown', king of England.[94] Henry continued to use parliament to strengthen his dynastic title. In 1404 he settled the succession on his sons and their issue, male and female, in order of age. In June 1406 he issued a charter sealed by the lords and the speaker of the commons entailing the crown on his sons and their heirs male. This belated attempt to give statutory force to Edward III's entail of the crown was revoked later in the year, and the position of the heir general reinstated.[95] The principle of succession through females was too well established in England. Given that Henry was blessed with four sons, the issue hardly seemed pressing. According to an early tradition, Henry himself had doubts about the validity of his title. Henry allegedly told his confessor that he had done penance for the usurpation and the death of Archbishop Scrope. He regretted he could not make restitution of the crown, but his sons would 'not suffer the regalia to go out of our lineage'.[96]

Henry V had no intention of letting loose his grip on the crown, but he was in a better position than his father to make amends. The young Henry had played no part in the betrayal of Richard, and as prince of Wales and earl of Chester he had sought to present himself as Richard's political heir. An early biographer of Henry V made a great deal of the story that Richard identified Henry as the subject of the prophecy that a future king of England, born in Wales, would do great deeds.[97] In the first year of his reign Henry arranged for Richard's reburial in Westminster abbey, borrowing some of the banners recently made for Henry IV's funeral.[98] It was both a noble act of reconciliation and a shrewd political move to staunch rumours that Richard was still alive. None the less Henry still had to face conspiracy and revolt. On the eve of his expedition to France in 1415, Henry discovered a plot which both looked back to the reign of Richard II and forward to the Wars of the Roses. The key conspirator was Richard, earl of Cambridge, the second son of Edmund of Langley, duke of York, and Richard's godson. It professed to seek a Mortimer succession, and involved Lord Scrope of Masham, Archbishop Scrope's nephew.[99] It was Henry's triumph at Agincourt that gave the house of Lancaster the appearance of a divine mandate, and stilled opposition for a generation.[100]

The ghost of Richard II could never be wholly exorcised.[101] Henry V's reign came to an abrupt end with his untimely death in 1422, leaving an infant son barely nine months old as heir to both England and France. Since none of Henry's brothers had legitimate issue the future of the house of Lancaster rested with the young and feeble Henry VI. Even after attaining his majority, Henry showed no real capacity for government, and remained childless until 1453, when the birth of a son and heir prompted the first of a series of bouts of psychotic derangement. In the circumstances there was a natural tendency to associate the misfortunes of the Lancastrian dynasty with the usurpation of Henry of Bolingbroke. In the course of the 1450s, if not earlier, Richard, duke of York, came to see himself as the rightful heir to the kingdom through his mother, Anne Mortimer. In presenting his claim to parliament in 1460 he accepted that Richard had resigned, but argued that Henry IV had then usurped the throne.[102] After his accession Edward IV, York's son, attributed all England's recent tribulations, the like of which 'hath not been seen or heard in any Christian realm', to Richard's deposition and murder.[103] The Burgundian chronicler Georges Chastellain likewise firmly associated the misfortunes of the house of Lancaster in the mid-fifteenth century to the revolution of 1399.[104] The debate over Richard continued. In Lancastrian circles he was remembered as a king who had sought to distort the English political tradition. In a manifesto of 1469 the opponents of Edward IV compared him to Richard II, along with Edward II and Henry VI, in his alienation of the magnates, indulgence of favourites, taxes, and tolerance of lawlessness.[105]

From the late sixteenth century the historical reputation of Richard II and the significance of 1399 were matters of great political note. Elizabeth I declared an identity with Richard II, and with good reason. As her long reign came to an end, a number of authors looked back to the last years of Richard's reign 'as a point of comparison for the uncertainty created by the coming change of dynasty'.[106] The most notable was William Shakespeare himself who in his cycle of history plays gave powerful expression to the notion that the troubles of the fifteenth century were the necessary consequence of Henry's usurpation. Conversely, the parliamentarians of the seventeenth century looked back to the assault on Ricardian absolutism in 1386 and 1388 as well as in 1399 for

The Coronation of James II, showing a portrait of Richard II (top left). (F. Sandford, The History of the Coronation of James II, *1687)*

precedent and inspiration. It was in the reign of James II that history came closest to repeating itself. In the Glorious Revolution of 1688–9 there was an invasion, a champion of liberties, the fiction of an abdication, and an empty throne. It is somehow fitting to see in an illustration of the coronation of James II, the last king to succeed by indefeasible hereditary right, the portrait of Richard, spectre-like, still fixed to his habitual choir-stall in Westminster abbey.[107]

NOTES

CHAPTER ONE

1. M. Meiss, *French Painting in the Time of Jean de Berry*, 2 vols (London, 1967), I, pp. 64–5.

2. *Chronicles of England, France and Spain by Sir John Froissart*, ed. T. Johnes, 2 vols (London, 1842), ii, pp. 703–4.

3. *Chronique de la Traison et Mort de Richart II*, ed. B. Williams (London, 1846); 'Translation of a French Metrical History of the Deposition of Richard II', ed. J.T. Webb in *Archaeologia*, 20 (1824) [hereafter 'French Metrical History']; J.J.N. Palmer, 'The authorship, date and historical value of the French chronicles on the Lancastrian Revolution', *Bulletin of the John Rylands Library*, lxi (1978–9), 145–81, 398–421.

4. 'French Metrical History', 152–4.

5. Froissart, *Chronicles*, ed. Johnes, i, p. 1.

6. See B. Tuchman, *A Distant Mirror. The Calamitous Fourteenth Century* (London, 1978), ch. 27.

7. G. Stow, 'Richard II in Jean Froissart's Chroniques', *Journal of Medieval History*, xi (1985), 333–45.

8. Froissart, *Chronicles*, ed. Johnes, ii, p. 709.

9. Froissart, *Chronicles*, ed. Johnes, ii, pp. 696–7.

10. For the point that the Rome manuscript version of Book I was 'undertaken at the time when Froissart was completing the second half of Book IV, which deals with the final moments of the reign of Richard II', see P.F. Ainsworth, *Jean Froissart and the Fabric of History. Truth, Myth, and Fiction in the Chroniques* (Oxford, 1990), p. 254.

11. Ainsworth, *Froissart and the Fabric of History*, pp. 211–13.

12. This fragmentary poem has often been regarded as of a piece with another fragment written in similar language, metre and tone called 'Mum and the Sothsegger': *Mum and the Sothsegger*, ed. M. Day and R. Steele (Early English Text Society, 199, 1936). There are good reasons for believing that they are separate, though related, works.

13. *English Historical Documents*, vol. IV. 1327–1485, ed. A.R. Myers (London, 1969), pp. 453–4.

14. *The Major Latin Works of John Gower. 'The Voice of One Crying' and 'The Tripartite Chronicle'*, ed. E.W. Stockton (Seattle, 1962).

15. M.B. Parkes, 'Patterns of scribal activity and revisions of the text in early copies of works by John Gower' in *New Science out of Old Books. Studies in Manuscripts and Early Printed Books in Honour of A. I. Doyle*, ed. R. Beadle and A.J. Piper (Aldershot, 1995), pp. 83–4.

16. For Usk, his career, and the new standard edition of his chronicle see *The Chronicle of Adam Usk, 1377–1421*, ed. C. Given-Wilson (Oxford, 1997).

17. *Chronicle of Adam Usk*, pp. 8–9, 30–1.

18. The extant chronicle began in 1337, but until 1377 is no more than 'a meagre continuation of the *Polychronicon*': M.V. Clarke and V.H. Galbraith. 'The deposition of Richard II', *Bulletin of the John Rylands Library*, xiv (1930), 131.

19. *The Kirkstall Abbey Chronicles*, ed. J. Taylor (Leeds: Publications of the Thoresby Society, 42, 1952), pp. 42–3, 75.

20. Clarke and Galbraith. 'Deposition of Richard II', 144–5.

21. *Chronica Monasterii de Melsa*, 3 vols, ed. E.A. Bond (Rolls Series, 1866–8), iii, p. 254.

22. *Scotichronicon by Walter Bower in Latin and English*, ed. D.E.R. Watt, vol. 8 (Aberdeen, 1987), pp. 20–1; A. Gransden, 'The date and authorship of John of Glastonbury's "Cronica sive Antiquitates Glastoniensis Ecclesie"' in *Legends, Traditions and History in Medieval England* (London, 1992), p. 295.

23. The *Liber Regius* is somewhat mysterious. William Sudbury and Richard Cirencester, monks of Westminster, both made reference to it in treatises in the late 1380s, and it was known (though not necessarily directly) to John Flete, monk of Westminster, in the mid-fifteenth century. A marginal note on Flete's manuscript states that it was produced by a monk of Bury St Edmunds for Richard II: *The History of Westminster Abbey by John Flete*, ed. J.A. Robinson (Cambridge, 1909), pp. 3–4. For a Bury St Edmunds manuscript chronicle of the kings of England which Richard II 'had compiled in his fourteenth year of his reign' see Corpus Christi College, Cambridge MS. 251, f. 16r. It is not the *Liber Regius*, but may be based on it.

24. *Historia Vitae et Regni Ricardi Secundi*, ed. G.B. Stow (Philadelphia, 1977); *Eulogium Historiarum sive Temporis*, ed. F.S. Haydon, vol. 3 (Rolls Series, 1863); A. Gransden, *Historical Writing in England. Volume II. c. 1307 to the Early Sixteenth Century* (London, 1982), p. 185.

25. The relevant portion of the St Albans chronicles is published as *Annales Ricardi Secundi et Henrici Quarti*

in *Johannis de Trokelowe et Henrici de Blaneforde, Monachorum S. Albani, necnon quorundum Anonymorum, Chronica et Annales*, ed. H.T. Riley (Rolls Series, 1866). See J. Taylor, *English Historical Literature in the Fourteenth Century* (Oxford, 1987), pp. 65–70; G.B. Stow, 'Richard II in Walsingham's Chronicles', *Speculum*, 59 (1984).

26. *Johannis Capgrave Liber de Illustribus Henricis*, ed. F.C. Hingeston (Rolls Series, 1858), p. xiv.

27. G.O. Sayles, 'The deposition of Richard II: three Lancastrian narratives', *BIHR*, liv (1981); C. Given-Wilson, 'The Manner of King Richard's Renunciation: a Lancastrian narrative?', *EHR*, cviii (1993).

28. Clarke and Galbraith, 'Deposition of Richard II', 144.

29. *Kirkstall Abbey Chronicles*, p. 45.

30. Clarke and Galbraith, 'Deposition of Richard II', 133; C. Given-Wilson (ed.), *Chronicles of the Revolution 1397–1400* (Manchester, 1993), p. 9.

31. For the strongest expression of this tendency see L.D. Duls, *Richard II in the Early Chronicles* (The Hague, 1975).

32. 'French Metrical History', 137–40.

33. *Traison et Mort*, pp. 180–3, 187.

34. *The Chronicle of Iohn Hardyng*, ed. H. Ellis (London, 1812), p. 354n. According to Walter Bower, Bolingbroke did likewise: *Scotichronicon*, viii, pp. 20–1.

35. *Chronicles of London*, ed. C.L. Kingsford (Oxford, 1905), p. 56.

36. C.M. Barron, 'The tyranny of Richard II', *BIHR*, 41 (1968), 14; *CCR 1397–9*, p. 505.

37. *Major Latin Works of John Gower*, pp. 309–10. His reference to verses mocking Gloucester, Arundel and Warwick in 1397 seems consistent with this claim.

38. F. Grady, 'The Lancastrian Gower and the limits of exemplarity', *Speculum*, 70 (1995), 552–75.

39. *Chronicle of Adam Usk*, pp. 136–43.

40. *Eulogium Historiarum*, iii, pp. 391–2.

41. *Chronicle of Adam Usk*, pp. 138–9.

42. G.O. Sayles, 'King Richard of England: a fresh look', *Proceedings of the American Philosophical Society*, 115 (1971), 28.

43. A cluster of works in the early 1970s, all archivally based, put Ricardian studies on a wholly new foundation: F.R.H. Du Boulay and C.M. Barron (ed.), *The Reign of Richard II. Essays in Honour of May McKisack* (London, 1971); A. Goodman, *The Loyal Conspiracy. The Lords Appellant under Richard II* (London, 1971); J.J.N. Palmer, *England, France and Christendom 1377–99* (London, 1972); J.A. Tuck, *Richard II and the English Nobility* (London, 1973). See now N. Saul, *Richard II* (New Haven, 1997) and A. Goodman and J.L. Gillespie (eds), *Richard II. The Art of Kingship* (Oxford, 1999).

44. J.B. Post, 'Courts, councils, and arbitrators in the Ladbroke manor dispute, 1382–1400', in R.F. Hunnisett and J.B. Post (eds), *Medieval Legal Records edited in Memory of C.A.F. Meekings* (London, 1978), pp. 323–4.

45. PRO, E 101/411/9.

46. M.J. Bennett, 'Edward III's entail and the succession to the crown, 1376–1471', *English Historical Review*, cxiii (1998), 580–609.

47. C.M. Barron, 'The tyranny of Richard II', *BIHR*, 41 (1968), 1–18.

48. *Annales Ricardi Secundi et Henrici Quarti*, p. 199. Walsingham is likewise held to be wholly prejudiced against John of Gaunt in the late 1370s and early 1380s. V.H. Galbraith stated firmly that 'sound criticism should treat as false anything detrimental' to Gaunt in Walsingham's chronicles which is not corroborated in other sources: *The Anonimalle Chronicle 1333 to 1381*, ed. V.H. Galbraith (Manchester, 1927), p. xli. He especially had in mind Walsingham's claim that Gaunt petitioned parliament in 1376 to 'make a law on the pattern of the French that no woman be heir to the kingdom': *Chronicon Angliae, 1328–1388*, ed. E. Maunde Thompson (Rolls Series, 1857), pp. 92–3. The fact that Edward III made an entail of the crown in 1376 must add to Walsingham's general creditworthiness.

49. PRO E 404/14/96, no. 411.

50. D.M. Bueno de Mesquita, 'The foreign policy of Richard II in 1397: some Italian letters', *EHR*, lvi (1941).

51. G.B. Stow, 'Chronicles versus records: the character of Richard II' in J.S. Hamilton and P.J. Bradley (eds), *Documenting the Past. Essays in Medieval History presented to George Peddy Cuttino* (Woodbridge, 1989), pp. 155–76.

52. Recent editions include *Historia Vitae et Regni Ricardi Secundi*, ed. G.B. Stow (Philadelphia, 1977); *The Westminster Chronicle 1381–1394*, ed. L.C. Hector and B.F. Harvey (Oxford, 1982); *Knighton's Chronicle 1337–1396*, ed. G.H. Martin (Oxford, 1995); *The Chronicle of Adam Usk, 1377–1421*, ed. C. Given-Wilson (Oxford, 1997). For important reassessments of fourteenth-century narratives see the work of J. Taylor, G.B. Stow, J.J.N. Palmer and C. Given-Wilson.

53. *Chronicle of Adam Usk*, pp. 12–13.

54. M.J. Bennett, 'The court of Richard II and the promotion of literature' in B. Hanawalt (ed.), *Chaucer's England. Literature in Historical Context* (Minneapolis, 1992), pp. 13–16.

55. *Historia Vitae et Regni Ricardi Secundi*, p. 134.

56. PRO, E 403/549, m. 6.

57. D. Gordon, *Making and Meaning: The Wilton Diptych* (London, 1993); D. Gordon, L. Monnas and C. Elam (eds), *The Regal Image of Richard II and the Wilton Diptych* (London, 1998).

58. *Westminster Chronicle*, pp. 118–21.

59. E.W. Kirsch, *Five Illuminated Manuscripts of Giangaleazzo Visconti* (London, 1991), p. 69, n. 2.

60. 'Mémoires de Pierre Salmon', troisième supplément in *Collection des Chroniques Nationales Françaises écrites en langue vulgaire du treizième au seizième siècle, avec notes d'éclaircissements*, tome xv, ed. J.A. Buchon (Paris, 1826).

61. C. Given-Wilson, 'Richard II, Edward II and the Lancastrian inheritance', *EHR*, cix (1994).

62. *Chronicle of Adam Usk*, pp. 64–5.

CHAPTER TWO

1. Froissart, *Chronicles*, ed. Johnes, i, p. 357; Walsingham, *Historia Anglicana*, i, p. 302; *Annales Ricardi Secundi et Henrici Quarti*, pp. 237–8.

2. Froissart, *Chronicles*, ed. Johnes, ii, p. 709.

3. N.H. Nicolas (ed.), *Testamenta Vetusta, being Illustrations from Wills*, 2 vols (London, 1826), i, pp. 66–77.

4. Bennett, 'Edward III's entail and the succession', 584–7.

5. Bennett, 'Edward III's entail and the succession', 588–94.

6. Froissart, *Chronicles*, ed. Johnes, i, 509.

7. Joshua Barnes, *The History of that Most Victorious Monarch Edward III . . .* (Cambridge, 1688), p. 898.

8. C.L. Kingsford (ed.), *A Survey of London by John Stow*, 2 vols (Oxford, 1908), i, pp. 96–7.

9. *Westminster Chronicle*, pp. 414–17.

10. Walsingham, *Historia Anglicana*, i, p. 334. J. Nelson, 'Kingship and empire' in J.H. Burns (ed.), *The Cambridge History of Medieval Political Thought c. 350–c.1450* (Cambridge, 1988), pp. 217–18.

11. Walsingham, *Historia Anglicana*, i, pp. 346–63. The letters were originally addressed to Edward III, but on arrival in England they were readdressed to Richard.

12. In 1383 the Abbot of Gloucester was granted a favour in return for celebrating masses for Edward II's soul on his anniversaries: *CPR 1381–5*, p. 273; J.M. Theilmann, 'Political canonisation and political symbolism in medieval England', *Journal of British Studies*, 29 (1990), 256.

13. Saul, *Richard II*, pp. 78–9.

14. *Westminster Chronicle*, pp. 22–3.

15. *Westminster Chronicle*, pp. 24–5.

16. *Westminster Chronicle*, pp. 68–9.

17. *Historia Vitae et Regni Ricardi Secundi*, p. 86.

18. *Westminster Chronicle*, pp. 68–81; *Historia Vitae et Regni Ricardi Secundi*, p. 81.

19. Tuck, *Richard II and English Nobility*, pp. 92–5; Saul, *Richard II*, pp. 131–4. It is noteworthy that the intrigue at the court of Milan in 1385, where Bernabó Visconti of Milan was assassinated by his nephew Giangaleazzo, aroused some interest in England: *Westminster Chronicle*, pp. 118–21.

20. Walsingham, *Historia Anglicana*, i, p. 156.

21. N.B. Lewis, 'The last medieval summons of the English feudal levy', *EHR*, lxxiii (1958); Saul, *Richard II*, p. 144.

22. Froissart, *Chronicles*, ed. Johnes, ii, pp. 53–4.

23. *Knighton's Chronicle*, pp. 336–9; *Westminster Chronicle*, pp. 140–1.

24. Walsingham, *Historia Anglicana*, i, p. 140.

25. *Eulogium Historiarum*, iii, p. 361.

26. This section of the chronicle presents a number of problems, not least in terms of chronology. Tout dismissed this report as one of many 'gross errors' in the account of the Parliament, and other historians have followed: T.F. Tout, *Chapters in the Administrative History of Mediaeval England*, 6 vols (Manchester, 1928), III, p. 396n; J.A. Tuck, *Richard II and the English Nobility* (1973), p. 205. T.B. Pugh, *Henry V and the Southampton Plot* (Southampton Record Series, xxx, 1988), pp. 73–4, examines the report in greatest detail. The continuation of the *Eulogium* may not have been the only chronicle which recorded Richard's nomination of Roger Mortimer as his heir. For a reference to a Glastonbury chronicle supporting the Mortimer claim, allegedly destroyed on the orders of Henry of Bolingbroke in 1399, see *Scotichronicon* viii, pp. 20–1, and Gransden, 'John of Glastonbury's *Cronica sive Antiquitates Glastoniensis Ecclesie*', p. 295.

27. It is instructive that Richard was already showing scant respect to his grandfather's last wishes with respect to the endowment of prayers for his soul: C. Given-Wilson, 'Richard II and his grandfather's will', *EHR*, xciii (1978), 320–1.

28. *Westminster Chronicle*, pp. 192–5. The passage appears under the year 1387. While work on the chronicle continued until 1396 or so, the likelihood is that the passage was written, at least in draft form, within a few years of 1387.

29. Goodman, *John of Gaunt*, pp. 114–15.

30. Goodman, *John of Gaunt*, p. 118.

31. *Historia Vitae et Regni Ricardi Secundi*, p. 166; Richard of Maidstone, 'The reconciliation of Richard II with the City of London' in *Political Poems and Songs relating to English History*, vol. 1, ed. T. Wright (Rolls Series, 1859), p. 285.

32. G.B. Stow, 'Richard II and the invention of the pocket handkerchief', *Albion*, 27 (1995), 221–35.

33. *Historia Vitae et Regni Ricardi Secundi*, ed. G.B. Stow Jr (1977), p. 166.

34. Walsingham, *Historia Anglicana*, ii, p. 149.

35. Walsingham, *Historia Anglicana*, ii, p. 148.

36. Walsingham, *Historia Anglicana*, ii, p. 156.

37. The notion that the king's subjects were the chief beneficiaries of the war is made explicitly in De Mézières, *Letter to Richard II*, which was presented to Richard in 1395. There is every reason to suppose that the notion was current among the peace-makers a decade earlier.

38. Walsingham, *Historia Anglicana*, ii, pp. 142, 151.

39. *Knighton's Chronicle*, pp. 420–3; Froissart, *Chronicles*, ed. Johnes, ii, pp. 331, 404.

40. As Given-Wilson observes, Richard did not begin to recruit retainers systematically until 1387: C. Given-Wilson, *The Royal Household and the King's Affinity. Service, Politics and Finance in England 1360–1413* (New Haven, 1986), p. 213.

41. *Westminster Chronicle*, pp. 138–9.

42. P.J. Eberle, 'The politics of courtly style at the court of Richard II' in G.S. Burgess and R.A. Taylor (eds), *The Spirit of the Court. Selected Proceedings of the Fourth Congress of the International Courtly Literature Society* (Woodbridge, 1985).

43. Favent refers to 'gold badges in the form of the sun and silver crowns': 'Historia siue narracio de modo et forma mirabilis parliamenti apud West-monasterium anno Domini millesimo ccclxxxvij, regni vero regis Ricardi secundi post conquestum anno decimo, per Thomam Fauent clericum indictata', ed. M. McKisack in *Camden Miscellany XIV* (Camden Society, 3rd series, 37, 1926), p. 4. The Westminster chronicle refers to 'gold and silver crowns': *Westminster Chronicle*, pp. 186–7.

44. The project may have been inspired by the similar scheme in the Grande Salle in the Cité in Paris: P. Binski, *Westminster Abbey and the Plantagenets. Kingship and the Representation of Power 1200–1400* (New Haven, 1995), p. 202.

45. *The Life of the Black Prince* by the Chandos Herald was commissioned around this time, though seemingly not by the king himself.

46. Binski, *Westminster Abbey and the Plantagenets*, p. 198.

47. *Annales Ricardi Secundi et Henrici Quarti*, p. 299; *Westminster Chronicle*, pp. 130–3, 154–7.

48. *CPR 1381–5*, p. 542.

49. *CPR 1385–9*, p. 78.

50. *Westminster Chronicle*, pp. 142–5, 158n–159n.

51. See in general R.H. Jones, *The Royal Policy of Richard II. Absolutism in the Later Middle Ages* (Oxford, 1968); N. Saul, 'Richard II and the vocabulary of kingship', *EHR*, cx (1995); S. Walker, 'Richard II's views of kingship' in R.E. Archer and S. Walker (eds), *Rulers and Ruled in Late Medieval England. Essays presented to Gerald Harriss* (London, 1995). pp. 49–63.

52. Walsingham, *Historia Anglicana*, i, p. 148.

53. *Knighton's Chronicle*, pp. 354–61. For the 'articles of accusation against Edward II', see C. Valente, 'The deposition and abdication of Edward II', *EHR*, cxiii (1998), 852–81.

54. J.S. Roskell, *The Impeachment of Michael de la Pole, Earl of Suffolk, in 1386 in the Context of the Reign of Richard II* (Manchester, 1984), pp. 49–50.

55. Lichfield Joint Record Office, Dean and Chapter Act Books I, f. 15.

56. *Historia mirabilis parliamenti*, p. 4.

57. *Westminster Chronicle*, pp. 186–7.

58. The king was attended at Nottingham by the archbishops of York and Dublin, the bishops of Durham, Chichester and Bangor, the duke of Ireland and the earl of Suffolk. The earl of Kent was also apparently present.

59. S.B. Chrimes, 'Richard II's questions to the Judges', *The Law Quarterly Review*, 72 (1956), 365–90.

60. M.V. Clarke, 'Forfeitures and treason in 1388' in M.V. Clarke, *Fourteenth Century Studies*, ed. L.S. Sutherland and M. McKisack (Oxford, 1937), pp. 126, 132.

61. Clarke, 'Forfeitures and treason in 1388', 132.

62. Goodman, *Loyal Conspiracy*, p. 21.

63. Clarke, 'Forfeitures and treason in 1388', 132.

64. Goodman, *Loyal Conspiracy*, p. 22.

65. *Knighton's Chronicle*, pp. 410–13.

66. *Westminster Chronicle*, pp. 212–15.

67. *Johannis Capgrave Liber de Illustribus Henricis*, ed. F.C. Hingeston (Rolls Series, 1858), p. 98.

68. J.N.L. Myres, 'The campaign of Radcot Bridge in December 1387', *EHR*, xlii (1927); J.L. Gillespie, 'Thomas Mortimer and Thomas Molineux; Radcot Bridge and the Appeal of 1397', *Albion*, vii (1975).

69. *Westminster Chronicle*, pp. 228–9. The year of Henry's birth is variously given as 1366 and 1367, but the former date is regarded as more likely: J.L. Kirby, *Henry IV of England* (London, 1970), p. 11. From the form of words used, the allusion would appear to be to Henry of Bolingbroke rather than either Gloucester, who was in his forties, or the earl of March who was still a young child. I thank Andrew Rayner for this point.

70. M.V. Clarke and V.H. Galbraith, 'The deposition of Richard II' in Clarke, *Fourteenth Century Studies*, p. 91.

71. Given-Wilson, *Chronicles of the Revolution*, p. 81.

CHAPTER THREE

1. For the possible rivalry between Gloucester and Derby over the succession see Clarke and Galbraith, 'Deposition of Richard II', 91. Richard kept the earls of Derby and Nottingham to stay with him in the Tower: *Knighton's Chronicle*, pp. 426–7.

2. *Westminster Chronicle*, pp. 234–5.

3. *Historia mirabilis parliamenti*, pp. 14–15.

4. *Westminster Chronicle*, pp. 236–69; *Knighton's Chronicle*, pp. 452–99.

5. *Westminster Chronicle*, pp. 278–9.

6. *RP*, iii, p. 236; B. Wilkinson, *Constitutional History of Medieval England 1216–1399. Vol. II: Politics and the Constitution 1307–1399* (London, 1952), p. 280.

7. Archbishop Neville was captured at Newcastle upon Tyne in June and remained in the custody of the mayor until 28 November, when he made a second escape abroad: *Westminster Chronicle*, pp. 342–5.

8. *Westminster Chronicle*, pp. 282–3.

9. *Westminster Chronicle*, pp. 310–13. Brembre sought to change the name of London to Troy: *Knighton's Chronicle*, pp. 500–1.

10. *Westminster Chronicle*, pp. 286–9.

11. *Westminster Chronicle*, pp. 288–91.

12. 'Morley versus Montagu (1399): A Case in the Court of Chivalry', ed. M.H. Keen and M. Warner in *Camden Miscellany XXXIV* (Camden Society, 5th series, 10, 1997), pp. 163–4. His partner as godfather was the chamber knight Sir Richard Stury.

13. *Westminster Chronicle*, pp. 290–3, 328–33; *Knighton's Chronicle*, pp. 500–3.

14. It may be significant that York and Basset were with the king at Lichfield in June 1387: Lichfield Joint Record Office, Dean and Chapter Act Books I, f. 15.

15. *RP*, iii, p. 251; *CPR 1385–9*, pp. 494–5; *CPR 1391–6*, p. 102.

16. Wilkinson, *Constitutional History of Medieval England*, ii, 283.

17. A list of 170 Sussex oath-takers, including clergy, gentry and burgesses, has survived. The oaths seem to have been taken in the local courts: N. Saul, 'The Sussex gentry and the oath to uphold the acts of the Merciless Parliament', *Sussex Archaeological Collections*, 135 (1997), 221–39.

18. *Westminster Chronicle*, pp. 342–3.

19. *Westminster Chronicle*, pp. 324–7.

20. Walsingham, *Historia Anglicana*, ii, pp. 157–8.

21. N.H. Owen, 'Thomas Wimbledon's Sermon: *Redde racionem villicacionis tue*', *Mediaeval Studies*, 28 (1966), esp. 183, 194; H.L. Spencer, *English Preaching in the Late Middle Ages* (Oxford, 1993), p. 67.

22. *Westminster Chronicle*, pp. 326–7.

23. *CPR 1385–9*, p. 468; *Knighton's Chronicle*, pp. 438–43.

24. *The Register of John Waltham, Bishop of Salisbury, 1388–1395*, ed. T.C.B. Timmins. (The Canterbury and York Society, 80, 1994), no. 129, p. 37.

25. *Westminster Chronicle*, pp. 354–7; Tuck, *Richard II and the English Nobility*, p. 135–6; R.L. Storey, 'Liveries and commissions of the peace 1388–90', in Du Boulay and Barron, *Reign of Richard II*, p. 132; N. Saul, 'The Commons and the abolition of badges', *Parliamentary History*, 9 (1990), 310–13.

26. Tuck, *Richard II and the English Nobility*, pp. 136–7.

27. *Westminster Chronicle*, pp. 368–73.

28. H.T. Riley (ed.), *Ingulph's Chronicle of the Abbey of Croyland with the continuations by Peter of Blois and anonymous writers* (London, 1893), p. 334.

29. *Westminster Chronicle*, pp. 374–5.

30. Tuck, *Richard II and the English Nobility*, p. 137. Richard was doubtless aware that in 1388 Charles VI of France, though still in his teens, had similarly declared himself of age and thrown off the tutelage of his uncles.

31. Tuck, *Richard II and the English Nobility*, p. 138.

32. Storey, 'Liveries and commissions of the peace 1388–90', 135.

33. Storey, 'Liveries and commissions of the peace 1388–90', 136–43.

34. John Gower, *Confessio Amantis*, Book 8, lines 2987–3043 in *The English Works of John Gower*, ed. G.C. Macaulay, 2 vols (London, 1900–1), ii, 469–74.

35. *Issues of the Exchequer, Henry III–Henry VI*, ed. F. Devon (London, 1847), p. 239.

36. Goodman, *Loyal Conspiracy*, p. 55.

37. Walsingham, *Historia Anglicana*, ii, pp. 193–4.

38. Goodman, *John of Gaunt*, p. 144.

39. *Westminster Chronicle*, pp. 406–9.

40. Queen Anne was inconsolable, taking to her chamber with her ladies and passing the days in weeping: *Westminster Chronicle*, pp. 408–11.

41. Tout, *Chapters*, iii, p. 460.

42. *Westminster Chronicle*, pp. 412–15; Goodman, *John of Gaunt*, p. 146.

43. *Proceedings and Ordinances of the Privy Council of England, vol. I. 1386–1410*, ed. Sir H. Nicolas (London, 1834), p. 18.

44. Storey, 'Liveries and commissions of the peace 1388–90', 146–7.

45. *Westminster Chronicle*, pp. 440–3. Northampton was released from prison, though not fully restored to citizenship of London.

46. *Ingulph's Chronicle of the Abbey of Croyland*, pp. 333–7; S. Walker, *The Lancastrian Affinity 1361–1399* (Oxford, 1990), p. 123.

47. *Ingulph's Chronicle of the Abbey of Croyland*, pp. 338–40.

48. *Issues of the Exchequer*, p. 238.

49. Saul, *Richard II*, p. 313.

50. *Westminster Chronicle*, pp. 414–17.

51. J.J.N. Palmer, 'England and the great western schism, 1388–1399', *EHR*, lxxxiii (1968), 517–19.

52. *Foedera*, vii, 672–5; *The Diplomatic Correspondence of Richard II*, ed. E. Perroy (Camden Society, 3rd series, 48, 1933), no. 120. The letter was sealed by all the lay lords.

53. St John's College, Cambridge, MS A7; Saul, *Richard II*, p. 237.

54. *Westminster Chronicle*, pp. 436–9, 158n–9n.

55. The rumour seems to have been sparked by the death of the earl of Pembroke. There was a prophecy that Thomas of Lancaster would achieve sainthood only after the extinction of the line of the men who had sat in judgement on them: *The Chronicle of England by John Capgrave*, ed. F.C. Hingeston (Rolls Series, 1858), p. 253.

56. J.L. Gillespie, 'Richard II: chivalry and kingship', in J.L. Gillespie (ed.), *The Age of Richard II* (Stroud, 1997), pp. 115–38.

57. John Dunbar, earl of Moray, apparently fought with the earl of Nottingham. Richard II granted him 200 marks, a silver cup and a gilt-covered ewer worth £139 11s 1d. Sir David Lindsay and Sir William Dalziell likewise received rewards: Sir James Balfour, *The Scots Peerage*, 9 vols (Edinburgh, 1904–14), vi,

p. 300. Andrew of Wyntoun recorded Sir David Lindsay's exploits while Richard was reigning 'in his flowris': Gillespie, 'Richard II: chivalry and kingship', 119. For Dalziell's bravura performance on field and during the banquet see *Scotichronicon*, viii, pp. 14–19.

58. *Westminster Chronicle*, pp. 436–7.

59. H.C. Maxwell-Lyte, *Historical Notes on the Great Seal of England* (London, 1926), pp. 206–7.

60. *Westminster Chronicle*, pp. 450–1. It may have been opportune that Henry of Bolingbroke, who had jousted well at St Inglevert, had set out on crusade the month previously: *Johannis Capgrave Liber de Illustribus Henricis*, p. 99.

61. *Westminster Chronicle*, pp. 450–1.

62. *Polychronicon Ranulphi Higden*, ed. C. Babington and J.R. Lumby, 9 vols (Rolls Series, 1889–95), viii, p. 490.

63. *Westminster Chronicle*, pp. 450–3.

64. *Westminster Chronicle*, pp. 454–5.

65. *History of Westminster Abbey by John Flete*, pp. 3–4; Corpus Christi, Cambridge, MS. 251. f. 16r.

66. *Westminster Chronicle*, pp. 454–5. Queen Anne granted an annuity at Bristol Castle on 21 March: *CPR 1391–6*, p. 72.

67. The 'old style' date 'March 1391'could refer to 1–24 March 1392 or 25–31 March 1391. The reference to the year as 14 Richard II [1390–1] confirms the matter.

68. Bodleian Library, Oxford, Bodley MS. 581, fos 9r–11r; *Four English Political Tracts of the Later Middle Ages*, ed. J.-P. Genet (Camden Society, 4th series, 18, 1977), pp. 22–3; H.M. Carey, *Courting Disaster. Astrology at the English Court and University in the Later Middle Ages* (London, 1992), pp. 102–3.

69. Bodleian Library, Oxford, Bodley MS. 581, fos 1r–3r; Genet, *Four English Political Tracts*, pp. 31–9; Carey, *Courting Disaster*, p. 102.

70. Bennett, 'Court of Richard II and the promotion of literature', 3–20.

71. 'Morley versus Montagu (1399): A Case in the Court of Chivalry' ed. M.H. Keen and M. Warner in *Camden Miscellany XXXIV* (Camden Society, 5th series, 10, 1997), p. 151.

72. BL, Additional MS. 5016; Cambridge University Library, MS. Ii VI 17.

73. *Annales Ricardi Secundi et Henrici Quarti*, p. 301.

74. Genet, *Four Political Tracts*, pp. 25–30, discusses some of the possibilities, eventually pressing the claims of William Thorpe, treasurer of York from 1393.

75. *Westminster Chronicle*, pp. 458–9.

76. Both men were greatly criticized, which may well be a measure of their influence. Bache was a theologian; when he first came into the royal service he followed the court on foot and refused preferment, but after his consecration as bishop of St Asaph in May 1390 he 'changed totally and became very arrogant': *Westminster Chronicle*, pp. 434–5. Burghill followed a

similar path, ending his days as bishop of Lichfield with the reputation as a miser: *Chronicle of Adam Usk*, pp. 248–50.

77. He is recorded as preaching on five separate occasions on the feast of St Edward the Confessor and once on the feast of St Edward the Martyr: Walker, 'Richard II's views on kingship', 59.

78. According to Adam of Usk, he had been expelled from the convent at Hailes 'for dabbling in the arts of healing and weaving spells': *Chronicle of Adam Usk*, pp. 134–5.

79. John Boor first appears as dean of the chapel royal in March 1389: *CPR 1388–92*, p. 15. Jean de Montreuil, a French chancery clerk centrally engaged in the peace negotiations in the mid-1390s, refers several times to the writings of 'maistre Jehan Boore', whom he clearly regarded as a sort of English 'historiographer royal': Jean de Montreuil, *Opera. Vol. II. L'oeuvre historique et polémique*, ed. N. Grévy, E. Ornato and G. Ouy (Torino, 1975), no. 220, lines 196–200, no. 221, lines 20–2. Montreuil came to England in 1394, and both Boor and Montreuil took part in the celebrations associated with Richard's marriage to Isabelle of France in 1396.

80. *Westminster Chronicle*, pp. 474–7; *Calendar of Letter-Books of the City of London. Letter Book H, c. 1375–1399*, ed. R.R. Sharpe (London, 1907), pp. 362–3. *Knighton's Chronicle*, pp. 536–9.

81. *City of London. Letter Book H*, p. 362n; C.M. Barron, 'The quarrel of Richard II with London 1392–7', in Du Boulay and Barron, *Reign of Richard II*, p. 178, n. 18.

82. *Westminster Chronicle*, pp. 456–7.

83. *Westminster Chronicle*, pp. 458–73; *Diplomatic Correspondence of Richard II*, no. 133.

84. *Register of John Waltham, Bishop of Salisbury*, no. A19. On 20 November Bishop Fordham of Ely issued similar instructions to the clergy of his diocese: Cambridge University Library, Register of John Fordham, bishop of Ely, fos 112v–113r.

85. *Knighton's Chronicle*, pp. 538–41.

86. *Westminster Chronicle*, pp. 480–3.

87. *Ingulph's Chronicle of the Abbey of Croyland*, pp. 345–8.

88. *Ingulph's Chronicle of the Abbey of Croyland*, pp. 345–8.

89. *RP*, iii, p. 286; Saul, *Richard II*, pp. 255–6.

90. He was visited there by representatives from Aquitaine protesting against the alienation of the duchy from the crown.

91. Barron, 'The quarrel of Richard II with London', 179–80.

92. In a Selby Abbey register there is a copy of part of a letter apparently written by the archbishop. It is dated in Rome 4 December 1391 and refers to an approach to the king and council 'for our right'. There is a reference to 'our dear brother' William Neville who may have brought letters from Richard to the archbishop earlier in the year: BL, MS. Cotton

Cleopatra D III, f. 193r. There is another letter from Archbishop Neville to the abbot of Selby dated 16 March 1392: BL, MS. Cotton Vitellius E.XVI, f. 122v. Neville died at Louvain at the end of May 1392: *Westminster Chronicle*, pp. 492–3.

93. *Westminster Chronicle*, pp. 484–7.

94. Goodman, *John of Gaunt*, p. 149.

95. Palmer, *England, France and Christendom*, p. 145.

96. Palmer, *England, France and Christendom*, pp. 154–8.

97. Goodman, *John of Gaunt*, p. 151. See in general C.J. Philpotts, 'John of Gaunt and English policy towards France 1389–95', *Journal of Medieval History*, 16 (1990).

98. Goodman, *John of Gaunt*, p. 151.

99. *Westminster Chronicle*, pp. 488–9.

100. Barron, 'The quarrel of Richard II with London', 180; *CCR 1389–92*, pp. 530–1.

101. Barron, 'The quarrel of Richard II with London', 180–1.

102. Barron, 'The quarrel of Richard II with London', 181–2.

103. N. Saul, 'Richard II, York, and the evidence of the king's itinerary', in Gillespie, *Age of Richard II*, p. 79. J.H. Harvey, 'Richard II and York', in Du Boulay and Barron, *Reign of Richard II*, pp. 206–7, overstates the time Richard spent in York.

104. *City of London. Letter Book H*, p. 375.

105. *Westminster Chronicle*, pp. 492–3.

106. *CCR 1389–92*, p. 466; *City of London. Letter Book H*, p. 377; *Westminster Chronicle*, pp. 494–5. The deputation was given this commission by the Londoners, though it was not empowered to act 'notwithstanding' the city's privileges, as the writ had requested: Barron, 'The quarrel of Richard II with London', 183.

107. According to the *Westminster Chronicle*, the decision to move the courts to York was taken on the advice of Archbishop Arundel and Bishop Waltham and at the urging of the duke of Lancaster and the earl of Huntingdon: *Westminster Chronicle*, pp. 492–3.

108. Barron, 'The quarrel of Richard II with London', 178–9.

109. The court was based at Rockingham Castle in early June. Their interest in the hunt is indicated not only by the presence of the earl of Rutland, the author of the *Master of the Chase*, but by the grant to the king's kinswoman Joan, countess of Hereford, of a licence to hunt in person with hunters and hounds for all game and venison in the king's forests: *CPR 1391–6*, pp. 70–1. At Nottingham on 29 June licence was given to Alexander Bache, bishop of St Asaph, for as long as he is the king's confessor, to hunt with five or six people in the king's forests: *CPR 1391–6*, p. 101.

110. A pardon at the earl of Derby's supplication is dated at Nottingham 4 July: *CPR 1391–6*, p. 116.

111. *CPR 1391–6*, pp. 98, 102.

112. *CPR 1391–6*, p. 131.

113. Barron, 'The quarrel of Richard II with London', 183–6; *City of London. Letter Book H*, p. 379.

114. *CPR 1391–6*, p. 166.

115. Barron, 'The quarrel of Richard II with London', 187.

116. Barron, 'The quarrel of Richard II with London', 189.

117. P. Nightingale, *A Medieval Community. The Grocers' Company and the Politics and Trade of London 1000–1485* (New Haven, 1995), p. 332.

118. *Knighton's Chronicle*, pp. 546–9; Richard of Maidstone, 'The reconciliation of Richard II with the City of London' in *Political Poems and Songs relating to English History*, vol. 1, ed. T. Wright (Rolls Series, 1859), pp. 282–300.

119. Barron, 'The quarrel of Richard II with London', 191.

120. This is the figure given by three chroniclers, and the amount received in the exchequer on 28 February 1393: Barron, 'The quarrel of Richard II with London', 194.

121. Barron, 'The quarrel of Richard II with London', 193.

122. *Anglo-Norman Letters and Petitions*, pp. 185–6.

123. Barron, 'The quarrel of Richard II with London', 194–5.

124. *Westminster Chronicle*, pp. 508–11.

125. F. Hepburn, *Portraits of the Later Plantagenets* (Woodbridge, 1986), p. 24.

126. *Diplomatic Correspondence of Richard II*, nos 150–1.

127. BL, Add. MS. 35115, fos 6r–12v.

128. *Westminster Chronicle*, pp. 510–11.

129. *Westminster Chronicle*, pp. 510–11.

130. Thus on 16 March 1393 he granted Richard of York 350 marks per annum. The duchess of York had specified 500 marks per annum: *CPR 1391–6*, p. 245.

131. BL, Add. MS. 35115, fo. 13v.

132. BL, Add. MS. 35115, fos 14r–15r.

133. W.T. Waugh, 'The Great Statute of Praemunire', *EHR*, xxxvii (1922), 174–5, 178–85; P. Heath, *Church and Realm 1272–1461. Conflict and Collaboration in an Age of Crises* (1988), pp. 215–17.

134. *RP*, iii, 299, 434.

135. For a growing appreciation of Waltham's role in the reconstruction of royal authority see Tout, *Chapters*, iii, 461–2; N. Saul, 'Richard II and the vocabulary of kingship', *EHR*, cx (1995), 869; Walker, 'Richard II's views on kingship', 54–6.

136. *Westminster Chronicle*, pp. 512–13.

137. *CPR 1391–6*, pp. 212, 242.

138. J.G. Bellamy, 'The northern rebellions of the later years of Richard II', *Bulletin of the John Rylands Library*, xlvii (1964–5).

139. Palmer, *England, France and Christendom 1377–99*, pp. 145–9.

140. R.C. Famiglietti, *Royal Intrigue. Crisis at the Court of Charles VI* (New York, 1986), pp. 1–4.

141. *Westminster Chronicle*, pp. 484–7.

142. Saul, 'Richard II and vocabulary of kingship', 857.

143. Waltham died on 18 September 1395. In recognition of his services, Richard insisted on his burial in Westminster Abbey. In his will Waltham mentions Sir William Scrope, who later became treasurer, Roger Walden and Lawrence Drew, who along with Scrope were members of the king's privy council in the late 1390s, and Janico Dartasso, the Basque soldier who remained loyal to Richard to the end: *Register of John Waltham, Bishop of Salisbury,* no. E1, pp. 214–17.

144. It is significant that one of the few books to survive which clearly belonged to him, MS. Bodley 581, contains both an edition of the *Secreta Secretorum,* a treatise of practical wisdom for princes, and works on divination.

145. Parkes, 'Patterns of scribal activity and revisions of the text in early copies of works by John Gower', 83–4.

CHAPTER FOUR

1. Maidstone, 'Reconciliation between Richard II and London', in *Political Poems and Songs,* I, p. 285.

2. F. Hepburn, *Portraits of the Later Plantagenets* (Woodbridge, 1986), pp. 13–24. In the late sixteenth century there was a very similar portrait in the royal collection. It may be that it was painted for Westminster Hall.

3. The altarpiece, which comprised five panels, and included representations of St Edward the Confessor, St Edmund and St George, was in the English College in Rome in the early seventeenth century. D. Gordon, 'The Wilton Diptych: an introduction' in Gordon, Monnas and Elam, *Regal Image of Richard II and the Wilton Diptych,* pp. 23–5.

4. BL, Royal MS. 12 E XXII, f. 132. The issue rolls record many payments to physicians and for medicine.

5. C.M. Barron, 'Richard II. Image and reality', in Gordon, *Making and Meaning. The Wilton Diptych,* p. 15; J.M. Bowers, 'Chaste marriage: fashion and texts at the court of Richard II', *Pacific Coast Philology,* 30 (1995), 15–26; R.W. Sullivan, 'The Wilton Diptych: mysteries, majesty and a complex exchange of faith and power', *Gazette des Beaux-Arts,* 129 (1997), 10–11.

6. J.H. Harvey, 'The Wilton Diptych – a re-examination', *Archaeologia* 93 (1961), pp. 5–5n.

7. *Thorne's Chronicle of Saint Augustine's Abbey Canterbury,* ed. A.H. Davis (Oxford, 1934), p. 674.

8. BL, Additional MS. 35115, f. 34r.

9. C.E. Woodruff, 'The sacrist's rolls of Christ Church Canterbury', *Archaeologia Cantiana,* xlviii (1936), 47–8.

10. Saul, *Richard II,* p. 318.

11. BL, Additional MS. 35115, f. 34r; *Westminster Chronicle,* pp. 516–17.

12. BL, Additional MS. 35115, fos 27r–29r.

13. J. Harvey, 'The buildings of Winchester College', in R. Custance (ed.), *Winchester College. Sixth Centenary Essays* (Oxford, 1992), pp. 77–127, at p. 84.

14. BL, Additional MS. 35115, f. 34r.

15. *Literae Cantuarienses,* ed. J.B. Sheppard, 3 vols (Rolls Series, 1887–9), iii, pp. 26–9.

16. BL, Additional MS. 35115, fos 28v–29r.

17. *Eulogium Historiarum,* iii, p. 369.

18. BL, Additional MS. 35115, fos 29r–30r.

19. The king commended him to Llandaff as 'a most virtuous man, of great sense and prudence in both spiritual and temporal matters': *Anglo-Norman Letters and Petitions,* ed. M.D. Legge (Anglo-Norman Text Society, 1941), pp. 61–2. The royal assent to his election is dated 18 August: *CPR 1391–6,* pp. 300, 319.

20. BL, Additional MS. 70,506, fos 122v–123r.

21. The king wrote a firm letter on the matter to the prior of Oxford on 12 July 1396: B. Jarrett, *The English Dominicans* (London, 1921), pp. 145–7.

22. PRO, E 403/547, m. 13.

23. *Westminster Chronicle,* pp. 516–17.

24. J. Steane, *Archaeology of the Medieval English Monarchy* (London, 1993), pp. 76–8.

25. Philpotts, 'John of Gaunt and English policy towards France', 376.

26. Saul, *Richard II,* p. 242.

27. *Westminster Chronicle,* pp. 516–19.

28. *CPR 1391–6,* p. 406. The earl of Arundel later claimed that he did not seek the pardon. Archbishop Arundel seems to have secured the pardon during Gaunt's absence overseas.

29. Given-Wilson, *Chronicles of the Revolution,* p. 196.

30. *Eulogium Historiarum,* iii, 369–70.

31. Though he was still not of full age, March performed homage for his English lands in February 1394: *CPR 1391–6,* p. 375.

32. Rymer, *Foedera,* vii, p. 763. The key phrase is 'si quem procreassemus'. The use of the pluperfect may be some indication that Richard was accepting the fact of his childlessness.

33. Palmer, *England, France and Christendom,* ch. 8.

34. *Westminster Chronicle,* pp. 518–19, 519n.

35. Palmer, *England, France and Christendom,* pp. 157–61; Philpotts, 'John of Gaunt and English policy towards France 1389–1395', 380.

36. Worcester Cathedral MS. A5, f. 371r.

37. Worcester Cathedral MS. A5, f. 374r. The prior of Worcester seems to have attended neither funeral, but sent representatives: Worcester Cathedral MS. A5, f. 374v.

38. At the beginning of July the countess of Derby died in child-bed and was buried at Leicester: *Westminster Chronicle,* pp. 520–1.

39. *Historia Vitae et Regni Ricardi Secundi,* p. 134.

40. M. Aston, *Thomas Arundel. A Study of Church Life in the Reign of Richard II* (Oxford, 1967), p. 327.

41. *Annales Ricardi Secundi et Henrici Quarti*, pp. 169, 424.

42. Steane, *Archaeology of the Medieval English Monarchy*, p. 59.

43. Binski, *Westminster Abbey and the Plantagenets*, p. 200.

44. Westminster Abbey Muniments, no. 5257A.

45. Binski, *Westminster Abbey and the Plantagenets*, pp. 200–1.

46. Binski, *Westminster Abbey and the Plantagenets*, pp. 200–1; Steane, *Archaeology of the Medieval English Monarchy*, p. 59.

47. *City of London. Letter Book H*, p. 412.

48. It may be noted, though, that the attorneys he nominated on 10 August included Archbishop Arundel and the earl of Arundel: *CPR 1391–6*, p. 500.

49. *Anglo-Norman Letters and Petitions*, pp. 74–6. The dating does not include the year, but given the itineraries of the four men 1394 seems the only possibility.

50. Tout, *Chapters*, iii, p. 487n.

51. Register of John Waltham, Bishop of Salisbury, no. 117. In a letter from about September 1394 Bishop Waltham refers to delays in organizing ships for transport to Ireland: *Anglo-Norman Letters and Petitions*, pp. 68–9. On his return from Milford Haven Bishop Waltham visited Glastonbury, possibly on the king's command. He was there on the vigil of St Edward the Confessor: *Register of John Waltham, Bishop of Salisbury*, p. 222.

52. J.L. Gillespie, 'Richard II: King of Battles?' in Gillespie, *The Age of Richard II*, p. 151.

53. Saul, *Richard II*, p. 277.

54. Saul, *Richard II*, p. 279.

55. J. Froissart, *Oeuvres*, ed. Kervyn de Lettenhove, 26 vols (Brussels, 1866–77), xv, p. 180.

56. *Register of John Waltham, Bishop of Salisbury*, no. 127.

57. Cambridge University Library, *Register of John Fordham, bishop of Ely*, f. 120v.

58. *Register of John Waltham, Bishop of Salisbury*, no. 128.

59. Gillespie, 'Richard II: King of Battles?', 152.

60. A. Cosgrove, *Late Medieval Ireland, 1370–1541* (1981), p. 22.

61. On 7 December payment was made to Robert Tapton valet, sent to the city of Chester 'with the greatest haste' to Lawrence Drew waiting there for passage to Ireland with certain ornaments for the king's chapel: PRO, E 403/549, m. 7.

62. Saul, *Richard II*, p. 280.

63. E. Curtis, *Richard II in Ireland 1394–5 and Submissions of the Irish Chiefs* (Oxford, 1927), pp. 93–4, 181–2.

64. D. Johnston, 'Richard II and the submission of Gaelic Ireland', *Irish Historical Studies*, 22 (1980), pp. 11–13; Saul, *Richard II*, p. 283.

65. Curtis, *Richard II in Ireland*, pp. 61, 152–3.

66. Curtis, *Richard II in Ireland*, pp. 74–5, 163–4.

67. Johnston, 'Richard II and the submission of Gaelic Ireland', 2.

68. Curtis, *Richard II in Ireland*, pp. 99–100, 186–7; J.L. Gillespie, 'Richard II: chivalry and kingship' in

69. Gillespie, *The Age of Richard II*, p. 152. The act was witnessed by three of Richard's closest clerical confidants: John Boor, dean of the chapel royal, John Burghill, the king's confessor, and Thomas Merks, monk of Westminster.

69. Curtis, *Richard II in Ireland*, pp. 137–9, 217–19.

70. *Rogeri Dymmok Liber contra XII Errores et Hereses Lollardorum*, ed. H.S. Cronin (London, 1922), pp. 3–5.

71. *Rogeri Dymmok Liber*, p. xvii.

72. *Rogeri Dymmok Liber*, p. xxx.n.

73. *CCR 1389–92*, pp. 530–1.

74. M. Aston, *Lollards and Reformers. Images and Literacy in Late Medieval Religion* (London, 1984), pp. 22–3.

75. According to Thomas Walsingham, the charges laid against the chamber knight Sir Richard Stury by the king at Eltham on 15 August were 'countenance of heresy': M. Aston, *Lollards and Reformers*, p. 22.

76. *Registrum Johannis Trefnant, Episcopi Herefordensis, A.D. 1389–1404* (Cantilupe Society, 1916), pp. 147–50.

77. PRO, E 403/551, m. 14: Harvey, 'Richard II and York', 207 n.24.

78. PRO, E 403/552, m. 1.

79. *Literae Cantuarienses*, iii, pp. 32–41.

80. *Calendar of Papal Registers, 1396–1404*, p. 67; B. Jarrett, *The English Dominicans*, p. 140.

81. *Literae Cantuarienses*, iii, pp. 50–3.

82. J.J.N. Palmer, 'The background to Richard II's marriage to Isabel of France (1396)', *BIHR*, 44 (1971), 2–5. On 3 April a serjeant-at-arms was paid to escort the French embassy from London to Ireland.

83. Palmer, 'Background to Richard II's marriage to Isabel of France', 8.

84. Philippe de Mézières, *Letter to Richard II. A Plea made in 1395 for Peace between England and France* (Liverpool, 1975), p. 30.

85. De Mézières, *Letter to Richard II*, pp. 35–8.

86. Palmer, *England, France and Christendom*, pp. 169–70.

87. E.F. Jacob, 'English Conciliar activity, 1395–1418', in *Essays in the Conciliar Epoch* (Manchester, 3rd edn 1963), 60–3.

88. M. Harvey, *Solutions to the Schism. A Study of some English Attitudes 1378 to 1409* (St Ottilien, 1983), p. 68.

89. E.F. Jacob, 'English conciliar activity, 1395–1418', in *Essays in the Conciliar Epoch* (Manchester, 1963), 59–60; Harvey, *Solutions to the Schism*, p. 64–6. The various participants in the debate are generally commendatory, where not flattering of the king's acumen and zeal for mother church. Early in 1399 the Cambridge masters addressed a letter on the schism to the king as 'the venerable lantern of princes and the special mirror of kings'.

90. A carpenter was sent at some expense to Ireland with a model ('cum quodam exemplario vocato patronu') made by Henry Yevele and Hugh Herland to show

the king by the model ('exemplarium') of the mode of building and foundation of a certain manor to be newly built for the king's residence at Isleworth for his approval: PRO, E 403/549, m. 6. Payments for work on the king's mansion at Isleworth were made from 17 November: PRO, E 403/549, m. 7. The site and whatever had been built may have been used in Henry V's foundation of Syon abbey.

91. *Annales Ricardi Secundi et Henrici Quarti*, pp. 184–5.

92. Harvey, 'The Wilton Diptych – a re-examination'.

93. The provision of French military assistance to Richard against his subjects was on the table for discussion as late as the spring of 1396. Palmer observes that Richard placed a low price on this aid, and in the end preferred an extra instalment of 100,000 francs. What seems remarkable is that it was under discussion at all: Palmer, *England, France and Christendom*, pp. 173–4.

94. De Mézières, *Letter to Richard II*, p. 39.

95. De Mézières, *Letter to Richard II*, pp. 51–3.

96. De Mézières, *Letter to Richard II*, p. 65.

97. PRO, C 115/K6684, fos 184v–185r.

98. De Mézières, *Letter to Richard II*, pp. 23–4.

99. J.R.S. Philipps, 'Edward II and the Prophets', in W.M. Ormrod (ed.), *England in the Fourteenth Century. Proceedings of the 1985 Harlaxton Symposium* (Woodbridge, 1986), p. 194.

100. BL, Harleian MS. 3988, fos 39–41.

101. De Mézières, *Letter to Richard II*, p. 101.

102. De Mézières, *Letter to Richard II*, p. 70.

103. De Mézières, *Letter to Richard II*, p. 71.

104. De Mézières, *Letter to Richard II*, p. 71.

105. Jean de Montreuil, De Mézières, *Letter to Richard II*, Opera. Vol. I. Epistolario, *ed. A. Combes (Torino, 1963), pp. 240–8; Jean de Montreuil*, Opera. Vol. III. Textes divers, appendices et tables, ed. N. Grévy-Pons, E. Ornato and G. Ouy (Paris, 1981), pp. 32–41.

106. De Mézières, *Letter to Richard II*, pp. xxxiii–iv; M. Keen, 'The Wilton Diptych: the case for a crusading context' in Gordon, Monnas and Elam, *The Regal Image of Richard II and the Wilton Diptych*.

107. M.V. Clarke, 'The Wilton Diptych' in Clarke, *Fourteenth-Century Studies*, p. 288.

108. Gordon, *Making and Meaning: The Wilton Diptych*, esp. pp. 59–60; Gordon, Monnas and Elam, *The Regal Image of Richard II and the Wilton Diptych*.

109. PRO, E 101/403/10, fos 35r–v.

110. PRO, E403/554, m. 15.

111. Rymer, *Foedera*, vii, pp. 820–30, 811–12.

112. *Annales Ricardi Secundi et Henrici Quarti*, p. 188.

113. PRO, E 101/403/10, fos 14v–15v, 35v.

114. Rymer, *Foedera*, vii, 812–13.

115. *Anglo-Norman Letters and Petitions*, pp. 67–8.

116. Froissart, *Chronicles*, ed. Johnes, ii, pp. 598 and 598n.

117. Froissart, *Chronicles*, ed. Johnes, ii, p. 599.

118. PRO, E 101/403/10, fos 19r–v.

119. A signet letter is dated there on that day: *Anglo-Norman Letters and Petitions*, p. 58.

120. PRO, E 101/403/10, fos. 20r–v.

121. The witness-list to a confirmation of a royal charter to Bristol on 1 April included the archbishops of Canterbury and York, the bishops of London, Salisbury and Worcester, the dukes of Aquitaine, York and Gloucester, the earls of Derby, Arundel and Northumberland, Roger Walden, the Treasurer, Sir Thomas Percy, the Steward, and Guy Mone, Keeper of the Privy Seal: H.A. Cronne, *Bristol Charters 1378–1499* (Bristol Record Society XI, 1946), pp. 98–100; *Calendar of Charter Rolls 1341–1417*, p. 353.

122. There is also record of his paying for the making of medicinal rings: PRO, E 101/403/10, f. 36r.

123. PRO, E 101/403/10, f. 36r. Among the clerks giving sermons over eastertide were the Dominican John Richard, the Carmelite Robert Marshal and the Augustinian William Betheley: PRO, E 101/403/10, f. 36r.

124. Saul, *Richard II*, p. 317. Harvey believes that the carved head of an emperor high on the south-east pier of the main crossing in the minster was a representation of Richard and an acknowledgement of his imperial ambitions: Harvey, 'Richard II and York', 213–14.

125. PRO, E 101/403/10, fos 20v–21v, 36r.

126. P. Chaplais, 'English diplomatic documents, 1377–99', in Du Boulay and Barron, *Reign of Richard II*, pp. 39–40.

127. PRO, E 101/403/10, fos 21v–25r.

128. PRO, E 101/403/10, fos 36r–v.

129. Rymer, *Foedera*, vii, 834; Tout, *Chapters*, iv, p. 3.

130. PRO, E 101/403/10, fos 25r–28r, 36v.

131. The safe-conduct from the king to the count of Saint Pol is dated 12 July at Woodstock: PRO, C76/81, m.11.

132. Froissart, *Chronicles*, ed. Johnes, ii, 610–11.

133. PRO, E 101/403/10, fos 28v–29r.

134. PRO, E 101/403/10, f. 36v.

135. PRO, E 101/403/10, fos 29r–v. Prior to leaving the kingdom, the great seal was delivered to John Scarle, keeper of the rolls, at Dover on the 6th: *CCR 1396–99*, p. 57.

136. PRO, E 101/403/10, fos 29v–30v. While there he heard, in St Nicholas's church, requiem masses for his mother on the 7th and for his grandmother on the 15th: PRO, E 101/403/10, f. 36v.

137. Froissart, *Chronicles*, ed. Johnes, ii, p. 611.

138. N. Valois, *La France et le Grand Schisme d'Occident*, 4 vols (1896–1902), iii, p. 108. The abbot of Westminster, charged with this mission, only made it as far as 'Benedict XIII' at Avignon. He was not willing to do homage as protocol required and so he returned immediately to England.

139. Valois, *La France et le Grand Schisme*, iii, p. 108 n.

140. PRO, E 101/403/10, fos 30d–32d.

141. PRO, E 101/403/10, f. 36v.

142. PRO, E 101/403/10, fos 36v–37r.

143. PRO, E 101/403/10, f. 37r.

144. PRO, E 101/403/10, f. 32d.
145. PRO, E 101/403/10, fos 32d–33.
146. *CCR 1396–99*, p. 65.
147. PRO, E 101/403/10, f. 37r.
148. Froissart, *Chronicles*, ed. Johnes, ii, p. 618.
149. *CPR 1396–99*, p. 29.
150. D. Johnston, 'The interim years: Richard II and Ireland, 1395–1399' in J. Lydon (ed.), *England and Ireland in the Later Middle Ages. Essays in Honour of Jocelyn Otway-Ruthven* (Blackrock, Co. Dublin, 1981), p. 178.
151. L. Mirot, 'Isabelle de France, reine d'Angleterre: Le marriage d'Isabelle et l'entrevue de Charles VI et de Richard II à Ardres', *Revue d'histoire diplomatique*, xix (1905), 84f; Froissart, *Chronicles*, ed. Johnes, ii, pp. 618–19.
152. Froissart, *Chronicles*, ed. Johnes, ii, p. 619.
153. Froissart, *Chronicles*, ed. Johnes, ii, p. 620.
154. She was born on 9 November 1389: L. Mirot, 'Isabelle de France, reine d'Angleterre: L'enfance de Isabelle de France', *Revue d'histoire diplomatique*, xviii (1904), 35.
155. Froissart, *Chronicles*, ed. Johnes, ii, pp. 620–1.
156. Froissart, *Chronicles*, ed. Johnes, ii, p. 621.
157. Froissart, *Chronicles*, ed. Johnes, ii, p. 21.

CHAPTER FIVE

1. *Annales Ricardi Secundi et Henrici Quarti*, p. 201.
2. P. Meyer, 'L'Entrevue de Ardres', *Annuaire Bulletin de la Société de l'Histoire de France*, xviii (1881), 209–24; L. Mirot, 'Isabelle de France, reine d'Angleterre: Le marriage d'Isabelle et l'entrevue à Ardres', 84f; Froissart, *Chronicles*, ed. Johnes, ii, pp. 618–19.
3. Valois, *La France et le Grand Schisme*, iii, p. 115 n. At Avignon Robert the Hermit received a commission to take a proposal from 'Benedict XIII' to Boniface at Rome: Valois, *La France et le Grand Schisme*, iii, pp. 116 and 116n.
4. Valois, *La France et le Grand Schisme*, iii, pp. 108–9. The agreement, copies of which survive at Paris and Rome, bears the date 5 November: Valois, iii, p. 109n.
5. J.J.N. Palmer, 'English foreign policy 1388–99' in Du Boulay and Barron, *The Reign of Richard II*, p. 103.
6. Palmer, 'English foreign policy 1388–99', 103–4.
7. Palmer, *England, France and Christendom*, p. 205.
8. On 5 November Richard wrote a letter to all kings and princes seeking safe passage for a chamberlain of the king of France and a clerk in the service of the duke of Burgundy who were setting off for distant parts.
9. Tuchman, *Distant Mirror*, ch. 27; Palmer, *England, France and Christendom*, pp. 204–7.
10. Froissart, *Chronicles*, ed. Johnes, ii, 621.
11. *Historia Vitae et Regni Ricardi Secundi*, p. 136. The king's pavilioner received a pardon for the loss of

tents and furnishings 'sunk by accident at sea': *CPR 1396–9*, p. 57.
12. Froissart, *Chronicles*, ed. Johnes, ii, 621; *Traison et Mort*, addendum 2, pp. 109–10.
13. *Historia Vitae et Regni Ricardi Secundi*, p. 136.
14. Gifts to court celebrities Margery Lady Moleyns and Sir Philip la Vache are dated at Eltham manor on 2 January: *CPR 1396–9*, p. 49.
15. *CPR 1396–9*, p. 46.
16. Dated Eltham, 2 January 1397: *CPR 1396–9*, p. 49.
17. Bueno de Mesquita, 'Some Italian letters', 629.
18. *Vita Ricardi Secundi*, 136–7; Froissart, *Chronicles*, ed. Berners, vi, 229–30.
19. PRO, E101/403/5.
20. According to the *Vita Ricardi Secundi*, the queen was crowned on the vigil of Epiphany, namely 5 January. The coronation had been scheduled for the 7th, while the Great Chronicle of London gives the date as the 8th: *Historia Vitae et Regni Ricardi Secundi*, pp. 136 and 202n; Aston, *Thomas Arundel*, p. 362. Arundel's bulls of appointment did not arrive until 10 January.
21. Hardyng, *Chronicle*, p. 344.
22. Walsingham, *Historia Anglicana*, ii, p. 222.
23. *CCR 1396–9*, p. 74. The summonses were issued on 30 November.
24. Froissart, *Chronicles*, ed. Johnes, ii, p. 599.
25. Bueno de Mesquita, 'Some Italian letters', 629. It is likely the Florentine who reported the preparations in January meant the earl of Rutland not the earl of 'Holland'.
26. *Calendar of Papal Letters*, iv, p. 300. According to Walsingham, Huntingdon secured from the pope a remarkable range of privileges: *Annales Ricardi Secundi et Henrici Quarti*, pp. 200–1.
27. PRO, E 364/32, m. 5d.
28. *CPR 1396–9*, p. 25.
29. Tout, *Chapters*, iv, 15; J.S. Roskell, *The House of Commons 1386–1421*, 4 vols (Stroud, 1993), i, pp. 110–11.
30. Tout, *Chapters*, iv, 17; *CPR 1396–9*, p. 141.
31. A. McHardy, 'Haxey's case, 1397: the petition and the presenter reconsidered' in Gillespie, *Age of Richard II*, pp. 93–114. It is noteworthy that on 27 January, during the parliamentary session itself, Haxey appeared among a group of notable royal clerks in the registration of a quitclaim of some property in Lincoln. Along with Mr William Waltham and Robert Ragenhill clerks, he was a feoffee of John Poppleton and Richard Holme clerks: *CCR 1396–9*, p. 77.
32. Along with Sir William Scrope, Haxey was Waltham's executor: *Register of John Waltham, Bishop of Salisbury*, no. E1, pp. 214–15.
33. Haxey acted as one of Nottingham's attorneys.
34. *CPR 1396–9*, p. 109. Still, it needs to be borne in mind that Haxey remained under a cloud until after the deposition, when he successfully petitioned for a reversal of the judgement against him.

35. *CPR 1396–9*, pp. 123, 141.

36. Gifts of jewellery were made by Lancaster, York and Gloucester, and the earls of Derby, Rutland, Huntingdon and March: *Traison et Mort*, addendum no. 2, pp. 108–13.

37. Froissart, *Chronicles*, ed. Johnes, ii, pp. 610–11.

38. *RP*, iii, 343; *CPR 1396–9*, p. 86.

39. Aston, *Thomas Arundel*, p. 299; PRO, C 270/25/29, 31.

40. PRO, E 364/30, m. 7; PRO, C 76/81, m. 5. On 28 March John Drax received a commission to deliver the fortress: Rymer, *Foedera*, vii, p. 853.

41. Johnston, 'Richard II and Ireland, 1395–1399', 188.

42. *CPR 1396–9*, p. 87. Green was associated with Sir William Bagot in a bond dated 16 February 1397: *CCR 1396–9*, p. 83.

43. Aston, *Thomas Arundel*, p. 299.

44. Aston, *Thomas Arundel*, p. 299; *Thorne's Chronicle*, p. 676.

45. Aston, *Thomas Arundel*, pp. 332–3.

46. Aston, *Thomas Arundel*, p. 335.

47. Aston, *Thomas Arundel*, p. 334.

48. *Literae Cantuarienses*, iii, pp. 50–3; Aston, *Thomas Arundel*, p. 331. The letters are undated, but the archbishop is named as Thomas, and '1396' appears in the margin. The most likely date is the end of 1396 in the old calendar, that is some time before 25 March 1397. The king's reply should be easier to date because it was written at Launde Priory in Leicestershire but no record of a visit has come to light. The king's movements in the second half of March 1397 are obscure.

49. PRO, C 270/25/29, 30, 31.

50. *The Episcopal Register of Bishop Robert Rede, O.P., Lord Bishop of Chichester, 1397–1415*, ed. C. Deedes, Part I (Sussex Record Society, vol. viii, 1908), pp. 71–2, from Reg. 2v. The year could be either 1397 or 1398. The archbishop is traditionally identified as Arundel, however, and the proceedings altogether fit better in 1397: Aston, *Thomas Arundel*, p. 299.

51. PRO, C 76/81, m.3; *CPR 1396–9*, pp. 109, 118. A signet letter was dated at Windsor on 8 May: PRO, C 81/1354/21.

52. PRO, E 364/30, m. 7.

53. *CPR 1396–9*, pp. 109, 143. Talbot was retained by the king with an annuity of 100 marks on 11 November 1397: *CPR 1396–9*, p. 252.

54. *Historia Vitae et Regni Ricardi Secundi*, p. 137.

55. PRO, C115/K6684, f. 197d.

56. On 16 April he obtained a pardon for a sum owing for the wardship and marriage of the son and heir of Thomas, earl of Stafford: *CPR 1396–9*, p. 111. As late as 29 June, he secured a royal mandate to the chancellor of Ireland to give him livery of his ward's lands in Ireland: *CCR 1396–9*, p. 138.

57. *CCR 1396–9*, p. 125; *CCR 1396–9*, pp. 123–4.

58. *Kirkstall Abbey Chronicles*, p. 73.

59. *Regesten der Pfalzgrafen am Rhein. Vol. I. 1214–1400,* ed. E. Winkelmann, A. Koch, J. Wille (Innsbruck, 1894), pp. 345, 354.

60. *Die Regesten der Erzbischöfe von Köln im Mittelalter. Zehnter Band 1391–1400 (Friedrich von Saarwerden)*, ed. N. Andernach (Düsseldorf, 1987), p. 486.

61. PRO, E 403/555, m.15.

62. The earl of Rutland claimed expenses for the period from 4 March until 11 July: PRO, E 364/31 m.1d. The two lords were paid identical sums on 21 July: PRO, E 403/555, m.18.

63. *Traison et Mort*, pp. 7, 127.

64. *Annales Ricardi Secundi et Henrici Quarti*, p. 201.

65. Payment to the messenger was made after 7 July but before the 10th: PRO, E 403/555, m.14.

66. *Annales Ricardi Secundi et Henrici Quarti*, p. 201.

67. *Annales Ricardi Secundi et Henrici Quarti*, p. 202.

68. *Annales Ricardi Secundi et Henrici Quarti*, pp. 203–6.

69. *CCR 1396–9*, p. 197. See also the letter to Llanthony Priory: PRO, C115/K6684, f. 196d.

70. *CCR 1396–9*, p. 208.

71. *CCR 1396–9*, p. 204.

72. *Traison et Mort*, pp. 121–6, 125n.

73. Palmer, 'French chronicles on the Lancastrian revolution', 400–5.

74. Froissart, *Chronicles*, ed. Johnes, ii, pp. 610–11.

75. There is evidence that Richard expected Mowbray to play a larger role in the appeal of treason than he was willing or able to do: Given-Wilson, *Chronicles of the Revolution*, pp. 91–2.

76. Given-Wilson, *Chronicles of the Revolution*, p. 55.

77. *Chronicle of Adam Usk*, pp. 20–1.

78. C. Philpotts, 'The fate of the truce of Paris, 1396–1415', *Journal of Medieval History*, 24 (1998), pp. 63–4.

79. It is noteworthy that the commons found the names of bishops and friars among 'the records of the last cursed parliament': *Chronicles of London*, ed. Kingsford, p. 56.

80. 'Mémoires de Pierre Salmon', troisième supplément in *Collections des Chroniques Nationales Françaises écrites en langue vulgaire du treizième au seizième siècle*, ed. J.A. Buchon (Paris, 1826), p. 11.

81. *Annales Ricardi Secundi et Henrici Quarti*, p. 199. Cf. Goodman, *Loyal Conspiracy*, p. 66.

82. *Annales Ricardi Secundi et Henrici Quarti*, pp. 202–3.

83. The embassy returned in early August, when Hervorst received a licence to export for his own use two cloths of scarlet and four pieces of worsted: *CCR 1396–9*, p. 148, where he appears as provost of the church of 'Zanton'. In the index, it is suggested that the church is Hauten, below Wesel on the Rhine: *CCR 1396–9*, p. 752.

84. PRO, E 404/14/96, no. 411.

85. Bueno de Mesquita, 'Some Italian letters', 633.

86. *Official Correspondence of Thomas Bekyngton*, 2 vols, ed. G. Williams (Rolls Series, 1872), I, pp. 287–9.

87. *CCR 1396–9*, p. 197.

88. *CCR 1396–9*, pp. 137–8.

89. *CCR 1396–9*, p. 208. Walsingham accurately summarizes this proclamation: *Annales Ricardi Secundi et Henrici Quarti*, pp. 206–7.

90. *CCR 1396–9*, p. 148.

91. Commissions of peace issued for Kent, Essex, Norfolk, Suffolk, Shropshire and Cambridgeshire on 22 July; and for Herefordshire, Gloucestershire, Worcestershire, Warwickshire, Sussex and Surrey on 27 July 1397: *CPR 1396–9*, pp. 227–9.

92. *Annales Ricardi Secundi et Henrici Quarti*, p. 206.

93. In the *Tripartite Chronicle*, Gower claims that 'England lost a shining light and grew wholly dark' when Gloucester was arrested and despatched to Calais, and that a hundred thousand people wept: *The Major Latin Works of John Gower*, p. 101.

94. Cambridge University Library, Register of John Fordham, bishop of Ely, f. 125v.

95. *Annales Ricardi Secundi et Henrici Quarti*, p. 207.

96. Westminster Abbey Muniments, no. 6221.

97. *CPR 1396–9*, pp. 176, 175.

98. PRO, CHES 2/70, m.7d.

99. *CCR, 1396–9*, p. 144.

100. PRO, C 115/K6684, f. 197d.

101. PRO, C 115/K6684, f.198; *CPR 1396–9*, p. 179. In a letter of 1 April 1398 the king further expressed for loan but deferred repayment: PRO, C 115/K6684, f. 203. On 6 May Llanthony agreed to cancel the debt in return for licence to appropriate a number of parish churches: PRO, C 115/K 6684, f. 206d.

102. *CPR 1396–9*, pp. 178–82.

103. The men of Lynn offered 400 marks, receipt of which was acknowledged on 11 September: PRO, E 34/1B/15/7/44; *CPR 1396–9*, p. 180. The dean and chapter of Lincoln promised a loan of £200, but no receipt has been found: PRO, E 34/1B/15/7/44/18. Gifts included £20 from Sir John Depeden, 20 marks from the abbot of Rievaulx, and 8 marks from the men of Doncaster: PRO, E 34/1B/15/7/47, 30, 23. For discussion see Barron, 'Tyranny of Richard II', 3, 3n.

104. Bret's account of travelling expenses began at Windsor. He left London on 1 August: PRO, E 364/36, m.1d.

105. *CPR 1396–9*, pp. 360, 193.

106. According to the Kirkstall chronicler, it was at a council at Nottingham on 23 July that the six earls made the appeal of treason: *Kirkstall Abbey Chronicles*, p. 74.

107. *RP*, iii, p. 449; Given-Wilson, *Chronicles of the Revolution*, pp. 214–15.

108. PRO, DL 28/1/9, f. 20v.

109. *RP*, iii, p. 449; Given-Wilson, *Chronicles of the Revolution*, pp. 214–15.

110. *RP*, iii, p. 450.

111. *RP*, iii, p. 451; Given-Wilson, *Chronicles of the Revolution*, pp. 216–17.

112. PRO, C 81/1354/22.

113. PRO, C 115/K6684, f. 198.

114. *CCR 1396–9*, p. 210.

115. J.L. Gillespie, 'Richard II's Cheshire archers', *Transactions of the Historic Society of Lancashire and Cheshire*, 125 (1974), p. 2; *CPR 1396–9*, p. 177.

116. The duke of York was likewise licensed to bring 100 men-at-arms and 200 archers: *CPR 1396–9*, p. 192.

117. J. Tait, 'Did Richard II murder the duke of Gloucester?' in *Historical Essays by Members of Owens College, Manchester, published in Commemoration of its Jubilee (1851–1901)*, ed. T.F. Tout and J. Tait (London, 1902), pp. 193–216. See also A.E. Stamp, 'Richard II and the death of the duke of Gloucester', *EHR*, xxxviii (1923), 249–51; R.L. Atkinson, 'Richard II and the death of the duke of Gloucester', *EHR*, xxxviii (1923), 563–4; H.G. Wright, 'Richard II and the death of the duke of Gloucester', *EHR*, xlvii (1932), 276–80; A.E. Stamp, 'Richard II and the death of the duke of Gloucester', *EHR*, xlvii (1932), 453; J. Tait, 'Richard II and the death of the duke of Gloucester', *EHR*, xlvii (1932), 726.

118. According to an early London chronicle, at St Bartholomew's tide Mowbray 'was at him': BL, Harleian MS. 3775, f. 86r.

119. *Chronicles of London*, ed. Kingsford, pp. 52–3. Walsingham accepts and repeats this story: *Annales Ricardi Secundi et Henrici Quarti*, p. 221.

120. Given-Wilson, *Chronicles of the Revolution*, pp. 219–20.

121. *Annales Ricardi Secundi et Henrici Quarti*, p. 208.

122. *Eulogium Historiarum*, iii, p. 372. Some time before 5 September Charles VI sent an embassy seeking Richard's support for the expedition to Italy: Bueno de Mesquita, 'Foreign policy of Richard II in 1397', 630.

123. *Knighton's Chronicle*, pp. 350–1.

124. BL, Harleian MS. 3775, f. 86r.

125. *Eulogium Historiarum*, iii, p. 372; Given-Wilson, *Chronicles of the Revolution*, p. 66.

126. BL, Harleian MS. 3775, f. 86r.

127. PRO, DL 28/1/9, f. 17r.

128. PRO, DL 28/1/9, fos 18v, 20r.

129. BL, Harleian MS. 3775, fos 87r–v.

130. Given-Wilson, *Chronicles of the Revolution*, p. 55.

131. BL, Harleian MS. 3775, f. 86v. The term may have been used in the account of the parliament used by the monk of Evesham and Adam of Usk. The monk of Evesham ends his account with the words, 'This is the end of that great parliament': C. Given-Wilson, 'Adam Usk, the Monk of Evesham and the Parliament of 1397–8', *Historical Research*, 66 (1993), 329.

132. *RP*, iii, p. 347, in Wilkinson, *Constitutional History of Medieval England*, ii, p. 305.

133. Tout, *Chapters*, iv, p. 24.

134. *Historia Vitae et Regni Ricardi Secundi*, p. 138; Given-Wilson, *Chronicles of the Revolution*, pp. 55–6.

135. *Historia Vitae et Regni Ricardi Secundi*, p. 139; Given-Wilson, *Chronicles of the Revolution*, p. 56.

136. *Annales Ricardi Secundi et Henrici Quarti*, p. 210; Saul, 'Richard II and the vocabulary of kingship', 854.

137. *Historia Vitae et Regni Ricardi Secundi*, p. 139; Given-Wilson, *Chronicles of the Revolution*, p. 56.

138. *Historia Vitae et Regni Ricardi Secundi*, p. 139; Given-Wilson, *Chronicles of the Revolution*, p. 56.

139. *Historia Vitae et Regni Ricardi Secundi*, pp. 139–40; Given-Wilson, *Chronicles of the Revolution*, pp. 56–7. See Given-Wilson's crucial emendation: p. 57n.

140. *Historia Vitae et Regni Ricardi Secundi*, p. 140; Given-Wilson, *Chronicles of the Revolution*, p. 57. A London chronicler refers to a 'foul affray' when the Cheshire men bent their bows to fire 'but they wist never where at': BL, Harleian MS. 3775, f. 86v.

141. *Historia Vitae et Regni Ricardi Secundi*, p. 140.

142. *Historia Vitae et Regni Ricardi Secundi*, p. 140; Given-Wilson, *Chronicles of the Revolution*, p. 57.

143. *Chronicle of Adam Usk*, pp. 26–7.

144. *Chronicles of London*, ed. Kingsford, pp. 38–9.

145. *Historia Vitae et Regni Ricardi Secundi*, p. 142; *Chronicle of Adam Usk*, pp. 26–7.

146. For evidence that Albemarle and the other lords identified themselves as the king's 'nurres' (foster-children) see *Annales Ricardi Secundi et Henrici Quarti*, p. 307; Atkinson, 'Richard II and the death of Gloucester', 564. Thomas Mortimer was the uncle of the earl of March; he joined Gloucester at Harringey and played a notable role in the action at Radcot Bridge: J.L. Gillespie, 'Thomas Mortimer and Thomas Molineux: Radcot Bridge and the Appeal of 1397', *Albion*, 7 (1975).

147. *Eulogium Historiarum*, iii, p. 375; Given-Wilson, *Chronicles of the Revolution*, pp. 66–7.

148. *Historia Vitae et Regni Ricardi Secundi*, pp. 142–3; Given-Wilson, *Chronicles of the Revolution*, pp. 58–9.

149. *Eulogium Historiarum*, iii, p. 375; Given-Wilson, *Chronicles of the Revolution*, pp. 66–7.

150. *Historia Vitae et Regni Ricardi Secundi*, p. 143; Given-Wilson, *Chronicles of the Revolution*, pp. 58–9.

151. *Annales Ricardi Secundi et Henrici Quarti*, p. 215.

152. *Historia Vitae et Regni Ricardi Secundi*, p. 143.

153. *Historia Vitae et Regni Ricardi Secundi*, p. 143; Given-Wilson, *Chronicles of the Revolution*, p. 59n.

154. *Eulogium Historiarum*, iii, p. 375; Given-Wilson, *Chronicles of the Revolution*, pp. 66–7.

155. *Eulogium Historiarum*, iii, p. 375; Given-Wilson, *Chronicles of the Revolution*, pp. 66–7. Burley was condemned to be hanged and drawn as well as beheaded, but since he was a Knight of the Garter the first part of the punishment was remitted: *Westminster Chronicle*, pp. 330–1.

156. *Annales Ricardi Secundi et Henrici Quarti*, p. 216.

157. *The Brut or Chronicles of England*, Part II, ed. F.W.D. Brie (Early English Text Society, original series 136, 1908), p. 354.

158. *Annales Ricardi Secundi et Henrici Quarti*, p. 216.

159. *Historia Vitae et Regni Ricardi Secundi*, p. 143; Given-Wilson, *Chronicles of the Revolution*, p. 59.

160. *Annales Ricardi Secundi et Henrici Quarti*, p. 217.

161. Froissart, *Chronicles*, ed. Johnes, ii, p. 657.

162. *Annales Ricardi Secundi et Henrici Quarti*, pp. 217–18.

163. *The Brut or Chronicles of England*, Part II, p. 354; Given-Wilson, *Chronicles of the Revolution*, p. 59n.

164. *Historia Vitae et Regni Ricardi Secundi*, p. 144; Given-Wilson, *Chronicles of the Revolution*, p. 60; BL, Harleian MS. 3775, f. 86v.

165. He was pardoned for this crime on 25 October 1398: *CPR 1396–9*, p. 427.

166. BL, Harleian MS. 3775, f. 87r.

167. Tait, 'Did Richard II murder the duke of Gloucester?', 210.

168. Tait, 'Did Richard II murder the duke of Gloucester?', 206–7.

169. Tait, 'Did Richard II murder the duke of Gloucester?', 206–8.

170. Given-Wilson, *Chronicles of the Revolution*, p. 79.

171. *CCR 1396–9*, p. 157. On 26 September Simon Blackburn, serjeant-at-arms, was sent to bring him to Westminster: *CCR 1396–9*, p. 159. According to a London chronicle the process against Lord Cobham took place on Monday: BL, Harleian MS. 3775, f. 87r. *CPR 1396–9*, p. 244.

172. *Chronicles of London*, ed. Kingsford, pp. 39–40.

173. *RP*, iii, pp. 353–4; *Historia Vitae et Regni Ricardi Secundi*, p. 144; Given-Wilson, *Chronicles of the Revolution*, pp. 60–1.

174. R.R. Davies, 'Richard II and the principality of Chester 1397–9' in Du Boulay and Barron, *Reign of Richard II*, pp. 256–9.

175. *Historia Vitae et Regni Ricardi Secundi*, p. 144; Given-Wilson, *Chronicles of the Revolution*, p. 60. For the background to the dispute, going back to the 1330s, see Holmes, *Estates of Higher Nobility*, pp. 14–19.

176. *Historia Vitae et Regni Ricardi Secundi*, p. 144; Given-Wilson, *Chronicles of the Revolution*, p. 61.

177. *Historia Vitae et Regni Ricardi Secundi*, pp. 144–5; Given-Wilson, *Chronicles of the Revolution*, p. 61. Note that according to the parliament roll and Adam of Usk, parliament did not meet on this day: Given-Wilson, *Chronicles of the Revolution*, p. 61n.

178. *Historia Vitae et Regni Ricardi Secundi*, p. 145; Given-Wilson, *Chronicles of the Revolution*, p. 61.

179. Froissart, *Chronicles*, ed. Johnes, ii, p. 657.

180. *Historia Vitae et Regni Ricardi Secundi*, p. 145; Given-Wilson, *Chronicles of the Revolution*, p. 61.

181. *Historia Vitae et Regni Ricardi Secundi*, pp. 145–6; Given-Wilson, *Chronicles of the Revolution*, p. 62.

182. *CPR 1396–9*, pp. 205, 281.

183. *CPR 1396–9*, pp. 200, 215–16.

184. *CPR 1396–9*, pp. 280–1.

185. *CPR 1396–9*, p. 220.

186. *CPR 1396–9*, pp. 211, 219, 250, 200.

187. *CPR 1396–9*, pp. 196, 198, 217–18, 221, 226, 222.

188. Given-Wilson, *Chronicles of the Revolution*, pp. 83–4.

189. Tout, *Chapters*, iv, 29.

190. *Traison et Mort*, pp. 11, 11n, 140, 140n.

191. *Major Latin Works of John Gower*, pp. 309–10.

CHAPTER SIX

1. C. Given-Wilson, 'Adam Usk, the Monk of Evesham and the Parliament of 1397–8', *Historical Research*, 66 (1993), 329–35.

2. *Kirkstall Abbey Chronicles*, p. 75. I have slightly adapted Taylor's translation.

3. *Annales Ricardi Secundi et Henrici Quarti*, p. 223.

4. The event is firmly dated by a London chronicle: BL, Harleian MS. 3775, f. 87r. PRO, DL 28/1/6, fos 8–9. For the general background see S. Dull, A. Luttrell and M. Keen, 'Faithful unto death: the tomb slab of Sir William Neville and Sir John Clanvowe, Constantinople 1391', *The Antiquarian Journal*, 71 (1991), pp. 181–2; Goodman, *John of Gaunt*, p. 163.

5. Harvey, 'Wilton Diptych – A re-examination', 27–8.

6. Bueno de Mesquita, 'Some Italian letters', 633–4.

7. PRO, E 101/320/17; D.M. Nicol, 'A Byzantine Emperor in England. Manuel II's visit to London in 1400–1401', *University of Birmingham Historical Journal*, xii (1969–70), 205.

8. Harvey, 'Wilton Diptych – A re-examination', 27–8. The letter is undated, but it was clearly written after the first session of parliament, and in all likelihood before the end of 1397.

9. *CPR 1396–9*, pp. 307–8.

10. PRO, E 403/560, m.2.

11. PRO, E 364/32, m.8d.

12. His last official act as archbishop of Canterbury was on the 15th. He probably left England around the 19th, when a safe conduct was issued to members of his entourage. Aston, *Thomas Arundel*, pp. 303, 372–3.

13. A.L. Brown, 'The Latin letters in MS. All Souls 182', *EHR*, lxxxvii (1972), 568–71.

14. *Annales Ricardi Secundi et Henrici Quarti*, pp. 218–19. The description of Arundel's passion in Walsingham's chronicle itself attests to an interest in presenting him as a martyr.

15. *CCR 1396–9*, p. 285.

16. *Foedera*, viii, p. 19; *CCR 1396–9*, p. 157.

17. *CCR 1396–9*, pp. 149–50.

18. Goodman, *John of Gaunt*, pp. 161–2.

19. *The Great Chronicle of London*, ed. A.H. Thomas and I.D. Thornley (London, 1938), pp. 76–7; Given-Wilson, *Chronicles of the Revolution*, p. 211. John Hall likewise testified that Mowbray informed him that the king and Albemarle ordered Gloucester's death: *Annales Ricardi Secundi et Henrici Quarti*, p. 309; Given-Wilson, *Chronicles of the Revolution*, p. 207.

20. The 'masters of the watch' were John Legh of Booths, Adam Bostock, Richard Cholmondeley, John Donne, Thomas Beeston, Thomas Holford and Ralph Davenport: Gillespie, 'Richard II's Cheshire archers', esp. 9–11, 13–14.

21. Davies, 'Richard II and principality of Chester', 268–9; P. Morgan, *War and Society in Medieval Cheshire, 1277–1403* (Manchester, 1987), pp. 199–201.

22. M.J. Bennett, 'Sir Gawain and the Green Knight and the literary achievement of the north-west Midlands: the historical background', *Journal of Medieval History*, 5 (1979), 63–88; M.J. Bennett, 'The historical background' in D. Brewer (ed.), *A Companion to the Gawain-Poet* (Woodbridge, 1997), esp. pp. 83–90.

23. BL, Additional MS. 35295, f. 260r; Clarke and Galbraith, 'Deposition of Richard II', 164.

24. *Annales Ricardi Secundi et Henrici Quarti*, pp. 218–19.

25. Clarke and Galbraith, 'Deposition of Richard II', 172.

26. *Chronicle of Adam Usk*, pp. 48–9; *Annales Ricardi Secundi et Henrici Quarti*, p. 208; *Mum and the Sothsegger*, Passus III, esp. lines 317f.

27. Froissart, *Chronicles*, ed. Johnes, ii, p. 658.

28. Given-Wilson, *Chronicles of the Revolution*, pp. 86–7.

29. In general see C. Given-Wilson, 'Richard II, Edward II and the Lancastrian inheritance', *EHR*, cix (1994), 553–74.

30. DL 28/1/10, f. 7r.

31. DL 28/1/10, f. 8r.

32. DL 28/1/10, fos 8v–9r.

33. A few days later Llanthony obliged Henry by granting a corrody to John Wykwelle, one of his servants: PRO, C115/K6684, fos 199r, 200r.

34. DL 28/1/10, fos 9v–10v.

35. A patent of 10 November is dated at Woodstock: *CPR 1396–9*, p. 274. Patents of 19–21 November are similarly dated: *CPR 1396–9*, pp. 259, 262, 271.

36. *Voyage au Purgatoire de St Patrice*, eds A. Jeanroy and A. Vignaux (Bibliothèque Méridionale publiée sous les auspices de la Faculté des Lettres de Toulouse, première série viii, 1903), pp. 12, 21.

37. 'Mémoires de Pierre Salmon', 11–13. The incident is undated, but the general chronology and the reference to Woodstock would indicate November 1397.

38. *Chronicles of London*, p. 54.

39. *The Episcopal Registers of the Diocese of St. David's 1397 to 1518*, ed. R.F. Isaacson, 2 vols (Cymmrodorion Record Series no. 6, 1917), i, p. 2.

40. On 26 November at Banbury he appointed the Cheshire clerk John Macclesfield keeper of the great wardrobe: *CPR 1396–9*, p. 266.

41. *CPR 1396–9*, p. 252.

42. On 22 November he appointed Thomas Daccombe sheriff of Somerset and Dorset: PRO, C 81/1354/25; Barron, 'Tyranny of Richard II', 14.

43. Tout, *Chapters*, iv, pp. 43n–44n.

44. PRO, C 81/1354/27; Barron, 'Tyranny of Richard II', 14.

45. Barron, 'Tyranny of Richard II', 7–8. In addition, a few fines 'made before the council' by retainers of the duke of Gloucester and the earl of Arundel were paid directly into the exchequer: Barron, 'Tyranny of Richard II', 8.

46. Barron, 'Tyranny of Richard II', 9–10.

47. Given-Wilson, *Chronicles of the Revolution*, pp. 86–7.

48. Froissart, *Chronicles*, ed. Johnes, ii, p. 661.

49. Thomas Clanvowe was sent to the French court with New Year gifts for the queen's father, mother, brother and uncles. He accounted for travel from 7 January, when he left the king's presence at Lichfield: PRO, E 364/32, m.1d.

50. *CPR 1396–9*, p. 286.

51. Bolingbroke appears to have been in London on 1 January, Pontefract on the 10th, Derby on the 17th, Stafford on the 24th and Shrewsbury on the 31st: PRO, DL 28/1/10, f. 2r. Between departure from London and arrival at Shrewsbury he visited Beverley, Bridlington and Tutbury: PRO, DL 28/1/10, f. 12r.

52. The pope had translated Arundel to the see of St Andrews and provided Walden to Canterbury in early November 1397. The bulls would not have arrived in England until December at the earliest: A.L. Brown, 'The Latin letters in MS. All Souls 182', *EHR*, 87 (1972), 569–70.

53. *CPR 1396–9*, p. 292. Davis, 'Richard II and Church', 345.

54. Several patents dated 21–3 January were issued at 'Heywood', including letters instructing the escheators to grant the new archbishop of Canterbury his temporalities: *CPR 1396–9*, pp. 280, 317. The place has been identified as Heywood in Cheswardine, Shropshire. It is more likely to have been Great Haywood in Staffordshire.

55. *RP*, iii, p. 360; Given-Wilson, *Chronicles of the Revolution*, pp. 86–7.

56. Corpus Christi, Cambridge, MS. 339, f. 48v.

57. Henry of Bolingbroke, duke of Hereford, received a pardon 'for all treasons', dated at Lilleshall on the 25th. *CPR 1396–9*, p. 280. Of the two remaining dukes, Gaunt is separately recorded as visiting Lilleshall after the parliament, while Mowbray absented himself completely from the Shrewsbury parliament.

58. *Chronicle of Adam Usk*, pp. 38–41.

59. *Voyage au Purgatoire de St Patrice*, p. 52; D.M. Carpenter, 'The pilgrim from Catalonia/Aragon: Ramon de Perellós, 1397' in M. Haren and Y. de Pontfarcy (ed.), *The Medieval Pilgrimage to St Patrick's Purgatory, Lough Derg, and the European Tradition* (Monaghan, 1988), pp. 99–119.

60. *Chronicle of Adam Usk*, pp. 38–9.

61. PRO, KB 9/179, mm.1–2.

62. *Chronicle of Adam Usk*, pp. 36–9.

63. *RP*, iii, p. 357; R.H. Jones, *The Royal Policy of Richard II. Absolutism in the Later Middle Ages* (Oxford, 1968), p. 86.

64. Given-Wilson, *Chronicles of the Revolution*, p. 85.

65. Given-Wilson, *Chronicles of the Revolution*, pp. 86–7.

66. *Chronicle of Adam Usk*, pp. 48–9.

67. *CPR 1396–9*, p. 339.

68. Given-Wilson, *Chronicles of the Revolution*, p. 88.

69. *CCR 1396–9*, pp. 281–2; J.A. Doig, 'Political propaganda and royal proclamations in late medieval England', *Historical Research*, 71 (1998), 259–60, 275–80.

70. Jones, *Royal Policy of Richard II*, p. 87.

71. *RP*, iii, 360–8; Given-Wilson, 'Richard II, Edward II and the Lancastrian inheritance', 560.

72. *RP*, iii, pp. 368–9; Given-Wilson, *Chronicles of the Revolution*, p. 88; Roskell, *House of Commons 1386–1421*, i, pp. 128–9.

73. Given-Wilson, *Chronicles of the Revolution*, p. 87.

74. Another interpolation in the doctored copy sought to give authority to the novel expedient of swearing oaths to uphold parliament's judgements. It was stated that the lords and commons were asked whether they agreed with oath-taking as 'a way of safety'. According to the interpolation, raising their right hands, they gave their assent with loud voices. J.G. Edwards, 'The parliamentary committee of 1398', *EHR*, xl (1925), 321–33; R. Butt, *A History of Parliament. The Middle Ages* (London, 1989), p. 439.

75. *Mum and the Sothsegger*, Passus IV; *English Historical Documents*, iv, pp. 453–4.

76. *Chronicle of Adam Usk*, pp. 38–41.

77. He was delivered from Shrewsbury to the custody of the abbot of Westminster in April 1399: *CPR 1396–9*, p. 584.

78. *Chronicles of Adam Usk*, pp. 38–9.

79. PRO, SC 6/774/7, mm.6d, 5d.

80. Repairs to a chamber in Delamere forest seem to be related to the king's visit: PRO, SC 6/774/7, m.6d.

81. *The Brut or Chronicles of England*, ii, p. 544.

82. Davies, 'Richard II and principality of Chester', 273.

83. Davies, 'Richard II and principality of Chester', 272.

84. A generous gift to the convent was noted: Corpus Christi, Cambridge, MS. 339, f. 48v.

85. PRO, DL 28/1/19, f. 2v.

86. *CPR 1396–9*, p. 285.

87. *CCR 1396–9*, p. 292.

88. Given-Wilson, *Chronicles of the Revolution*, p. 89.

89. Patents were dated at Worcester from 28 February to 7 March, and at Gloucester from 6 to 14 March: *CPR 1396–9*, pp. 315–17.

90. A patent dated at Worcester on 4 March was originated by the king at Hanley: Maxwell-Lyte, *Great Seal*, p. 250.

91. *CPR 1396–9*, p. 315.

92. *CPR 1396–9*, p. 315.

93. The outcome of the election was apparently reported on 3 March: Davis, 'Richard II and the Church', 345, 359, n.30.

94. *CCR 1396–9*, p. 290.

95. Given-Wilson, *Chronicles of the Revolution*, p. 89.

96. The group included Sir Thomas Fleming, Sir Richard Kirkby, Sir Richard Hoghton, Sir John Croft and Sir John Ashton: *CPR 1396–9*, pp. 321, 324.

97. *Historia Vitae et Regni Ricardi Secundi*, p. 149. The protagonists had spent the winter incarcerated in the

Tower of London. The order to deliver them from the Tower is dated 24 February 1398:*CCR 1396–9*, p. 245.

98. *CPR 1396–9*, p. 361. The date of the grant would seem to be 27 March, not 27 April as in the margin.

99. *Mum and the Sothsegger*, Passus II, lines 35–43.

100. Maxwell-Lyte, *Great Seal*, p. 250.

101. *CPR 1396–9*, p. 365.

102. *CCR 1396–9*, p. 288.

103. *CCR 1396–9*, p. 277. Sir Edward Charlton must have felt totally hounded. Briefly imprisoned in the autumn of 1397, he entered an obligation to sue for the king's grace and pay a fine of 500 marks in the quinzaine of Easter, that is 21 April. He seems to have paid the amount by the beginning of March:*CCR 1396–9*, pp. 159, 286.

104. *Oxfordshire Sessions of the Peace in the Reign of Richard II*, ed. E.G. Kimball (Oxfordshire Record Society 53, 1983), pp. 82–9.

105. Myres, 'Campaign of Radcot Bridge'.

106. He retained two more of Gaunt's men, Richard Chelmswick and Alan Norreys, at Windsor on 22 April: *CPR 1396–9*, pp. 330, 328.

107. The duke of Albemarle made a grant at Windsor castle on 25 April: *CPR 1396–9*, pp. 342–3. The dukes of Lancaster and Hereford seem to have accompanied the king from Windsor to London on the 28th: *Anglo-Norman Letters and Petitions*, pp. 104–5.

108. PRO, E 403/561, m.13.

109. PRO, E 30/332.

110. *English Historical Documents*, iv, pp. 174–5.

111. PRO, E 101/328/1, m.2d.

112. *Deutsche Reichstagsakten unter König Wenzel. Dritte Abtheilung 1397–1400*, ed. J. Weizsäcker (München, 1877), pp. 60–1.

113. Valois, *La France et le Grand Schisme d'Occident*, iii, pp. 127–30; H. Kaminsky, 'Cession, subtraction, deposition: Simon de Cramaud's formulation of the French solution to the Schism' in J.R. Strayer and D.E. Queller (eds), *Post Scripta. Essays on Medieval Law and the Emergence of the European State in Honor of Gaines Post* (Rome: Studia Gratiana vol. XV, 1972), pp. 293–317.

114. D. Johnston, 'The interim years: Richard II and Ireland, 1395–1399' in J. Lydon (ed.), *England and Ireland in the Later Middle Ages. Essays in Honour of Jocelyn Otway-Ruthven* (Blackrock, Co. Dublin, 1981), esp. pp. 188–90, p. 194, fn. 94.

115. *CPR 1396–9*, p. 336.

116. M.J. Bennett, 'Richard II and the wider realm' in A. Goodman and J. Gillespie (ed.), *Richard II. The Art of Kingship* (Oxford, 1999), pp. 202–4.

117. *Anglo-Norman Letters and Petitions*, pp. 104–5.

118. The correspondent adds that he has been informed that there was to be shortly a great assembly of prelates and clergy. It was around this time, too, that the decision to arrange a meeting of churchmen in

London on 1 June, the morrow of Ascension, became publicly known. On 28 April the king wrote to the prior of Llanthony requesting his attendance at the meeting: PRO, C115/K6684, f. 203d.

119. Rymer, *Foedera*, viii, p. 36.

120. On 23 May payment was made to various clerks for their work in listing jewels in the king's treasury at Westminster that had formerly belonged to Queen Anne, the duke of Gloucester and the earl of Arundel: PRO, E 403/560, m.2. In 1385 Richard is recorded as visiting Westminster abbey twice, at night and unannounced, to inspect the crown jewels. On one occasion he was accompanied by the king of Armenia: *Westminster Chronicle*, pp. 130–3, 154–7.

121. Given-Wilson, *Chronicles of the Revolution*, p. 89.

122. The group who considered a petition of Sir Ralph Basset of Drayton were the chancellor (Edmund Stafford, bishop of Exeter), the treasurer (Guy Mone, bishop of St Davids), the earl of Worcester, the keeper of the privy seal (Richard Clifford), the clerk of the rolls, Mr Ralph Selby, Sir John Bushy, Sir Henry Green, Sir John Russell and Robert Farington clerk: Maxwell-Lyte, *Great Seal*, p. 85.

123. *CPR 1396–9*, p. 331.

124. PRO, C 67/30, m.19.

125. *CPR 1396–9*, p. 341.

126. *CPR 1396–9*, pp. 363–4.

127. The loan had been requested on 23 July 1397 and granted by 5 September. Repayment was to be made by Easter 1398. On 1 April the king had written thanking the prior but deferred payment: PRO, C 115/K6684, fos 197v, 198r, 203r, 206v; *CPR 1396–9*, p. 342.

128. The patent was dated 6 May: Maxwell-Lyte, *Great Seal*, p. 146.

129. *CPR 1396–9*, p. 329.

130. Davies, 'Richard II and the church', 352.

131. *CPR 1396–9*, p. 350. Commissioners were appointed to assist the bishop of Worcester and the abbot of Tewkesbury in the face of persons raising resistance and rebellion, in collection of moiety of a tenth of benefices, 19 September. From its position in the register this item should be dated 22 Richard II and not, as in the text, '21': PRO, C 115/K6684, f. 204d.

132. *CPR 1396–9*, p. 365. See Saul, *Richard II*, p. 443.

133. *CPR 1396–9*, p. 365.

134. *CPR 1396–9*, p. 366.

135. *CPR 1396–9*, p. 368.

136. *CCR 1396–9*, p. 310.

137. *CPR 1396–9*, p. 346.

138. *CPR 1396–9*, p. 352. The patent is dated at Coventry on the 25th, but Richard was already at Lichfield on the 24th: *Proceedings and Ordinances of Privy Council*, i, p. 80.

139. *Proceedings and Ordinances of Privy Council*, i, pp. 79–80.

140. PRO, C 270/25/34. A licence for the election was granted on 10 May: *CPR 1396–9*, p. 338.

141. Davies, 'Richard II and the church', 347–51.

142. Davies, 'Richard II and the church', 348. The translations continued. Thomas Peverel, bishop of Ossory in Ireland, was translated to Llandaff.

143. Davies, 'Richard II and the church', 352.

144. Davies, 'Richard II and the church', 352.

145. *Proceedings and Ordinances of Privy Council*, i, pp. 80–1. Ferriby's accounts reveal him bringing the council's report on convocation to the king at Lichfield, carrying the king's letter back to London, and returning with the council's response to the king, finding him at Flint castle, presumably around 10 June: PRO, E 403/559, m.14.

146. The curialist Tideman, bishop of Worcester, was at his manor of Blockley on 30 May, and it is possible that the court was in this part of the West Midlands: Worcester Cathedral MS. A5, fos 392v–393r.

147. *CPR 1396–9*, p. 349.

148. The king was at Chester briefly in June: Davies, 'Richard II and principality of Chester', 272.

149. Roger Bruyn, a young Cheshire gentleman, performed homage to him for his inheritance on 11 June: BL, Harleian MS. 2022, f. 40d.

150. PRO, C 270/25/35.

151. PRO, E 403/559, m.14. The payment for travel expenses which was made on 31 July included a further journey on the king's command from Stafford to London, and then a return with the council's response from London to Shrawardine.

152. The correspondent likewise reported that the duke of Exeter, captain of Calais, was at his post, and that all the soldiers and men of the lordship were obedient and ready to respond to his commands: *Anglo-Norman Letters and Petitions*, pp. 271–3. Legge dates the second letter to 1399, which is clearly wrong. Corpus Christi fell on 29 May in 1399, but on 6 June in 1398. The anniversaries of the deaths of Queen Anne and the Black Prince were 7 and 8 June respectively.

153. PRO, C 270/25/36.

154. On 18 June messengers were paid for making proclamation throughout the realm that all retainers of Gloucester, Arundel and Warwick had to appear before the king's council and sue for pardons: PRO, E 403/559, m.10.

155. *CCR 1396–9*, p. 392.

156. *Anglo-Norman Letters and Petitions*, p. 262. In the autumn the sum of 4,000 marks was deposited at Chester abbey for distribution: Davies, 'Richard II and principality of Chester', 261.

157. On 3 June payment was made for the dispatch of a privy seal letter to Lord Berkeley summoning him to attend the council at Nottingham on the morrow of St Peter the Apostle: PRO, E403/559, m.8. The feast of SS Peter and Paul is 29 June. There was a council at Shrewsbury on the morrow of St Peter ad Vincula (1 August).

158. *Eulogium Historiarum*, iii, p. 378.

159. Clarke, *Fourteenth-Century Studies*, pp. 105–6, 112–14. The petitions may be as early as the Nativity of St John the Baptist and probably no later than August. The oaths to observe the statutes and judgements made in parliament do not include reference to the decisions taken on 16 September. The accounts of the city of Norwich record a supplication presented to the king at Leicester by Sir Edmund Thorpe, Sir Edmund Noon, Sir Robert Berney, Sir Ralph Shelton: *Select Records of the City of Norwich*, p. 51. This supplication may be the submission of Norfolk. The king was at Leicester for a few days at the end of July and again in autumn.

160. *CPR 1396–9*, p. 433.

161. He had in his company the archbishop of Canterbury, the bishops of London and Salisbury, and others: PRO, C 270/25/37.

162. PRO, C 270/25/38. The witnesses were the archbishop of Dublin and the bishops of London and Carlisle.

163. Worcester Cathedral MS. A5, fos. 396r–v.

164. *CPR 1396–9*, p. 402. On the 27th a writ of aid was dispatched to provide for the expenses of Surrey's household in Ireland, until his arrival there: *CPR 1396–9*, p. 400.

165. On 24 May Surrey had been granted the wardship of the lands of the Irish lord Richard Talbot of Molaghide, during the minority of his son Thomas, while Edmund Holland, who was to accompany Surrey to Ireland, was granted an annuity of 100 marks. *CPR 1396–9*, pp. 344, 347.

166. *CPR 1396–9*, p. 408. See also *CPR 1396–9*, p. 431.

167. *CPR 1396–9*, p. 408.

168. PRO, DL 28/1/10, fos 11d, 21, 17–18, 22d–23.

169. In late July he appointed Robert King and Stephen Wodesham as mason and carpenter at Holt, and commissioned them to take skilled workmen from other counties to work on the castle: *CPR 1396–9*, p. 402.

170. Davies, 'Richard II and principality of Chester', 266–7, 273.

171. PRO, C 81/1354/28.

172. PRO, C 1/69/281.

173. *CPR 1396–9*, p. 580.

174. Cheshire R.O., DCH R/4 (Unclassified).

175. PRO, CHES 2/73, m.1.

176. PRO, C 81/1354/31; PRO, C 270/25/39.

177. Lichfield Dean & Chapter, AB I, fos 52d–53.

178. *Traison et Mort*, p. 150.

179. *Traison et Mort*, p. 149.

180. BL, Additional MS 25,288, f. 46r.

181. The patent is dated 10 September, Westminster: *CPR 1396–9*, p. 505.

182. PRO, DL 28/1/6, f. 39r.

183. Bueno de Mesquita, 'Some Italian letters'.

184. C. Phillpotts, 'The fate of the truce of Paris, 1396–1415', *Journal of Medieval History*, 24 (1998), 65–6.

185. *Traison et Mort*, p. 149.
186. *Traison et Mort*, p. 158.
187. Given-Wilson, *Chronicles of the Revolution*, p. 90.
188. Given-Wilson, *Chronicles of the Revolution*, pp. 91–2.
189. Given-Wilson, *Chronicles of the Revolution*, p. 92.
190. *Traison et Mort*, p. 158, where Nuneaton is rendered 'Nonnetes.'
191. *CPR 1396–9*, p. 514.
192. 'Excestre' would seem to be 'Leicester': *Traison et Mort*, pp. 158–9.
193. *Traison et Mort*, p. 159.
194. *CPR 1396–9*, p. 416.
195. *CPR 1396–9*, p. 429.
196. *Traison et Mort*, p. 159.
197. *Traison et Mort*, pp. 161–2.
198. *CPR 1396–9*, pp. 439, 420.
199. *CPR 1396–9*, p. 422.
200. *CPR 1396–9*, p. 440.
201. *CCR 1396–9*, p. 339.
202. *CPR 1396–9*, pp. 417, 425.
203. Froissart, *Chronicles*, ed. Johnes, ii, pp. 667–8.
204. PRO, E 403/561, m.4.
205. *RP*, iii, p. 423.

CHAPTER SEVEN

1. *Eulogium Historiarum*, iii, p. 378.
2. *Chronicle of Adam Usk*, pp. 74–7.
3. PRO, C 67/30, m.3.
4. PRO, CHES 2/70, m.7d; 'Calendar of Recognizance Rolls of the Palatinate of Chester' in *Thirty-Sixth Report of the Deputy Keeper of the Public Records* (1875 for 1874), appendix 2, p. 99; Davies, 'Richard II and principality of Chester', 261n.
5. *CPR 1396–9*, p. 123. J. Pichon, *Mémoire sur Pierre de Craon* (Paris, 1860).
6. Froissart, *Chronicles*, ed. Johnes, ii, pp. 667–8.
7. PRO, E 403/561, m.1.
8. Salisbury left on 18 October, and Carlisle the following day. They returned on 6 December and 28 November respectively. PRO, E 403/561, m.1; PRO, E 364/32, mm.1d, 5d.
9. J.C. Laidlaw, 'Christine de Pizan, the earl of Salisbury and Henry IV', *French Studies* 36 (1982), 129–43.
10. The gifts were made soon after their arrival on 6 November: PRO, E 403/561, m.4. On 14 November the earl of Worcester was paid for escorting persons coming from France on the king of France's business: PRO, E 403/561, m.4.
11. Davies, 'Richard II and the church', 355.
12. *CCR 1396–9*, pp. 354–5.
13. Davies, 'Richard II and the church', 355. Davies notes that the select council included three bishops 'notable for their recent connections with the Roman curia'.
14. Davies, 'Richard II and the church', 355.
15. *Traison et Mort*, pp. 159–61.
16. *Chronicle of Adam Usk*, pp. 76–7; *Calendar of Papal Letters*, v, pp. 259–60.
17. Davies, 'Richard II and the church', 355–6.
18. *CCR 1396–9*, pp. 366–7.
19. PRO, E 403/561, m.10.
20. The chamberlain of Oxford paid 8*d* to the herald making the proclamation: *Munimenta Civitatis Oxonie*, ed. H.E. Salter (Oxford Historical Society, 1920), p. 277.
21. *Historia Vitae et Regni Ricardi Secundi*, p. 151.
22. For Hilario Doria, see D. Nicol, 'A Byzantine emperor in England. Manuel II's visit to London in 1400–1401', *University of Birmingham Historical Journal*, xii (1969–70), 206–7.
23. The marquis of Dorset, who was under contract to lead a retinue to Aquitaine, had been specifically instructed to wait on the king until the Monday after Epiphany: *CCR 1396–9*, p. 354. Sir John Stanley was at Lichfield on Christmas Eve: Lichfield Joint Record Office, B/A/1/7, fos 122 r–v.
24. Jean de Villeroy was paid on 23 March for taking New Year gifts to the king and the duchess of Gloucester: R. Vaughan, *Philip the Bold. The Formation of the Burgundian State* (London, 1962), p. 108. Richard received a horse from the duke of Berry: PRO, E403/561, m.11.
25. Manuel II must have planned the visit well before he heard of Richard's overthrow. He left Constantinople on 10 December 1399: Nicol, 'A Byzantine emperor in England', 210.
26. *CCR 1396–9*, pp. 367–8; A. Heales, *The Records of Merton Priory in the County of Surrey* (London, 1898), p. 292. Froissart gives an account of a meeting of clergy to discuss the king's 'position of neutrality between popes', but says that it was held at Westminster. According to him, the king's spokesman was the bishop of London. He claims that the king himself spoke eloquently: Froissart, *Chronicles*, ed. Johnes, ii, p. 675.
27. *Chronicles of London*, p. 52. It is unfortunate that the conversation is undated. Since it took place at Lichfield, it must have been some time between Christmas 1397 and New Year 1399. The focus on Albemarle and Bolingbroke is little guide. Richard had set the earl of March's claims of blood at a discount long before his death in summer 1398. Over this period, too, Albemarle's star was in the ascendant.
28. *Four English Political Tracts*, pp. 22–3.
29. 'Mémoires de Pierre Salmon', 7–10.
30. J. Alexander and P. Binski (ed.), *Age of Chivalry. Art in Plantagenet England 1200–1400* (London, 1987), p. 524.
31. The term used is 'mutaciones'. *Chronique du religieux de Saint-Denys 1380–1422*, ed. M.L. Bellaguet (Paris, 1840), ii, pp. 696–7; Given-Wilson, *Chronicles of the Revolution*, p. xviii.

32. *Annales Ricardi Secundi et Henrici Quarti*, pp. 233–4. He was specifically compared to the 'bull' of British prophetic tradition.

33. *Eulogium Historiarum*, iii, p. 380.

34. *Annales Ricardi Secundi et Henrici Quarti*, pp. 237–8.

35. P. Strohm, *England's Empty Throne. Usurpation and the Language of Legitimation, 1399–1422* (New Haven, 1998), pp. 6–14.

36. M.V. Clarke and V.H. Galbraith, 'The deposition of Richard II' in Clarke, *Fourteenth-Century Studies*, pp. 60–1.

37. Bennett, 'Richard II and wider realm', 202–4.

38. *Annales Ricardi Secundi et Henrici Quarti*, p. 229.

39. A. Goodman, *John of Gaunt. The Exercise of Princely Power in Fourteenth-Century Europe* (London, 1992), pp. 166–7.

40. S. Armitage-Smith, *John of Gaunt* (London, 1904), pp. 463–4. Goodman, *John of Gaunt*, pp. 167–8, presents good reasons for not dismissing Gascoigne's story out-of-hand.

41. PRO, E 403/561, m.11. The payment was certainly made before 20 January, the date of the next set of entries. Payment was made at the same time to a squire going on the king's secret business to Henry of Bolingbroke in France.

42. Worcester Cathedral, MS. A5, f. 398r. Lord Bardolf was among the lords asked to attend: Norfolk R.O., Hare 5013, 218 x 3.

43. Worcester Cathedral, MS. A5, f. 396r.

44. *The Episcopal Registers of the Diocese of St David's 1397–1518. Vol. 1. 1397–1407*, ed. R.F. Isaacson (Cymmrodorion Record Series 6, 1917), pp. 96–8. On 14 February the archbishop of Canterbury sent the orders to the bishop of London, who on the 24th sent them to the bishop of St David's: *Registers of the Diocese of St David's*, i, p. 102. But see the order to archbishops of Canterbury and York for moderation of statute of provisors, dated at Coventry on 16 December 1398: *CCR 1396–9*, pp. 366–7.

45. *Anglo-Norman Letters and Petitions*, p. 152. The editor, unaware of the council of 13 January, has incorrectly dated the letter as 'late 1398'.

46. Worcester Cathedral MS. A5, f. 398r.

47. PRO, C 81/1354/31; Barron, 'Tyranny of Richard II', 15.

48. Worcester Cathedral MS. A5, f. 398r.

49. BL, Additional MS. 7096, fos 165v–166r; Clarke and Denholm-Young, 'Kirkstall Chronicle', 111–12; Barron, 'Tyranny of Richard II', 15.

50. T.F. Kirby (ed.), *Wykeham's Register*, 2 vols (Hampshire Record Society, 1896, 1899), ii, p. 488. Barron, 'Tyranny of Richard II', 15.

51. Barron, 'Tyranny of Richard II', 13.

52. Clarke and Denholm-Young, 'Kirkstall Chronicle', 105.

53. PRO, C 76/83, m.6.

54. *CCR 1396–9*, p. 365.

55. *A Calendar of the Register of Richard Scrope, Archbishop of York, 1398–1405*, ed. R.N. Swanson, 2 vols (York, 1981–5), ii, p. 35.

56. *Register of Richard Scrope, Archbishop of York*, ii, pp. ii–iii, 34–5, 3–4.

57. Walsingham dates his death as 3 February, while Adam of Usk has the 4th: *Annales Ricardi Secundi et Henrici Quarti*, p. 232; *Chronicon Adae de Usk*, ed. E. Maunde Thompson (Oxford, 1904), p. 24; J.B. Post, 'The obsequies of John of Gaunt', *Guildhall Studies in London History*, 5 no. 1 (1981), 1–2.

58. *Kirkstall Abbey Chronicles*, p. 76.

59. Post, 'Obsequies of John of Gaunt', 4.

60. Post, 'Obsequies of John of Gaunt', 2–3. Post prefers the 16th, but the account of the keeper of the wardrobe gives the 15th: PRO, E 361/5, mm.10–10d.

61. *Annales Ricardi Secundi et Henrici Quarti*, p. 232; *Kirkstall Abbey Chronicles*, p. 76.

62. PRO, E 361/5, mm.10–10d. Exeter did some business with John Catesby 'at the interment of the duke of Lancaster' on Passion Sunday.

63. Norfolk Record Office, Hare 5013, 218 x 3.

64. He obtained licence to leave England on the 18th: PRO, C76/83, m.4.

65. On 20 February he was at Newcastle under Lyme, just across the Cheshire border: PRO, C 76/83 m.6.

66. *Chronicles of London*, p. 53.

67. *Chronicles of London*, p. 53.

68. Given-Wilson, *Chronicles of the Revolution*, pp. 92–3.

69. *RP*, iii, pp. 372–3.

70. Froissart, *Chronicles*, ed. Johnes, ii, p. 676.

71. *Annales Ricardi Secundi et Henrici Quarti*, pp. 232–3.

72. *CFR 1391–9*, p. 293–7; Tuck, *Richard II and Nobility*, p. 210; Saul, *Richard II*, p. 404.

73. R.E. Archer, 'The estates and finances of Margaret of Brotherton, c. 1320–1399', *Historical Research*, 60 (1987), 264–80.

74. *CPR 1397–9*, pp. 580–1. The duchess's Irish lordships remained in Richard's hands: *CPR 1397–9*, p. 572.

75. PRO, E 101/411/9.

76. John Michell, serjeant-at-arms, seems to have been employed more or less continuously at this task. In October he took £2,000 to Chester for the veterans of Radcot Bridge; in December he carried 8,000 marks to Coventry and Lichfield; in the same month he delivered 2,000 marks to John Ikelington, the king's treasurer at Holt; and in February he delivered him a further 1,000 marks: PRO, E403/651, mm.3, 7, 14.

77. *Annales Ricardi Secundi et Henrici Quarti*, p. 233.

78. *Annales Ricardi Secundi et Henrici Quarti*, p. 230.

79. The king's request to the prior of Worcester and his reply are dated respectively 1 February and 4 March: Worcester Cathedral MS. A5, f. 396r. The king's request to the prior of Rochester and his reply are dated respectively 1 May and 19 May: BL, Cotton MS. Faustina C.V, fos 88v–89r.

80. Payment was made between 5 and 26 March for the expense of moving his household to Canterbury. Easter Sunday was the 30th. The bishop of London was at King's Langley on the 26th, which would seem to indicate that the king had either not set out or had already returned by that date: *Registers of the Diocese of St David's*, i, p. 104.

81. *Eulogium Historiarum*, iii, pp. 379–80.

82. *Annales Ricardi Secundi et Henrici Quarti*, pp. 231–2; *Eulogium Historiarum*, iii, p. 380.

83. PRO, E 403/561, m.16.

84. Clarke and Denholm-Young, 'Kirkstall Chronicle', 110; *Calendar of Papal Letters*, v, p. 259.

85. *Eulogium Historiarum*, iii, p. 380. *Annales Ricardi Secundi et Henrici Quarti*, pp. 299–300. Walsingham implies that Richard discovered the holy oil during Archbishop Arundel's time. The story may thus be out of sequence, perhaps brought to mind when Richard removed the gold eagle to take with him to Ireland.

86. *Annales Ricardi Secundi et Henrici Quarti*, p. 238.

87. *A Collection of all the Wills, now known to be extant, of the Kings and Queens of England*, ed. J. Nicholls (London, 1780), pp. 191–201.

88. *Eulogium Historiarum*, iii, p. 380.

89. Froissart, *Chronicles*, ed. Johnes, ii, p. 681.

90. BL, Cotton MS. Cleopatra, F. III, f. 12; Barron, 'Tyranny of Richard II', 16n. A patent dated at Windsor on the 24th indicates that Albemarle and Westmorland also transacted some business together: *CPR 1396–9*, p. 556.

91. *Traison et Mort*, pp. 166–7.

92. *Traison et Mort*, pp. 163–5.

93. A number of issues under the date 10 June relate to the payment of the debts of Lady Courcy and Agnes Courcy and gifts on their departure for France: PRO, E 403/562, mm.11–12. Froissart blamed the 'Londoners' for expelling Lady Courcy and all the French ladies: Froissart, *Oeuvres*, ed. Kervyn de Lettenhove, 26 vols (Brussels, 1867–77), xvi, pp. 189–90.

94. *Anglo-Norman Letters and Petitions*, no. 370, pp. 431–2.

95. He was at Kidwelly on 10 May: PRO, DL 29/584/9240.

96. PRO, E 364/37, m.3d.

97. On 16 May at Dublin Robert Farington clerk received £180 from the duke of Surrey for work on the castle: PRO, E 364/34, m.9.

98. PRO, E 403/652, mm.3, 10.

99. Norfolk Record Office, Hare 5013, 218 x 3.

100. PRO, E 403/561, m.14; *Calendar of Select Pleas and Memoranda of the City of London, A.D. 1381–1412*, ed. A.H. Thomas (Cambridge, 1932), p. 262; *CPR 1396–9*, p. 576.

101. 'French Metrical History', 13. It is possible that Peter de Craon was Creton's companion.

102. *Kirkstall Abbey Chronicles*, p. 76.

103. *CCR 1397–9*, p. 505.

104. *Annales Ricardi Secundi et Henrici Quarti*, p. 239.

105. *Chronicle of Adam Usk*, pp. 76–7.

106. *Annales Ricardi Secundi et Henrici Quarti*, pp. 239–40.

107. 'French Metrical History', 23n.

108. 'French Metrical History', 22–4. The main contingents may have arrived from a number of ports. On 28 May the earl of Salisbury received money for shipment of men from Poole: PRO, E 364/34, m.6d.

109. 'French Metrical History', 27–31.

110. *Annales Ricardi Secundi et Henrici Quarti*, p. 239. For the career of Janico Dartasso, see S. Walker, 'Janico Dartasso: chivalry, nationality and the man-at-arms', *History*, 84 (1999), 31–51.

111. *Annales Ricardi Secundi et Henrici Quarti*, p. 240.

112. 'French Metrical History', 31–2.

113. 'French Metrical History', 35–6.

114. 'French Metrical History', 37–44.

115. PRO, E 364/34, m.7d.

116. J.L. Kirby, *Henry IV of England*, p. 11.

117. *Chronicles of London*, p. 53.

118. J.A. Tuck, 'Richard II and the Border Magnates', *Northern History*, iii (1968).

119. Froissart, *Chronicles*, ed. Johnes, ii, pp. 681–2. William Norham was from Northumberland. At the time of the Percies' rebellion against Henry IV in 1403 Norham obtained an audience with the king to upbraid him for his usurpation and misrule: *Eulogium Historiarum*, iii, pp. 380, 397.

120. Aston, *Thomas Arundel*, p. 374.

121. He was in the keeping of Sir John Shelly, Exeter's retainer: *The Brut or the Chronicles of England*, p. 357.

122. *The St Albans Chronicle 1406–1420*, ed. V.H. Galbraith (Oxford, 1937), pp. 134–5.

123. BL, Additional Charters 3,066, 3404. Orléans lost a silver plate when he entertained English guests on 1 December 1398: BL, Additional Charter 46.

124. *Choix de pièces inédites relatives au règne de Charles VI*, ed. L. Douët-d'Arcq (Paris, 1863), 157–60; Given-Wilson, *Chronicles of the Revolution*, pp. 112–14.

125. Henry would probably have found French aid a political liability in England. It would have been more in his interest to claim that he had support in France but had declined offers of assistance. Jean Petit claims that he boasted to the English lords that he had a puissant friend and ally in France and read them the letters of alliance with Orléans: A. Colville, *Jean Petit. La Question du Tyrannicide au commencement du xvme siècle* (Paris, 1932), p. 337. Walsingham claims that he declined offers of support from the French: *Annales Ricardi Secundi et Henrici Quarti*, p. 241.

126. *The Chronicles of Enguerrand de Monstrelet*, ed. T. Johnes, 2 vols (London, 1849), i, 16–23.

127. *Chronique du religieux de Saint-Denys 1380–1422*, ii, pp. 700–7; Given-Wilson, *Chronicles of the Revolution*, pp. 109–11. Henry moved with some expedition to keep his promise. On 22 August, in one of his first acts after Richard's surrender, he transferred the custody of Deerhurst priory from Sir John Russell to Richard Wyche, a clerk: *CPR 1396–9*, p. 589.

128. Froissart's account of the descent on England, it must be said, is wrong in almost every particular. He reports a landing in Plymouth and a march overland to London. It may be that Froissart himself confused a number of episodes. It has been suggested, though on no firm grounds, that Henry may have crossed to England incognito at some point. Froissart may simply have drawn too firm inferences from news of key events, like the surrender of Bristol to Bolingbroke, which perhaps reached him in advance of a full account of the revolution.

129. S.K. Walker, 'Letters to the duke of Lancaster in 1381 and 1399', *EHR*, cvi (1991), 75–9. The keeper of the realm issued a commission on 3 July to recover Pevensey from the king's enemies: *CPR 1396–9*, p. 596. For the career of Sir John Pelham, see N. Saul, *Scenes from Provincial Life. Knightly Families in Sussex 1280–1400* (Oxford, 1986), pp. 70–2.

130. PRO, DL 42/15, f. 74; Tuck, *Richard II and Nobility*, p. 214; DL 29/728/11987, m.10.

131. Walsingham and the Kirkstall chronicle independently give this date: *Annales Ricardi Secundi et Henrici Quarti*, p. 244; *Kirkstall Abbey Chronicles*, pp. 77, 121. The continuator at Crowland adds the touch that it was at night-time: *Ingulph's Chronicle of the Abbey of Croyland*, p. 353. Adam Usk dates Henry's landing on 28 June: *Chronicle of Adam Usk*, pp. 52–3. This earlier dating has found some favour: J. Sherborne, 'Richard II's return to Wales, July 1399', *Welsh History Review*, vii (1974–5), 389. Saul cites evidence from the Westminster Abbey Liber Niger that Henry was at Pickering by the 4th: Saul, *Richard II*, p. 408n. Usk, though, probably had in mind the date of the first proclamation regarding the invasion. News of Bolingbroke's proposed invasion adequately explains the garrisoning of castles prior to 4 July.

132. Matthew Danthorpe the hermit had begun to build a chapel by 1 October 1399, and had done so 'without licence': *CPR 1399–1401*, p. 209. The cross bore representations of the crucifixion and the coronation of the Virgin Mary, and a number of coats-of-arms, including that of Ralph Neville, earl of Westmorland: G.R. Park, *The History of the Ancient Borough of Hedon in the Seigniory of Holderness and East Riding of the County of York* (Hull, 1895), pp. 210–12; M.T. Craven, *A New and Complete History of the Borough of Hedon* (Driffield, 1972), p. 49. The chronicler of Meaux abbey records the landing at the place at the site of the former village of Odd iuxta Ravenser: *Chronica Monasterii de Melsa*, iii, p. 254.

133. *Kirkstall Abbey Chronicles*, p. 77; *Chronicon Abbatie de Parco Lude. The Chronicle of Louth Park Abbey, with Appendix of Documents*, ed. E. Venables and A.R. Maddison (Lincolnshire Record Society, 1891), p. 43.

134. The marble tomb exuded oil continuously for sixty-one days and nights. It is unclear whether this was an auspicious portent: *The Historians of the Church of York and its Archbishops*, ed. J. Raine, 3 vols (Rolls Series, 1879–96), iii, p. 288. The mayor of Hull allegedly stated that he had taken an oath to the king and that nothing would separate him from his allegiance save death: T. Gent, *Annales Regioduni Hullini or the History of the Royal and Beautiful Town of Kingston-upon-Hull* (London, 1735), p. 94.

135. Clarke and Galbraith, 'Deposition of Richard II', 179. The Dieulacres chronicle is the sole source for an oath to the Percies on 'the relics of Bridlington'. He could be referring to the oath at Doncaster, which may have been taken on a reliquary containing some of the bones of St John of Bridlington.

136. *Kirkstall Abbey Chronicles*, p. 77.

137. *Kirkstall Abbey Chronicles*, p. 77; Clarke and Galbraith, 'Deposition of Richard II', 171.

138. Clarke and Galbraith, 'Deposition of Richard II', 179.

139. For an alleged oath taken at Knaresborough, later recalled among members of the circle of Archbishop Scrope, see Thomas Gascoigne, *Loci et Libro Veritatum*, ed. J.E.T. Rogers (Oxford, 1881), p. 230.

140. 'French Metrical History', 159–63.

141. *Kirkstall Abbey Chronicles*, p. 77.

142. Clarke and Galbraith, 'Deposition of Richard II', 179; *Chronicle of Iohn Harding*, pp. 349–50. In his manifesto of 1405 Archbishop Scrope of York claimed that he swore a similar oath at Chester: *Historians of the Church of York*, iii, p. 304.

143. Gascoigne, *Loci et Libro Veritatum*, p. 230.

144. *Chronicle of Iohn Harding*, p. 350. Harding is a late source, but some of what he says (pp. 351–4) appears in the Percies' manifesto of 1403.

145. *Historians of the Church of York*, ii, pp. 295–6.

146. *A Collection of Royal and Historical Letters during the Reign of Henry IV. Vol. 1. 1399–1404*, ed. F.C. Hingeston (Rolls Series, 1860), i, p. lxxxviii.

147. *Wykeham's Register*, ii, p. 491.

148. *Traison et Mort*, p. 180.

149. The letter, apparently received around 24 July, sought a loan: J.H. Tillotson, *Monastery and Society in the Late Middle Ages. Selected Account Rolls from Selby Abbey, Yorkshire, 1398–1537* (Woodbridge, 1988), p. 63.

150. *Traison et Mort*, pp. 180–3.

151. *Traison et Mort*, p. 183.

152. For a sympathetic assessment of York and his predicament in 1399 see D. Biggs, '"A wrong whom conscience bid me to right." A reassessment of

Edmund of Langley, duke of York, and the usurpation of Henry IV', *Albion*, 26 (1994), 253–74.

153. *Traison et Mort, pp. 183–4; PRO, E 403/562, m.14.*

154. BL, Additional MS. 25,288, f. 50v.

155. *CPR 1396–9*, p. 586.

156. PRO, E 403/562, m.13.

157. *Ingulph's Chronicle of the Abbey of Croyland*, p. 353.

158. Given-Wilson, *Chronicles of the Revolution*, pp. 247–51.

159. *CCR 1396–9*, p. 507.

160. CUL, Register of John Fordham, bishop of Ely, f. 191v.

161. *CCR 1396–9*, p. 509–10.

162. BL, Additional MS 25,288, fos 50v–51r.

163. Biggs, 'Reassessment of Edmund of Langley', 259.

164. *CCR 1396–9*, p. 510.

165. *Wykeham's Register*, ii, p. 490.

166. Walker, 'Letters to the duke of Lancaster in 1381 and 1399', 75–9. Walker has shown that the Pelham letter, hitherto believed to be from 'Joan' Pelham to her husband, is actually from John Pelham to Henry of Bolingbroke.

167. Biggs, 'Reassessment of Edmund of Langley', 258.

168. *Chronicon Adae de Usk*, ed. Thompson, pp. 37–8, 102.

169. *Kirkstall Abbey Chronicles*, pp. 77–8.

170. Post, 'Ladbroke manor dispute, 1382–1400', 289–339, at p. 323.

171. R. Somerville, *History of the Duchy of Lancaster. Vol. 1. 1265–1603* (London, 1953), p. 136. It was Smart who had been sent by Bagot to Henry of Lancaster with the news of the sequestration of his estates.

172. Records of the Borough of Nottingham. Vol. 1. 1155–1399, ed. W.H. Stevenson (London, 1882), pp. 358–61.

173. *Chronicle of Adam Usk*, pp. 52–3. Both the monk of Evesham and the Kirkstall chronicler claim that Henry had 100,000 men at Bristol: *Historia Vitae et Regni Ricardi Secundi*, p. 154; *Kirkstall Abbey Chronicles*, p. 78. According to Creton, the earl of Salisbury received reports that Henry had 60,000 men in arms: 'French Metrical History', 66–7. Walsingham also numbers the insurgents at 60,000: *Annales Ricardi Secundi et Henrici Quarti*, p. 245.

174. *Traison et Mort*, p. 183. Usk claims that some of the forces withdrew at Shrewsbury after Henry had declared that Cheshire would not be pillaged: *Chronicle of Adam Usk*, pp. 54–5.

175. *CCR 1396–9*, pp. 522, 512.

176. *Chronicle of Adam Usk*, pp. 52–3; Mum and the Sothsegger, Passus II, lines 113–34.

177. *Chronicle of Adam Usk*, pp. 138–9. The anonymous poet recalls Henry's readiness to hear the grievances of the people: *Mum and the Sothsegger*, Fragment M, lines 143–51.

178. *Historians of Church of York*, ii, p. 295; 'French Metrical History', 47–55.

179. *Annales Ricardi Secundi et Henrici Quarti*, p. 244.

180. *Historia Vitae et Regni Ricardi Secundi*, p. 154.

181. *Kirkstall Abbey Chronicles*, p. 78.

182. *Historia Vitae et Regni Ricardi Secundi*, p. 154.

183. A routine letter by Guy Mone, bishop of St David's, dated at Dublin on 8 July, was presumably written in advance of the news of Bolingbroke's landing. It was a response to a letter written by the bishop of Hereford on 18 June: *Episcopal Registers of St David's*, i, pp. 118–21.

184. PRO, E 364/34, m.7d; G.O. Sayles, 'Richard II in 1381 and 1399', *EHR*, xciv (1979), 822–3.

185. PRO, CHES 2/73, m.1; Davies. 'Richard II and principality of Chester', 275.

186. 'French Metrical History', 75. Creton referred to a delay of eighteen days in Ireland. He may well have been counting the days between his own departure from Ireland and the king's arrival at Conway. Creton probably had little understanding of the geography of Wales, and seems to have believed that Richard traversed Wales in one night.

187. Saul, *Richard II*, p. 411. Some scholars have argued for an even earlier arrival date: Sayles, 'Richard II in 1381 and 1399', 823; Sherborne, 'Richard II's return to Wales', 391–3. Yet the earliest reference to activity indicating the king's presence in Wales is 29 July: PRO, E 361/5, m.26d.

188. *Chronicle of Adam Usk*, pp. 58–9, 52–5.

189. PRO, E 361/5, m.26d.

190. *Episcopal Registers of St David's*, i, pp. 120–1.

191. 'French Metrical History', 76–8. Creton names Sir Stephen Scrope, Janico Dartasso and William Ferriby. The Dieulacres chronicle names the seven commanders of the Cheshire bodyguard: Clarke and Galbraith, 'Deposition of Richard II', 172. Another possible companion was Peter Legh of Lyme, another Cheshire man and royal favourite. He was subsequently arrested in Cheshire disguised in a monk's habit. He may have been sent into the principality to raise loyalist forces.

192. William Egerton was appointed by the earl of Salisbury as keeper of Harlech castle on 30 July. It is unlikely that he was in a position to prepare it for the king's arrival: PRO, CHES 2/73, m.1.

193. 'French Metrical History', 95.

194. 'French Metrical History', 96.

195. 'French Metrical History', 93–7.

196. 'French Metrical History', 97.

197. 'French Metrical History', 98–103. For Creton, Albemarle was the great traitor, observing that for this act he 'hath been much despised; not a soul hath held him in estimation from that time; and it is no wonder; for it is a long while since any man of high employ hath been seen to do such a thing as to attempt the undoing of his rightful lord, and the accomplishment of his will upon him'.

198. *Eulogium Historiarum*, iii, p. 381.

199. BL, Additional Charter 5,829. There is a large seal impaling on the left the arms of St Edward the

Confessor impaled with England, and on the right the arms of Bohun.

200. *Chronicle of Adam Usk*, pp. 52–5. Charlton joined Henry at Leominster: *Historia Vitae et Regni Ricardi Secundi*, p. 155.

201. *Historia Vitae et Regni Ricardi Secundi*, p. 155.

202. *English Historical Documents*, iv, p. 179.

203. *Chronicle of Adam Usk*, pp. 54–5. Henry's grant to John Norbury of any goods forfeited by John Lowick is dated at Leominster on 31 July. Perhaps Henry made a verbal promise on the 31st and confirmed it in writing at Leominster three days later: BL, Additional Charter 5,829.

204. 'French Metrical History', 104–6.

205. *Historia Vitae et Regni Ricardi Secundi*, p. 155.

206. *Chronicle of Adam Usk*, pp. 86–7. Froissart relates a similar story: Froissart, *Oeuvres*, ed. Kervyn de Lettenhove, xvi, p. 187.

207. PRO, SC 6/774/10, m.2d; *Historia Vitae et Regni Ricardi Secundi*, p. 155.

208. *Chronicle of Adam Usk*, pp. 54–5.

209. 'French Metrical History', 122–4. Creton claims that there were 100,000 marks in gold coin as well as jewels and other treasure at Holt.

210. Clarke and Galbraith, 'Deposition of Richard II', 171–2.

211. *Chronicle of Adam Usk*, pp. 54–7.

212. *Chronicle of Adam Usk*, pp. 56–7. Peter Legh is mentioned in the lullaby allegedly used by the Cheshire guard to calm Richard: Clarke and Galbraith, 'Deposition of Richard II', 164.

213. 'French Metrical History', 106–9.

214. *Annales Ricardi Secundi et Henrici Quarti*, p. 249; *Historia Vitae et Regni Ricardi Secundi*, p. 155.

215. 'French Metrical History', 119–22.

216. 'French Metrical History', 114–16.

217. 'French Metrical History', 125–9. Despite the testimony of the 'Record and Process' and of Walsingham, it is most unlikely that Archbishop Arundel accompanied Northumberland on his mission to Conway. Both Creton and the Kirkstall chronicle present Northumberland as acting alone. According to Creton, Archbishop Arundel appeared only at Flint. A number of chronicles, understandably, confuse or conflate the events at Conway and Flint: *Historia Vitae et Regni Ricardi Secundi*, p. 155.

218. 'French Metrical History', 129–30.

219. 'French Metrical History', 130–2.

220. 'French Metrical History', 133–7.

221. Clarke and Galbraith, 'Deposition of Richard II', 173; J. Sherborne, 'Perjury and the Lancastrian revolution of 1399', *Welsh History Review*, xiv (1988), esp. 232.

222. 'French Metrical History', 137–40.

223. 'French Metrical History', 140–2.

224. 'French Metrical History', 142–5.

225. 'French Metrical History', 145–9.

226. 'French Metrical History', 149–50.

227. According to the Liber Niger Quarternus of Westminster abbey, Richard was captured on 14 August, and this may indicate the date on which he found himself Northumberland's prisoner at Flint: Taylor, *English Historical Literature in the Fourteenth Century*, p. 188.

228. 'French Metrical History', 150–1.

229. 'French Metrical History', 151.

230. In addition to Salisbury, the bishop of Carlisle, Sir Stephen Scrope, Janico Dartasso and William Ferriby, Creton names the son of the countess of Salisbury, whom Richard had knighted in Ireland, and Henry of Monmouth, Bolingbroke's son: 'French Metrical History', 151–6.

231. Creton felt sure that both Albemarle and Worcester had betrayed the king. He expressed his belief that Henry's removal of Albemarle from the office of constable of England and his stripping away of the ducal title was done 'to blind the world, that no one might think that he knew anything of the affair or of the treason, rather than for any other cause': 'French Metrical History', 157–8.

232. 'French Metrical History', 157–9.

233. *Eulogium Historiarum*, iii, p. 127.

234. 'French Metrical History', 151, 159–63.

235. 'French Metrical History', 163–4. Creton and the unnamed French knight in whose company he had come to England were very fearful, and sought protection, granted by Henry himself, through the good offices of Lancaster Herald: 'French Metrical History', 164–7.

236. 'French Metrical History', 167–8.

237. 'French Metrical History', 170–3.

238. *Annales Ricardi Secundi et Henrici Quarti*, p. 249.

239. There are problems with the dating. According to the monk of Evesham, Archbishop Arundel and Northumberland went to Richard at Conway on Sunday 17 August: *Vita Ricardi Secundi et Regni Ricardi Secundi*, p. 155. Most sources concur that Richard was a prisoner at Chester by the 16th: Saul, *Richard II*, p. 416: Davies, 'Richard II and principality of Chester', 278.

240. *Chronicle of Adam Usk*, pp. 90–1.

241. 'French Metrical History', 168–70.

CHAPTER EIGHT

1. Froissart, *Chronicles*, ed. Johnes, ii, p. 701.

2. F. Lehoux, *Jean de France, duke de Berri*, 3 vols (Paris, 1966–8), ii, p. 417n.

3. Meiss, *French Painting in the Time of Jean de Berry*, i, pp. 64–5.

4. Nicol, 'A Byzantine emperor in England', 208–10, 216–18.

5. '[W]hich castell Kyng Richard had rioly repeiret, and made with hertes of frestone betwene ich lope,

with crownes and cheynes about theire nekkes, for he lovit wele that place': *The Brut or the Chronicles of England*, ed. F.W.D. Brie, Part II (EETS original series 136, 1908), p. 544.

6. *The Brut or the Chronicles of England*, ii, p. 545.

7. 'French Metrical History', 173–5.

8. PRO, E 364/36, m.6.

9. *Vita Ricardi Secundi et Regni Ricardi Secundi*, p. 155; PRO CHES 2/73, m.7.

10. 'French Metrical History', 152–4.

11. *CCR 1396–9*, pp. 520–1.

12. *CCR 1397–9*, p. 522.

13. Norfolk Record Office, Hare 5013, 218 x 3.

14. C. Barron, 'The Deposition of Richard II' in J. Taylor and W. Childs (eds), *Politics and Crisis in Fourteenth-Century England* (Gloucester, 1990), pp. 132–49.

15. BL, Harleian MS. 3775, f. 87v; *Chronicle of Adam Usk*, pp. 60–1.

16. *Chronicle of Adam Usk*, pp. 60–1.

17. *CPR 1396–9*, p. 592.

18. Morgan, *War and Society in Medieval Cheshire*, p. 204.

19. 'French Metrical History', 176–8. In Creton's account, the Welsh are generally presented as loyal to Richard, while the English are regarded as hostile. He probably included the men of Cheshire among the 'Welsh'.

20. *Historia Vitae et Regni Ricardi Secundi*, p. 156.

21. 'French Metrical History', 175–6.

22. 'French Metrical History', 176–7.

23. Richard had reputedly spent 30,000 marks on a gown of cloth of gold studded with pearls and other jewels: *Historia Vitae et Regni Ricardi Secundi*, p. 156.

24. J.M. Rigg, 'Muniments of the Corporation of the City of Salisbury', in *Historical Manuscripts Commission. Report on Manuscripts in Various Collections IV* (1907), pp. 192–3. The city of Norwich seems to have made a similar submission: T. John, 'Sir Thomas Erpingham, East Anglian society and the dynastic revolution of 1399', *Norfolk Archaeology*, xxxv (1970), 101.

25. 'French Metrical History', 178–9.

26. 'French Metrical History', 179.

27. *Chronicon Adae Usk*, p. 179.

28. *Historia Vitae et Regni Ricardi Secundi*, p. 157; *Traison et Mort*, p. 215n.

29. *Traison et Mort*, p. 215.

30. *Chronicle of Adam Usk*, pp. 80–3.

31. In general, see R.L. Storey, 'Episcopal king-makers in the fifteenth century' in R.B. Dobson (ed.), *The Church, Politics and Patronage in the Fifteenth Century* (Gloucester, 1984), pp. 82–98.

32. BL, Cotton MS. Vespasian F VIII, fos 70, 77.

33. 'French Metrical History', 137–40.

34. G.E. Caspary, 'The deposition of Richard II and the canon law' in *Proceedings of the Second International Congress of Medieval Canon Law, Boston College, 12–16 August 1963*, ed. S. Kuttner and J.J. Ryan

35. (Monumenta Juris Canonici. Series C: Subsidia, Vol. 1. Vatican City, 1965), pp. 189–201, at p. 198.

35. He states that the panel considering precedents for deposition worked on the assumption that Richard 'was prepared to abdicate': *Chronicle of Adam Usk*, pp. 62–3.

36. Valente, 'Deposition and abdication of Edward II', 852–81.

37. *Chronicle of Adam Usk*, pp. 62–3.

38. *Chronicle of Adam Usk*, pp. 62–3; Caspary, 'Deposition of Richard II and canon law', 189. The deposition of Adolphe of Nassau, King of the Romans, in 1298 seems also to have been considered: Caspary, 'Deposition of Richard II and canon law', 192.

39. Caspary, 'Deposition of Richard II and canon law', 197.

40. *Chronicle of Adam Usk*, pp. 62–3.

41. Caspary acknowledges that the papal decretal 'began with a detailed specification of the charges, while the crimes and deficiencies of Richard were listed in a separate schedule of objections, as well as in his instrument of abdication, so that the sentence of deposition could afford simply to resume them'. The first paragraphs are thus not conclusive, even though phrases are echoed ('nulla . . . possunt tergiversatione celari'). Richard is generally held to be 'insufficientem penitus et inutilem'. 'But with the dispositive clauses, the agreement in meaning, syntax and phraseology becomes positively dramatic': Caspary, 'Deposition of Richard II and canon law', 191.

42. Caspary, 'Deposition of Richard II and canon law', 201.

43. *Chronicle of Adam Usk*, pp. 62–3.

44. Caspary, 'Deposition of Richard II and canon law', 200.

45. Caspary, 'Deposition of Richard II and canon law', 200–1.

46. In the risings of 1400 the aim was to restore Richard II. In December 1402, however, Sir Edmund Mortimer announced that he had allied with Owain Glyndwr to restore Richard, or, if Richard were dead, to establish his nephew the earl of March, the right heir to the crown, on the throne: *Original Letters Illustrative of English History*, ed. H. Ellis, second series, 4 vols (London, 1827), i, pp. 24–6.

47. 'French Metrical History', 200. Creton may not be reliable on this point, but it is very probable that within the ruling family at least York, Albemarle and his brother Richard, later earl of Cambridge, were considered closer to the crown than the Mortimers.

48. *Chronicle of Adam Usk*, pp. 62–3.

49. *Chronicle of Adam Usk*, pp. 64–5.

50. *Chronicle of Adam Usk*, pp. 64–5.

51. *English Historical Documents*, iv, p. 407.

52. *English Historical Documents*, iv, p. 407.

53. *English Historical Documents*, iv, pp. 407–8.

54. G.O. Sayles, 'The deposition of Richard II: three Lancastrian narratives', *BIHR*, liv (1981), 257–70. C. Given-Wilson, 'The Manner of King Richard's Renunciation: a "Lancastrian Narrative"?', *EHR*, cviii (1993), 365–70.

55. Sayles, 'Three Lancastrian narratives', 267; Given-Wilson, *Chronicles of the Revolution*, p. 42.

56. *Annales Ricardi Secundi et Henrici Quarti*, p. 286.

57. Clarke and Galbraith, 'Deposition of Richard II', 173.

58. *Chronicle of Adam Usk*, pp. 66–9.

59. *Traison et Mort*, pp. 221–2.

60. *RP*, iii, p. 417; *English Historical Documents*, iv, p. 408.

61. *RP*, iii, p. 417; *English Historical Documents*, iv, p. 408.

62. *Chronicle of Adam Usk*, pp. 66–9.

63. *RP*, iii, pp. 417–18; *English Historical Documents*, iv, p. 408.

64. *RP*, iii, p. 418; *English Historical Documents*, iv, p. 409.

65. *RP*, iii, pp. 418–19; *English Historical Documents*, iv, p. 409.

66. *RP*, iii, p. 419; *English Historical Documents*, iv, pp. 410–11.

67. *RP*, iii, pp. 419–20; *English Historical Documents*, iv, pp. 411.

68. *RP*, iii, p. 419; *English Historical Documents*, iv, pp. 410–11.

69. *RP*, iii, p. 419; *English Historical Documents*, iv, pp. 411–12.

70. *RP*, iii, p. 419; *English Historical Documents*, iv, p. 410.

71. *RP*, iii, p. 420; *English Historical Documents*, iv, p. 411.

72. *RP*, iii, pp. 420-1; *English Historical Documents*, iv, p. 411.

73. *RP*, iii, p. 421; *English Historical Documents*, iv, p. 412.

74. *RP*, iii, p. 419; *English Historical Documents*, iv, pp. 410–11.

75. *RP*, iii, p. 421; *English Historical Documents*, iv, p. 412.

76. *RP*, iii, p. 421; *English Historical Documents*, iv, p. 412.

77. *RP*, iii, p. 420; *English Historical Documents*, iv, p. 411.

78. *RP*, iii, p. 420; *English Historical Documents*, iv, p. 411.

79. *RP*, iii, p. 420; *English Historical Documents*, iv, p. 412.

80. C.M. Barron, 'The tyranny of Richard II', *BIHR*, xli (1968).

81. *Collection of Wills of Kings and Queens of England*, pp. 191–201.

82. *RP*, iii, pp. 423–4; *English Historical Documents*, iv, p. 412.

83. *RP*, iii, p. 424; *English Historical Documents*, iv, p. 413.

84. Sayles, 'Three Lancastrian narratives', 269; Given-Wilson, *Chronicles of the Revolution*, p. 166; *English Historical Documents*, iv, p. 413.

85. *Chronicle of Adam Usk*, pp. 68–9.

86. *Chronicle of Adam Usk*, pp. 70–1.

87. Sayles, 'Three Lancastrian narratives', 269–70.

88. H.G. Richardson, 'The elections to the October Parliament of 1399', *BIHR*, 16 (1938–9), 137–43.

89. *English Historical Documents*, iv, p. 413.

90. *English Historical Documents*, iv, p. 414.

91. *Chronicle of Adam Usk*, pp. 66–9.

92. *El Victorial. Crónica de Don Pero Nino, Conde de Buelna*, ed. J. de Mata Carriazo (Madrid, 1940), p. 183.

93. *Chronicle of Adam Usk*, pp. 84–5.

94. *English Historical Documents*, iv, p. 415.

95. P. Heath, *Church and Realm 1272–1461. Conflict and Collaboration in an Age of Crises* (London, 1988), p. 244; A. Rogers, 'Clerical taxation under Henry IV 1399–1413', *BIHR*, xliv (1973), 126–7.

96. Storey, 'Episcopal king-makers in the fifteenth century', 88–9.

97. *Wykeham's Register*, ii, pp. 491–2.

98. Walsingham and Froissart date the creation of the knights to the 11th: *Annales Ricardi Secundi et Henrici Quarti*, p. 291; Froissart, *Chronicles*, ed. Johnes, ii, p. 698. Uniquely Usk attests Richard's presence at the investiture of the knights, and dates the event to the 12th: *Chronicle of Adam Usk*, pp. 70–1. Payments made to a number of English and foreign heralds for their role in ceremonies on Sunday the 12th support Usk on this point: PRO, E 403/564, m.2.

99. *Chronicon Adae Usk*, ed. Thompson, p. 187.

100. *Chronicle of Adam Usk*, pp. 72–3.

101. *Chronicle of Adam Usk*, pp. 72–5.

102. *Chronicon Ade Usk*, ed. Thompson, pp. 189–90.

103. Roskell, *House of Commons 1386–1421*, i, p. 209.

104. *Chronicles of London*, pp. 50–1.

105. *Chronicle of Adam Usk*, pp. 76–9.

106. *Chronicle of Adam Usk*, pp. 84–5.

107. *RP*, iii, p. 426.

108. *RP*, iii, p. 426.

109. E.F. Jacob, *The Fifteenth Century 1399–1485* (Oxford, 1969), p. 23.

110. Given-Wilson, *Chronicles of the Revolution*, pp. 204–5.

111. *Chronicle of Adam Usk*, pp. 78–9.

112. Despenser styles himself earl of Gloucester as late as 27 October: 'Private indentures for life service in peace and war 1278–1476', ed. M. Jones and S. Walker in *Camden Miscellany*, XXXII (Camden Society, fifth series 3, 1994), pp. 123–4.

113. On the 19th Merks made submission to the archbishop of York in the presence of the abbot of Westminster, two canons of York and other clerks: *Register of Archbishop Scrope*, ii, p. 362.

114. *Chronicle of Adam Usk*, pp. 82–5.

115. Roskell, *House of Commons 1386–1421*, i, pp. 69–70.

116. *Chronicle of Adam Usk*, pp. 82–3.

117. *RP*, iii, 434.

118. *RP*, iii, 453.

119. *Chronicles of London*, p. 56.

120. Kirby, *Henry IV*, p. 77.

121. *Chronicle of Adam Usk*, pp. 78–9.

122. *Chronicle of Iohn Harding*, p. 356.

123. Given-Wilson, *Chronicles of the Revolution*, pp. 252–3.

124. *Annales Ricardi Secundi et Henrici Quarti*, p. 320.

125. Matthew Danthorpe had begun to build a chapel before 1 October 'without licence': *CPR 1399–1401*, p. 209.

126. The point is made in Given-Wilson, *Royal Household and the King's Affinity*, pp. 225–6.
127. Walsingham states how England had to mourn in a short time the deaths of the best father and most promising son, in whom the hopes of the commons were placed, and a most noble mother who excelled all the women around in prudence, modesty and holiness: *Annales Ricardi Secundi et Henrici Quarti*, p. 321.
128. *Vita Ricardi Secundi et Regni Ricardi Secundi*, p. 156. For the scroll 'containing magic arts' see *Annales Ricardi Secundi et Henrici Quarti*, p. 301.
129. Henry wrote to five towns in the north Midlands – Leicester, Nottingham, Derby, Shrewsbury and Stafford – asking them to send him armed men: D. Crook, 'Central England and the revolt of the earls, January 1400', *Historical Research* 64 (1991), p. 409.
130. Crook, 'Central England and the revolt of the earls', 404–5.
131. *Traison et Mort*, pp. 238–58; *Chronicle of Adam Usk*, pp. 88–9; H. Hutchinson, *The Hollow Crown* (London, 1961), p. 234.

CHAPTER NINE

1. *Proceedings and Ordinances of Privy Council*, i, 107; J.H. Wylie, *History of England under Henry IV*, 4 vols (London, 1884–98), i, pp. 116–17.
2. Wylie, *Henry IV*, i, p. 115.
3. *Eulogium Historiarum*, iii, p. 387.
4. Clarke and Galbraith, 'Deposition of Richard II', 174.
5. *Traison et Mort*, pp. 248–51.
6. A.P. Stanley, 'On an examination of the tombs of Richard II and Henry III at Westminster Abbey', *Archaeologia*, xlv (1880).
7. PRO, E 403/564, m.10; Saul, *Richard II*, pp. 427–8.
8. *Select Cases in the Court of King's Bench under Richard II, Henry IV and Henry V*, ed. G.O. Sayles (Selden Society, lxxxviii, 1971), p. 212; Saul, *Richard II*, p. 427.
9. John Waltham, bishop of Salisbury, and Sir John Golafre, had expressly wished to be buried elsewhere: N. Saul, 'Richard II and Westminster Abbey', in W.J. Blair and B. Golding (eds), *The Cloister and the World. Essays in Medieval History in Honour of Barbara Harvey* (Oxford, 1996), pp. 210–12.
10. *Collection of Wills of Kings and Queens of England*, pp. 191, 194.
11. *The Chronicle of Fabian, which he nameth the Concordaunce of Histories . . .* (London, 1559), p. 378.
12. Harvey, 'Wilton Diptych – A re-examination', 27–8.
13. *Chronicle of Adam Usk*, pp. 64–5.
14. 'French Metrical History', 97–8.
15. *RP*, iii, p. 150; Saul, *Richard II*, p. 119.
16. *Four English Political Tracts*, pp. 22–3; Walker, 'Richard II's views on kingship', 52.

17. *RP*, iii, p. 347; *English Historical Documents*, iv, p. 405.
18. *Chronicles of London*, p. 52.
19. *Chronicles of London*, p. 31. John Ikelington, clerk of the king's treasury at Holt obtained acquittances in 1400 and 1402 for sums of 65,000 marks and 946 marks 4s 4d which were disposed on Richard's verbal instructions: *Foedera*, vii, pp. 162, 181.
20. Given-Wilson, *Royal Household and King's Affinity*, pp. 214–23.
21. A. Goodman, 'Introduction' in Goodman and Gillespie, *Richard II. The Art of Kingship*, p. 4.
22. Given-Wilson, *Royal Household and King's Affinity*, p. 226; Barron, 'Deposition of Richard II', 138–9.
23. The phrase is from Richard's letter to Albert of Bavaria: Harvey, 'Wilton Diptych – A re-examination', 28.
24. Eberle, 'Richard II and the literary arts' in Goodman and Gillespie, *Richard II. The Art of Kingship*, pp. 247–8.
25. It is possible that Richard gave some intimation of his larger ambitions to parliament in 1395, when he sent Lawrence Drew to explain the 'honourable deed of conquest and the purpose he had undertaken on the settlement' of Ireland, and when he himself addressed parliament in February 1397 with regard to the peace with France and a proposed expedition to Italy, and was commended for 'his honourable purpose' by the commons: *Proceedings and Ordinances of Privy Council*, i, p. 58; Roskell, *House of Commons 1386–1421*, i, pp. 110–11.
26. *Mum and the Sothsegger*, Passus I, lines 32–7.
27. Clarke and Galbraith, 'The deposition of Richard II', 60–1.
28. *Annales Ricardi Secundi et Henrici Quarti*, p. 201.
29. 'French Metrical History', 110.
30. Strohm, *England's Empty Throne*, pp. 6–13.
31. *Chronicle of Adam Usk*, pp. 90–1.
32. *Incerti Scriptoris Chronicon Angliae de Regnis Trium Regum Lancastrensium, Henrici IV, Henrici V, et Henrici VI*, ed. J.A. Giles (London, 1848), p. 12; *Traison et Mort*, appendix H, pp. 297–8.
33. 'French Metrical History', 110–13.
34. According to Creton, 'not a soul hath held him in estimation from that time': 'French Metrical History'. p. 99. The count of Saint Pol went one step further, and hanged Albemarle in effigy at the gates of his castle: Monstrelet, *Chronicles*, i, p. 24.
35. He offers no comment on York's defection, and relates with some relish how Dorset had written secretly to Henry in France: *Traison et Mort*, p. 186.
36. *Traison et Mort*, appendix H, p. 297.
37. *Chronicle of Adam Usk*, pp. 76–7. In his famous sermon of 1387/8 Thomas Wimbledon had made allusion to Rehoboam: Owen, 'Thomas Wimbledon's sermon', 183.
38. It is worth noting, too, that some of his closest associates – Suffolk and de Vere in the late 1380s,

and Albemarle and Scrope in the late 1390s – were likewise childless. The patent creating Scrope earl of Wiltshire in 1397 shows some consciousness of his lack of heirs of his body. The form of the grant is 'to him and his heirs male in perpetuity', without the usual restriction to his issue: *Complete Peerage*, xii, part 2, p. 731.

39. *Annales Ricardi Secundi et Henrici Quarti*, p. 215.

40. In a recent conference paper Alison McHardy showed that John Scarle, who later became Henry IV's first chancellor, was clearly disaffected with Richard by 1397.

41. C. Given-Wilson, 'Richard II and the higher nobility' in Goodman and Gillespie, *Reign of Richard II*, pp. 112–13.

42. *Annales Ricardi Secundi et Henrici Quarti*, p. 201.

43. In a book prepared for the king in 1391, he is praised as a prince who 'has not declined to taste of the fruit of the subtle sciences for the prudent government of himself and his people'. On the epitaph to his tomb he is described as 'prudens ut Omerus' ['prudent as Homer'].

44. *RP*, iii, p. 418; *English Historical Documents*, iv, p. 409.

45. *RP*, iii, p. 421; *English Historical Documents*, iv, p. 412.

46. *RP*, iii, p. 419; *English Historical Documents*, iv, pp. 410–11.

47. Given-Wilson, 'Richard II, Edward II, and the Lancastrian inheritance', 554–5, 570–1.

48. *RP*, iii, pp. 417–18; *English Historical Documents*, iv, p. 409.

49. *RP*, iii, p. 418; *English Historical Documents*, iv, p. 409.

50. *RP*, iii, pp. 418–20; *English Historical Documents*, iv, pp. 409, 411.

51. *RP*, iii, p. 420; *English Historical Documents*, iv, p. 411.

52. *Chronicles of London*, p. 34.

53. Given-Wilson, *Chronicles of the Revolution*, pp. 204–5.

54. The old adage, 'Vox populi, vox Dei', presumably had some currency in 1399: E. Peters, 'Vox populi, vox Dei' in E.B. King and S.J. Ridyard (eds), *Law in Medieval Life and Thought* (Sewanee, 1990), pp. 110–16.

55. K.B. McFarlane, *Lancastrian Kings and Lollard Knights* (Oxford, 1972), pp. 54–5.

56. Bennett, 'Edward III's entail and the succession to the crown', 596–9.

57. For a powerful statement of the importance of ideas in the politics of late medieval England see J. Watts, *Henry VI and the Politics of Kingship* (Cambridge, 1996).

58. *Wykeham's Register*, ii, pp. 491–2.

59. *Records of the Borough of Nottingham*, i, pp. 358–61.

60. 'French Metrical History', 133–4.

61. *Chronicle of Adam Usk*, pp. 140–1.

62. Jacob, *Fifteenth Century*, p. 23; P. McNiven, 'Legitimacy and consent: Henry IV and the Lancastrian title', *Mediaeval Studies*, 44 (1982), 474–5, 481–2.

63. G.L. Harriss, 'Medieval doctrines in the debates on supply, 1610–1629' in K. Sharpe (ed.), *Faction and Parliament. Essays on Early Stuart History* (Oxford, 1978), pp. 73–4.

64. G.L. Harriss, 'Political society and the growth of government in late medieval England', *Past and Present*, 138 (1993), 56.

65. The phrases are from Harriss, 'Political society and growth of government', 34, 57.

66. Sir John Fortescue, *De Laudibus Legum Anglie*, ed. S.B. Chrimes (Cambridge, 1949), pp. 78–81.

67. The use of the term 'revolution' in respect of 1399 has been well explored, though to rather different ends, in J. Gillespie, 'Clio in Arachne's web: historians weave the revolution of 1399', *Medievalia et Humanistica*, forthcoming.

68. *Select Cases in Court of King's Bench under Richard II, Henry IV and Henry V*, pp. 111–14.

69. *Select Cases in Court of King's Bench under Richard II, Henry IV and Henry V*, pp. 122–5.

70. Monstrelet, *Chronicles*, i, p. 20.

71. A.L. Brown, 'The reign of Henry IV: the establishment of the Lancastrian regime' in S.B. Chrimes, C.D. Ross and R.A. Griffiths (eds), *Fifteenth-Century England 1399–1509. Studies in Politics and Society* (Manchester, 1972), p. 24.

72. *RP*, iii, p. 428; *Chronicles of London*, p. 61.

73. *Chronicle of Adam Usk*, pp. 136–43, xlvi–xlvii.

74. *RP*, iii, p. 458; McFarlane, *Lancastrian Kings and Lollard Knights*, p. 89.

75. McFarlane, *Lancastrian Kings and Lollard Knights*, pp. 88–90.

76. McFarlane, *Lancastrian Kings and Lollard Knights*, pp. 97–9.

77. *Select Cases in Court of King's Bench under Richard II, Henry IV and Henry V*, pp. 122–5.

78. *Foedera*, viii, pp. 255–6; *CPR 1401–5*, pp. 126–9.

79. *Eulogium Historiarum*, iii, pp. 389–94. P. McNiven, *Heresy and Politics in the Reign of Henry IV. The Burning of John Badby* (Woodbridge, 1987), p. 97.

80. *Eulogium Historiarum*, iii, p. 397.

81. *Historians of Church of York*, ii, pp. 304–11; *Eulogium Historiarum*, iii, pp. 405–6.

82. P. McNiven, 'The betrayal of Archbishop Scrope', *Bulletin of the John Rylands Library*, 54 (1971–2), 173–213; P. McNiven, 'The problem of Henry IV's health, 1405–1413', *English Historical Review*, c (1985), 747–72.

83. *Johannis Capgrave Liber de Illustribus Henricis*, pp. 108–9.

84. Brown, 'Reign of Henry IV', 11.

85. McNiven, *Heresy and Politics in the Reign of Henry IV*, pp. 80–1, 93.

86. *Chronicle of Adam Usk*, pp. 242–3.

87. Lehoux, *Jean de France, duke de Berri*, ii, p. 420n.

88. A. Tuck, 'Henry IV and Europe: a dynasty's search for recognition', in R.H. Britnell and A.J. Pollard (eds), *The McFarlane Legacy. Studies in Late Medieval Politics and Society* (New York, 1995), pp. 107–25; S.P. Pistono, 'The accession of Henry IV: effects on

Anglo-Flemish relations 1399–1402', *Tijdschrift voor Geschiedenis*, 89 (1976), 465–74.

89. P. Morgan, 'Henry IV in the shadow of Richard II', in R.E. Archer (ed.), *Crown, Government and People in the Fifteenth Century* (Stroud, 1995), esp. pp. 9–11.

90. 'French Metrical History', 87–95; Strohm, *England's Empty Throne*, p. 109.

91. *Eulogium Historiarum*, iii, p. 396. Percy was allegedly frustrated by their naive loyalism, pointing out that he had played a major part in expelling Richard and installing Henry, and that his main aim was to secure good governance.

92. Trinity College, Cambridge, MS. R.5.35 [726], f. 414r.

93. *Eulogium Historiarum*, iii, pp. 389–94.

94. *Select Cases in Court of King's Bench under Richard II, Henry IV and Henry V*, pp. 111–14; *Original Letters Illustrative of English History*, ed. H. Ellis, second series, vol. 1 (London, 1827), pp. 24–6.

95. Bennett, 'Edward III's entail and the succession to the crown', 600.

96. Capgrave, *Chronicle of England*, p. 302.

97. *Thomae de Elmham Vita et Gesta Henrici Quinti*, ed. T. Hearne (Oxford, 1727), p. 5.

98. J.H. Wylie and W.T. Waugh, *The Reign of Henry the Fifth*, 3 vols (Cambridge, 1914–29), i, pp. 209–11.

99. T.B. Pugh, *Henry V and the Southampton Plot* (Gloucester, 1988).

100. Even Albemarle achieved his quietus at Agincourt. As McFarlane memorably wrote: 'he was held to have made atonement for his disloyalty by dying of suffocation on the ground at Agincourt': McFarlane, *Lancastrian Kings and Lollard Knights*, p. 67.

101. In general see M. Aston, 'Richard II and the Wars of the Roses' in Du Boulay and Barron, *Reign of Richard II*, pp. 280–317.

102. *The Politics of Fifteenth-Century England. John Vale's Book*, ed. M.L. Kekewich, C. Richmond, A.F. Sutton, L. Visser-Fuchs and J.L. Watts (Stroud, 1995), pp. 195–200.

103. *RP*, v, p. 464.

104. A. Goodman, 'Introduction', 2.

105. *The Politics of Fifteenth-Century England. John Vale's Book*, p. 213.

106. A. Gross, *The Dissolution of the Lancastrian Kingship. Sir John Fortescue and the Crisis of Monarchy in Fifteenth-Century England* (Stamford, 1996), pp. 2–4.

107. F. Sandford, *The History of the Coronation of . . . James II* (London, 1687), between pp. 102 and 103.

INDEX

Abbeville, 53
Abingdon, 77, 115
Agincourt, 207
Albany, duke of, 206
Albermarle, duke of, *see* Edward, earl of Rutland, duke of Albemarle, duke of York
Albion, 169
Alexandria, 74
Aleyn, William, of Ashby by Lutterworth, 130
Alfred the Great, king of England, 18
Aljubarotta, 23
Amiens, 45, 46,
Angoulême, Edward of, elder brother of Richard, 19
Anjou, 70
Anne of Bohemia, first wife of Richard, 11, 20; her seal (illust.), 21; Anne and Richard in Rome altarpiece (illust.), 21; 32; Anne and Richard in charter initial (illust.), 37; 43, 49; died, 57, 62, 63, 71, 79, 81, 129, 193, 213 n.40, 214 n.66, 225 n.120
Aquitaine, 14, 35, 39, 46, 52, 60, 61; rebellion in 62; 70, 186, 214 n.90, 227 n.23
Aragon, John, king of, 115
Aragon, Yolande of, 69
Ardres, 81; 'Field of Cloth of Gold', marriage and peace celebrations at Ardres likened to, 82–3
Armenia, 24
Armenia, king of, *see* Leo de Lusignan
Antwerp, Lionel of, *see* Lionel of Antwerp
Arthur, king of Britain, 22, 49, 67; Arthurian tradition, 73, 74
Arundel castle, 92, (illust.), 93
Arundel, Thomas, bishop of Ely, archbishop of York, archbishop of Canterbury: portrait of, in initial (illust.), 101; treats with Richard on parliament's behalf, 27; promoted to see of York, 33; 34, 38, 45, 47, 54, 60; obtains pardon for brother 61, 216 n.28; 66; support for Richard, 68–9; celebrates Richard's second marriage, 81; crowns new queen 83; protects Haxey, 86; still king's man, 88; enthronement at Canterbury, 88–9; convocation and concern with Lollardy, 89; secures brother's surrender, 91; alleged role in conspiracy, 92; 93, 95; parliamentary attack on, 100; denied hearing and condemned to exile, 100–1, 223 n.12; left England, 110–11; translated to St Andrews by pope, 224, n.52; residence at

Utrecht and makes contact with Henry, 151; lands in England with Henry, 154; at Chester, 171; acting chancellor to Henry, 171; 173–4; preaching on behalf of Henry (illust.), 174; 177, 183, 185; deceived by Richard, 198; 198, 204; pleads for life of Archbishop Scrope, 204; 215 n.107, 217 n.48, 218 n.121, 219 n.20, 220 n.48, 220, n.50
Arundel, Sir William, 95
Ashbourne, Dr Thomas, 112
Ashton, Sir John, 224 n.96
Avignon, 3, 19, 79, 82, 125
Aylesbury, 48

Babylon, 73
Bacharach, 90
Bache, Alexander, bishop of St Asaph, 44, 214 n.76, 215 n.109
Bacon, John, 26
Badcock, Walter, monk, 44
Bagot, Sir William, 88, 98, 113, 115, 120; Richard discusses renouncing the crown, 139; 145; exhorts Bolingbroke to look to his interests, 151; 157, 175, 186, 220 n.42, 231 n.171
Bamme, Adam, mayor of London, 44
Bampton, 123–4
Banbury, 114, 223 n.40
Bangor, bishop of, 212 n.58
Bannockburn, 22
Barcelona, 69
Bardolf, Lady, 171
Bardolf, Lord: attendance at Gaunt's funeral, 145; in Ireland, 148; submits to Henry, 162
Barking abbey, 79; shrine of St Alburgie, 79
Barnet, 143
Barnwell priory, 34
Barron, C. M., 116
Basset, Lord, 28, 32, 212 n.14
Basset, Sir Ralph, 225 n.122
Bath, 112
Bath and Wells, 34; bishop of, 80
Bath, Order of, 185
Bavaria, Albert of, count of Holland, 110
Bavaria, duke of, 10
Bavaria, Rupert of, count palatine of Rhine, 90
Bavaria, William of, count of Ostrevant, 42
Beauchamp family, 158
Beauchamp, Sir John, of Holt, 28, 31; impeached and executed, 32
Beauchamp, Thomas, earl of Warwick, 29, 87, 90; arrested at feast in London, 91; alleged conspiracy, 92; followers in arms,

94–5; 96, 102; 105; trial and confession, 105–6; escorted to Chester, 114; lands and jewels seized, 106, 111; followers, 115–16; 121; 128, 135, 136; released and joined Henry, 172; 185
Beauforts, 88
Beaufort, Henry, bishop of Lincoln, son of John of Gaunt, 128, 129, 130, 143, 160
Beaufort, John, earl of Somerset, marquis of Dorset, 83, 88, 96, 101, 106, 114; attendance at Gaunt's funeral, 143; encourages Bolingbroke to challenge for his rights, 151; mobilises, 156, 227 n.23, 235 n.35
Beaulieu abbey, 60
Beaumaris, 163
Beaumaris castle, 68
Beaumont, John, Lord, 28, 52, 64, 70, 79
Bede, the Venerable, 169
Bedfordshire, 141
Beeston, Thomas, 223 n.20
Benedict XIII, anti-pope, 125, 218 n.138, 219 n.3
Berkeley, 159, 161
Berkeley, Thomas, Lord, 182, 226 n.157
Berkshire, 115, 128
Bermondsey priory, 112
Berners, Sir James, 31; executed, 34
Berney, Sir Robert, 226 n.159
Berry, Jean, duke of, 1, 3, 52; at the marriage, 81; 151, 153, 170, 205
Betheley, William, Augustinian friar, 218 n.123
Beverley, 117, 224 n.51; shrine of St John of, 117, 154
Binski, P., 63
Blackburn, Simon, 222 n.171
Black Prince, *see* Edward of Woodstock, prince of Wales
Blake, John, 32
Blockley, 226 n.146
Blount, Sir Thomas, 35; in plot to kidnap Henry IV, 189
Bohemia, 135
Bohun, Eleanor, duchess of Gloucester, wife of Thomas of Woodstock, 112; memorial brass (illust.), 112; death of, 189; tribute to, 235 n.127
Bohun, Joan, countess of Hereford, 215 n.109
Bohun, Mary, countess of Derby, first wife of Henry of Bolingbroke, 62, 114, 216 n.38
Boissay, Robert de, 143
Bolingbroke, Henry of, *see* Henry IV, king of England